The Adult is Parent to the Child

to the Child

Transactional Analysis with Children and Young People

Edited by
Keith Tudor

Russell House Publishing

Published in 2008 by
Russell House Publishing Limited
4 St George's House
Uplyme Road
Lyme Regis
Dorset
DT7 3LS

Tel: 01297 443948
Fax: 01297 442722
e-mail: help@russellhouse.co.uk

British Library Cataloguing-in-Publication Data:

A catalogue record of this book is available from the British Library

ISBN: 978-1-905541-17-1

Typeset by TW Typesetting, Plymouth, Devon
Printed by Biddles Ltd, Kings Lynn

Russell House Publishing

Russell House Publishing aims to publish innovative and valuable materials to
help managers, practitioners, trainers, educators and students.

Our full catalogue covers: social policy, working with young people, helping
children and families, care of older people, social care, combating social
exclusion, revitalising communities and working with offenders.

Full details can be found at rhttp://www.russellhouse.co.uk/ and we are
pleased to send out information to you by post. Our contact details are on
this page.

We are always keen to receive feedback on publications and new ideas
for future projects.

To Saul and Esther

And in fond and appreciative memory of Brian,
Sue and Petrûska

For their inspiration, creativity, advocacy and humanity.

Contents

List of Figures, Boxes and Illustrations

Introduction

Keith Tudor

There's no such thing as a child. This may appear a strange and somewhat stark sentence. Nonetheless, it makes the point that we cannot be with or think about a child without, in effect, acknowledging that they are initially dependent on adult nurture and care and, in any case, are part of a system. This system may be, and include parent, carer, family, extended family, community, school, culture and society – all singular or plural. This book acknowledges children's context in its range of chapters which encompass the social environment, parents, school, legislation, and residential settings, as well as different forms of therapy.

Whilst children are dependent on adults, they do not 'belong' to adults, even – especially – their parents. As Gibran (1923/1926: 20) puts it: 'And though they are with you yet they belong not to you.' Similarly, knowledge about 'the child' and 'child development' does not belong to any one discipline or profession. This book acknowledges this perspective in bringing together nineteen professionals with a range of backgrounds, training, experience, expertise, and interest.

What brings us – and this book – together is a common experience and interest in transactional analysis (or TA). In our various ways we find TA a helpful framework for understanding our work with children in context and want to share this with a wider audience, not least as TA has a long history of working with children. Thus the aims of the book are:

- To communicate how TA is and can be used with children and young people in context, across a wide range of settings.
- To bring TA to a wider audience including parents, educators, health care professionals, and others involved in organisations concerned with the lives, well-being, care and treatment of children and young people.
- To bring a wider and contemporary view of TA both to a general audience, as well as to those who are familiar with TA but perhaps less familiar with its application to work with this population.
- To put therapeutic, educational and organisational work with children and young people back on the map within TA and within the wider professional fields encompassed by the book. We hope that this text will be considered core reading not only on TA training courses but on all courses training professionals to work with children and young people.

Transactional analysis

TA is a way of understanding what happens between and within people. Although its roots are in psychotherapy, TA is more than another 'school' of or approach to therapy. For example, it provides a theory of communication, which has been extended to analysing systems and organisations, fields of TA which are also represented in this book. For the reader who is unfamiliar with TA, Chapter 1 stands as an introduction to its basic concepts (see also Mountain, 2004).

From the early days of transactional analysis (TA) its practitioners have been writing about their work with children (see Mannell, Piehl and Edwards, 1968; James, 1969; Piehl, 1969) and about the implications of theory for child development (Amundson, 1978; Levin, 1988a, 1988b). In 1988 a special themed issue of the international *Transactional Analysis Journal* was devoted to the subject of 'TA and Children' (Bonds-White, 1988) and, in 2005, a special themed issue of the journal on 'TA and Education' (Newton, 2005) had three articles on working with children. A number of books have been written directly for children, translating, as it were, TA concepts into a language, with images and stories accessible to children. Eric Berne himself, the founder of TA, wrote a book for children, *The Happy Valley* (Berne, 1968), a moral tale of conscience, in which Berne's ideas about personality and ego states can be detected. Claude Steiner, a close colleague of Berne's, followed this up in 1977 with *The Warm Fuzzy Tale*, which translates and introduces the concept of strokes which, in turn, derive from a human hunger for recognition. In a series of illustrated workbooks aimed at 'Tots', 'Kids' and 'Teens', Alvyn Freed (1973, 1971, 1976, respectively) brought various TA concepts, especially from a problem-solving perspective, to bear on aspects of children's and young people's lives and relationships. In a rare book, Kleinewiese (1988) offers a series of visual representations of ego states in order to facilitate therapeutic and educational work with children. These and other TA books for children are summarised in Appendix 1. A recent book published in Italian introduces relevant and contemporary theory from TA and developmental psychology about children and child development by means of a tale which parallels Saint Exupéry's *The Little Prince* (Giusti, 2006).

In addition, over 50 articles have been published in the *Transactional Analysis Journal* and its predecessor, the *Transactional Analysis Bulletin*, which are summarised in Appendix 2. These represent a range and depth of work with children and young people across the different fields of applications of transactional analysis: clinical (psychotherapy), counselling, educational and organisational, a range which is represented in Parts I and III of this book.

However, judging by the attitude of some colleagues particularly towards therapeutic work with children and young people, both outside and within TA, this history does not appear very present. There are a number of reasons for this:

• Some ignorance of this history. Part of my motivation as editor for producing this current book has been both to reclaim TA history, and to represent present practice within different fields of applications, and from diverse perspectives within TA.

- In TA training, there is a general lack of focus on or reference to work with children and young people. TA training is generic, in that it prepares students for working with the general population, and yet in psychotherapy training, for instance, most of the elements of that training – theory, practice and supervision – focus on individual work with *adult* clients. In the UK it is only in the past ten years that some candidates presenting for their certifying TA examination, have presented their work with children and, in a number of cases, this has been challenged and even opposed by their supervisors. This book seeks to rectify this situation by applying theory to practice and practice to theory, and, in doing so, to support the next generation of practitioners, especially but not exclusively transactional analysts, who may work with children and young people.

- A certain anxiety about practitioners in whatever field working with minors, an anxiety which may be more heightened in those who have little or no experience of such work. When working with minors, certain legal, professional and ethical requirements need to be taken into account, as well as the personal impact of the work on the practitioner. These requirements are considered throughout the book and are addressed specifically in Chapters 5 and 12. In this way this book aims to inform, educate, support, stimulate and challenge practitioners, trainers and supervisors alike.

- The way in which professions are organised and regulated, which, in the case of psychotherapy in the UK, is currently viewing child psychotherapy as a postgraduate (even a post postgraduate) activity, the implications and requirements of which are presented and discussed in Chapter 12 and Appendix 5.

The structure of the book

Drawing on contributions from experienced TA practitioners in all fields of TA, this book describes the state of the art and science of transactional analysis with children and young people.

Following this introduction **Chapter 1** introduces transactional analysis, written especially for the reader who is unfamiliar with TA. Written by a friend and colleague, Graeme Summers, and myself, we introduce fundamental TA concepts – ego states, transactions, scripts and games – which are referred to throughout the book. We also introduce two other concepts in TA which are also referred to in various chapters in the book and are of particular relevance to working with children: a model for systemic assessment, and a note on contracts and contracting. This introduction to TA acts as a reference point for the book as a whole.

Part One takes as its inspiration from Winnicott's dictum that 'There's no such thing as a baby – only a mother and a baby.' The child or young person cannot be understood outside of or separate from their environmental context and, being a child, her or his context includes society, family, school, the law, and institutions, each of which are represented in the first five chapters. In **Chapter 2**, Trudi Newton, an educationalist and a Teaching and Supervising Transactional Analyst (TSTA), draws on the image of the village, both real and virtual, to discuss changing paradigms in education and society. She assesses the implications of recent research and thinking in education, neuroscience and positive psychology for a social environment which supports the healthy development of children and young people. In **Chapter 3**, Diane Hoyer and Laura Hyatt, two colleagues who have both trained in TA and have worked together in the UK's National Society for the Prevention of Cruelty to Children, argue the importance of working with children and their parents. Drawing on child development theory and non-directive play therapy as well as TA, they present their work in this field through a discussion of their use and development of TA frameworks, and especially the 'treatment triangle'. In most cultures in the world school is a major influence on the acculturation of children into society. In **Chapter 4**, Pete Shotton, a transactional analyst, certified both as an educationalist and as a psychotherapist, describes his work in an inner city boys' high school. As the manager of a team of mentors his work helps boys to recognise their social and emotional needs in the context of a diverse and dynamic school culture and the wider social context of a multicultural community in a post 9/11 world. The social environment includes both the laws and mores of society and, in **Chapter 5** Mica Douglas and I focus on UK law and social policy as it pertains to and influences thinking and practice about child protection. Drawing on our experience both as social workers and as psychotherapists (Mica is also a manager of a child protection agency), we summarise and comment on relevant legislation and policies, and discuss a number of parameters to therapeutic work with children. We also consider the concept of protection within TA, and conclude with some ideas about ethical decision-making for practitioners, especially therapists in private practice, faced with issues of child protection. One aspect of child protection has been the establishment of institutions for the protection, care and, where needed, the treatment of children. In the final chapter in this first part of the book, Anita Mountain, also doubly certified, in organisational and psychotherapy applications of TA, and a TSTA in both, describes her work over ten years as a consultant to a social services establishment housing and supporting young people. This unique work encompassed: the development of a therapeutic environment and the social milieu; the establishment of therapeutic contracts and treatment plans for the residents; professional development for the staff; and organisational analysis and development. Some of the assessment sheets developed and used by the author are reproduced in Appendix 4.

The chapters in **Part Two** focus specifically on therapeutic practice with children and young people. In the first chapter of this part of the book, I present a number of TA concepts also based around the 'treatment triangle' of contracts and contracting, diagnosis or assessment, and the therapy itself, with reference to case examples and my therapeutic work with one child in particular. In doing so, I offer some comments on the development of TA theory and models, especially with regard to diagnosis. In the first of three chapters which focus more specifically on ongoing clinical work with children, **Chapter 8**, appropriately enough, discusses the first meeting between a child and psychotherapist. Echoing Berne's (1966) reflections prior to the first meeting of a group, Dolores Munari Poda, an experienced child psychotherapist and a TSTA, also reflects on certain therapeutic considerations prior to the first *tête-à-tête* between therapist and child. Her account is rich with case material and illustrations from children. A number of Italian TA colleagues are not only working with children and young people across all fields of application, but are also developing the practice, theory and the method of child psychotherapy. Most of this material is only available in Italian and I am delighted to have the original work of both Munari Poda and that of another Italian colleague, Maria Assunta Giusti (**Chapter 18**), published here in English. The next two chapters discuss the impact of attachment. In **Chapter 9** Kath Dentith and Jean Lancashire, both experienced social workers in childcare and clinical transactional analysts, discuss their clinical work with children who have been fostered and adopted. To this they bring their understanding and integration of attachment theory and TA. **Chapter 10** focuses on TA with adolescents. Mark Widdowson, a certified transactional analyst with a lot of experience of working with adolescents, especially in public sector settings, brings his own direct style of work with young people to the tone of this chapter which addresses you, the reader, directly. Some reflections on the concept of 'Inner Adolescent' are followed by some initial considerations about working with adolescents from a contextual perspective, drawing on UK social legislation, and the chapter concludes with practical examples of TA therapy and of working with a group of adolescents from a psycho-educational perspective. In **Chapter 11**, Diane Hoyer and Laura Hyatt present the application of their work (outlined in Chapter 3) with children and parents, including three clinical vignettes. This also includes the application of a positive parenting strategy, developed by Hoyer the explanatory notes for which form Appendix 5. The final two chapters in this part focus on the necessary qualities, attributes and skills of the child psychotherapist, and are both written by certified transactional analysts who have undertaken additional training in order to further their work as therapists working with children. In **Chapter 12** Mica Douglas, a certified transactional analyst and child care worker and manager (see Chapter 5), describes her transition to becoming a child psychotherapist. In describing this journey, Douglas encompasses the personal and the practical implications of making this change, as well as commenting on the TA theory she has found helpful in so doing. There is a debate within the health and social services in the UK and in the United Kingdom Council for Psychotherapy (UKCP) about the provision of child psychotherapy and the requirements for training as a child psychotherapist. I am grateful to the UKCP and, in particular, Alex Walker-McClimens for permission to reproduce in Appendix 6 its key document on *Psychotherapy with Children* which outlines principles, aims and guidelines for training. One of the requirements of and challenges for the practitioner working with children is to be able to play and to be creative. In **Chapter 13**, Roger Day, who, subsequent to his TA training and certification, has trained and qualified as a play therapist, offers practical applications of TA and play therapy, including the therapeutic use of play objects, drawing, creative games and, influenced by gestalt therapy, experimentation.

In **Part Three**, six chapters develop different elements of TA theory with reference to work with children and young people. Its title acknowledges the research involved in such developments (and especially and specifically that reported in Chapter 16), and that this theory development and research encompasses all TA fields of application: the organisational, the clinical (psychotherapy), counselling, and the educational. In 1962 Berne published a short article on the 'Classification of Positions' in which he defines a 'position', a term he adopted from Klein (1962: 23) as 'the fundamental variable of human living.' He continues: 'The subject of all positions are particulars of the polarity I-Others, and their predicates are particulars of the polarity OK – not OK.' Putting these predicates together produces the four 'life positions' or, what some authors refer to as 'existential life positions': 'I'm OK, You're OK'; 'I'm OK, You're not OK'; 'I'm not OK, You're OK'; 'I'm not OK, You're not OK'. Although 'They', those others, is implied in 'You' and, indeed, in his original article Berne makes this explicit, it was not until his last work, published posthumously in 1972, that Berne extended the concept of the two-handed position to include the third party 'They': 'I'm OK, You're OK, They're OK', and so on. In **Chapter 14** Davidson, a certified transactional analyst from the organisational field of TA, elaborates this theory with reference to his own development of the 'OK square', in which he maps the eight different three dimensional positions. This model first appeared two years ago in an article on systems and processes in organisations, published in the *Transactional Analysis Journal* (Mountain and Davidson, 2005). Here Davidson illustrates it using examples of young people especially in groups and gangs. In doing so, Davidson brings a sensitivity to this practical application of the concept of life positions, as well as some useful references to the political sphere. One of Berne's particular contributions was in making theory accessible. Following in the tradition of Bettleheim and others, Berne and some of his colleagues (see, for example, Karpman, 1968) took and discussed a number of fairy tales or stories as conveying certain psychological and cultural messages. Subjecting these to a transactional analysis, through his independent, other world, 'Martian' thinking, Berne identified a number of characteristic life stories or scripts, and offered alternative readings. In the same spirit, in **Chapter 15**, Marie Naughton, a certified transactional analyst in psychotherapy, who works as a school counsellor, takes as her starting point the fairy tale *Sleeping Beauty* and, specifically, the figure of the twelfth fairy. In a chapter which considers Berne's concept of script theory in the light of more recent narrative approaches to therapy, Naughton likens the role of the counsellor to that of the twelfth fairy in its transforming influence in the lives of children and young people. In **Chapter 16** Jim Allen, TSTA, and recent past president of the International Transactional Analysis Association, expands Crossman's (1966) concepts of permission and protection to include resilience. Like Newton in Chapter 2, Allen draws on the tradition of positive psychology and, citing his own and other people's research, extends these concepts to include permissions to make meaning and to find cultural nurturance. In the second part of the chapter Allen focuses on the significance of the environment in promoting resilience, and reports on research amongst a group of 'severely artistically-talented youth', which found certain factors which promote a culture of permission and protection. In **Chapter 17** Susannah Temple, a certified transactional analyst in the educational field, considers child rearing and growing up from a particular TA perspective. She presents her 'functional fluency' model of human social functioning (Temple, 1999, 2004) to illustrate human psychological development and to highlight the benefits of positive child rearing relationships.

In nearly fifty years – Berne's first article on transactional analysis was published in 1958 – TA has grown both organisationally and theoretically. Over the years a number of schools, traditions and perspectives have developed within TA. In common with other theoretical approaches to the fields of psychotherapy and counselling, education and organisational development, there is much discussion within TA about its identity and its development: What is TA? What are its commonalities? What are the differences and tensions within it? The last two chapters in this part represent theoretical developments in TA psychotherapy. In **Chapter 18** Maria Assunta Giusti, a qualified CTA and an experienced child psychotherapist who has worked with disturbed children for nearly 30 years, writes about a new methodology for working with children and parents. This chapter draws on the psychoanalytic tradition within TA and integrates insights from self psychology and developmental psychology. In **Chapter 19** Paul Kellet, a certified transactional analyst in psychotherapy, explores a developing perspective in TA, that of relational transactional analysis. Drawing on object relations, self psychology and Lacanian psychoanalytical theory, Kellett reflects on his therapeutic relationship with a young man in terms of a developing sense of self and theory of self. His honest account of his own reflections on and fantasies in his work owes much and contributes to the methodology of relational TA (see Hargaden and Sills, 2002).

Finally, in a book which emphasises context, I also want to acknowledge the context and contribution of my own family, the contributing authors and the publisher. In *Principles of Group Treatment* Berne (1966: 64) discusses the necessary preparation a group therapist must take before running a group. He goes on to pose some questions about the therapeutic relationship:

> *First, in regard to his own development, he should ask himself: 'Why am I sitting in this room? Why am I not at home with my children, or skiing, or skin-diving, or playing chess, or whatever else my fancy might dictate?'*

These are good questions for the busy practitioner – and in my experience most practitioners are busy – and also for the busy author or editor. I thank my family and, with regard to this particular project, especially my children, Saul and Esther, for their patience – as well as their impatience – with a sometimes absent father. Like Topsy this book 'just growed', enhanced and interrupted by developments and new ideas which became new chapters, and by life events which interrupted the process but which, like any crisis, gave rise to new opportunities – and chapters, and I want to acknowledge the patience of the contributors, especially those who wrote and submitted their chapters promptly and early on in this process. Thanks also go to Geoffrey Mann at Russell House for his enthusiasm for this project and his positive response to its scope which might have daunted other publishers. A final acknowledgement goes to all the children and young people who appear in these pages, with permission, and suitably anonymised and disguised, without whose experience, stories and reflections we, as practitioners and readers, could not continue to learn and develop.

References

Amundson, N.E. (1978) Developmental Principles and TA with Children. *Transactional Analysis Journal*, 8, 142–3.

Berne, E. (1958) Transactional Analysis: A New And Effective Method of Group Therapy. *American Journal of Psychotherapy*, 11, 292–309.

Berne, E. (1966) *Principles of Group Treatment*. New York: Grove Press.

Berne, E. (1975) *What Do You Say After You Say Hello?* Harmondsworth: Penguin. (Original work published 1972)

Berne, E. (1968) *The Happy Valley*. New York: Grove Press.

Bonds-White, F. (Ed.) (1988) TA and Children [Special issue]. *Transactional Analysis Journal*, 18: 2.

Crossman, P. (1966) Permission and Protection. *Transactional Analysis Bulletin*, 5: 19, 152–4.

Freed, A.M. (1971) *TA for Kids*. Sacramento, CA: Jalmar Press.

Freed, A.M. (1973) *TA for Tots (and Other Prinzes)*. Sacramento, CA: Jalmar Press.

Freed, A.M. (1976) *TA for Teens and Other Important People*. Sacramento, CA: Jalmar Press.

Hargaden, H. and Sills, C. (2002) *Transactional Analysis: A Relational Perspective*. London: Brunner-Routledge.

Gibran, K. (1926) *The Prophet*. London: Heinemann. (Original work published 1923)

Guisti, M.A. (2006) *La Piccola Principessa* [The Little Princess]. Rome: Istituto di Analisi Transazionale/Associazione Italiana di Analisi Transazionale.

James, M. (1969) Transactional Analysis With Children: The Initial Session. *Transactional Analysis Bulletin*, 8: 29, 1–2.

Karpman, S. (1968) Fairy Tales and Script Drama Analysis. *Transactional Analysis Bulletin*, 7: 26, 39–43.

Kleinewiese, E. (1988) *Circle-Face Symbols*. Berlin: Institut für Kommunikationstherapie.

Levin, P. (1988a) *Becoming The Way We Are* (3rd edn). Deerfield Beach, FL: Health Communications.

Levin, P. (1988b) *Cycles of Power*. Hollywood, CA: Health Communications.

Mannell, S.B., Piehl, W. and Edwards, M. (1968) TA with Children and Adolescents. *Transactional Analysis Bulletin*, 7: 28, 84–5.

Mountain, A. (2004) *The Space Between: Bridging the Gap Between Workers and Young People*. Lyme Regis: Russell House Publishing.

Mountain, A. and Davidson, C. (2005) Assessing Systems and Processes in Organizations. *Transactional Analysis Journal*, 35: 4, 336–45.

Newton, T. (Ed.) (2005) TA and Education [Special issue]. *Transactional Analysis Journal*, 34: 3.

Piehl, W. (1969) TA with Children. *Transactional Analysis Bulletin*, 8: 32, 98.

Steiner, C. (1977) *The Warm Fuzzy Tale*. Rolling Hill Estates, CA: Jalmar Press.

Temple, S. (1999) Functional Fluency for Educational Transactional Analysis. *Transactional Analysis Journal*, 29: 3, 164–74.

Temple, S. (2004) Update on the Functional Fluency Model in Education. *Transactional Analysis Journal*, 34: 3, 197–204.

Tudor, K. (1991) Children's Groups: Integrating TA and Gestalt Perspectives. *Transactional Analysis Journal*, 21, 12–20.

CHAPTER 1

Introducing Transactional Analysis

Graeme Summers and Keith Tudor

This chapter stands as an introduction to transactional analysis (TA) especially for the reader who is unfamiliar to TA for whom the chapter aims:

- To provide knowledge of the basic concepts of TA, including, through some guided reflections, its application to their own lives.
- To provide a contemporary view and reading of TA.
- To provide an introduction to the concepts and theories referred to throughout the book and, thereby, to make the book more accessible.

Transactional analysis is a way of understanding what happens between and within people. Since its conception in the 1950s by Eric Berne (1910–1970) it has evolved from its origins as a form of psychotherapy to include other, well-established applications in the fields of counselling, education and organisational development.

One of Berne's concerns was to make complex ideas and concepts, especially those from psychoanalysis, accessible to the lay person (see Berne, 1957/1971). Thus, he described the structure of personality in terms of Parent, Adult and Child *ego states*; the psycho-social model of human development in terms of *life script*; the stimulus-response model of human communication in terms of *transactions*; and Freud's concept of repetition-compulsion in terms of the *psychological games* people play (Berne, 1964/1968). These four concepts represent the fundamental theory of TA on which diverse theory and practice has been developed. During Berne's life other TA practitioners, influenced by radical psychiatry, gestalt therapy and ideas about radical parenting and regression therapy, developed what came to be known as 'schools' of TA. In the 35 years since Berne's death, TA theorists and practitioners have continued to develop the theory, techniques and practice of TA, developments and differences which are represented by the different contributors to this book. From its humble beginings as a seminar group meeting in San Francisco, TA has developed organisationally. Now the International Transactional Analysis Association (ITAA), a non profit educational organisation, with a system of accreditation, has practitioners, teachers and supervisors in over 65 countries (see www.itaa-net.org).

There are a number of introductions to TA (Stewart and Joines, 1987; Lapworth, Sills and Fish, 1993; Stewart, 2000; Tudor and Hobbes, 2007). In this introduction we take a co-creative perspective on TA, based on previous work (Summers and Tudor, 2000). For those who are interested to read about Eric Berne there are two biographies (Jorgenson and Jorgenson, 1984; and Stewart, 1992). For those who are interested in attending an introductory (TA '101') training course see details on the ITAA's website (www.itaa-net.org) and, in the UK, the website of the Institute of Transactional Analysis (www.ita.org.uk).

Co-creative TA

Co-creative TA is a contemporary perspective on TA that integrates recent developments in philosophy and psychology. Co-creative TA updates the four core concepts of TA theory – ego states, transactions, games and scripts – to provide models of:

- Personality – a way of understanding yourself and others.
- Relationship – ways of initiating or maintaining creative contact with other people.
- Confirmation – understanding and influencing repeating patterns of positive or negative interactions and their predictable outcomes.
- Identity – ways of understanding yourself in the context of your past and present culture and shaping the "stories' you construct about yourself, others and life.

These four models interact to give a clear and consistent framework for understanding what

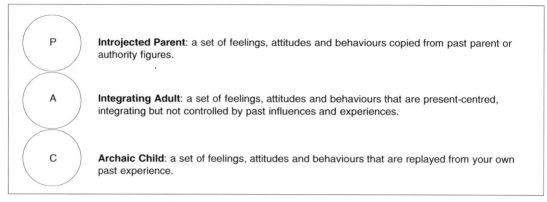

Introjected Parent: a set of feelings, attitudes and behaviours copied from past parent or authority figures.

Integrating Adult: a set of feelings, attitudes and behaviours that are present-centred, integrating but not controlled by past influences and experiences.

Archaic Child: a set of feelings, attitudes and behaviours that are replayed from your own past experience.

Figure 1.1   The ego state model of personality (structural model) (Lapworth, Sills and Fish, 1993)

happens within and between people. Each model describes both healthy and dysfunctional patterns and can be used to generate effective strategies to support personal and professional development. We explore each concept in turn.

Ego states (Co-creative personality)

Personality can be thought of as our 'sense of self' created through movement within and between ego states.

Ego states

An ego state is a set of feelings, attitudes and behaviours. It is a 'possible state of self': a potential way of being or relating that is co-created through our interactions with others. Berne identified three types of ego states (Figure 1.1).

The development of ego states

In the course of healthy human development we integrate experience throughout life. From infancy onwards we are naturally proactive and, with adequate support, will get what we need and reject what we don't need or negotiate 'good enough' compromises. We are innately motivated to be curious and seek attachment, competence and mutual recognition. Much of this can be achieved through the vitality of healthy inter-dependent relationships which help to regulate our feelings and needs. Healthy interactions include 'rough and tumble' and recovery from difficult or traumatic experiences. With repetition, these interactions become

generalised and encoded in emotional memory. These emotional memories support us to use and create sets of feelings, attitudes and behaviours that are effective in dealing with the challenges and opportunities that life presents. These are 'Integrating Adult' ego states.

However, most of us will have had situations in which we were not helped to manage particular feelings and needs. When our experience becomes unmanageable we can split our sense of self, creating two sets of feelings, attitudes and behaviours that are disconnected from our usual sense of who we are. This is an attempt to manage the mismatch between our need for support and the lack of appropriate response from a significant other. We simultaneously create a Parent and Child ego state. The Child ego state is like a snapshot of ourselves attempting to cope with more than we could manage. The Parent ego state is a set of feelings, attitudes and behaviours copied, as it were, from the parent figure or other person we were relating to at the time. Note that, on the basis of these definitions, anybody, however young, can be thought of as having Parent, Adult and Child ego states. Over the years, Berne developed his ideas, and other TA authors since have continued to develop these ideas and concepts in order to understand different and various aspects of human personality. The basic diagram (Figure 1.1) has been developed to incorporate different levels or orders of personality (first, second and third). When referring to these developments and introducing more complex ideas, the contributing authors to this book explain their use of such terms and concepts.

Also, the precise nature and development of ego states is the source of some debate within the TA community, and this is reflected in the different authors' contributions to this book. Basically, there are two views on ego state development, both of which derive from Berne's original work. The first is that, as Parent, Adult and Child ego states all represent different aspects of the structure of personality, they may all be developed. Thus new, positive messages are viewed as being introjected into a developing Parent ego state. Similarly a person may make a new, positive decision 'in Child' about an old, unhelpful or abusive message they received as a child and in this sense develop their Child ego state. This view and model is represented in the chapters by Hoyer and Hyatt, Mountain, and Dentith and Lancashire. The other view takes Berne's (1961/1975: 76) definition of the Adult ego state – 'characterized by an autonomous set of feelings, attitudes, and behavior patterns which are adapted to the *current* reality' (our emphasis) – as its starting point and argues that Parent and Child ego states represent, respectively, past, unintegrated introjects from parental figures, and fixated, unresolved archaic experiences. As these are resolved and integrated, they form part of an ongoing, expansive and integrating part of the personality we may call the Adult or, as Berne originally named it, the *neopsyche* (see Tudor, 2003). This model is represented in the chapters by Tudor (Chapter 7), Naughton, and Temple.

Ego states in everyday life

Parent, Adult and Child are not people inside us. They are possible (and probable) ways of being and relating which are influenced by our choices, our expectations based on past experience, and our present situation. However, some TA writers use the phrase 'in her Child', 'in his Parent' and so on. We think this is confusing and so tend to write 'in' in inverted commas to make the point that these are ways of understanding personality and personal history rather than active figures.

Consider a time when you dealt with a problem or challenging situation creatively. You probably accessed resources from within yourself as well as accessing resources around you. Even though you may have been profoundly challenged or emotionally distressed, you were responsive, resourceful and creative. What did you feel? What attitude did you have? What did you do? At such moments you are probably in Adult 'flow': in good contact with yourself and your environment.

Now consider a situation in which you got stuck. In hindsight you recognise that the set of feelings, attitudes and behaviours you brought to that situation were not useful. Perhaps at a different time you might have managed the situation much more effectively. The probability here is that you were approaching the situation from a Parent or Child ego state: a familiar but unhelpful set of feelings, attitudes and behaviours.

It is not surprising that people tend to act out of Parent or Child ego states at times of stress or anxiety since these are familiar ways of attempting to manage difficult experiences. These regressive ego states are often at the heart of problematic or unfulfilling relationships at home and work. Example: Alan is eleven years old and about to begin secondary school. He begins to initiate fights with his younger sister in a way which he used to do six years ago. John, his father, feels frustrated and considers punishing Alan by sending him to bed early. Here we might hypothesise that, in response to the challenge of starting a new school, Alan has 'regressed' from his normal eleven year old self (Adult) to being like he was at five years old (Child).

Using ego states

Here we highlight three ways of using ego states.

1. *Develop awareness*

Knowing 'where you are coming from' is enormously useful. Sometimes this awareness alone is sufficient to help you interrupt a defensive Parent or Child response and approach a situation from Adult instead. There are four clues that you can use to help identify which ego state you (or others) may be using at any given point in time:

- Behavioural – are you behaving in a parental or child-like way e.g. telling someone off (Parent) or sulking (Child)? Example: Alan starts to initiate fights like he did when he was five years old.
- Social – are others around you behaving in a complementary fashion? If others are being child-like, this might indicate that you are operating from a Parent ego state. Example:

John feels like treating Alan as though he is a younger child. This appears to be a Parent response that complements Alan's child-like behaviour.

- Historical – does your attitude or behaviour remind you of one of your parent figures, or yourself when you were younger? Example: We know from the narrative above that Alan's behaviour is similar to his behaviour when he was younger. John recognises that his initial response was to punish Alan in the way that he had been punished by his own father.
- Felt sense (originally referred to as 'phenomenological') – do you feel as if you are one of your parent figures, or as if you are younger than you actually are? Example: We could only discover this through asking Alan how old he feels when he is initiating a fight (assuming he was both able and trusting enough to tell us).

Note that 'in' Adult we may behave in a parent or child-like way because it is appropriate, effective, or just good fun. This is different from compulsively responding from Parent or Child which is usually ineffective, defensive and limiting. You may use the four questions above to help identify which ego state you (or others) are coming from. Notice the situations in which you are more likely to move into each of the three types of ego state.

2. *Strengthen and expand your Integrating Adult*

Our greatest potential for personal and professional development lies in developing our strengths rather than improving our weaknesses. It is important to know and exercise your natural and cultivated strengths. In which situations do you thrive? What triggers your Adult ego state? In what conditions do you enjoy and maintain Adult flow? Which sets of feelings, attitudes and behaviours do you use?

The answers to these questions will be very personal, reflecting your uniqueness as an individual. These are important questions because they help us focus on health, strength and vitality. It is also essential to draw on healthy Adult resources in order to manage our areas of weakness and our potential to use Parent or Child defences. These are also useful questions to ask of people with whom you are working, similarly, in order to help them identify strengths as well as stuck or sore points.

When in Adult flow we will naturally explore and expand our range of being and relating because we are curious about ourselves, others and life. We will invent and test new possibilities, expanding our relational, emotional, intellectual or technical capacities. At times this may involve managing and 'working through' our Parent and Child defences against the fear and excitement this new learning might provoke. Example: One of Alan's strengths is in his determination to be like bigger boys. He will often take necessary and appropriate developmental risks because he wants to be more grown up. Alan and John can find ways to build on this strength in order to help Alan manage his anxiety and excitement about starting 'big' school. One of John's strengths is in his willingness to discuss these difficulties with his wife even though he finds this uncomfortable.

3. *Manage or 'work through' Parent or Child defences*

It is important to stay respectful of yourself even when you notice that you compulsively move into Parent or Child ego states. Recognise that you created these ego states (out of awareness) as an attempt to manage what felt unmanageable at the time. You might still use these ego states in the present for the same reason. It may be that adopting this compassionate attitude towards yourself (and others) helps you move out of Parent and Child more quickly.

'Working through' means learning how to tolerate more of your experience with fresh support that was previously unavailable. Interestingly, learning to feel intense pleasure or excitement can be as challenging as feeling anger, fear and sadness. This healing process is one of expanding your Adult capacity to experience and manage previously repressed feelings, needs and desires so reducing the compulsion to use Parent and Child defences at times of difficulty or change. Example: why has Alan regressed to five years old? John and his partner remember the difficulties Alan had in starting primary school and wonder if some of those feelings are re-stimulated at the thought of this next move. This 'connection' and the support of his partner helps John tolerate his own frustration and to find out what Alan needs from him now. Here John learns how to contain his Parent impulses and develop his capacity to be with his son in new (Adult) ways.

Transactions (Co-creative relationship)

A transaction is an exchange between people that consists of a stimulus and a response. Transactions are the building blocks of relationship to which both (or more) parties contribute.

From a TA perspective, there are three main types of transaction: parallel, crossed and ulterior. Each type of transaction has, according to Berne (1966) a corresponding rule of communication.

Parallel transactions

These are transactions in which the vectors are parallel, and the ego-state addressed is the one from which the recipient responds.

Both these types of transactions are parallel yet each build very different kinds of relationship. Healthy present-centred relating consists of Adult – Adult transactions. Problematic or unhealthy relating consists of transactions involving Parent and Child ego states, a common example being the Parent – Child transaction. Berne (1966: 223) summarises this in his first rule of communication: 'as long as the vectors are parallel, communication can proceed indefinitely.'

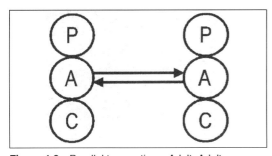

Figure 1.2   Parallel transactions: Adult–Adult

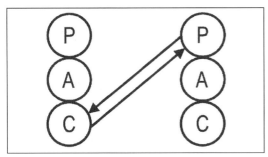

Figure 1.3   Parallel transactions: Parent–Child

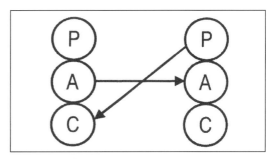

Figure 1.4   Crossed transactions

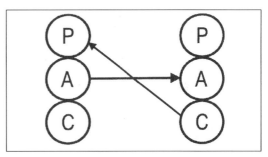

Figure 1.5   Crossed transactions

Crossed transactions

When people cross transactions the vectors are no longer parallel, and the ego state addressed is not the one from which the recipient responds. Figures 1.4. and 1.5 show two examples of crossed transactions.

A crossed transaction is a moment of change, often marked by a pause in the conversation. It is a way of switching from healthy to unhealthy relating or vice versa. Stewart and Joines (1987: 65) summarise Berne's second rule of communictaion: 'When a transaction is crossed, a break in communication results and one or both individuals will need to shift ego-states [sic] *in order for communication to be re-established.'*

Ulterior transactions

Here, in order to conceptualise the ulterior transaction, we distinguish between social and psychological level messages (see Figures 1.6 and 1.7)

The social level messages are explicit and represented by solid arrows; the psychological level messages are implicit and represented by dashed arrows. Berne's (1966: 227) third rule of communication states that: 'The behavioural

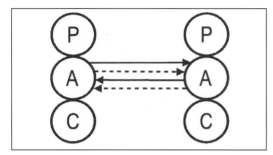

Figure 1.6   Ulterior transactions

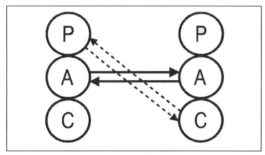

Figure 1.7   Ulterior transactions

outcome of an ulterior transaction is determined at the psychological and not at the social level.' In other words: the non-verbal messages we give and receive often have the most impact. We can give and receive healthy (Adult) and unhealthy (Parent or Child) ulterior messages. Parent or Child psychological messages are often hidden by apparent Adult-Adult social level messages. Example: Alan and his father had intitially got into a Parent-Child parallel transaction initiated by Alan's provocative behaviour. We speculate that Alan's ulterior message to his father might be 'contain me'. In order to break their negative pattern Alan's father needs to be firm but fair and supportive. He needs to guide his son's behaviour away from destructive 'acting out' and help him manage his anxieties about starting school. This would constitute crossing the transaction by inviting and supporting Alan to behave age appropriately (Adult) as he faces this new challenge.

Recognition

Any transaction involves an exchange of recognition between people. This is significant because it is a poweful motivation for people to interact and was one of a number of human

hungers which Berne (1970/1973) identified. Recognition may vary in intensity or significance and be verbal or non-verbal, positive or negative, and conditional or unconditional.

Strokes

Berne used the word 'stroke' to describe a unit of recognition because our first recognition as infants often comes through physical touch. Later, Steiner (1974), drawing an analogy with the economic world, suggested that social and cultural patterns mediated through the family creates a certain 'stroke economy' which is maintained by means of five restrictive rules:

- Don't give strokes when you have them to give.
- Don't ask for strokes when you need them.
- Don't accept strokes if you want them.
- Don't reject strokes when you don't want them.
- Don't give yourself strokes.

Using transactions

1. Build Adult–Adult relationships

Discover and use Adult triggers. Enjoy Adult-Adult transactions. Use positive ulteriors. Negotiate for what you want. Develop secure attachments.

2. Cross problem transactions

Use your own impulses to respond from Parent or Child as information about the other person. Reject invitations to respond from these ego states. Respond from an Adult ego state. Tolerate the discomfort of temporarily breaking communication. Allow the other person time to move to Adult. Validate old realities. Create and support new possibilities.

3. Use positive and useful recognition

Catch yourself and others doing things right. Give, ask for and receive positive and useful feedback. Work out your own stroke economy. Reject it and unhelpful feedback.

Games (Co-creative confirmation)

A game, or psychological game (to distinguish it from forms of structured play), is a pattern of transactions that is used to confirm positive or negative feelings and beliefs about self or others. It is, according to Berne (1964/1968: 44), 'an ongoing series of complementary ulterior transactions progressing to a well defined predictable outcome.' Again, from a co-creative perspective, games are co-created by both parties: just as it takes two to tango, it also takes two to tangle.

Structure of games

The structure of a positive or negative game can be described using the game plan which was developed by James (1973), and comprises a series of questions:.

1. What keeps happening to me over and over again?
2. How does it start?
3. What happens next?
4. (Mystery question)
5. And then?
6. (Mystery question)
7. How does it end?
8a. How do I feel?
8b. How do I think the other person feels?

The feelings and attitudes created at the end of a game are described as the game 'payoff'.

Positive games

In TA games are traditionally viewed as negative, although Berne (1964/1968: 143) himself defined a good game as: 'one whose social contribution outweighs the complexity of its motivations . . . [therefore] a "good" game would be one which contributes both to the well-being of the other players and to the unfolding of the one who is "it".' Consider a relationship with someone you know that is consistently satisfying. Now use the above gameplan to map out the sequence of the pattern you manage to co-create with this person over and over again. Finally consider the mystery questions:

4. What is my secret message to the other person?
6. What is the other person's secret message to me?

Typical responses to this approach are that such patterns start with a sense of anticipation,

welcoming and re-connection. The middle phase often involves sharing, exploring, honesty and creative co-operation. Such patterns often end with satisfaction, confirmation, and well-being. Common ulteriors include 'I like you', 'I trust you' and 'I respect you'. In satisfying relationships such patterns create a framework for intimate and productive contact.

Negative games

Now use the above game plan to consider a repetitive negative pattern that occurs over and over with another person. Here you are describing the structure of a game where the payoff is to end up with familiar negative feelings and attitudes towards yourself and/or others.

The drama triangle

The structure of a negative game can also be described using the drama triangle (Karpman, 1968).

All three game roles are, in TA terms, inauthentic and are played from Parent or Child ego states. Negative games often involve a switch in game roles as the game is played out.

Examples of negative games are:

- 'Now I've got you' – in which one person exploits another person's mistakes or weakness for psychological gain, and the other party allows this.
- 'Kick me' – doing things badly until eventually people feel obliged to put you down.
- 'Why don't you?' – offering unsolicited advice which often leads to a reponse of . . .
- 'Yes, but . . . ' – acting as if you needed help and then refusing every suggestion.
- 'After all I've done for you'- doing too much and then feeling resentful.

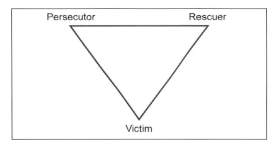

Figure 1.8 The drama triangle (Karpman, 1968)

Characteristics of negative games

Negative games are repetitive, involve negative ulterior transactions, often include a moment of surprise or confusion and end with the players experiencing familiar bad feelings and attitudes. They can be played at different degrees of intensity.

The advantages of games

People play positive and negative games to regulate feelings, structure time, confirm beliefs about self and others, get recognition, and maintain connections to other people.

Using game theory

1. Develop and savour positive games

Pay attention to relationships that work well. Understand your explicit and implicit contribution to positive outcomes. Savour satisfaction and ask yourself how you can repeat this in other areas of your life.

2. Change negative games

Celebrate awareness as you use hindsight, midsight, insight, and foresight to become aware of and name negative games. Dis-invest in the negative payoff. Use the 'winners' triangle' (Choy, 1990) to respond from Adult instead of Parent or Child, that is, be assertive and potent instead of persecutory, responsive instead of rescuing, and proactively vulnerable instead of being a victim. Adjust or reaffirm goals, agreements and positive aspects of relationship. Learn from the game. Create alternative forms of structure, stimulation and recognition. Example: Alan has initiated a game of 'Kick me' as an attempt to manage his discomfort about going to his new school. Alan's father is tempted to 'punish' as expected but is seeking a way to interrupt the sequence of this negative game and invite Alan into a positive game of 'I can do it' which will reinforce Alan's sense of himself as capable of growing up and facing challenges with courage, creativity and support.

Scripts (Co-creative identity)

A personal script or life script is the set of beliefs we make about ourselves, others and life and the decisions we make based on these beliefs. It is a way of understanding how we define ourselves within the context of past and present cultural influence. As Cornell (1988: 281) defines it: 'Life script is the ongoing process of a self-defining and sometimes self-limiting psychological construction of reality.'

Script messages

Our 'psychological construction' influences and is influenced by messages we receive from others and the culture and sub-cultures within which we live. These messages may be positive or negative in intent or impact and can be classified in five main ways:

- Attributions e.g. 'You are . . . ' – characteristics ascribed to you by others e.g. shy, clever, stupid, likeable.
- Injunctions e.g. 'Don't . . . ' – prohibitive messages (often non-verbal).
- Permissions e.g. 'You can . . . ' – messages which encourage or support options.
- Counter-injunctions e.g. 'You should . . . ' – prescriptive messages, usually given directly, such as 'Work hard', 'Be good', 'Do your best'.
- Modelling e.g. 'Here's how to . . . ' – modelling by others showing how to fulfil other script messages.

Co-creative script matrix

The script matrix, originally developed by Steiner (1966) is, in effect, a personal map on which people can note and trace their developmental history through the influences of their parents, family, friends and culture. The matrix below (Figure 1.9) helps map script messages from *and to* significant others. This can be used to reflect on formative co-created influences early in life or to reflect on current relationships.

The traditional script matrix maps messages to and from two parents to the child or subject. The co-creative script matrix can be used to map influences in terms of any social construct important to you e.g. regarding gender, class, race, age, etc. (see Naughton and Tudor, 2006) so important questions may be: What binary construct is most significant to you (male-female, black-white, disabled-able-bodied, working class-middle class, gay-straight)? What messages do people give to you? What messages do you give others?

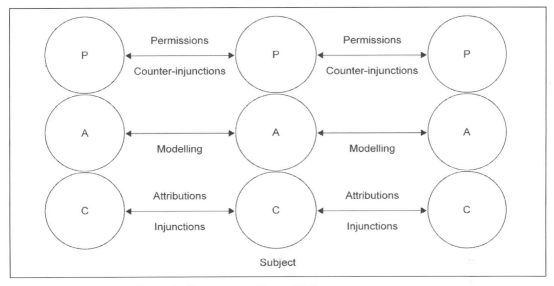

Figure 1.9   Co-creative script matrix (Summers and Tudor, 2000)

Script responses

The messages we receive from different people, and sometimes the same person, may be contradictory. In addition, we are not passive recipients and will therefore respond to messages we receive with our own creative and adaptive capacities. This means that even in difficult circumstances we have scope for forming our own conclusions and making personal decisions. Sometimes these beliefs and decisions are not cognitive or even conscious but can be characterised as emotional, instinctive or intuitive responses to our opportunities and limitations in a given situation. As you reflect on your experience, consider what beliefs and decisions have you made (in or out of awareness) in response to script messages? Are there any you have already changed or want to change? Also, script formation is a two way process . . . so what influence do you want to have on others or your culture?

Using script theory

1. Identify script messages and responses

Identify past and present script messages i.e. attributions, injunctions, permissions, counter-injunctions and modelling. Use the script matrix to map these out in terms of significant relationships and broader cultural patterns.

Identify and infer the beliefs and decisions you have made in the context of these influences.

2. Update script messages, beliefs and decisions

Experiment with alternative beliefs and decisions about you and your life. Take into account your natural strengths, interests and your social identity. Notice what happens when you define yourself differently. Seek and use messages and relationships that support the beliefs and decisions that feel right for you. See the bigger picture: understand that your personal change may be emotional, cognitive, and behavioural as well as being part of broader social, political and spiritual processes. Example: John experiences a dilemma. He wants to help his son to face challenges rather than regress – but he also wants him to be able to ask for and use support rather than just pretending to 'be strong'. In this process John has needed to question his own 'be strong' attitude to parenting and the appropriateness of copying what he had learned from his own father. As he works through this dilemma with Alan, he and his son are co-creating new identities for each other and engaging in a broader social process of redefining what it means to be male – in which being courageous and adventurous can also include sharing vunerability and requesting and receiving help when needed.

Summary

This introduction to TA emphasises the co-created nature of personality (ego states); relationships (based on transactions); how we confirm or discount each other (through games); and our identity (or life script). On the basis of these fundamental concepts TA has, over the past 50 years, developed enormously. From its roots in psychoanalysis and cognitive behavioural therapy, a number of other traditions have influenced TA, for a summary of which see Tudor and Hobbes (2007). TA has been influenced by and has influenced the theory and practice of radical psychiatry (see Steiner, 2000); it has developed innovative ideas about and practice in working with severely disturbed people (see Schiff et al., 1975); it has close links to gestalt psychology and its therapy (see Goulding and Goulding, 1979); it is viewed by some as an integrative psychotherapy (e.g. Erskine and Moursund, 1988; Clarkson, 1992); and it is actively involved in the current interest in relational psychotherapy (see Hargaden and Sills, 2002) – and the contributors and chapters in this book reflect this diversity.

Where a contributing author refers to another concept in TA (which does not appear in this introduction) she or he introduces it. A number of authors refer to the same concept and, to save repetition, two key concepts are briefly introduced and summarised.

Systemic assessment

As is apparent from the structure of the book, 'context counts'. To paraphrase John Donne, 'no child is an island, entire of herself'. It's not possible to work with a child or a young person without viewing her or him in her or his environmental context. To represent this Clarkson and Fish (1998) developed a model for the overlapping sub-systems in the life of child which they conceptualised as a tool for a systemic assessment and planning of TA child psychotherapy (Figure 1.10).

A number of the contributors to this book refer to this model as a conceptual map for a systemic way of thinking about working with a child or young person *in context*.

Contracts and contracting

TA is based on what is known as 'the contractual method', a contract being a mutually agreed statement of change or, as Berne (1966: 362) puts it: 'An explicit bilateral agreement to a well-defined course of action'. The contract, the process of contracting, and the contractual method is the basic therapeutic method of TA and maintains an openness between therapist and client on the basis that the outcome, process and method of therapy is negotiated, agreed and re-negotiable. Of particular relevance to working with children is the concept of the three-handed or three-cornered contract (English, 1975) (Figure 1.11).

Originally developed in the context of training, English conceptualised and designed this, as an antidote to, as she viewed it (p. 383), 'various additional and mutually contradictory expectations [on the part of] participants based on subtle promises that have been made deliberately or unknowingly [by the organisers]'. As working with children as minors clearly involves a third party (parent/s, carer/s) – and, not unusually, even fourth and fifth parties (school, social services departments, and so on), this concept has been found to be most useful in clarifying complex relationships, expectations and agreements (see Tudor, 2006).

Again, over the years, the theory of contracts in TA has been developed and, indeed, has influenced the broader, generic field of psychotherapy and counselling (see Sills, 2006).

References

Berne, E. (1961) *Transactional Analysis in Psychology*. New York: Grove Press.

Berne, E. (1966) *Principles of Group Treatment*. New York: Grove Press.

Berne, E. (1968) *Games People Play*. Harmondsworth: Penguin. (Original work published 1964)

Berne, E. (1971) *A Layman's Guide to Psychiatry and Psychoanalysis*. Harmondsworth: Penguin. (Original work published 1957)

Berne, E. (1973) *Sex in Human Loving*. Harmondsworth: Penguin. (Original work published 1970)

Berne, E. (1975) *What Do You Say After You Say Hello*. London: Corgi Press.

Choy, A. (1990) The Winner's Triangle. *Transactional Analysis Journal*, 20: 1, 40–6.

Clarkson, P. (1992) *Transactional Analysis Psychotherapy: An Integrated Approach*. London: Routledge.

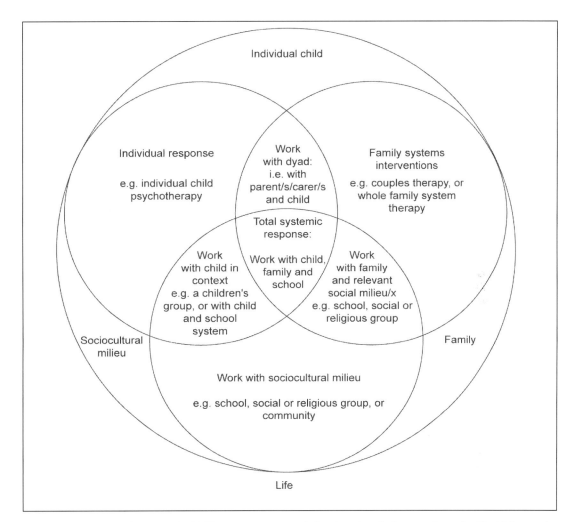

Figure 1.10   A model for systemic thinking, assessment and planning of socio-therapeutic work with children and young people (based on Clarkson and Fish, 1988)

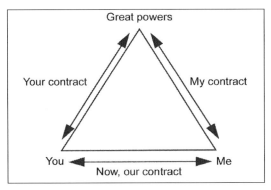

Figure 1.11   The three-cornered contract (English, 1975)

Clarkson, P. and Fish, S. (1988) Systemic Assessment and Treatment Considerations in TA Child Psychotherapy. *Transactional Analysis Journal*, 18: 2, 123–32.

Cornell, W.F. (1988) Life Script Theory: A Critical Review from a Developmental Perspective. *Transactional Analysis Journal*, 18: 4, 270–82.

Cornell, W.F. and Hargaden, H. (Eds.) (2005) *From Transactions to Relations*. Haddon Press.

English, F. (1975) The Three-cornered Contract. *Transactional Analysis Journal*, 5, 383–4.

Erskine, R. and Moursund, J. (1988) *Integrative Psychotherapy in Action*. Newbury Park, CA: Sage.

Goulding, M. and Goulding, R. (1979) *Changing Lives Through Redecision Therapy*. New York: Brunner-Mazel.

Hargaden, H. and Sills, C. (2002) *Transactional Analysis: A Relational Perspective*. London: Routledge.

James, J. (1973) The Game Plan. *Transactional Analysis Journal*, 3: 4, 14–17.

Jorgensen, E.W. and Jorgensen, H.I. (1984) *Eric Berne: Master Gamesman*. New York: Grove Press.

Karpman, S (1968) Fairy Tales and Script Drama Analysis. *Transactional Analysis Bulletin*, 7: 26, 39–43.

Lapworth, P., Sills, C. and Fish, S. (1993) *Transactional Analysis Counselling*. Bicester: Winslow.

Naughton, M. and Tudor, K. (2006) Being White. *Transactional Analysis Journal*, 36: 2, 159–71.

Schiff, J.L. et al. (1975) *Cathexis Reader: Transactional Analysis Treatment of Psychosis*. New York: Harper and Row.

Sills, C. (ed) (2006) *Contracts in Counselling* (2nd edn). London: Sage.

Steiner, C. (1966) Script and Counterscript. *Transactional Analysis Bulletin*, 5: 18, 133–135.

Steiner, C. (1974) *Scripts People Live: Transactional Analysis Councelling*. London: Sage.

Steiner, C. (2000) Radical Psychiatry. In Corsini, R.J. (Ed.) *Handbook of Innovative Therapy*. Chichester: Wiley.

Stewart, I. (1992) *Eric Berne*. London: Sage.

Stewart, I. (2000) *Transactional Analysis Counselling in Action*. (2nd edn) London: Sage.

Stewart, I. and Joines, V. (1987) *TA Today*. Nottingham: Lifespace.

Summers, G. and Tudor, K. (2000) Cocreative Transactional Analysis. *Transactional Analysis Journal*, 30: 1, 23–40.

Tudor, K. (2003) The Neopsyche: The Integrating Adult Ego State. In Sills, C. and Hargaden, H. (Eds.) *Ego States*. London: Worth Reading.

Tudor, K. (2006) Contracts, Complexity and Challenge. In Sills, C. (Ed.) *Contracts in Counselling and Psychotherapy*. (2nd edn) London: Sage.

Tudor, K. and Hobbes, R. (2007) Transactional Analysis. In Dryden, W. (Ed.) *The Handbook of Individual Therapy*. (5th edn) London: Sage.

PART ONE

There's No Such Thing as a Child:
Children and Young People in Context

CHAPTER 2

Building the Virtual Village: Working with the Social Environment

Trudi Newton

I am writing this on the veranda of an ancient farmstead in the Western Cape province of South Africa. As I write, I can see people moving around the farm's open spaces – many people, men and women, far more than you would see on a mechanised farm in Britain, tending horses, pigs and cattle, working on the combine, doing domestic tasks around the farm buildings. I am reminded that last weekend, in the transactional analysis (TA) training group in Cape Town, someone mentioned the African saying 'It takes a village to raise a child'. It does.

What does this saying convey to you? To me it evokes a culture in which compassionate communal networks encourage and support all members and no one is isolated. In my internal landscape of the 'village' all the inhabitants are known and recognised; defined boundaries make for security, structure and safety; there are varied contacts and relationships with clear responsibilities; there is wisdom, shared history, stories and sayings of the community often held and remembered by 'people to go to'. Health, learning and spiritual needs are all accounted for, stages in development are acknowledged, peer groups (from little kids to the elderly) are recognised and appreciated. Above all there is acceptance, interdependence, a sense of belonging – and freedom. A community, or a society, that shows these qualities is what I mean by a virtual village.

But today, in western society, that picture of community which many of us carry in our heads – a caring, supportive, understanding group, an idealised family – has become fragmented for us as we continue to expand our individualised, independent, isolated ways of life.

And perhaps the village was not always as good a thing as the saying suggests. Some in the training group believed that the 'village' could engender a fear of individuality and of thinking for oneself, rather than the benevolent picture I have evoked. Their 'village' meant domination, smothering, fear of challenge or novelty,

demands for compliance and penalties for rebellion.

So how do we create an appropriate 'village' in a modern, 21st century, western capitalist society where the equivalent of the visible African village has become a thing of the past? My aim in this chapter is to discuss TA as a framework for understanding what happens in normal healthy development and thriving, and how we can use that understanding to create an environment that has the characteristics of my 'virtual village'. The context I refer to is the formal education setting, from kindergarten through primary to secondary phase, looking at what the environment needs to take account of so as to promote the emotional health which is a precursor to real learning.

Promoting thriving in school

Somehow we need to find a balance between our contemporary focus on individual autonomy and the benefits of community that we can sense in 'the village'. What we do know, and what resonates for us in that saying, is that the social environment beyond the immediate family is paramount to how children develop. It acknowledges the significance of the wider social environment as well as the contained family one. Communities raise children, not nuclear families, and communities are responsible for providing and sustaining what children need for growing up, and what grownups need in order to do the bringing-up.

A learning environment, such as playgroup, nursery or school, is usually a child's first experience of social life outside the home. Our education system provides the social institution which has the closest contact with children for most of their formative years and is the best placed to observe and recognise difficulties that interfere with a child's development. As Heller (2000: 22) puts it:

Schools are uniquely placed to ... recognise social and emotional difficulties and to address needs which are interfering with the learning process ... (often) masked by misleading behaviour which may repel rather than attract help and understanding. The challenge is to produce conditions in which troubled pupils feel safe enough to reveal their needs and in which someone pays attention and responds appropriately.

Heller is discussing counselling services in schools. This is an important area but it is not always possible for teachers or support staff to refer all troubled children to experienced and empathic helpers. Sometimes emotional difficulties or gaps in development that appear are perceived by the 'big people' as behaviour problems that are beyond help and result in 'labelling' of the child. When this happens responses sometimes focus on 'fixing' the child through behavioural techniques, or interventions that remove the child from the environment, and send a message that they are at fault in some way.

An alternative approach is to consider the whole environment – how things would look if all was going well – and identify what resources the child/teacher/class/school have, or need, to change the system and promote a positive outcome.

Rackets and games are played out in the classroom, just as they are in the home and school is a place where the alternatives of self-determination, autonomy and interdependence can be fostered (Frazier, 1971). As we observe the links between environment and development, how does a TA approach facilitate an understanding of the learning process, both emotional and cognitive? How can knowing, thinking and using TA promote thriving?

TA offers an enormous potential for positive, blame-free, working methods. In an important article clarifying and proposing a new taxonomy with regard to games and rackets, Marilyn Zalcman (1990) argued that within the TA community we need to look to our educational and organisational colleagues for information about normal processes of learning and development in order to counteract the emphasis in the literature on pathology. She suggested that educational and organisational practitioners could incorporate into transactional analysis theory 'what learning theories and research on normal human behaviour [can] ... tell us about how people process information' (p. 17).

Since then it seems many educational practitioners have written about using TA as a model for understanding healthy development and exploring what is needed in a child's environment to achieve this – and what is needed to fill gaps in development at later stages (see, for instance, Clarke and Dawson, 1989/1998; Temple, 2000; Pierre, 2002; and see Emmerton and Newton, 2004 for a review of educational TA literature).

This chapter draws on ideas from many TA writers and practitioners as well as other psychologists and sociologists such as Martin Seligman (1991, 1995, 2002) and, more recently, Sue Gerhardt (2004), to examine how we can engage with educational culture to develop and maintain a social environment that promotes health. It includes a new model to integrate what we have learned, and links this to current thinking and research from other approaches.

Where we are now

We know what the current situation is. Although many schools achieve an inclusive learning culture, many others, primary, secondary and even nursery schools, particularly in inner city areas, have high rates of exclusions for unacceptable behaviour. Absenteeism is a major problem, as is antisocial behaviour and bullying among young men and increasingly among young women; susceptibility to addictions, conduct disorders, Attention Deficit Hyperactive Disorder and Obsessive Compulsive Disorder and evidence of links between these and personality disorders in adulthood are indicators that all is not well. Some schools claim they have to cope with too many children who are 'beyond'. Even without going so far, it is clear that many teachers and schools are struggling to do what they consider to be their primary job, i.e. teaching to a required standard, while at the same time coping with children whose only way of showing their distress and isolation is through challenging behaviour. While much superb work is done with individual children by school counsellors and support staff, there is a more general problem of holding together seemingly incompatible aims and meeting the varied needs of children to enable them to benefit from the school environment. Teachers may feel they are expected to be like social workers or surrogate parents, coping with conflicting expectations, being sympathetic while still maintaining traditional standards and exercising authority (Devlin, 1995).

Responses to these challenges often rely on a system of behavioural contracts, rewards and sanctions which increasingly are being shown not to attain the required outcome:

> . . . there is a growing number of youngsters for whom the 'normal', mainstream approaches to managing behaviour simply do not work. Invariably the perspectives used in understanding and responding to these cases are drawn from classic cognitive/behavioural theory – the standard, default mode for many schools across the country.
>
> (Barrow, Bradshaw and Newton, 2001: 4)

These authors invite us:

> . . . to consider the possibility that the children 'beyond' are actually telling us something about the limitations of conventional responses to difficult behaviour. Techniques that can 'work' for many children for much of the time can leave us bereft of ideas and success when it comes to those most difficult cases. The outcome can be to damn kids, and that can hold only fears for the future. The notion that instead we damn adults in schools for not doing it right is equally futile – they are our best hope. In responding to the challenge of increasing the inclusive capacity of schools, we need to take a more critical look at the theory, technique and practice of what we do.
>
> (ibid: 4)

There are some important factors to note here:

- Evidence does not support the theory that simple behavioural techniques work in the long term. Observation indicates that while small children may respond well for a while to this approach alone, older children soon learn that if they don't want the proffered rewards, and don't care about the sanctions, there is little the 'big people' can do. Research in the field of behavioural science has shown that not all animals respond as expected (Seligman, 2002).
- The cause of disruptive behaviour may not simply be poor learning about expectations and consequences but the expression of a need or developmental gap in the only way the child knows; this may be dramatic and disturbing but can nevertheless respond to a different approach (Newton and Wong, 2003).
- Significantly, many behavioural methods model a social ethic and a social environment in which work, productivity and money, not people as valued individuals or relationships as key to change and development, are the

priority. This may be the key factor in the present situation and no amount of reinforcing the behavioural response in answer to yet more evidence of crisis is going to be effective.

We need a different paradigm and a different solution – a new way forward. Some recent writing challenges conventional thinking:

- Oliver James (2003) points out that increasing wealth does not link to an increased sense of well-being beyond a certain point. He even gives a figure – £16,000 per annum – as the income level above which there appears to be no significant improvement in either mental health or happiness. Advanced capitalism, he says, and its associated social pressures, are making us 'ill' rather than healthy. It is also true that within developed nations the poorest classes are more liable to be mentally ill than the richer ones. He says: 'The implications are profound. If, after our physical welfare, our well-being is what matters most, then personal or national economic growth should cease to be the primary goal of the majority of people or politicians in developed nations'. Taking account of our increasing understanding of how our emotional environment in childhood affects our psychological development, James' conclusion is that we should make meeting the needs of children, rather than economic growth, our priority.
- Frank Furedi in *Therapy Culture* (2003) proposes that we have arrived at a place where we define all difficult or complex aspects of social life in terms of 'deficit' or 'suffering' and the need for care, rather than looking for the resilience and resourcefulness that people and communities exhibit. Furedi has been widely criticised for advocating a return to a culture of the 'stiff upper lip' but I believe this is a misunderstanding of his thesis. His concern is not with counselling or psychotherapy where it is genuinely needed but with the growing cultural expectation of an 'inability to cope' in any adversity, small or large, and the definition of problems as invariably requiring some kind of professional psychological intervention for the individual. We can learn a lot from his ideas. Why are we so quick to 'label' and to assume the existence of trauma? How can we learn to listen to a range of emotional language and allow for supportive structures and problem-solving through friendship, family, school and community?

- Most recently and, I believe, most crucially, Sue Gerhardt (2004) in *Why Love Matters* brings together recent research on how early relationships and interactions affect brain development in infants, in particular for forming a consistent narrative and a sense of self and for developing social intelligence and relationships. The importance of her book lies in its demonstration, through clear accessible explanations, of the connection between an infant's interactions with care-givers and the physical development of the brain. The main line of reasoning is that children develop their own regulatory strategies that enable them to deal with discomfort and adversity from having experienced the attention and engagement of an adult (usually, but not necessarily, the mother) through reciprocal, conversation-like interaction (see also Stern, 1985). This is a biochemical process: by regulating the flow of cortisol, these interactions promote the development of the pre-frontal cortex, which Gerhardt (2004: 41) calls the 'social brain' and enable the child to acquire a sense of self and, eventually, to create a social self and a consistent narrative. This is not the same, she notes, as having a happy childhood. She describes the implications for parents, educators and the wider community; attention to early care, awareness of the training, professionalism and understanding needed by childcare workers. Like James, Gerhardt draws attention to the question of what we are sacrificing in our work and achievement based culture – and shows how environmental-neurological-developmental mechanisms operate.

All these writers reflect on factors that indicate a desperate and troubled situation, explore and note the significance of the social environment in normal development – away from a theory of families and/or genetics as being the only source of good or ill.

Let's pause for a moment and consider how our village would look if we were to take account of what James, Furedi and Gerhardt are saying. We would have a society in which each person's well-being was more important than financial prosperity; in which everyone's resources were recognised and supported; and in which children grew up in an environment that promoted their mental as well as physical well-being, and understood how this was to be done. We have

removed lead from petrol and tartrazine from soft drinks – can we now reduce the level of what Gerhardt (2004: 57) refers to as 'corrosive cortisol' in children's brains?

To return to the specific environment of school – what happens there between children and adults is a microcosm or, more accurately, a fractal of the surrounding culture. When things go wrong, reactions tend to focus on 'fixing the kids'. While this often results in individual changes (an inside to outside process), we also need to consider changing the culture that engendered the difficulties in the first place (the outside to inside process). Changing a school culture may start with a small shift in attitude, but to be effective it must be based on a belief in everyone's value and potential – see, for example, Pete Shotton's (2004) description of a mentoring team making themselves available to all pupils and staff with no formal referral system.

An alternative approach

An important recent perspective is the contribution from the emerging positive psychology movement. The best known proponent of this movement is Martin Seligman, recognised for the concept of 'learned helplessness' (Seligman, 1975). In fact, Seligman also proposed 'learned optimism', the capacity of young children to acquire problem-solving and self-supportive strategies and so overcome obstacles (Seligman, 1991, 1995). The positive psychology movement began within behavioural psychology but now enjoys a wider base, through research, writing and educational activities promoting the idea of mental health and well-being as the natural state for human beings, rather than passivity, victimhood, anxiety or general malaise.

Positive psychology includes the study of positive emotion, positive character traits, and positive institutions. As the science behind these becomes more firmly grounded, Dr Seligman is now turning his attention to training positive psychologists, individuals whose 'practice will *make the world a happier place, in a way that parallels clinical psychologists having made the world a less unhappy place'* (Seligman, 2004, my italics). We need both – ways of making the world a less unhappy place for those in distress, and ways of making the world a happier place for everyone. An example of the latter from the Positive Psychology Center is a curriculum developed for high school students. The major goals are to increase positive emotion, character strengths, citizenship and sense of meaning or purpose in young people. The curriculum emphasises that experiences which increase meaning often involve connection to others and causes that are larger than ourselves; students develop plans for engaging in activities, individually or with others, that increase their sense of meaning and fulfillment (Seligman, 2004b). The Center also investigates the development of 'well-being indicators' to set alongside economic indicators for influencing government policy (see also James, 2003).

If we agree that there are strong indications that we need to change the social paradigm, and to work with the social context, not only with individuals and families, and that there is increasing evidence that we can begin to specify how to do that, what contribution can TA make to this process? James Allen (2003: 141) has associated the positive psychology movement with what he calls the transactional analysis positive psychology (practitioner) style. This approach 'focuses on health, good feelings, hope, gratitude, flow, intimacy, mindfulness and repair of ruptures in communication'. Like solution-focused approaches in education (Barrow, 2004) and appreciative enquiry (Watkins and Mohr, 2001) this style privileges resourcefulness, potential and resilience.

There are many similarities between positive psychology and co-creative TA (Summers and Tudor, 2000). Both employ the constructivist principles that meaning constantly evolves through dialogue and discourse creates systems; 'we participate in co-creating the universe that we experience' (Mahoney, 2002). Both share an emphasis on openness, interdependence, joint responsibility and engagement with the present moment. Summers and Tudor propose the idea of TA practitioners becoming 'transactional designers'. Rather than being subject to a 'given' situation we can cooperatively create new possibilities for the social environment that take account of all members.

We have a very flexible and creative system with some significant strengths, in particular:

- A focus on interaction and observable change.
- A positive philosophy of being in charge (Temple, 1999).
- Accessible language for describing ideas and ways of working.

- Coherent theory that takes account of dynamics of relationships.
- Teachable models that offer a practical way to devise new methods of working.

Like positive psychology, TA can be taught effectively to children (Hellaby, 2004; Barrow, 2005), to school staff, including support staff (Lerkkanen and Temple, 2004; Shotton, 2004; Wong and Bradshaw, 2004) and to school managers (Rosewell, 2003; Barrow, 2004).

We have a contextual model in TA, where concepts are continually being developed to analyse and transform new situations. Above all TA is a social model (Berne, 1961; Moiso, 1998). Allen (2003) has noted the *usefulness* of core TA concepts; and we are well placed to 'name, describe and explain' what we see. Allen (2003, 2004) also points out the biological and neural basis for relationships, and shows how environmental input changes brain chemistry. How can we use atunement and resonance to modify neural networks in beneficial ways? We need to create and implement new strategies for our virtual village, for working with the environment (outside to inside) *as well as* with individuals (inside to outside).

Healthy development

In this section I describe a model that brings together some ideas for looking at what is happening when things are going right. For each part of the diagram I cite TA contributions that support this approach, emphasising health and promoting thriving.

The genesis of this diagram lies in an idea by Julie Hewson, first published in *ITA News* (1990) (see Figure 2.1). The aim of the diagram is to relate TA concepts visually, showing how they connect with child development. Starting from the original symbiosis with mother or other primary caregiver, the stroking environment determines the child's frame of reference and existential position, resulting in script decisions and, later, in the adaptations developed to keep these in place, and in the strategies of rackets and games which aim to reinforce the script. This results in the script or racket system, inviting the recreation or re-establishment of symbiosis, and so on. While, as Hewson states (1990), the model works at different levels of abstraction, the diagram nevertheless has a strong visual impact

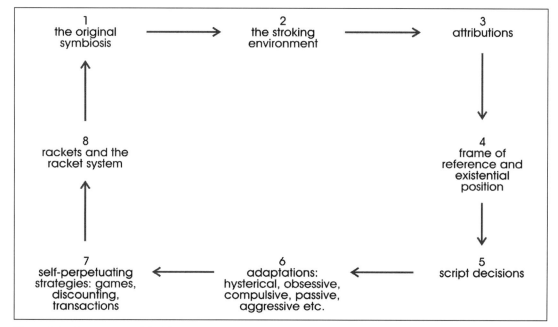

Figure 2.1   A systems model of TA

and aids understanding of the relationship between these practical concepts. It is also useful in offering a framework for holding all these ideas together.

In my development of the diagram (see Figure 2.2) I have added an outer cycle, to represent normal healthy growth, including concepts which emphasise strength and resourcefulness. I have also added two inner cycles, the preventive cycle – preventing the formation of negative script patterns and supporting healthy development up to 6–7 years old, and the restorative cycle, addressing and supporting change of any limiting patterns that have become established.

A systems model

Here I describe the stages of the model (with reference to the numbers in Figure 2.2). In some ways this is work in progress and the selection of TA models is not necessarily complete. I hope that by bringing together the 'positive' concepts that have been found effective by TA educational practitioners, and by presenting it in this way here, that other practitioners are stimulated to add their own ideas for creative practice.

1. Symbiosis

This describes the uneven relationship between infant and carer that can be necessary for a while but becomes unhealthy if continued into childhood. A better model – of normal dependency – was suggested by Woollams and Brown (1978) in which all the carer's egostates are involved. Gerhardt (2004: 39) says that the baby has to be invited to participate in human culture, to be 'welcomed into the world', and that the best way to do this is by making child-carer interaction pleasurable. Both Stern (1985) and Gopnik et al. (1999) suggest, in different ways, that the child is an active agent in this very early stage, not simply a passive recipient of care. As Moiso (1998: 1) puts it: 'The unit for transactional analysis is not just the stimulus, but the stimulus-plus-response dyad, thus emphasising the reciprocity of cause and effect within the interplay of relationships'. The *need to belong* is primary for human beings:

> *Within the Bernian perspective of the essential human hungers, there are three existential and natural drives that guide each person from birth until death: the drive to*

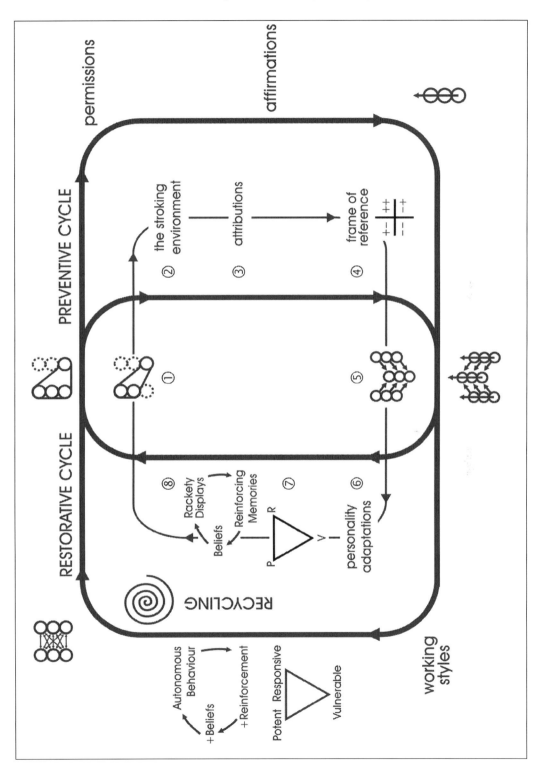

Figure 2.2 Building the social environment

belong, the drive to be, and the drive to become. From this perspective we may then recognise sequentially that there are three permissions that are essential to the child:

1. To belong, in order to acquire a base for affective and emotional OKness.

2. To be, in order to acquire security and self-esteem through one's own means.

3. To do, in order to acquire a functional 'pro-activity' in terms of achieving one's goals and aspirations . . .

We can thus define the quality of life as the result of three factors: belonging, being, and becoming. Belonging involves the individual's having a place within the environment and with others and provides the foundation and meaning for being and becoming . . . I exist, I act, and I am not alone!

(ibid: 7)

This pleasurable reciprocity and resulting sense of 'welcome' and belonging will happen when the mother's or carer's child is involved through touch and play – this is how a positive stroking environment becomes established.

2. The stroking environment

The stroking environment determines what strokes are available, withheld or unavailable and, therefore, what strokes the infant will expect and try to get later. Stroking, or recognition, is the base of all human relationships and the means by which a baby is welcomed and invited to participate in the family and the world. Strokes are first given through touch – the baby feels himself safely held and literally 'stroked' as parents and others enjoy handling and talking to him. Gradually touch gives way to language as the main way that strokes are conveyed:

Strokes are our language. They are the way we bond in our families and wider groups, they are the source of well-being (and stimulate endorphins in the process), and they fine-tune our intuition to tell us what we, and others, need. Through language we construct our reality; strokes are our means of building, sustaining or changing the whole range of groups we belong in.

(Newton, 2002: 95)

Language may even have evolved as a kind of 'vocal stroking' that enabled bonding between family and group members. One effect of physical stroking is the release of opiates (endorphins) within the body, resulting in a sense of pleasure and well-being and so enhancing bonding. Similarly smiling and laughing also stimulate opiate production. Gerhardt (2004: 41) explains how this happens:

When the baby looks at his mother (or father), he reads her dilated pupils as information that her sympathetic nervous system is aroused, and she is experiencing pleasurable arousal. In response his own nervous system becomes pleasurably aroused and his own heart rate goes up. These processes trigger off a biochemical response . . . (here she describes the biochemical process). So, by this technical and circuitous route we discover that the family's doting looks are triggering off the pleasurable biochemicals that actually help the social brain to grow.

Following and expanding Levin-Landheer's (1982) work on stages of development and affirmations, Clarke and Dawson (1989/1998) offer a brilliant guide for parents, carers and professionals to what children need for healthy growth. With principles of normal development as a guide, for each stage they detail particular strokes the infant, child or adolescent needs to receive – by words, touch, attitude or other non-verbal means. These supportive messages, known as developmental affirmations, are important to the child and, at the same time, are valuable to parents, carers and teachers, enabling them to learn through giving these messages and by their own child listening in (Barrow, Bradshaw and Newton, 2001). Thus the infant and growing child internalises permissions to belong, to be and then to do, think and feel.

3. Working with attributions

As with the stroking environment, affirmations support each person in being themselves, and give permission to be who you are, to find your own way of doing things, to get help, to feel what you feel, and so on – rather than taking on a 'label' of being clever/stupid, shy/outgoing, favoured/not favoured. This is not the same as 'positive reinforcement', although there are some superficial similarities. Nor is it the same as giving children material things or letting them rule the family (see Clarke et al., 2004). Mountain (2004: 59–60) suggests that stroking creates the 'emotional safety' that precedes positive reinforcement, and that building these 'concepts for thriving' should be celebrated at every stage.

4. Frame of reference – and existential life position

These permissions promote a sense of well-being, so that the child's frame of reference, culturally situated as it will be, includes a belief in potential and a positive attitude that can be expanded as information is acquired and sorted. The possibility increases of an 'I'm OK, You're OK' life position becoming the default mode. Virginia Satir used the terms 'I count/don't count, You count/don't count' (see Allen, 2003). A similar concept is that of 'accounting' (Clarke and Dawson, 1998; Temple, 1999, 2004). The child who belongs and knows that they count will find it natural to adopt an 'I'm OK, You're OK' stance with family members, peers and at school. 'Accounting' or 'counting', rather than 'OKness', may make it easier to translate this idea to a wider milieu, and to see the connection with how we both are affected by the socio-cultural environment, and also affect it (Allen, 2003). Nevertheless, OKness is an effective concept to teach. In his last book, Berne (1972) described three life positions: 'I'm OK, You're OK, They're OK', 'I'm not OK . . .' and so on – which brings the wider context into the equation. Davidson (1999) has developed this concept into what he calls 'three-D OKness' – an important concept for schools in addressing the implications of basing a behaviour programme on the (eight) combinations of these three-handed life positions (see Newton, 2004b; Chapter 14).

Physis, the urge to life and growth, has sometimes been a neglected human drive within TA writing (see Clarkson, 1992b). We can relate physis to the idea of 'resilience' as an important factor in a person's ability to regulate their emotions and sense of self and value (see Allen, 1998; Furedi, 2003; Gerhardt, 2004) and to use this to recover from 'not-OK' experiences.

5. Script

The scene is now set in the life of each little person for the creation of their unique personal story. We all need to find explanations and make meaning of our experience and so create our own story and source of self-definition (Montuschi, 2004). Scripts are not just sources of limitation and pain; as part of our sense of self and our place with others they also contain essential information about how to survive and thrive. Script can be a source of resilience and learning. Hay (1997) suggested an autonomy matrix (shown under the script matrix at 5 on Figure 2.2) to set alongside the familiar script matrix as a way of diagramming the permissions and supportive messages that have been taken in from carers and from culture and history. I have

added 'physis' arrows for the 'supporters': in order to encourage growth in a new generation the 'bringers up' themselves need to experience their own life force and sense of self.

The gap between the arrows in Figure 2.2 (at 5) represent the view that the child/subject is decisional and active about what they take in from their environment – and therefore, what they take into their script. This has become known as the 'physis gap'.

Another recent development of script theory proposes a co-operative, co-creative model (Summers and Tudor, 2000) where everyone who is part of the little person's social world has influence on script formation, the lines of the matrix are horizontal and the arrows go both ways. In other words it is *relationship* which is key in script decisions and beliefs (cf. Moiso, 1998). Emotional security depends more on having a consistent and internally coherent narrative than on the actual story itself (see Gerhardt, 2004). The story may play a crucial role in creating a secure sense of self, or it may be a by-product of the positive relationships and good feedback from others.

6. Adaptations

We all make adaptations to social life depending on our script decisions. Clarkson (1992a) proposed that these are an advantage to be appreciated and maximised; she suggested that the qualities of agreeableness, excellence, endurance, experimentation and speed be respected and fostered as social responses to 'the web of messages we received about how to survive and thrive regarding how we should help other people, good standards to aim for, ways in which we should be reliable and dependable, the importance of having a go and doing our best and how to make good use of time' (Napper and Newton 2000: 7.3). Similarly, Hay (1996) emphasises the positive working styles associated with each counterscript driver. Understanding pupils' developing styles, their associated preference for thinking, feeling or doing (Ware, 1983) and social needs for recognition and acceptance (Joines and Stewart, 2002), can be a powerful tool for intervention (see Harding, 2004). Children can be encouraged to enjoy their own styles and ways of working, and stroked for their thinking, responsiveness to others and ability to do things while also facilitating their use of less preferred modes.

7. Games

Though they are ineffective attempts at intimacy, games are a sign of life. The most elegant way of diagramming the game, the drama triangle (Karpman, 1968) has given rise to the idea of the winners' triangle, which recognises the validity or good intention of each role and proposes ways of implementing responsiveness, assertiveness and vulnerability in place of the game roles (Choy, 1990). The drama and winners' triangles are a straightforward tool for teaching to primary age pupils, promoting empowerment and problem-solving. This has been demonstrated recently in a TA programme for schools where these were favoured models and almost every child involved shared an example of conflict resolution using the triangles (Newton, 2004a; Barrow, 2005).

Even more significantly, Le Guernic (2004) has developed a triangle of social roles, showing how stories can enable children to choose positive relationship models and so move towards personal growth and autonomy. Thus a child can be the hero of their own story, benefiting from the help and direction given by others and learning to offer help and direction to others too. Le Guernic presents a reading of fairy stories that contributes to the 'healthy, functional aspects of our personal reality' which Cornell (1988) calls our 'psychological life plan'.

8. The racket system or script system

This is like a cross section of the script. One of Zalcman's (1990) suggestions is that we need a positive version of the racket system. In *TA Today* Stewart and Joines (1987) describe an autonomy system – an updated system after learning or therapeutic intervention. I prefer the idea that each of us has already internalised a positive system based on good experiences and reinforced by positive memories of similar experiences, and that we can learn to make that our natural practice. Both systems are laid down in childhood (Hellaby, 2004). So what enables us to stay with the positive system and not go to our racket system? It helps to have had repair of disturbance modelled for us while we are small so that we are able to draw on self-stroking and permissions. Neural pathways can be modified through positive interventions and new regulatory strategies developed (Gerhardt, 2004). It also helps to have healthy behaviours, and healthy responses to our behaviour, modelled for us by parents, teachers and others at any age. This demonstrates for us that we can make choices to draw on our positive experiences and build up good memories to feed our response to new situations.

As this cycle of normal development is completed we can find illustrations of healthy behaviour based on all ego states in the functional fluency model (Temple, 1999, 2004), including the naming of positive control (structuring), and positive adaptation or socialisation (cooperation). Transactions, the stimulus-plus-response dyad (Moiso, 1998) are where these positive behavioural modes become visible in everyday interactions:

> *Transactional analysis may, therefore, help promote the healthy integration of autonomous individuals within their cultural and political groups, developing healthy individuality with the capacity for belonging, intimacy, and social responsibility. Specifically, a model of belonging combined with personal responsibility offers a healthy contrast to the contemporary development of what appear to be increasingly smaller and tighter social and political groupings that seem to be the basis for increasingly paranoid social structures that are replacing the narcissistic societies of recent decades.*
>
> (Moiso, 1998: 7)

Positive systems

Taking up Zalcman's (1990) suggestion, here I consider two cycles which contribute to positive development – and to the development of positive systems.

The restorative cycle

I deal with the restorative cycle first because, although developmentally it refers to later concepts, it is observable behaviours that draw attention to a need and this is when practitioners may be asked to intervene. Schools, for instance, may seek help as pupils' distress or alienation shows up in games and rackets.

While the aim of the preventive cycle in Figure 2.2 is to enable small children to develop in as healthy a way as possible by offering the kind of 'engaged care' that promotes autonomy and OKness, the restorative cycle is based on a belief that damage can be repaired and developmental gaps filled. This is where a 'cultural shift' can take place in working alongside school staff, and where school based interventions can be most effective, offering a very different view of 'difficult' pupils. With older children in school there is a need for recognition of the reasons for problems and the influence of the environment in exacerbating or relieving them:

> *In our work with schools we have noticed a common theme. In working on pupil behaviour the conventional approaches continue to make their mark but often colleagues present instances where the approaches fall short of success and need to be reminded that relying on a single perspective limits effective work with children.*
>
> *Where we have started to introduce concepts drawn from Transactional Analysis, something else happens. As an alternative model it illustrates, through familiar experience, new ways of understanding behaviour and new ways of creating different insights into challenging situations.*
> (Barrow, Bradshaw and Newton, 2001: 4)

We know that people can experience a resonance that leads to change, in a therapy setting or through encountering someone who really 'sees' them. A key model here is re-cycling (Levin-Landheer, 1982; Clarke and Dawson, 1989/1998; Barrow, Bradshaw and Newton, 2001; Barrow and Newton, 2004). The understanding that earlier stages of development can be re-visited and gaps or disruption repaired, that a child who has difficulties can be offered new opportunities and another chance to thrive, is often a liberating moment for parents, schools and support services. This approach can be reinforced by teaching models such as the winners' triangle, working styles, 'straight' transactions and functional fluency.

An example of the restorative cycle in practice is a new programme currently being used in primary and secondary schools, often with pupils at risk of exclusion from school, or in PRUs (Pupil Referral Units). Named TAPACY (TA Proficiency Award for Children and Young People) it enables pupils to learn and apply TA concepts such as transactions, drama and winners' triangles, working styles and strokes to solve problems, resolve conflict and understand and take charge of their own behaviour. They then have to create portfolios of evidence and share and explain these to peers and adults. Based on the TA principles that everyone can learn and change, the TAPACY is underpinned by a series of core beliefs, including:

- Teaching and learning are interchangeable activities – not prescribed roles.

- Individuals learn in different ways and have different preferences for demonstrating what they have learnt.
- Adults delivering sessions establish a relationship based *on learning alongside* children and young people.
- Genuine learning is about creating unique understandings and insights which arise through exploration between teacher and learner.

The emphasis throughout the process is on promoting the centrality of the learner and the process of learning in a context that is permission giving and promotes diversity and inclusion (Barrow, 2005). Results from the first pilot are extremely encouraging. Most of the pupils involved have a history of exclusion, public care experience, recent bereavement, or erratic parenting and many are regarded in school as 'difficult' or 'problems'. Nevertheless they were able to adeptly explain their actions, thinking, and feeling in transactional analysis terms and tell their stories of difference and change; it was very clear that they are determined to grow.

The TAPACY is an example of everyone – children and adults – learning together, demonstrating effectiveness, modelling a better future, and spreading ideas between peers.

> *Children can quickly learn (and create) new languages, and language change is one way to change an educational culture. Sharing transactional analysis with kids, and listening to them, starts to make a new story, not just for them but for us.*
> (Newton, 2004a)

The preventive cycle

A clear need is for all staff who work with young children to be appropriately and professionally trained (Gerhardt, 2004). When parenting in the home is inadequate, and parents or carers have insufficient emotional resources to cope with their children, usually due to having been poorly parented themselves, the supportive interventions our educational and social services offer need to rest on a secure understanding of the causes and processes of disruption and ways of responding appropriately to individual need. One example of this working in the UK has its origins in France, where *Écoles Maternelle* have been shown to make a significant and lasting difference to the attainment and integration in school of children of immigrant families (see

Allen, 1998). These pre-schools are staffed by highly trained professionals. Such findings contributed to the setting up in Britain of the Sure Start programme, designed to support children and families at risk through a whole range of initiatives from health, social services, education and voluntary organisations. Early indications are that these interventions are working. In Sure Start areas, for families who access the services, there is a fall in the number of children on the child protection register, a rise in children's attainment and a reduction in behaviour problems in nursery schools (see DfEE, 2005). These examples illustrate the importance of taking seriously the quality of care. The understanding and perspective we have in TA can contribute to training of staff. Work with early years professionals demonstrates how effective this can be (Wong and Bradshaw, 2004) as do many examples of behaviour support teams basing their services to nursery staff and play workers on TA models. The response is invariably positive, and putting the learning into practice effective. Staff appreciate the accessibility and practicality of the concepts and the OK-OK ambience of the training.

It is often the case that staff employed as care or play workers, for instance, are not expected to be highly trained, or offered training that answers their own need for some real understanding of children's behaviour. Introducing them to the concepts of affirmations and stages of development offers something that can be understood through observation of the children they work with and also invites personal development for themselves. When supported by positive information about strokes and life positions this provides a coherent way of choosing new options for interacting with a child.

An example of the preventive cycle in practice is the story of Nathan (Newton and Wong, 2003). At three years and ten months old Nathan was aggressive, hardly spoke or communicated with other children or adults in any way, had little or no sense of his own body (for instance apparently not feeling pain) and never smiled. The skilled staff at the nursery where he was placed worked patiently and conscientiously with him but were making little progress and parents of other children were pressing for him to be excluded. When two members of a behaviour support team visited the nursery they joined the staff in doing a holistic assessment of Nathan's situation, identifying that he had not completed the

developmental tasks of 'being' and 'doing'; in other words he had not been 'welcomed into the world' or 'invited to participate' by his birth family. Learning about stages and cycles of development helped the nursery staff to understand how they could enable Nathan to experience the 'baby' and 'toddler' stages in the positive way that his family home had been unable to support. After seven months Nathan was smiling, talking, playing with other children, doing social tasks such as tidying or setting lunch tables, and became a much loved child in the nursery.

Conclusion

As Summers and Tudor (2000) suggest, perhaps we need to see ourselves as transactional *designers* as well as transactional analysts and share this potential for radical change with others. The skills of analysis can be used to diagnose but in deciding what sort of environment we want for our children we also need to consciously design for the future.

I have offered some ideas about what it means to live and work in a virtual village. Many of us already do – we know how it feels to live as part of a supportive community, not necessarily physically close, but attuned and responsive to each other's needs. We experience structure, support, acceptance, empathy and cooperation through different forms of contact. Affirming the importance of these things can look like 're-inventing the wheel' (Gerhardt, 2004: 216). Maybe we need to do that – to take a fresh look at our priorities and decide the sort of society we want to be part of. Constructing virtual villages requires planning, energy and suitable tools and materials. The energy and materials are already to hand in every human community. Transactional analysis offers an accessible language for planning together with many useful tools for cooperative building.

References

Allen, J.R. (1998) Of Resilience, Vulnerability, and a Woman Who Never Lived. *Child and Adolescent Psychiatric Clinics of North America*, 7: 1, 53–71.

Allen, J.R. (2003) Concepts, Competencies and Interpretive Communities. *Transactional Analysis Journal*, 33: 2, 126–47.

Allen, J.R. (2004) *Transactional Analysis Today: Current Understanding of its Biological Underpinnings*. Workshop notes. ATAA Conference, Canmore, Canada.

Barrow, G. (2004) Taking the Drama out of a Crisis: How School Managers Use Game Theory to Promote Autonomy. In Barrow, G. and Newton, T. (Eds.) *Walking the Talk: How TA is Improving Behaviour and Raising Self-Esteem*. London: David Fulton.

Barrow, G. (2005) *TAPACY: Transactional Analysis Proficiency Award for Children and Young People*. Watford: Institute of Developmental Transactional Analysis.

Barrow, G. and Newton, T. (2004) (Eds.) *Walking the Talk: How TA is Improving Behaviour and Raising Self-Esteem*. London: David Fulton.

Barrow, G., Bradshaw, E. and Newton, T. (2001) *Improving Behaviour and Raising Self-Esteem in the Classroom: A Practical Guide to Using TA*. London: David Fulton.

Berne, E. (1961) *Transactional Analysis in Psychotherapy*. New York: Grove Press.

Berne, E. (1972) *What Do You Say After You Say Hello?* New York: Grove Press.

Blair, T. (2004, 11 November) Speech on Childcare to the Daycare Trust, *The Guardian*. Available on line at: http://politics.guardian.co.uk/labour/story/0.1348945.00.html

Choy, A. (1990) The Winners Triangle. *Transactional Analysis Journal*, 20: 1, 40–6.

Clarke, J.I. and Dawson, C. (1998). *Growing Up Again*. (2nd edn) Center City, MN: Hazelden. (Original work published 1989)

Clarke, J.I., Dawson, C. and Bredehoft, D.J. (2004) *How Much is Enough? Everything You Need to Know to Steer Clear of Overindulgence and Raise Likeable, Responsible, and Respectful Children*. New York: Marlowe and Company.

Clarkson, P. (1992a) In Praise of Speed, Experimentation, Agreeableness, Endurance and Excellence: Counterscript Drivers and Aspiration. *Transactional Analysis Journal*, 22: 1, 16–20

Clarkson, P. (1992b) Physis in Transactional Analysis. *Transactional Analysis Journal*, 22: 4, 202–9.

Cornell, W. (1988) Life Script Theory: A Critical Review From a Developmental Perspective. *Transactional Analysis Journal*, 18: 4, 270–82.

Davidson. C. (1999) I'm Polygonal OK. *INTAND Newsletter*, 7: 1, 6–9.

Devlin, A. (1997) *Criminal Classes*. London: Waterside.

DfEE (2005) *Early Impacts of Sure Start Local Programmes on Children and Families. Report of the Cross-sectional Study of 9 and 36 Month Old Children and Their Families*. London: HMSO.

Emmerton, N. and Newton, T. (2004) The Journey of Educational Transactional Analysis from its Beginnings to the Present. *Transactional Analysis Journal*, 34: 3, 283–91.

Frazier, T.L. (1971) The Application of Transactional Analysis Principles in the Classroom of a Correctional School. *Transactional Analysis Journal*, 11: 4, 16–20.

Furedi, F. (2003) *Therapy Culture: Cultivating Vulnerability in an Uncertain Age*. London: Routledge.

Gerhardt, S. (2004) *Why Love Matters: How Affection Shapes a Baby's Brain*. London: Brunner-Routledge.

Gopnik, A., Meltzoff, A.N. and Kuhl, P. (1999) *The Scientist in the Crib*. New York: Morrow.

Harding, A. (2004) Have I Got the Right Hat on? Using TA to Deliver High Quality Individual Tuition. In Barrow, G. and Newton, T. (Eds.) *Walking the Talk: How TA is Improving Behaviour and Raising Self-Esteem*. London: David Fulton.

Hay, J. (1996) *Transactional Analysis for Trainers*. Watford: Sherwood Publishing.

Hay, J. (1997) The Autonomy Matrix. *INTAND Newsletter*, 5: 1, 7.

Hellaby, L. (2004) Teaching TA in the Primary School In Barrow, G. and Newton, T. (Eds.) *Walking the Talk: How TA is Improving Behaviour and Raising Self-Esteem*. London: David Fulton.

Heller, F. (2000) Creating a Holding Environment in an Inner City School. In Barwick, N. (Ed.) *Clinical Counselling in Schools*. London: Routledge.

Hewson, J. (1990) A Heuristic Systems Model for TA. *ITA News*, 26, 2–5.

James, O. (2003, 17 May) Children Before Cash. *The Guardian*.

Joines, V. and Stewart, I. (2002) *Personality Adaptations*. Nottingham: Lifespace Publishing.

Karpman, S. (1968) Fairy Tales and Script Drama Analysis. *Transactional Analysis Bulletin*, 7: 26, 39–43.

Le Guernic, A. (2004) Fairy Tales and Psychological Life-Plans. *Transactional Analysis Journal*, 34: 3, 216–22.

Lerkkanen, M-K. and Temple, S. (2004) Student-teachers' Professional and Personal Development Through Academic Study of Educational Transactional Analysis. *Transactional Analysis Journal*, 34: 1, 253–71.

Levin-Landheer, P. (1982) The Cycle of Development. *Transactional Analysis Journal*, 12: 2, 129–39.

Mahoney, M.J. (2002) Constructivism and Positive Psychology. In Snyder, C.R. and Lopez, S.J. (Eds.) *The Handbook of Positive Psychology*. New York: Oxford University Press.

Moiso, C. (1998) Being and Belonging: An Appreciation and Application of Berne's Social Psychiatry. *The Script*, 28: 9, 1, 7.

Montuschi, F. (2004) Interventions on the Script in the School Setting. *Transactional Analysis Journal*, 34: 1, 205–8.

Mountain, A. (2004) *The Space Between: Bridging the Gap between Workers and Young People*. Lyme Regis: Russell House Publishing.

Napper, R. and Newton, T. (2000) *TACTICS – Transactional Analysis Concepts for all Trainers, Teachers and Tutors + Insight into Collaborative Learning Strategies*. Ipswich: TA Resources.

Newton, T. (2002) Grooming, Gossip and Saying Hello. In Leach, K. (Ed.) *Conference Papers of the Annual Conference of the Institute of Transactional Analysis*. Edinburgh: ITA.

Newton, T. (2004a) Editorial. *Transactional Analysis Journal*, 34: 3, 194–6.

Newton, T. (2004b) 3–D OK-ness for Schools: Developing Positive School Cultures Through Three Dimensional Acceptance. In Barrow, G. and Newton, T. (Eds.) *Walking the Talk: How TA is Improving Behaviour and Raising Self-Esteem*. London: David Fulton.

Newton, T. and Wong, G. (2003). A Chance to Thrive: Enabling Change in a Nursery School. *Transactional Analysis Journal*, 33: 1, 79–88.

Pierre, N. (2002) *Pratique de l'Analyse Transactionnelle Dans la Classe avec des Jeunes et dans les Groupes* [Using transactional analysis in class with young people and groups]. Issy les Moulineaux ED ESF.

Rosewell, N. (2003) I'm OK, My School's OK. *Emotional Literacy Update*, 2: 5, 5.

Seligman, M. (1991) *Learned Optimism: How to Change Your Mind and Your Life*. New York: Knopf.

Seligman, M. (1995) *The Optimistic Child: Proven Programme to Safeguard Children from Depression and Build Lifelong Resistance*. New York: Houghton Miffin.

Seligman, M. (2002) *Authentic Happiness: Using the New Positive Psychology to Realize Your Potential for Lasting Fulfillment*. New York: Free Press.

Seligman, M. (2004a) Seligman Bio. Positive Psychology Centre. University of Pennsylvania. Available online at: www.ppc.sas.upenn.edu/bio.htm

Seligman, M. (2004b) Positive Psychology Centre: Overview of Activities, University of Pennsylvania. Website: www.ppc.sas.upenn.edu/index.htm

Seligman, M. and Beagley, G. (1975) Learned Helplessness in the Rat. *Journal of Comparative and Physiological Psychology*, 88, 534–41.

Shotton, P (2004) Saying Hello: Establishing a Pastoral Mentoring Service in an Inner-City Secondary School. In Barrow, G. and Newton, T. (Eds.) *Walking the Talk: How TA is Improving Behaviour and Raising Self-Esteem*. London: David Fulton.

Stern, D. (1985) *The Interpersonal World of the Infant*. New York: Basic Books.

Stewart, I. and Joines, V. (1987) *TA Today*. Nottingham: Lifespace Publishing.

Summers, G. and Tudor, K. (2000) Co-creative Transactional Analysis. *Transactional Analysis Journal*, 30: 1, 23–40.

Temple, S. (1999) Functional Fluency for Educational Transactional Analysts. *Transactional Analysis Journal*, 29: 3, 164–74.

Temple, S. (2000) The Stroke Management Map. *ITA News*. 56: 1

Temple, S. (2004) Update on the Functional Fluency Model in Education. *Transactional Analysis Journal*, 34: 3, 197–204.

Ware, P. (1983) Personality Adaptations: Doors to Therapy. *Transactional Analysis Journal*, 13: 1, 11–9.

Watkins, J.M. and Mohr, B.J. (2001) *Appreciative Inquiry*. San Francisco, CA: Jossey-Bass.

Wong, G. and Bradshaw, E. (2004) It Doesn't Matter What Age You Are It's the Stage You Are that Counts . In Barrow, G. and Newton, T. (Eds.) *Walking the Talk: How TA is Improving Behaviour and Raising Self-esteem*. London: David-Fulton.

Woollams, S. and Brown, M. (1978) *Transactional Analysis*. Ann Arbor, MI: Huron Valley Institute Press.

Zalcman, M. (1990) Game Analysis and Racket Analysis: Overview, Critique and Future Developments. *Transactional Analysis Journal*, 20: 1, 4–19.

CHAPTER 3

Working with Children and Parents

Diane Hoyer and Laura Hyatt

There are varied and interweaving reasons why therapeutic work with children is so vital – reasons which, indeed, have informed the publication of this book. Our own work and therapy has led us to conclude that therapeutic and social work with families is equally important. By families we mean parents, carers, siblings, and other key adults, and, in this chapter, 'children' includes young people. Here we describe the principles which underpin our interventions. We explain our methods for integrating child development and counselling/therapeutic theories into practice, and describe our use of knowledge, skills, and experience in contracting, assessment and treatment work. In doing this, we draw on our training in transactional analysis (TA) encompassing psychodynamic and cognitive-behavioural theory, as well as in child development theory and in non-directive play therapy. In Chapter 11 in the second part of the book, we present three vignettes which illustrate our work with children and their parents.

We value children as individuals with varied needs stemming from their early life history and/or current life experience. Integral to our work is the concept of balance, that is: aiming to develop and maintain stability in order to work through the impact of trauma to promote personal happiness and safety, and the well-being of society. Both of us have worked for the National Society for the Prevention of Cruelty to Children (NSPCC) in the UK, an organisation which promotes the protection of children through individual treatment work, family support, parenting programmes, and public education. Di continues to do so, Laura has moved into private practice.

The impact of abuse on child development has been well documented (see Daniel et al., 1999). We work with children of all ages who have suffered various types of abuse, including those displaying abusive behaviours. Whilst our work is child-centred, we work systemically with parents and professionals to optimise positive outcomes for children. By considering children in the context of *their* environment (ecosystem) we can strengthen their resilience, and diminish the impact of negative influences by encouraging insight and change in the key adults. In this chapter, we consider a number of theories that have influenced our work. We say more about how we work and why we work in this way.

Transactional analysis

TA has a major influence on our interventions. Here we give some definitions and examples of key TA concepts which are significant in our work. Our assessment relies heavily upon two developmental theories: ego state growth and development from birth onwards (Levin, 1974) and the development of personality adaptation (Ware, 1983). Together these reflect, as Joines and Stewart (2002: 27) put it: 'a combination of two factors: (1) what is innate at birth, and (2) how the person is interacted with in the first six years of life.'

Ego state theory underpins our work as therapists, in particular our observations of clients, and choice of therapeutic interventions. As therapists we can and do select our transactions for optimum therapeutic benefit. For example, one young person had been given the message from her parents that 'Parents are always right'. Her therapist asked her if this was true. This here-and-now challenge from the therapist's Adult ego state, using a level tone of voice without particular emotional content, activated the client's Adult ego state, and she reflected that, no, it wasn't true as no one is perfect and gets everything right.

Script theory influences our assessments as well as subsequent therapy. Early script decisions can be detrimental to healthy development, and so we address such thoughts, feelings, and behaviours through redecision work (Goulding and Goulding, 1979) whereby the client is able to identify conflicting or confusing messages and to resolve their impact by making a new decision in favour of autonomy. Ware's (1983) theory of personality adaptations specifies how a particular personality is likely to think, feel and behave, and identifies how to make contact with people most effectively thus, for example, to make contact with a person with a paranoid personality adaptation through thinking. The process communication model (Kahler, 1978) enables us to access the most beneficial channels of communication for each personality adaptation, thus, for instance, with the same adaptation, being requestive. Once these communication channels are established, permissions, affirmations, and positive strokes (praise) anchor therapeutic interventions and build self-esteem in clients.

Our knowledge base also includes theoretical information on the impact of abuse, in particular child sexual abuse. Sgroi (1982: 109) summarises the issues associated with this abuse:

- 'Damaged goods' syndrome.
- Guilt.
- Fear.
- Depression.
- Low self-esteem and poor social skills.
- Repressed anger and hostility.
- Impaired ability to trust.
- Blurred role boundaries and role confusion.
- Pseudomaturity, coupled with failure to accomplish developmental tasks.
- Self-mastery and control, that is, the lack of self-mastery and negative use of control.

Developmental theory

Our work with children is governed by awareness of three essential aspects of child development:

1. Genetic influences (biological development, temperament).
2. Life experiences (physical, emotional, cognitive development) – in TA terms: life script, life position, injunctions.
3. Here-and-now relationships (social development) – which we understand in terms of ego state assessment, and the process communication model (Kahler, 1978).

We recognise that there are various debates relating to the value of therapy for children before they have attained various developmental 'tasks'. We, however, work from the perspective

that where these 'tasks' are lacking, it is our role within therapy to facilitate the development of these areas (see Winnicott, 1971). So, for example, a child without appropriate trust could benefit from a dependable and reliable person to *be* with. A child without healthy attachment could benefit from a consistently respectful, protective, and encouraging relationship. A child without object constancy could benefit from a relationship that reflects differences in experience, activity, and location. A child without use and understanding of language could benefit from a relationship that both names and explains objects and processes. A child without symbolic play could benefit from an effective and attuned commentary on their play. A child without a clear sense of time, that is, before, during, and after, could benefit from clear explanations and examples of time such as prediction. This sequence often reflects the order of our interventions.

Working with children we ask ourselves: 'Are we "repairing" or 'creating'?' Is there an existing set of schemas that we are challenging, or are we introducing new concepts? We see two general theories here:

Theory 1:   There is a developmental process which incidents such as abuse interrupt, causing trauma. This, in turn, alters the developmental pathway, if not offered correction.

Theory 2:   There is a developmental pathway that is already interrupted due to parenting deficits. This 'interruption' leads to vulnerability and abuse, which compounds the developmental difficulty.

The differentiation between these two theories informs treatment direction. Thus those children with adequate development prior to abuse can benefit from cognitive-behavioural techniques because their 'being' and 'doing' tasks are intact. Children with existing developmental difficulties have not attained such resources and understanding. They, therefore, require therapy which focuses on the development of self through somatic, physiological and experiential interventions.

Alongside these interventions, work with the parents improves their capacities both to recognise and to meet these needs for their children. Support work also identifies the developmental needs of parents and carers, and explores ways of meeting these without undermining the development of children.

Therapeutic play

Play therapy complements TA and developmental theory by harnessing non-verbal expression to promote development and release from trauma. In many of our interventions play therapy has its place by offering less intrusive opportunities to challenge behaviours and attitudes. In some cases this prevents the development of a harmartic script, and in others offers a safe environment in which the child can practise new ways of being. Therapeutic play offers an opportunity to work with the child in a number of ways:

1. By offering an uninterrupted, safe, consistent, and child-focused environment, the child is likely to present aspects of their temperament and personality. This enables the therapist to assess their 'natural' traits such as introvert/ extrovert. For example, observing the child's proximity to, and involvement of the therapist. An extrovert child is more likely to initiate conversation, an introverted child is likely to retain their personal space.
2. By linking the play experiences to the child's life experiences in a gentle reflective style, the therapist enables the child to make tentative and even concrete representations of their 'trauma' through symbolic play, art, drama and other media. This process strengthens the child's understanding of 'fantasy versus reality', and helps them to move on or to let go of issues. It also enables the therapist to assess the developmental capacity of the child, through the careful use of specific questions or phrases, for instance, to assess the child's concept of time, reversibility, object constancy, third person perspective and so on. With this information the therapist is then able to plan interventions that meet current developmental needs, and to encourage the child to develop further: "So right now it's difficult for you to see how your mum felt about that, but in the future your thinking will grow to help you do that."
3. By reflecting on the active process in the room the child can gain a sense of their self in relation to 'other', a vital component for children who have not achieved healthy

separation as part of their developmental process. As above, it offers the therapist the opportunity to assess development and, in response, to offer the child a repertoire of relationship and self-efficacy skills that promote interpersonal relationships: "You look really surprised about what happens when you put water in the sand. Your mouth and eyes are wide open", "You seem unsure of what to say. That's OK. Many children feel like that. Sometimes it helps to say how your body feels right now."

Why we work with children

Children have the right to grow up in safety and security, and to have all their developmental needs met, that is: physical, emotional, cognitive, social, educational, and spiritual needs. This is enshrined in the United Nations (UN) *Convention on the Rights of the Child* (UN, 1989). This includes positive, healthy and competent parenting to inform the child's global development. For children without such experiences, the potency of therapeutic interventions can strengthen substantially their life chances.

Underpinning our interventions are three specific factors: philosophy, benefits, and professional responsibility.

Philosophy

We believe that the welfare of the child is paramount. In the UK this is reflected in *The Children Act 1989* (DoH, 1989). Our work takes the development of the child into account. We believe that child development is a process that requires parental understanding in order to promote healthy growth (Illsley-Clarke and Dawson, 1998). Unrealistic expectations feed parental anger, child resentment, and low self-esteem.

Benefits

There are significant benefits to be gained from working with children, for the child, the child's parents and siblings, and for society.

Benefits for the child

TA, with its emphasis on process and awareness of developmental needs, along with play therapy techniques, has many benefits for the child. It offers the therapist varied theories and methods which support a range of interventions relevant to:

- The temperament and personality of the child – through knowing their personality adaptations (Ware, 1983) and a greater range in working with the child using the appropriate communication channels (Kahler, 1978).
- The cognitive and language capacity of the child – by, for example, re-naming good and bad 'strokes' as 'warm fuzzies' and 'cold pricklies' (Steiner, 1974; Freed, 1991), using the child's language and their understanding of time past, present, and future.
- The emerging 'self versus other' conflicts of the child – by giving permissions and modelling: "It's OK for you to be you and me to be me" and "We can share/both get what we need" (Crossman, 1966).
- The physical, play, and social needs of the child – by providing a safe and secure environment, through time structuring which provides play activities (Berne, 1966) and by responding positively to the child's invitation to play (West, 1992).
- The dynamic nature of the therapeutic relationship – by attuning to the child through the use of one's own ego states and transactions (Hughes, 1998).

Underpinning all of the above is a simple time factor. From the stance that our adult functioning is derived primarily from parenting received in childhood, reinforced through our frame of reference and life script, our work with children has the significant advantage of *timeliness*. By working with children in, or chronologically close to, their developmental 'optimum', we can achieve change swiftly. This seems to occur for a number of reasons:

- The natural curiosity and pre-occupation of children at each developmental stage is utilised.
- The neurological capacity for change is at its greatest in the young brain.
- There is limited 'baggage' from unhealthy parental introjects, which become reinforced over time.
- Children are generally free of the responsibilities that can limit therapeutic change in adults e.g. family, relationships, work, and financial commitments, although in

some cases children are young carers of parents with disabilities, or have been placed in the parental role by adults.

Benefits for parents

The model we use recognises the vital role played by parents and carers, i.e. their role in the developing script of the child (ego state theory). We undertake sessions, meetings, and agreements with these key players, in order to optimise the outcome for each child. This involves gaining their perspectives through developing trust, and demonstrating empathy with them. It also involves a great deal of 'therapeutic education' in helping them to gain a greater understanding of how to parent their children, and alongside this being available to desensitise, or work through issues that arise for them. Common examples of issues for parents include:

- Reluctance to explore 'Whose problem is it?' 'Who needs to change?'
- Both denial and acknowledgement of their own abuse issues and feelings such as anger and fear.
- Resistance to changing unhealthy patterns of parenting.
- Fear of being disempowered.
- Lack of available energy or motivation to change.

Alongside the child resuming their healthy developmental pathway, our work often enables parents to resolve their own issues. Although direct work with parents is not the primary focus of our organisation, our efforts in this area continually demonstrate the benefits of such interventions. The healing experienced by these parents also ripples outwards to siblings and other relatives (see Chapter 11 and Appendix 4).

Benefits for society

It follows then, that changes in parental attitude and behaviour, through greater awareness, understanding and skill, will lead to providing for children's *needs* rather than their *wants*. We hope that in time this will be echoed in society in general.

Our focus on child development enables us to promote 'needs led' interventions with schools, health workers, social workers, and police by giving specific examples of techniques, strategies, and philosophies that optimise the life chances of children. One issue that emerges repeatedly is the disparity between developmental and chronological needs of children. Age, used as an assessment tool in an arbitrary manner with little insight, cannot gauge accurately the needs and abilities of individuals, and can result in inappropriate expectations or interventions.

Professional responsibility

The third factor relates to the specific place children have in society. They are defined as 'minors' with adults making decisions on their behalf and undertaking duties of care for them. As such, children have a limited autonomy to meet their own needs or, indeed, to know their own needs in a society so driven by wants. Therefore, it falls to parents and professionals to safeguard the development of children. If an adult chooses not to come into therapy to make life changes, there is little society can do. However, when a child is seen to have specific health or care needs, it is seen as neglectful not to provide for them.

How we work with children

We adhere to the basic philosophy of TA which states that: people are OK (they have worth, value and dignity); everyone has the capacity to think (except people with severe brain damage) and, therefore, to decide, re-decide and change. Our style of intervention follows the treatment triangle of contracting, diagnosis/assessment and treatment direction (Guichard, 1987) (see Figure 3.1).

The concept of the treatment triangle ignited our creativity. We pictured a coloured triangle

with the primary colours of red, yellow and blue in separate corners. When they come together and mix at the centre of the triangle, they become the colour brown, which can signify 'grounding', a pathway, or solidity. The treatment triangle is dynamic. Any imbalance between the three processes thus impacts upon the progress made with a particular client.

Further, we see the triangle as a three-dimensional object, leaning in to support itself, with its own secure base and central core – and thus a pyramid. We find this a useful metaphor for the need for secure attachment, strong identity, and potential for growth. For us the image of a pyramid encapsulates the strengths of equality, growth, development, identity, and interdependency.

We discuss each aspect of the treatment triangle, giving examples from practice.

Contracting

Contracts need to be valid and effective. Steiner (1974) identifies four requirements of contracting reflecting:

- Mutuality
- Consideration of the therapist's services
- Potency
- Adherence to professional ethics

Clients therefore need to have sufficient cognitive capacity to understand what they are agreeing to and therapists need to demonstrate their trustworthiness in terms of behaviour and decision-making. Given the age of our client group, this process often includes a third party such as a parent (English, 1975) and an exploration of the decision-making competence of children which in the UK was, until recently, referred to as 'Gillick competence' (Gillick, 1986) (see Chapter 5 for further details).

We draw up a business contract and a therapeutic contract, having first carried out a developmental assessment to inform us of the level at which we need to interact. We aim to create healthy dynamics within 'multilateral contracts' aware that 'there is a danger that in work with the child the counsellor will become the 'great power'/influence such that the parent is marginalised and put on the same level as the child, thus undermining the family structure' (Tudor, 1997: 160).

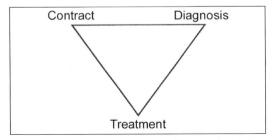

Figure 3.1 The treatment triangle (Guichard, 1987)

According to Levin (1974) children begin to have the capacity to understand and reason from an early age (18 months to 3 years). Our experience of working with young children confirms that this depends upon their developmental environment. Because of this we use language carefully and check a child's comprehension through questions, tasks and play. The use of open questions is dependent on developmental considerations, for example, younger children may need a selection of options, rather than a 'blank canvas' such as "How do you feel?" Whilst we acknowledge that the use of language is critical to the process of TA, the initial stages of some work are more dependent on non-verbal communication with the child or verbal communication with a third party consistent with early developmental need. For example, the therapist modelling potency, protection and permission, whilst initially involving a parent in the session, offers an opportunity for the child to begin to develop trust in the therapy.

In the business contract, we are obliged by social work legislation e.g. *The Children Act 1989* to provide information to the child about access to information, reporting child protection concerns, and how to access complaints procedures. We set limits (non-negotiable requirements) to prevent harm to themselves (the client), to others (this includes *us* – which we say explicitly to some children), or to property. Mindful that burdening the child with 'rules' can disempower them, we adhere to the maxim 'contact before contract'. We ensure that children sufficiently understand the 'practicalities' in order to feel secure e.g. how to get to sessions, where and when they will be there, and for how long. We undertake regular reviews of the work, emphasising to the child and to parents that their views will be considered, in planning and ending the work. We see endings as a cause for celebration of redecision, relearning, and cure.

The therapeutic contract is negotiated with the child and reflects their understanding of why they have been referred. In our experience, children often want to 'please others' including us, and form a close attachment to us. In some ways this is fostered by our unconditional acceptance of them. It is important for us initially to separate out other people's views of the child, and to give them permission to have their own needs and feelings. It remains our role however, to assess when to reflect the reality of others'

views, in order to develop a shared understanding between child and therapist. It is equally important to separate fantasy and reality when discussing expectations and goals in order to prevent children gaining the impression that the therapist has a 'fix-it' role.

Other aspects of contracting are more concerned with the therapeutic process and are therefore negotiable such as how much water to put in the sand tray with a child who has not yet developed the ability to predict. Our professional experience determines whether to follow through on issues as they arise, mindful of the stated, overall contract. It can be helpful to contract for a wider exploration of issues as they surface, if the therapist assesses this as appropriate. In general we use the analogy 'Trust the taxi driver to take the best route'. As therapists we take responsibility for driving the process and having a certain knowledge of the territory; however, from time to time, we also check the destination and the route with the client. In doing this we draw on Lee's (1997) ideas about process contracting. This demands that the therapist makes an immediate assessment of client need, and engages in a respectful questioning of whether to work on issues as they arise.

Sometimes there is a conflict regarding the therapeutic relationship and the professional responsibility of the therapist to take charge of the process. This can mean that the child is not always consulted, for example, regarding self-harm, when we make decisions regarding a possible psychiatric referral. Therapeutically it is helpful for the therapist to model self-care behaviours, and especially for a 'parentified' child to have the therapist take appropriate responsibility.

Assessment/diagnosis

The term 'assessment' is used to be consistent with social work models of intervention. Diagnosis is a medical term more commonly used in psychotherapy. In our experience children are more familiar with the term 'assessment'.

We undertake a systemic assessment at the beginning of the work with a child using Clarkson and Fish's (1988) systemic model (see Chapter 1). One advantage of this model is that it locates the child within their immediate family and also the social context, and it prefigures and is compatible with the *National Framework for Assessment* (DoH, 2000) used by social workers.

The systemic model is also useful in assessing whether the child is carrying the 'sick' role in the family (Campos, 1986) and gives options for the therapist to consider where the therapeutic and/or social work needs to be focused (see also Massey and Massey, 1988).

We collate information about the child's circumstances and development from files and written information held by agencies, from meetings with the referrer and carers, and from interacting directly with the child. The latter requires observation skills and a knowledge of child development in order to assess developmental need and the effect of trauma. It is important to hear the words and note the silences of the client as well as rhythms and intonation of speech, facial expressions, posture, proximity to self and others, agitation, and passivity.

We also assess in terms of the impact of genetic influences, life experience, and here-and-now relationships on the presenting functioning of the child. There has to be sufficient balance between these for the process of development to continue. Too much emphasis on temperament fails to validate the child's capacity to make and sustain change, and ignores the fact that natural bias or predisposition are not in themselves indicators of outcome. For example, a shy child can learn assertiveness and leadership skills. Too much emphasis on life experiences fails to harness the energy of the present and future, or to recognise individual traits such as deflection and decisiveness. For instance, a child who witnessed domestic violence can choose not to show aggression as an adult. Too much emphasis on the here-and-now fails to validate the child's internalisation of life events, and therefore neglects the opportunity to anchor feelings, responses or thoughts in the past. For example, the child who is discouraged from discussing life events may question their own memories of 'self'. They may also sense reluctance on the part of the worker to 'go there', that is, to hear traumatic detail.

As the assessment process is dynamic and ongoing, an objective balance needs to be maintained during both the process of collation and analysis. For example, a focus on life experiences as described by parents can become deterministic and can neglect the child's current functioning, resourcefulness, and resilience in overcoming negative life experiences.

A common difficulty in assessment is that parents can be overly concerned about words and phrases used by the child and automatically associate these with abuse. We determine the meaning for the child through assessing their language in direct discussion, observation of affect, along with feedback from parents and others regarding the context of such use of language. An abuser's name could cause distress for parents, yet the child could be using it appropriately e.g. when describing events, or expressing feelings.

Whilst assessment generally precedes treatment, both are continuous and have a dynamic relationship with the other (as reflected by our perspective on the treatment triangle above). In our work, we undertake an initial assessment and continue to assess progress throughout the treatment. This can lead to tensions from an organisational perspective as, statistically, they tend to be seen as separate processes. It is important not to lose sight of the child's perspective and understanding in this, and say, for instance, "Let's play for six weeks", rather than to burden them with defining assessment and treatment. Assessment leads to a treatment plan using, especially, the theory of personality adaptations (Ware, 1983) and process communication theory (Kahler, 1978). Identifying the client's main and secondary personality adaptations provides us with information about their strengths and weaknesses, and how to make and keep contact with them (Stewart, 1996).

One of us (LH) has worked with children who, due to the impact of trauma, tend to hold their bodies stiffly and show little emotion: they have learned that to show feelings makes them vulnerable to further abuse. They may also be responding to functional Controlling Parent messages that feelings are not OK. Using the process communication/personality adaptations model gives the information that they have a 'Be Strong' driver and that the communication sequence is, according to Ware (1983): behaviour (open door) thinking (target door) feeling (trap door). Following this, my treatment plan has been to work with freeing up behaviour through play so that the child learns to feel comfortable in their body and in taking up space. Alongside this I contact their thinking and give them positive messages about what they do, and then move on to working on feelings with them. One child I worked with was so freed up that she was chosen to lead the Easter Parade through her village, which she undertook with confidence and enjoyment.

Therapy/treatment

We prefer the term 'therapy' to 'treatment' as children associate 'treatment' with illness, and this can imply that the problem lies solely with the child. By contrast, 'therapy' suggests to us growth and nurture.

Our philosophy is that everyone has the capacity to change and that change is a process. Current research in neuroscience and genetics shows that the processes of being, thinking and doing develop alongside one another but have differing significance and usefulness at key times in development. Genetics highlights that predisposition (temperament) and adaptation (personality) will influence the process of change in individual children. Our treatment work recognises the developmental, personality, and relational needs of the child (and the parent) within any given process, and offers clinical interventions to complement these, in short: 'when to use what'.

Many children we work with have confusion about whom and how to trust, having had their trust abused by an adult with a duty of care for them, or having been 'groomed' to believe what adults say. Because of this, we see the therapeutic relationship as being important in developing and relearning *appropriate* trust and caution, to regain self-esteem, and to practice self-protective skills. Trust is built when the therapist maintains boundaries, is reliable, potent, and consistent.

It is important to show empathy, in terms of understanding what the child is experiencing and seeing how their world is for them. This is developed through reflecting the perspective or 'feelings' of toys or objects being thrown, ridiculed, nurtured or praised within the play, and showing how Adult perceptions can lead to positive changes in behaviour. This could be described as 'systemic empathy' when the child then applies this learning within their home situations.

A similar process needs to take place for parents, as sometimes children pick up non-verbal messages or misinterpret verbal information e.g. "he's the man of the house". We work with the parents, empowering them to take responsibility for their comments or actions, and reduce the impact on the child by, for example, saying directly to the child: "You're little so you don't have to take care of me."

Empathy is not an easy concept to grasp or develop and we are helped by Hargaden and Sills' (2002: 35) view that 'empathy is a combination of skill and technique and a reflection of who we are and how we are ourselves'. As well as having skill, it is important for therapists to maintain empathy for themselves by experiencing it in their own therapy, and in receiving supportive clinical supervision. We cannot stress enough the importance of developing congruent empathy for those working therapeutically with children.

How we work with parents

As has already been highlighted in this chapter, for therapeutic work with children to be effective, simultaneous work with parents needs to take place. Given that children need appropriate affirmations in order to progress for themselves, they need to hear these from other significant adults as well as the therapist. During discussions with parents we highlight these needs. However, we often find that the parents' own unmet needs compete with the here-and-now needs of their children. We then assist parents in giving themselves permission to get their needs met appropriately from other adults or in their own therapy. If parents have the internal resources to make changes, they can create a new functional Nurturing Parent through self-reparenting techniques (see James, 1974).

Parents also need to have an understanding of child development. The following examples reflect the struggles of parents who have limited knowledge of children's needs, and unrealistic expectations of their development, which are common themes within our work with parents.

Skills in working with parents

There are common skills required for working with parents. The following examples occur frequently within our work.

Communication skills

TA provides a model of communication by recognising individual transactions within communication and identifying verbal and non-verbal cues. This model is equally effective with children and parents. However, some communication skills required for working with children and parents differ. Social expectations impact upon the depth of conversation and, the timing of questions to a greater extent with adults. For example, initially a greater time may be spent in complementary transactions to establish rapport. With a child we may reflect their presentation more directly, with an adult we may simply comment that they seem uncomfortable.

Ultimately the aim is for effective communication to take place between the parent and child exclusive of the therapist. It is necessary therefore for a parent to be attuned to their child. A lack of attunement to the child can prevent the child recovering from trauma (and give them injunctions such as 'Don't Feel', 'Don't Be You'), and encourages the child to adapt to the needs of the adult in order to survive the family environment. Consequently the child learns conditional OKness i.e. "As long as I don't mention Granddad's name, Mummy will be OK and then I'll be OK." Recognising the shifts in ego states and employing tools to help ground parents in the here-and-now during discussions strengthens their Adult ego state(s), thus promoting positive outcomes for children.

Creating and maintaining boundaries

The existence of boundaries is a primary need in order to create security in relationships. Whereas we have commented that with adults it is initially important to build rapport and 'sameness', with children this initial period is often spent in establishing boundaries. This serves to reinforce the differing social expectations of adults and children. For many of the children we work with this is a particular struggle as they want to build 'sameness' by either testing potency or treating the therapist as a peer.

Similarly, we regularly need to educate parents in how to deal with these issues confidently and aside from their own emotions to save children from feeling the need to be the parent. This can include modelling of phrases and body language to acknowledge power and identity differences between parents and children e.g. "It's my job as a grown-up to make sure that you get enough sleep".

Assessment skills

It is essential to assess and analyse information from a variety of perspectives in order to inform the treatment direction. We endeavour to work alongside parents recognising that this may not always be possible for a number of reasons including:

- The parents' being a risk to the child and others.
- Their lack of motivation.
- Their mental health issues.
- Their attitude to the child.

It may be necessary to assess practical constraints that prevent meaningful work with parents, such as availability or timescales. Further to this, in order to demonstrate that the main focus is on the child, work with parents may need to be kept to a minimum. It may be more appropriate to refer such work to another agency.

Parents gain assessment skills through the process of TA being modelled by the therapist, learning such skills as observation and reflection e.g. "I notice you're looking tired". These skills are transferable into everyday relationships promoting Adult resourcefulness within communication and problem solving.

Summary

Working with children and families is a constant challenge, but also a privilege in terms of optimising children's futures. Within our model, it is essential to maintain a focus on genetic influences, life experiences, and here-and-now relationships, in order to promote holistic development within the child. The continuing challenge is to use our knowledge and skills to satisfy the following dimensions:

- The competing needs of children and families.
- Treatment timescales, styles and parameters.
- Societal demands, for instance, with regard to human rights, *The Children Act 1989*, and so on.
- Organisational structures, including procedures, administration, and caseload management.

For the child development pyramid to successfully reach a peak, therapy requires a high level of supervision that covers clinical, ethical and procedural issues in a collaborative, flexible style, and that allows for the dynamic processes that continue within the child, their ecosystem, the therapist, the organisation, and wider society. However, the view from the top of this peak, when a piece of work reaches a positive outcome, continually inspires us to develop our services to children and families.

References

Berne, E. (1966) *Principles of Group Treatment*. New York: Grove Press.

Campos, L.P. (1986) Empowering Children: Primary Prevention of Script Formation. *Transactional Analysis Journal*, 16; 1, 18–23.

Clarkson, P. and Fish, S. (1988) Systemic Assessment and Treatment Considerations in TA Child Psychotherapy. *Transactional Analysis Journal*, 18: 2, 123–32.

Crossman, P. (1966) Permission and Protection. *Transactional Analysis Bulletin*, 5: 19, 152–4.

Daniel, B., Wassell, S. and Gilligan, R. (1999) *Child Development for Child Protection and Child Care Workers*. London: Jessica Kingsley.

Department of Health (1989) *The Children Act*. London: HMSO.

Department of Health (1998) *Human Rights Act*. London: HMSO.

Department of Health (2000) *Framework for Assessment*. London: The Stationery Office.

English, F. (1975) The Three-Cornered Contract. *Transactional Analysis Journal*, 5: 4, 383–4

Freed, A.M. (1991) *TA For Tots and Other Prinzes*. Sacramento CA: Jalmar Press.

Gillick v. West Norfolk Health Authority (1986) AC 112, [1985] 3 All England Law Reports 402.

Goulding, M.M. and Goulding, R.L. (1979) *Changing Lives Through Redecision Therapy*. New York: Grove Press.

Guichard, M. (1987) *Writing the Long Case Study*. Workshop presentation, EATA Conference, Chamonix.

Hargaden, H. and Sills, C. (2002) *Transactional Analysis: A Relational Perspective*. London: Brunner-Routledge.

Hughes, D. (1998) *Building the Bonds of Attachment*. Northvale, NJ: Jason Aronson.

Illsley-Clarke, J. (1998) *Self-esteem: A Family Affair*. Center City, MN: Winston Press/Hazelden. (Original work published 1978)

Illsley-Clarke, J. and Dawson, C. (1998) *Growing Up Again: Parenting Ourselves, Parenting Our Children*. (2nd edn) Center City, MN: Hazelden.

James, M. (1974) Self Reparenting: Theory and Process. *Transactional Analysis Journal*, 4: 3, 32–9.

Joines, V. and Stewart, I. (2002) *Personality Adaptations*. Nottingham: Life Space Publishing.

Kahler, T. (1978) *Transactional Analysis Revisited*. Little Rock, AR: Human Development Publications.

Lee, A. (1997) Process Contracts. In Sills, C. (Ed.) *Contracts in Counselling*. London: Sage.

Levin, P. (1974) *Becoming the Way We Are*. Menlo Park, CA: Trans Pubs.

Massey, R.F. and Massey, S.D. (1988) A Systemic Approach to Treating Children With Their Families. *Transactional Analysis Journal*, 18: 2, 110–22.

Sgroi, S. (1982) *Handbook of Clinical Intervention in Child Sexual Abuse*. Massachusetts/Toronto: Lexington Books.

Steiner, C. (1974) *Scripts People Live: Transactional Analysis of Life Scripts*. New York: Grove Press.

Stewart, I. (1996) *Developing Transactional Analysis Counselling*. London: Sage.

Tudor, K. (1997) A Complexity of Contracts. In Sills, C. (Ed.) *Contracts in Counselling*. London: Sage.

United Nations. (1989) *Convention on the Rights of the Child*. Geneva: UNCORC.

Ware, P. (1983) Personality Adaptations: Doors to Therapy. *Transactional Analysis Journal*, 13: 1, 11–9.

West, J. (1992) *Child-Centred Play Therapy*. London: Arnold.

Winnicott, D.W. (1971) *Playing and Reality*. London: Tavistock/Routledge.

CHAPTER 4

Context Counts: Working with Young Muslim Men in a Post 9/11 World

Pete Shotton

Ahmed is 15. He has asked to speak to me because he has recently got into trouble for an act of vandalism while on a school trip to a university. This is the first time he has ever been in trouble in school. He was on the trip because he is classified as gifted and talented. He is expected to perform well in his exams. He came to the UK from Iran at the age of 10. He spoke no English but is now fluent. He is intelligent, articulate and popular with teachers and classmates. He wants me to help him to find out why he did something so bad. He tells me that he has let down his parents, his school and his religion. He recognises the pressure of expectations that are placed on him. What puzzles him is that when he looks back at what he did he doesn't feel bad. He tells me that he feels 'normal, instead of some super-achieving genius'.

Andrew is 12. His father also came to this school, and was taught by a number of teachers who are still on the staff. Andrew is a wiry, sandy-haired white boy with a second name that suggests Irish heritage. I have been asked to talk to him because he has been getting older boys to chase him by calling them 'pakis' and 'terrorists'. He tells me that they can't take a joke and that names don't hurt. He also tells me that he wouldn't call his best friend Farouk those names because it would really upset him.

Ali is 14. His father, who came to the UK in his teens, is Iraqi. His mother is white, of Welsh heritage. When people meet Ali, they are often confused. He appears to be a young white British male and yet his name reveals his dual heritage. He has been referred to me because of his anger. He has often been in serious confrontations with teachers and other boys. He tells me that he hasn't been in a mosque for years and he doesn't know if he'd call himself a Muslim. He doesn't know how he'd describe himself. He says he doesn't care what happens in Iraq, although he is aware that members of his father's family are there. He has thought about changing his name, but doesn't see why he should. He is loyal to his friends, loves basketball and says that he wants to be left alone. He regularly books one-to-one counselling sessions and says that this has helped him to stop fighting and, rather, to pursue his ambition of becoming an actor.

Adnan is 16, of Pakistani heritage and about to take his GCSE exams. He loves the music of Metallica and Jimi Hendrix. He says he 'can't see the point of anything'. He goes to lessons at the mosque after school each day and can only keep in touch with his friends, who are from other ethnic and cultural backgrounds, by chatting to them online.

Ajmal is also about to take his exams. He says he has stopped doing his coursework and he doesn't know why this is. As I ask him about his life he tells me he is Kurdish, from Northern Iraq. He shows me a web page he has made which tells of his witnessing the torture of his aunt when he was seven years old. It also describes the journey he made to the UK at the age of 8 via Turkey and Germany. Finally, it tells the story of Kurdistan and the part the British played in dividing up his homeland. His father has returned to Iraq to play a part in the setting up of a new government. Ajmal says he doesn't want to go back. He wants to stay in the UK and become a doctor. After telling me his story we negotiate an extension with his teacher and he completes his coursework.

These portraits are composite ones, based on real people and real events that I have encountered in my work.

For the past seven years I have led a team of mentors in an inner city multicultural high school for boys aged 11–16. The main focus of our work is the pastoral welfare of the boys. This chapter describes certain aspects of the work that the Mentor Team has done over the past six years and demonstrates how I have used transactional analysis (TA) models and ideas to impact on the process of developing relationships and understanding and meeting the needs of a culturally diverse pupil cohort. I also recognise and consider the influence of external factors, including major world events, on the school and its population.

From the beginning I have used TA in order to provide a shared philosophy and approach and because it has a range of tools for working at organisational, educational and therapeutic levels. Moreover, TA gives a methodology for understanding, healing and developing human relationships, all qualities which have been vital to our work.

The school

The school was originally built in the 1930s as a state grammar school for boys. It is now a comprehensive school. It continues to function as a boys' school as there are two large girls' schools on the same side of the city, both of which predominantly serve the requirements for single sex education of a growing Muslim community. There are 1,100 boys in the school, from 26 different ethnic/cultural groups, and with 30 languages other than English spoken at home. Between 50 per cent and 60 per cent of the boys qualify for free school meals, compared to a national average of 14.8 per cent (Department for Education and Science, 2004). Over 60 per cent of the boys are Muslims. A significant minority of the boys are refugees or asylum seekers or first generation immigrants to the UK. Over 80 per cent of the pupil population live outside the area where the school buildings are located. This area is a mixture of private and council housing with a mainly White British population. This means that the school is located in a community, but is not seen as part of the community.

The school is a caring, lively and affirming place. Before I became a mentor it was one of a number of schools I regularly worked in as a peripatetic support teacher and I was touched and impressed by the level of regard that teachers had for the boys. I was also aware that this was a school with a traumatic history, still dealing with the grief and recriminations resulting from a racist murder which had taken place there in the 1980s. There is an awareness in the school of both the positive and the negative extremes which can emerge in a place where those from diverse and different cultural backgrounds are required to develop, to co-exist and to learn. Looking at this in TA terms, the school's culture and ethos has a major part to play in the formation of script decisions. The phrase 'context counts' was originally coined by the family systems therapist, Virginia Satir, and is said to have inspired Berne's (1972/1975) addition of the third-handed position 'They're OK' to his more famous phrase 'I'm OK, You're OK' (see below and Chapter 14). It also appears and is acknowledged in a recent article by Naughton and Tudor (2006) who, through their use of co-creative script matrices for a young Asian man and a White female therapist, demonstrate the impact and power of messages about culture and identity which are given by and conveyed through teachers and schools.

The school culture

I have described the multicultural nature of the school in the broad statistical terms of home language and cultural groupings. What this means in an everyday sense is illustrated in this typical description of a contact record for one day (in which the names have been changed):

1. *Ranjit (Sikh, Year 8) and Kieron (White, Irish heritage, Year 8) reported theft of a mobile phone belonging to a classmate. Investigated and recovered from another classmate.*
2. *Year 9 Anger management group. Rashid (Mixed heritage Iranian/English) Chris (White English) Curtley (Jamaican) Bilal (Pakistani) Roy (Mixed heritage Afro Caribbean/English) and Kassim (Mixed heritage Pakistani/English). Group meets with me for one lesson (55 mins.) to discuss relationships in school/home/peer group and their feelings and responses.*
3. *One-to-one 30–minute session with Omar (Year 7, Libyan, refugee) experiencing anxiety.*
4. *Child protection meeting concerning Osman (Year 10, Somali) apparently living alone because guardian (believed to be uncle or older brother) has gone to another part of the country.*
5. *Year 11 Peer mentor training. Stephen (Nigerian) Qasir, Parvez and Kashif (all Bengali) Dan (White, English) Viraj (Sri Lankan) and Abdi (Somali). Teaching session on strokes.*

There is a rich variety of cultural background and life experience within this client group. What they have in common is that they are all teenage boys, they live in the same city and they attend the same school.

Context

So far I have described the specific and complex organisation that is the school, given a taste of the diverse backgrounds and issues manifested by the pupils and alluded to the potential influence of the school and its staff on the pupils' lives. As a worker in this system it is easy to feel overwhelmed by the range of needs, issues, behaviours, opinions and attitudes that I encounter. In order to understand and create a context for the issues which are impacting upon the boys and how best to offer support I use the model for overlapping sub-systems in the assessment and planning of TA child psychotherapy (Clarkson and Fish, 1988) (see

Chapter 1). I see this model as a map on which I can locate the issues that the boys bring to me. There are three overlapping sub-systems: the individual child, the family system and the socio-cultural system, which would include groupings such as school, peer group and religious affiliations, located within the larger system of life. These sub-systems overlap, creating four further areas in which issues and interventions can be located. All of the areas identified in this model are constantly changing and developing and therefore will take on different significance and importance at different times for different individuals. However, as well as enabling me to map and work with boys' individual profiles, this model gives me the opportunity to examine and appreciate the more wide ranging effects of the school sub-system and the global system of life. In the title of this chapter I refer to a 'post 9/11 world'. As Clarkson (1992: 230) puts it: 'life', 'fate' or 'acts of God' contribute the unexpected and unpredictable events which impinge on human lives, such as death, disease and disasters', a list to which I would add politics and global conflict. I draw on this systemic perspective to frame discussions in the rest of this chapter about a necessary awareness of life outside school; work in school; and how I use TA to work with individuals and groups in school.

Life

A growing awareness of life is a vital part of the experience of the boys that I work with. During the time that they attend the school they move from childhood into young adulthood. They develop their understanding of the cultural, social and political dynamics that impact upon their lives, while at the same time working towards defining and developing their own individual identities. As I have already stated, a clear majority of the boys in school are Muslim and have family links in other parts of the world. The destruction of the World Trade Centre in New York, the conflicts in Afghanistan and Iraq, the Tsunami of 2004, the earthquake in Pakistan, and the London bombings in 2005, have all been significant events in the life system for these boys. Some sections of the media have made much of the fact that the London bombers were young British Muslims. This has prompted the British government to set up a Commission on Integration and Cohesion with regard to minority

and immigrant communities. Whatever the intentions behind this body, its very existence links the actions of the bombers to these communities, and implies that a lack of integration and cohesion is a cause of the problem. Omaar (2006: 3) describes the dilemma of integration:

> It is a question that is a fundamental part of what it is to be Muslim in the modern world – especially a Muslim living in the West. Does your Muslim identity and loyalty supersede loyalty to your nation? Do you feel Muslim first and Somali, British, French or Dutch second? Can the two identities really co-exist? My (Muslim) second name also says something about the often hidden aspect of Muslim lives in this post September 11 world. Integration, at least as it is seen from the perspective of Muslims coming to and living in the West, is often about denying or even abandoning half of ourselves.

TA provides a language and model for understanding the potential impact of this process on the young men that I work with. Exploring the issues with a group of 15-year-olds in school, I talked about cultural messages in terms of a Parent ego state and asked them what Parent message they thought they were getting from the media and politicians. They came up with the message "If you are young and you look like a Muslim, you're dangerous. You'd better behave yourself and be like us". They identified the injunctions: Don't be close, Don't be you, and Don't belong. In exploring TA as a social psychiatry, Moiso (1998: 1) highlights the importance of belonging:

> Let us remember that in transactional analysis, the healthy relationship is one in which two individuals put themselves on equal terms and base their negotiations on the specific characteristics of autonomy of the Adult: awareness, as the capacity to know how to distinguish self from other; spontaneity, as the capacity to act on one's motivations in the first person; and intimacy, as the capacity to open oneself to another in an authentic exchange of experience and feelings.
> We can thus define the quality of life as the result of three factors: belonging, being and becoming. Belonging involves the individuals having a place within the environment and with others; being concerns who and how a person is as an individual; and becoming relates to what a person does to attain individual aims and aspirations. Belonging provides the foundation and meaning for being and becoming.

It therefore follows that in order to create a healthy environment in which the boys can learn and develop we need to let them know that they belong.

Work in school

After the family, school is the social institution which has the closest contact with children for most of their formative years. The primary and increasingly demanding purpose of a school is clearly educational. At the same time, schools are uniquely placed to observe their pupils, to recognise social and emotional difficulties and to address needs which are interfering with the learning process and could continue into adulthood. Realising the potential of this position is not at all simple. Emotional and social needs are essentially private, unclear even to the individual experiencing them, and at school they are often masked by misleading behaviour which may repel rather than attract help and understanding. The challenge is to produce conditions in which troubled pupils feel safe enough to reveal their needs and in which someone pays attention and responds appropriately.

(Heller, 2000: 22)

This quote from Heller is one that I often use with staff to explain the context for social and emotional provision alongside learning in school. The Mentor Team is still a relatively new development in the school and using this quotation is my way of saying 'We belong here'.

When I began working at the school I had 20 years' experience as a teacher in a variety of classroom, pastoral and support posts. I was in my fourth year of TA training and I was also working in private practice as a psychotherapist. Three other members of staff were appointed to the team and, at my request, were trained in TA to an introductory (TA 101) level. They all had experience of working with young people in a variety of settings but none of them had worked for a sustained period in a mainstream school. Over the years, team members have left to move on to other roles in education and new mentors have been appointed. I have qualified in TA in both education and psychotherapy fields of application and have continued to use TA models to provide a structure for training, supervision and practice within the team.

I invite new colleagues to recognise that we all have life experiences that enable us to understand, and empathise with, a teenage client group. I also stress that these experiences are part of knowing ourselves and understanding our aptitude and motivation for working with this age group. In working with adults who are keen to work with young people I often encounter a

dynamic whereby the adults confuse their own 'teenage' frame of reference with what they believe to be an attuned response to the young person's needs. They impose the message "I know who you are because I was once like you" rather than asking the questions "Who are you and what is it like to live your life?" It is important that we know and understand ourselves in order that we can create the space to know and understand others. I regularly discuss with colleagues any transference and countertransference issues that may be emerging from and impacting upon our relationships with our client group.

We work dynamically, effectively and successfully with the boys. I believe that this is because of our awareness of, and regard for, difference, and our willingness to be part of a process of meeting, learning about and engaging with them as they define themselves.

What follows is a description of the way that I use TA theory to facilitate this process.

Working with TA

The three core beliefs of TA underpin our work and are a potent and vital force for ensuring change and growth in ourselves, our clients and the school as an organisation. When I work with boys I often begin the session by writing them on the board:

- People are OK.
- People can think – and therefore choose their destiny.
- People can change.

These statements rarely go unchallenged. The boys often focus on what they perceive to be power imbalances in school in favour of teachers, which means they have or perceive that they have no choice. Often this leads to discussions about the options they have in any given situation, the different individual responses and the potential for different outcomes. Using these statements as a starting point for the work has an immediate impact, encouraging reflection, challenging previously held beliefs, and promoting the idea that school is a place where pupils and teachers work collaboratively to 'co-create' an ethos or culture. Summers and Tudor (2000: 24) summarise the principles of constructivism that are relevant to a co-creative transactional analysis:

- *Meaning constantly evolves through dialogue.*
- *Discourse creates systems (and not the other way around).*
- *Therapy is the co-creation, in dialogue, of new narratives that provide new possibilities.*
- *The therapist [mentor] is a participant-observer in this dialogue.*

The fact that we give the boys the opportunity to recognise the part they play in the co-creative process gives them the permission and power to choose and change their destiny if they wish.

As this is a co-created process it is important that I promote the same beliefs to school staff. Part of my role is to work with staff formally through training. I run programmes covering the work of the Mentor Team, mediation and conflict resolution, and working therapeutically in the school environment. I also work with staff informally by way of everyday contact in the corridors and classrooms. I find that informal contact is valuable and effective because the relationship is also based on the motivation of the other member of staff wishing to find out about the way that I and the team work. I am open to discussion and, because we have a philosophical and practical methodology for the work, I am able to demonstrate how our interventions are part of a structured approach to establishing mutually respectful relationships in school. For example, pointing out to a colleague the difference between saying to a pupil "You are an idiot!" and saying to him "You are behaving like an idiot" can have a profound influence on that colleague's practice, affecting their experience of themselves as leaders in the educational process, and their relationship with their pupils. Also, in pointing this out I am modelling confrontation in the sense of raising awareness, as opposed to making an adversarial intervention. In this way I, my team, and the young people and staff that we work with, can all influence language and behaviour and invite a collaborative approach in school, a strategy which, ultimately, gives permission to and empowers all.

I have previously referred to the impact of world events on the everyday life of the boys. A question I still find myself asking, as a therapeutic worker in this environment, concerns the implications of me as a white man, rooted in my country and culture of origin, supporting my multicultural client group in confronting, challenging and coming to terms with cultural messages and choosing to define themselves. Am

I the 'right' person to be doing this work? This is a question that resonates throughout organisations offering care, support and education in Western society, in that we operate in a world of increasing mobility, fluidity and conflict with a client group which is becoming more diverse and less likely to conform to or understand the dominant culture's norms. Using the drama triangle (Karpman, 1968) as a template, there is a danger that positive intention can be used to justify the righteous imposition of values (Persecutor), unbidden and patronising caretaking (Rescuer) and viewing the other (Victim) as less resourceful, less able to develop and less able to make autonomous decisions. We need to be aware of these dangers in order to avoid becoming 21st century missionaries. We also need to be aware of ways to develop productive, collaborative and mutually beneficial working relationships with our clients. TA provides many models for understanding ourselves and our relationship to others. I have found the existential life positions (Berne, 1962) to be particularly helpful as a model for myself and for my client group. By identifying two fundamental views of self (I am OK and I am not OK) and two views of the other (You are OK, you are not OK), it is possible to identify four life positions from which individuals can view the world and identify their place, or position, in it:

1. I am OK, You are OK (I+U+)
2. I am not OK, You are OK (I-U+)
3. I am OK, You are not OK (I+U-)
4. I am not OK, You are not OK (I-U-)

'Every game, script and destiny . . . is based on one of these four basic positions' (Berne, 1962: 3). This is a simple and profound idea, using everyday language to provide a framework for self-analysis, for understanding conflict in relationships and for changing our 'destiny'. I find that these are qualities that appeal to teenage boys. I teach the model to boys and teachers, adapting and combining Ernst's (1971) OK corral (Figure 4.1) with Karpman's (1968) drama triangle (Figure 4.2), and Choy's (1990) winner's triangle (Figure 4.3) into what I refer to as the OK matrix (Figure 4.4).

First I set out the life positions and discuss the characteristics, attitudes and behaviours they might associate with the life positions (Figure 4.1).

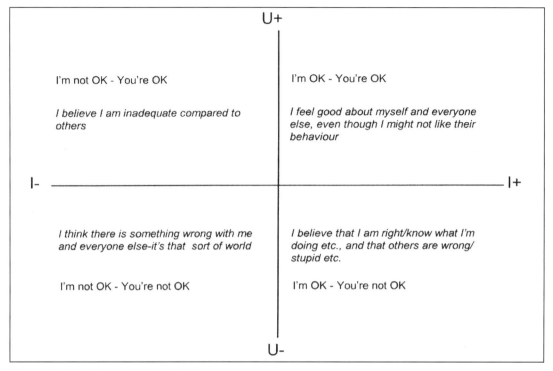

Figure 4.1   The OK corral (Ernst, 1971)

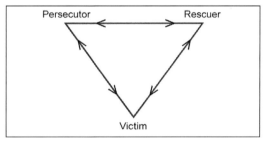

Figure 4.2   The drama triangle (Karpman, 1968)

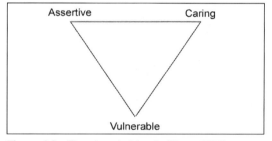

Figure 4.3   The winner's triangle (Choy, 1990)

I then teach the roles and dynamics of the drama triangle (Figure 4.2) and combine these roles with their respective life positions.

I then introduce the 'winner's triangle' (Choy, 1990) (Figure 4.3). These roles provide the opportunity to explore and discuss change, development and growth; to confront repeated negative patterns of behaviour; and to offer positive alternatives to the drama triangle roles, again linked to life positions.

Combining all three models provides a template for a process of developing autonomy (Figure 4.4).

By tilting the OK Corral on its axes, I emphasise the aspirational nature of the model through setting the position 'I'm OK, You're OK' above the other three positions. On a social level, this diagram stimulates discussion and offers a model (I'm OK, You're OK) for 'getting on with' others. I see this as a vital model for those of us who have chosen to work with teenagers, and for our client group, which is why I have included the concept of *physis*, which Berne (1947, 1957: 68) describes as 'the force of Nature, which eternally strives to make things grow and to make growing things more perfect'. What this requires of us is

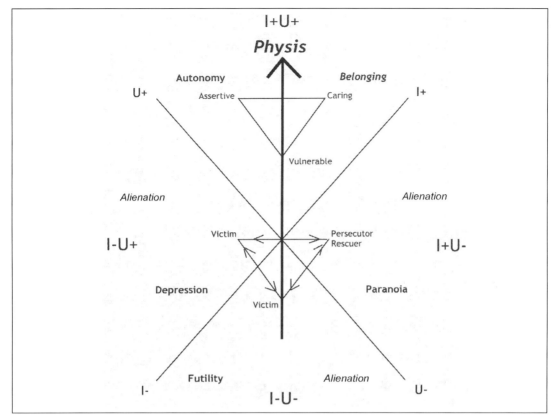

Figure 4.4 The OK matrix

not only to *act* from an 'I'm OK, You're OK' position, but also to think, feel and behave 'I'm OK, You're OK', and to recognise, analyse and learn from those times when we do not think, feel or behave 'I'm OK, You're OK'. This is especially true within a multicultural setting. As Hargaden and Sills (2002: 106) point out:

> *Within Transactional Analysis we have theoretical models that allow for diversity and health to coexist. Paradoxically, these very strengths also point to an inherent weakness, which is that we can ignore difference. It can seem almost as though by believing in 'I'm OK, You're OK' we can make it happen. Although the intention is honourable, it is misguided and easily leads to discounting behaviour that amounts to racism.*

A key part of 'I'm OK, You're OK' is the recognition of difference, through the polarities of 'I' and 'You' or 'other', and a willingness to find out more about and honour those polarities. If we do not acknowledge these differences then we miss out on experiencing the variety and the value of human diversity and recognising our own unique contribution. In TA terms, this involves being aware of the impact of our own personal and cultural scripts on ourselves, and on our relationships with others. Understanding this can be a demanding and painful process.

I grew up in a predominantly white working class community where the attitudes that were modelled towards other cultures were at best patronising and at worst mistrustful and hostile. Many of the boys I work with have grown up in families who experienced these discriminatory attitudes and carry equally negative cultural script messages about the dominant white culture that I belong to. I sometimes experience transferential feelings towards boys which are rooted in the racist cultural messages I was subjected to in my own childhood. I find these feelings disturbing. In owning them and describing them I feel vulnerable, and protective towards the community that I grew up in.

Awareness review

- Am I aware of the impact of my past upon the assumptions that I make about culture, identity, morals, etc.?
- Can I identify dominant and minority groups in wider society and in the area(s) in which I live and work? Can I identify power imbalances and discrimination in the relationship between these groups, and can I see ways in which these practices are perpetuated?
- What can I do to enhance my learning about the groups from which my client group and colleagues come?
- Am I open to a wide range of challenging and perhaps contradictory views of the world expressed by my client group and my colleagues?
- How can I adapt and extend the theories and models of teaching, learning and pastoral care that I use in order to develop my understanding of, and responses to, my clients?
- How might my way of being with clients recognise and address the societal and political implications of their situation?
- How might my way of being with clients recognise and address the emotional and psychological implications of their situation?

Box 4.1   Awareness review (adapted from Lago and Thompson, 1996)

However, to deny the existence of the feelings would be to ignore what Lago and Thompson (1996: 14) describe as 'the profound and often unconscious impact our own cultural heritage has upon our attitudes and perceptions towards others, especially those who are racially and culturally different to ourselves'.

If I am going to work effectively and honestly with my clients from an 'I'm OK, You're OK' position then it is important that I acknowledge the prejudices that form part of my upbringing. I can only confront and change that which I can see. The challenge of working in a multicultural setting is an ever-changing process, in response to which I use a questionnaire in order to raise awareness and stimulate effective practice in school (Box 4.1).

In answering these questions it is clear that as mentors, educators and for some of us as therapists, our work is, of necessity, about our professional and personal development as much as that of our clients, and that this mutual and co-creative development is appropriate in an 'I'm OK, You're OK' school ethos. Our work is also about being aware of a wider context to school and maintaining an 'I'm OK, You're OK' *and* 'They're OK' position so that we can hear and understand the concerns, hopes and aspirations of our client group as they are often 'They'. The importance of hearing their voices is summed up in this passage from the autobiography of Rageh Omaar, a writer and broadcaster, born in Somalia, a British citizen and a Muslim (2006: 215):

Muslims are unfamiliar to and seen as alien by so many people in this country, their experiences as individuals whether working as a travel agent on a high street or living as a mother in a suburb, as a recently arrived refugee or as an educated woman in a youth centre, or as a businessman in Edgeware Road are rarely heard. And yet, without allowing these voices in politics, on our streets, in our schools, in our newspapers and on our televisions we are all lost. It is only when the voice of the individual is lifted above the waves of condemnation that all of us can begin to see more clearly and perhaps start to realize that our worlds are not actually in conflict after all.

References

Berne, E. (1957) *A Layman's Guide to Psychiatry and Psychoanalysis*. New York: Ballantine Books. (Original work published 1947)

Berne, E. (1961) *Transactional Analysis in Psychotherapy*. New York: Grove Press.

Berne, E. (1962) Classification of Positions. *Transactional Analysis Bulletin*, 1: 3, 23.

Berne, E. (1975) *What Do You Say After You Say Hello?* London: Corgi. (Original work published 1972).

Clarkson, P. and Fish, A. (1988) Systemic Assessment and Treatment Considerations in TA Psychotherapy. *Transactional Analysis Journal*, 18: 2, 123–32.

Clarkson, P. (1992) *Transactional Analysis Psychotherapy: An Integrated Approach*. London: Routledge.

Choy, A. (1990) The Winner's Triangle. *Transactional Analysis Journal*, 20: 1, 40–6.

Department for Education and Science (2004) *Trends in Education and Skills. National Statistics 2004*. Available online at www.dfes.gov.uk

Ernst, F.H. (1971) The OK Corral: The Grid for Get-on-With. *Transactional Analysis Journal*, 1: 4, 231–40.

Hargaden, H. and Sills, C. (2002) *Transactional Analysis A Relational Perspective*. London: Brunner Routledge.

Heller, F. (2000) Creating a Holding Environment in an Inner City School. In Barwick, N. (Ed.) *Clinical Counselling in Schools*. London: Routledge.

Karpman, S. (1968) Fairy Tales and Script Drama Analysis. *Transactional Analysis Bulletin*, 7: 26, 39–43.

Lago, C. and Thompson, J. (1996) *Race, Culture and Counselling*. Buckingham: Open University Press.

Moiso, C. (1998) Being and Belonging. *The Script*, XXVIII: 9, 1–2.

Naughton, M. and Tudor, K. (2006) Being White. *Transactional Analysis Journal*, 36: 2, 159–71.

Omaar, R. (2006) *Only Half of Me: Being a Muslim in Britain*. London: Penguin Books.

Summers, G. and Tudor, K. (2000) Cocreative Transactional Analysis. *Transactional Analysis Journal*, 30: 1, 23–40.

Child Protection

Mica Douglas and Keith Tudor

Child protection, like health protection, refers to those legal and fiscal controls, together with other regulations or policies, and voluntary codes of or frameworks for practice, aimed at the prevention of child abuse and the promotion of the positive well-being of children. This chapter examines this aspect of the context of working with children, through a number of discussions, beginning with some definitions of child abuse. This is followed by a review of relevant legislation, and discussion of a number of implications for practice: contracts, confidentiality, the therapist's duty of care, disclosure, referral, working with child witnesses, and the status of therapist's notes. As a concept transactional analysis (TA) has valued the importance of 'protection' and, in the third part of the chapter, this concept is discussed with reference to working with children. Drawing on these discussions, the chapter concludes with some reflections on ethical decision-making with specific reference to therapists working with children in independent, private practice.

A therapist is working in private practice with Katie, a 13-year-old girl who has been referred by her parents. They are concerned that she has low self-esteem, little confidence, and is anxious about the next two or three years when she is going to be taking exams and deciding her future. Katie agrees that she needs some emotional support and wants to come to therapy to have time for herself to look at things that are bothering her. After six or seven weeks of therapy, Katie's demeanour has changed. She is excited, says she has a secret, and is acting just like teenagers do when they are in love for the first time. Eventually she discloses to you that a teacher at school is spending

extra time with her, and he has told her that she is special. She knows that they cannot have a relationship because of his position; he has offered friendship, and they are sending text messages to each other on a daily basis. Katie tells you that he has asked her to send him a photograph of herself via her mobile phone, and they have planned to meet in the school holidays at his home because, he says, people would not understand it if they were seen together in town. Katie has told nobody about her teacher apart from you, her therapist.

This scenario poses particular ethical dilemmas for therapists working with children, especially for those working in independent, private practice on whom there is no legal duty to report abuse, although there are moral, ethical, and professional issues, codes and frameworks to consider (see Box 5.1). It is important to note this distinction in the therapist's working context as it is commonly misunderstood by therapists, supervisors and trainers. We return to the implications of this distinction later in the chapter.

Bearing this initial scenario in mind, this chapter looks at the wider legal context of child protection and the moral, ethical and professional issues posed for therapists, as well as their duties of care. We discuss this with regard to therapists working in agencies that do have a legal duty to report abuse, as well as those in independent, private practice. We offer this summary of relevant legislation and legal issues in the spirit of offering an increased knowledge and awareness of how the law affects the work of therapists working with children, viewing, as Jenkins

Legislation, statutory regulations, national and local government policies		Codes/frameworks of ethics and professional practices
govern		regulate/advise
Statutory workers e.g. social workers	Therapists working in statutory and voluntary agencies	Therapists working in independent practice

Box 5.1 The different contexts for therapists working in statutory and voluntary agencies, and in independent, private practice

(2002a) puts it, the legal system as the *terrain* which impinges on the *content* that is therapy. Knowledge and comprehension of relevant law and legal issues are not only educational objectives, they are consistent with most ethical and professional practice guidelines. Also, in 2003, the United Kingdom Council for Psychotherapy (UKCP) published training guidelines for *Psychotherapy with Children* (reproduced in Appendix 6) which state that trainees will need to demonstrate knowledge of legal issues such as child protection. For further information and details about many of the issues discussed in this chapter we also recommend the work of Jenkins (1997, 2002b) and Daniels and Jenkins (2000).

The chapter also discusses a model of decision-making about ethical issues that can support therapists in reaching decisions that are in the best interests of the child. At this stage it might be useful for you, the reader/practitioner, to make a mental note of your initial reactions and responses to this initial scenario and to see if, by the end of the chapter, they are any different.

Definitions of abuse

Practitioners working with children need some working definitions of child abuse in order to support their thinking and help with diagnosis of a problem (see Figure 5.2). A more detailed list of the signs and symptoms of each kind of abuse is in Appendix 3.

Referring to our case vignette at the beginning of this chapter, alarm bells are likely to be ringing for the therapist with regard to emotional abuse. At the very least the teacher is abusing his power and position of trust in a way that is likely to lead to emotional abuse, if nothing else.

The legal context in the United Kingdom

There is no single piece of legislation that covers child protection in the United Kingdom. Instead there is a myriad of laws and guidance that are continually being amended, updated and revoked through new legislation and interpretation by the courts that then becomes case law. Not all laws cover all parts of the UK, which comprises England, Wales, Scotland, Northern Ireland and the Channel Islands, whose legal systems vary in different areas.

Legislation covering child protection can be divided into two main categories:

1. Civil law – comprising:
   - Public law, that puts in place systems and processes in order to minimise the risk of children coming to harm, and lays out what action should be taken if children are at risk.
   - Private law, that deals with family proceedings such as divorce and contact.
2. Criminal law – that deals with people who have offended, or are at risk of offending against children.

Abuse and neglect – is harm being inflicted on a child by another person or by a failure to act and prevent harm.

Physical abuse – may involve hitting, shaking, throwing, poisoning, burning or scalding, drowning, suffocation, or otherwise causing physical harm to a child. This definition would include 'fabricated and induced illness' (FII) which deliberately causes ill-health to a child.

Sexual abuse – involves forcing or enticing a child or young person to take part in sexual activities, whether or not the child is aware of what is happening. The activities may involve any inappropriate physical contact or involving a child in looking at, or in the production of, pornographic material, or in encouraging a child to behave in sexually inappropriate ways.

Emotional abuse – is the persistent ill-treatment of a child that causes severe and adverse effects on the emotional development of the child. Emotional abuse may involve: being consistently over-critical; conveying to a child that they are worthless, unloved or inadequate, or valued only insofar as they meet the needs of another person; only giving a child conditional strokes; causing a child to frequently feel frightened; or the exploitation or corruption of children.

Neglect – is the persistent failure to meet a child's basic physical and/or psychological needs, likely to result in the serious impairment of the child's health or development. This may be about failure to provide adequate food, shelter and clothing or unresponsiveness to a child's basic emotional needs.

Box 5.2   Definitions of child abuse

Children Act 1989

The current child protection system is based on the *Children Act 1989* (hereafter 'the *Act*') which was introduced in an effort to reform and clarify the then existing plethora of laws affecting children. The *Act* enshrined a number of key principles that inform practice today. One of them was the 'paramountcy principle', which means that, when making any decisions about a child's upbringing, the child's welfare takes precedence. The *Act* also placed a duty on courts to take into account the wishes and feelings of the child, and determined that the courts should not make an 'Order' about an outcome under the act unless this would be better for the child than making no Order at all. The *Act* also introduced the concept of 'parental responsibility', which sets out the rights, duties and responsibilities of the parent or carer of the child.

At the time the *Children Act 1989* was hailed by the then Lord Chancellor, Lord Mackay of Clashfern, as 'the most comprehensive and far-reaching reform of child law which has come before Parliament in living memory' (quoted in NSPCC, 2005).

Whilst local authorities have a mandatory duty to investigate if they are informed a child may be at risk, there are no mandatory reporting laws in the UK that require professionals to report their suspicions to the authorities. Most professional bodies issue to their members guidance which sets out what they should do if they are concerned about the welfare of a child with whom they come into contact. For psychotherapists and counsellors, the absence of reporting laws does not make the task of what to do about concerns they may have any easier because any child protection issue is an ethical rather than a legal one.

Relevant legislation 1989–2004

Since the *Children Act 1989* many other new laws have been passed which have made amendments to that Act, and which are currently in force:

- The *United Nations Convention on the Rights of the Child 1989* which was ratified by the UK in December 1991. The convention includes the right to protection from harm, the right to express views and have them listened to, and the right to care and services for disabled children or children living away from home.

- Although the UK government has said that it regards itself bound by the demands of the *Convention*, and refers to it in child protection guidance, it has not become part of UK law (see Lyon et al., 2003).

- The *Human Rights Act 1998* incorporates the European Convention of Human Rights into UK law. Whilst it does not specifically mention children's rights, children are covered by this legislation as they are 'persons' in the eye of the law, just as adults are (Bainham, 2005). This *Act* makes it unlawful for public authorities to act in a manner which is incompatible with the rights and freedoms contained in the *Act*.

- *The Education Act 2002* includes a provision (Section 175) requiring school governing bodies, local education authorities and further education institutions to make arrangements to safeguard and promote the welfare of children.

- Section 120 of the *Adoption and Children Act 2002* amends the *Children Act 1989* by expanding the definition of 'harm' to include 'witnessing domestic violence'.

- The death of Victoria Climbié and subsequent report (Laming, 2003) has helped shift the emphasis of child protection to prevention work and the integration of systems between agencies working together to that end. The government has a ten year strategy setting national standards for the health and care of children. The tragic and unnecessary death of Victoria Climbié revealed to the world, once again that, although many different professionals were involved in the life of this child, they did not share information or talk to each other sufficiently enough to build a complete picture of the horror Victoria was suffering. As with previous child deaths, each of the workers involved suspected the dangerous situation that the child was in, but each one only had a partial picture of the risks to the child. The government's response to the Victoria Climbié Inquiry Report led to the *Children Act 2004*.

Keeping children safe from harm requires professionals and others to share information. However, there is a need to balance that requirement with the need for children and young people to share confidences. The challenge for therapists and all professionals interested in protecting children is how to get that right for the child.

Children Act 2004

The *Children Act 2004* does not replace or even amend much of the *Children Act 1989*. Instead it sets out the process for integrating services to children so that every child, not only children known to the care system, can achieve five outcomes:

1. Being healthy – including mental, emotional, sexual, physical health.
2. Staying safe – from injury, death, bullying, discrimination, crime, neglect, violence and sexual exploitation, combined with a secure and stable base.
3. Enjoying and achieving – including personal, social, educational development, attending and enjoying school and recreational activities.
4. Making a positive contribution – gaining self confidence, learning to deal with significant life changes and challenges, engaging in decision-making and in law-abiding and positive behaviour, developing positive relationships and enterprising behaviour.
5. Achieving economic well-being – living free from poverty, engaging in training or further education and living in decent homes and sustainable communities.

These aims were identified by children and young people as the things they would like for themselves, and are consistent with the results of research into factors or abilities which define children's and young people's positive mental health conducted by the Mental Health Foundation (DES, 2003):

- The ability to develop psychologically, emotionally, creatively, intellectually and spiritually.
- The ability to initiate, to develop and to maintain mutually satisfying personal relationships.
- The ability to become aware of and to empathise with others.
- The ability to use and to enjoy solitude.
- The ability to play and to learn.
- The ability to develop a sense of right and wrong.
- The ability to face problems and setbacks and to learn from them – in ways that are age-appropriate.

The 2004 *Act* also paves the way for agencies to set up information-sharing databases. Section 58 of the *Act* outlines restrictions on punishment and what is considered reasonable force for a parent to use against a child. This *Act* did not go as far as to outlaw smacking, but it removes most defences that a parent, or someone acting as one, may use to justify child battery when charged with this criminal offence.

There is also a wealth of legislation designed to protect children from adults who pose a risk to them. Here we consider two pieces of legislation which are relevant to therapists and to consideration of our initial case vignette, regarding: criminal records, and sexual offences.

Criminal Record Bureau checks

The *Protection of Children Act 1999* created a single system for identifying people unsuitable to work with children. It made it mandatory for employers to check this list, which is administered by the Criminal Records Bureau (CRB), when employing someone in a post involving the care of children, and also made it an offence to employ anyone on the list. Thus, as a safeguard for young and vulnerable clients, therapists who work with children, in the context of an organisation, do have to conform to legal requirements of an enhanced CRB check. Usually, this is applied for by the organisation that is employing people to work with children or is offering placements. Therapists working with children in private practice are not covered by this legislation and, therefore, are not required to obtain a CRB check. However, many do, partly on a principle of equity, identifying with colleagues in the public and voluntary sector and, partly, to reassure parents and carers of children that, as therapists, they have nothing to hide.

Sexual Offences Act 2003

This was introduced to update the legislation relating to sexual offences against children. It includes the offences of grooming, abuse of position of trust, trafficking, and covers offences committed by British citizens whilst abroad. It also updated the *Sex Offenders Act 1977* to strengthen the monitoring of offenders on the sex offenders' register.

There are a number of other legalities of which the practitioner working with children needs to be aware, including, famously, 'Gillick competence' which is now referred to as 'Fraser competence' (see below).

Fraser competence

This refers to the child being of sufficient age and understanding that they may be treated for all intents and purposes as if they were 16 years old. 'Children' are defined as being under 16, and 'young people' as between 16 and 18. The term 'Gillick competence' derived from judgements made in 1985 and 1986 in the House of Lords that held that a doctor may lawfully prescribe contraception for a girl under 16 years of age without the consent of her parents. Lord Scarman ruled that parental rights to determine medical treatment for a child below 16 'terminates if and when the child achieves a sufficient understanding and intelligence to enable him or her to understand fully what is proposed' (Hansard 3A 11 ER 402 [HL]). The underlying principle is that parental rights yield to the child/young person's right to make up their own mind *when* they have sufficient understanding and intelligence to be capable of doing that. This ruling (Gillick v West Norfolk and Wisbech Area Health Authority, 1986) marked a major advance in the rights of children and young people. Until recently, this ruling was referred to as the 'Gillick ruling', after the person, Victoria Gillick, who brought the original action questioning the health authority's right to treat children, and, specifically, to provide contraception, without parental consent. As the ruling went against her, it was somewhat ironic that the measure of competence was subsequently named after her. In response to Mrs Gillick's request that this ruling should not be so named, it is now known as the 'Fraser ruling' and the mark of the child's competence as 'Fraser competence', renamed after Lord Fraser who ruled on the original case.

Having summarised the relevant legislation relating to children, we now consider a number of implications for practice, regarding: contracts, confidentiality, the therapist's duty of care, disclosure, referral, working with child witnesses, and case notes. In this part of the chapter we focus principally on the implications for therapeutic practice, although these may apply equally to practitioners working in other fields of application such as education.

The implications of child protection legislation and policy for therapeutic practice

Contracts

Since its inception, TA has been characterised by its contractual method, for the most recent discussion of which see various contributions in Sills (2006). For therapists working with children, the principle of 'Fraser competence' is of great significance and importance as it means that, if the child meets the 'Fraser test' of having sufficient understanding and intelligence to understand what is proposed, such as meeting for counselling, then the therapist can make a contract to do this. This test elaborates one of the four basic requirements for a contract to be legally valid, identified by Steiner and Cassidy (1967):

- Mutual consent – In a therapeutic context, this implies a clear and understandable offer on the part of the therapist of what they will give, in return for some agreement on the part of the client about what is the focus of the work and how both therapist and client will work together to achieve defined outcomes. Of course, when parents are party to this, mutual consent becomes three-handed, and such consent may be withdrawn. In order to protect the child and the therapy, it is important, as Steiner (1971: 134) puts it, that this 'is adequately dealt with by an agreement with the parents that the child will not discontinue treatment unless both he and the guardians consent to it.'
- Valid consideration – This refers to the benefit conferred by both the therapist (amelioration, cure) and the client (payment and/or attendance, active participation). In the context of working in an agency this may be as simple as the therapist offering a service to a child or young person who meets the criteria of the agency and, for their part, the client attending and participating, as agreed. In private practice it usually involves a three-cornered contract (English, 1975) including a parent or carer who is paying for the child's therapy.
- Competency – This refers to the ability of the parties to enter into a contract and is, therefore, often mediated in the case of legal minors and, for Steiner and Cassidy, certain levels of

dysfunction and intoxication. The principle of 'Fraser competence' provides a clear basis for assessing the competence of 'minors' to decide for themselves. In practice, even if a child is capable of making this kind of therapeutic contract, many therapists seek to involve the parents in consultation, especially with regard to contracts and to reviews, unless this is clearly inappropriate.

- Lawful object – This refers to the broader consideration that, as Steiner and Cassidy (1969: 31) put it: 'The contract must not be in violation of law or against public policy or morals.' In practice, a lot of the time, this point in contracting comes down to personal ethics, with practitioners ignoring minor offences or considering them not serious enough to warrant a rupture in the therapeutic relationship (see below for further discussion of ethics and ethical decision-making).

Confidentiality

Confidentiality is often viewed as the cornerstone of any therapeutic relationship. When working with a child, as with any client, it is important that they know the limits of confidentiality. Whilst therapists differ as to the importance they place on confidentiality, it is important to note that there are always limits to confidentiality (see Jenkins, 1997, 2002b). Our own view is that confidentiality can be overstated at the cost of ignoring other moral or ethical principles, such as the duty of care, for instance, to assess the risk of harm to a child.

This is not to say that, in response to any concern or worry, therapists should or would breach the client's confidence. It is more that, if a pattern of behaviour emerges, therapists would and probably should talk this through in supervision and, maybe, with a child protection worker. In thinking about whether or not to breach confidentiality because of a concern you as a practitioner may have for a child's welfare, it is useful to know where you stand in law. The law does not prevent you from sharing information with another practitioner or agency:

- If those likely to be affected consent.
- If the public interest in safeguarding the child's welfare over-rides the need to keep the information confidential.
- If disclosure is required under a court order or other legal obligation. (See DfES, 2005)

One of the recommendations of the Victoria Climbié Inquiry was that:

> The Government should issue guidance on the Data Protection Act 1998, the Human Rights Act 1998, and common law rules on confidentiality. The Government should issue guidance as and when these impact on the sharing of information between professional groups in circumstances where there are concerns about the welfare of children and families.
>
> (Laming, 2003)

There is a common law 'duty of confidence', which has developed over time through case law. The courts have found a duty of confidence to exist:

- Where a contract provides for information to be kept confidential.
- Where there is a special relationship between parties, such as patient and doctor, solicitor and client, teacher and pupil.
- Where an agency or government department such as the Inland Revenue collects and holds personal information for the purpose of its functions.

However, this duty of confidence is not absolute and disclosure can be justified:

- If the information is not confidential in nature.
- If the person to whom the duty is owed has expressly or implicitly authorised the disclosure.
- If there is an over-riding public interest in disclosure.
- If disclosure is required by the law or a specific court order.

A duty of confidence may be owed to a child or a young person in their own right. A young person aged 16 or over, or a child who has the capacity to understand and make their own decisions, may give or refuse consent to a disclosure. In other cases, that is a child under 16 who is not 'Fraser competent', their parent, or a person with parental responsibility for them should consent or not on their behalf. Also, concerns about a child's welfare also take precedence over the *Data Protection Act 1998* and the *Human Rights Act 1998* which respects individual rights to privacy unless disclosure is necessary to protect the welfare of a child (see DfES, 2005). For further discussion on confidentiality see Palmer (2002) and Hayman (1965, 2002).

Duty of care

Therapists owe a duty of care to clients (see Jenkins, 1997). The standard of care required must meet the ordinary and reasonable standards of those who practice in the same field. According to case law (Bolam vs. Friern HMC, 1957) this is defined as the standard of a competent, respected professional. In the *Ethics and Professional Practice Guidelines* produced by the European Association for Transactional Analysis (EATA) (1998), this duty of care is linked explicitly to the concept of protection (Clause A): 'It is the primary protective responsibility of EATA members to provide their best possible services to the client and to act in such a way as to cause no harm intentionally or by negligence.'

The therapist has a greater duty of care towards child clients than towards adult clients. During therapy sessions with children the practitioner is acting *in loco parentis*, and has full responsibility for the safety and welfare of the child during this time. This also means that if a child wishes to leave a therapy session part way through, the practitioner has to ensure that there will be adequate supervision of the child until they are returned to the relevant responsible adult. The United Kingdom Council for Psychotherapy (UKCP) is currently developing a *Code of Ethics for Working Psychotherapeutically with Children and Young People* which includes guidance on training, supervision, insurance, touch, and complaints (UKCP, in press, 2007).

Disclosure

This somewhat clinical term belies the nature of some of what children disclose. A large part of the preparation for working with children and young people is in order to be able to deal with practitioner's own emotional responses, as well as anything it evokes for them personally when a child discloses (see Chapter 12). Examples of disclosure might include when:

- A child tells someone what is happening to them.
- Someone else tells you, as a practitioner, about something they have seen or heard.
- An adult or child tells you that they have hurt a child.
- A parent or carer tells you that they are having problems in meeting their child's needs.

A therapist was told by a father that he was physically abusing his children. After talking through the issues with her supervisor, she sought advice from social services and breached confidentiality to let them know the children were being hurt. Understandably, the client was furious and left therapy. A few months later he returned to resume his work. He said he had realised that he had told the therapist because he needed someone to stop him. This was not an easy situation to deal with, and it took a lot of courage and some sleepless nights on the part of the therapist to take the action she took.

As this vignette illustrates, acting on disclosure is not easy. Some factors which may cause the practitioner to pause or stop taking action include:

- Concern about breaching confidentiality.
- The child's attempt to bind the practitioner to secrecy.
- Doubt about the child's truthfulness.
- Fear about being wrong, or that there may be other reasons for the child's behaviour.
- Anxiety about taking responsibility for triggering a chain of events.
- Unresolved feelings, which may be transferential, counter-transferential or co-transferential.
- Resentment about being put in this position when the practitioner did not choose to be a social worker.
- Uncertainty about and fear of procedures and consequences.
- Concern that social services won't do anything, or that the child isn't going to get the protection and help they need.
- Not wanting to interfere in family life.

For a therapist working within the context of an agency, there is often more clarity about what to do when a child protection issue arises because there are clear legal responsibilities and protocols. In private practice the issues are sometimes less clear because the practitioner is not bound by the same laws and, in the absence of a clear policy on reporting disclosed abuse, some or all of the above can influence their decision-making.

In both statutory or voluntary agency settings, the therapist, as the responsible adult, would talk to their supervisor or line manager to clarify what, if any, action needs to be taken. Therapists working with children do need to be prepared to take action and, therefore, to be aware of what action they would take. Even though the therapist would – and should – keep the child informed, any action taken is likely to disrupt the therapeutic relationship. For example, if a child discloses an allegation of abuse, therapeutic work with the child should be stopped and the allegation reported to the police and the local authority social services department so that it can be investigated and the child can be kept safe. In those circumstances the child will need to be interviewed by someone trained in interviewing children for evidential purposes. If, after investigation, the Crown Prosecution Service (CPS) decides that it would not be in the public interest to have a court hearing or that there is not enough evidence to proceed, then therapy with the child can be resumed. If, however, the child is going to be a witness in a prosecution, and if it is in the child's best interests, therapy can resume as long as it is done in accordance with Home Office (HO), Department of Health (DoH) and CPS (2001) *Practice Guidance on the Provision of Therapy for Witnesses Prior to a Criminal Trial*. For further discussion on the legal and therapeutic implications of disclosure and non disclosure see Jenkins (1997) and Bell-Boulé and Roche (2002).

In either working context, to continue working with a child who has disclosed abuse could jeopardise the gathering of evidence and, potentially, the CPS's ability to prosecute the perpetrator. One school counsellor carried on working with a child after a disclosure because she 'thought it was her job to listen to the child's story'. As the therapist had entered into a dialogue with the child about the actual offence, the police could not be certain of the distinction between the child's evidence and what was the result of the child's discussion with the counsellor who was untrained in working with child protection procedures.

It is generally very difficult for a child to share with anyone what has happened or what is still happening to them because it generates such divided loyalties. Featherston and Evans (2004) identify some of the barriers to sharing that children experience (see Box 5.3).

Featherston and Evans (2004) also make a number of suggestions as to what to say and do when a child or parent does disclose abuse (see Box 5.4, below).

Referral

Children have a right to be safe and well and to be able to rely on adults around them to protect

---

Barriers to children sharing worries

- Feeling there is no one to talk to (who will listen and can be trusted).
- Fear of not being listened to, understood, taken seriously or being believed.
- A belief in self-reliance.
- A sense of futility about sharing problems and a belief that nothing will change.
- Embarrassment.
- Not wanting to burden others.
- Fear of getting oneself or someone else into trouble.
- Adults trivialising or over-reacting and making matters worse.
- Fear of lack of control.
- Limited knowledge of formal helping services and what they do.
- Stigma of involvement with formal agencies.

Box 5.3 Barriers to children sharing worries (Featherston and Evans, 2004)

---

them. A child's therapist may be the first adult to provide consistency, security, safety and/or protection. Indeed, these may be the qualities of the therapist which the child experiences and which helps them to disclose to the therapist in the first place. As one practitioner in the life of the child, the therapist may well have one small piece of the jigsaw, and other professionals involved, such as the GP, teacher, dentist, and so on, may hold other pieces. One of the particular lessons from the Victoria Climbié Inquiry was that the various professionals and agencies involved had not shared information or concerns with each other, and that each thought that what they had was not enough to take further action. The recommendations of the Inquiry included:

- Recommendation 6: That local authority committees of Members for Children and Families 'must ensure the services to children and families are properly co-ordinated and that the inter-agency dimension of this work is being managed effectively.'
- Recommendation 8: That a director should be 'responsible for ensuring that inter-agency arrangements are appropriate and effective.'
- Recommendation 13: That the Department of Health 'must establish a 'common language' for use across all agencies to help those agencies to identify who they are concerned about, why they are concerned, who is best placed to respond to those concerns, and what

- React calmly.
- Don't stop a child or parent who is talking freely about what has happened.
- Observe and listen, but don't ask for more information.
- Keep responses short, simple, slow and gentle.
- Avoid making comments or judgements about what is shared.
- Be aware of your non-verbal messages. For example, whilst looking shocked may be appropriate, the child may read such a reaction as conveying disbelief, or confirming that their problem is too big for other people to deal with.
- If you have difficulty in understanding the child or parent's communication, reassure them that you will find someone who can help.
- Tell the child or parent that what they are saying is important, that they have done the right thing by telling you, that you will do your best to help, and that what they've said is so important that you need to talk with someone else about it.
- Tell the child or parent what will happen next – and be honest.
- Make a written note of a) what is said, b) who is present, and c) anything else that happens after the child or parent has spoken to you.

Box 5.4   What you might say or do following disclosure (from Featherston and Evans, 2004)

outcome is being sought from any planned response', and 'must make clear in cases that fall short of an immediately identifiable section 47 label that the seeking or refusal of parental permission must not restrict the initial information gathering and sharing. This should, if necessary, include talking to the child.'

- Recommendation 14: That the National Agency for Children and Families 'should require each of the training bodies covering the services provided by doctors, nurses, teachers, police officers, officers working in housing departments, and social workers to demonstrate that effective joint working between each of these professional groups features in their national training programmes.'
(Laming, 2005)

There are a number of good reasons for making a referral:

- That adults, in our view, have a general, social responsibility to protect children.
- That, if children and families are given help, this can stop a child from being further harmed.
- That not to report serious concerns may be tantamount to condoning abuse and neglect, and is to act as a bystander (see Clarkson, 1996)

If a practitioner has a concern about a child they are working with is being abused, neglected or in some way unprotected, then they should:

- Identify the concern.

- Sort out why they have concerns, based on what they have seen, heard from others, and what has been said to them directly.
- Be as clear and specific as they can about the causes of such concerns. (This may include their instinct that something just does not seem to be right.)

How do we make decisions about genuine anxieties or concerns we may have about child clients? There may be times when, as a therapist, you have concerns about a child or a young person that prove unfounded or, when you raise these concerns with the client, there is a simple explanation. There may be other times, however, when a child or a young person is completely unaware that they are at risk, or are putting themselves at risk, and are vulnerable. This could be the situation with our vignette at the beginning of the chapter. It may be that in talking to this child, she becomes aware of the dangers and responds in ways that reassure you about how seriously she takes the potential threat from her teacher. On the other hand, she may ignore or minimise your concerns and become defensive. In any case it is useful to seek support and to make links with a social worker from the local authority or the NSPCC, either of whom could talk through any concerns before you commit to reporting them. There are also a number of trained social workers within the TA community who may be willing to share their child protection knowledge and experience with colleagues. Box 5.5 offers some guidance for therapists faced with 'niggles', worries, evident abuse and disclosure.

Nature of concern	Support, supervision and consultation	Action
A niggle or feeling that something is not right.	Your supervisor.	None at this stage.
A worry about a child protection issue persists.	Your supervisor or manager. A social worker or designated child protection worker in your agency (if appropriate). The child, if they are 'Fraser competent', and could shed light on the issues that concern you.	Talk through the issues with social services anonymously.
Abuse of some kind is evident to you.	Your supervisor, manager, professional body or insurance company for support and legal advice. Also discuss your concerns with the child, as appropriate to their age and understanding; and with their parents, with a view to seeking their agreement to make a referral to social services, unless that would put the child at further risk.	Telephone the social services or the police for them to investigate. Follow up in writing within 48 hours. When you make a referral agree with the recipient what the child and their parents will be told by whom and when.
If child discloses abuse.	As above Social services, and police.	As above. Make provision to resume work at a later date with the child, if they and their parents are open to that. You may be asked by social services to provide information or to be involved in assessment. You may also be asked to provide help or a specific service to the child as part of an agreed plan, which could be therapy.

Box 5.5 Levels of concern about possible abuse

When making a referral, practitioners need to be aware of the additional workload involved and, as child protection procedures are often long and involved, that this may continue for some time.

Therapy with child witnesses

In the situation where a child or young person has disclosed abuse and the case is prosecuted, the child may be called as a witness. Under guidelines contained in the *Practice Guidance on the Provision of Therapy for Child Witnesses Prior to a Criminal Trial*, a child can receive therapy as long as the actual offence is not talked about until after the trial. What can be done is work to help the child reduce their stress about the impending trial and the 'treatment of associated emotional and behavioural disturbance that does not require the rehearsal of abusive events' (HO,

DoH, CPS, 2001: 18). One of the authors (MD) works with children who have suffered trauma, such as rape, on any post-traumatic symptoms they have. I do therapeutic work to alleviate some of the physical and emotional distress that has resulted from the offence. Therapeutic work of this nature can be very successful in reducing nightmares, flashbacks, and to help the child feel safe again in the world. Of course, as the trial looms, a child's distress often increases again, so it is important that they have the consistency of a therapeutic relationship and coping strategies to support them through the difficult time ahead. Once the court case is over, the actual offence can be addressed.

Case notes

When working with a child who is going to be a court witness, the therapist must maintain records of therapy, including video and audio tapes as well as notes, so that they can be produced for the court if required. Detailed requirements are contained in the pamphlet *Practice Guidance on the Provision of Therapy for Child Witnesses Prior to a Criminal Trial* (HO, DoH, CPS, 2001). The child needs to be told about notes and their status at the outset of any work where the child is going to be a witness, and helped to understand that their confidentiality cannot be guaranteed. This does not mean that all is lost if a court order is made regarding your case notes as there is a defence of public interest immunity (see below).

There are a number of points to bear in mind when courts or other legal officials ask to see a practitioner's case notes:

- If the defence request access to confidential client files, the therapist should refuse, and anticipate that a witness summons may be issued for attendance at court with files. Any such request should always be put in writing.
- The material to be disclosed must be both relevant and necessary for the purposes of a police investigation.
- Any request from the Police or CPS must be in writing and contain:
  - The identity and contact details of the police disclosure officer and the officer dealing with the case.
  - A summary of the case and the details of the offences being investigated.
  - A statement of the relevant information which is sought from the records in order to pursue all reasonable lines of enquiry, and why that information is thought likely to be relevant to the investigation.
  - A statement of how failure to disclose relevant information would prejudice or delay the investigation.
- If a child is a witness in a trial and either the prosecution or defence believe that something in your notes may be able to be used by them to discredit the witness (i.e. the defence) or to strengthen the prosecution case (i.e. the CPS) either can apply to the judge who may then request to see the file. It is generally not advisable to refuse this request from a judge. They may wish to look through the files to decide if there is any relevant and material information contained in them. If the judge does not identify anything relevant and material then the practitioner should be able to

leave court with the files, nothing having been disclosed from them.
- It is possible to argue against notes being read either by the CPS or the defence barristers and being used in court on the basis of public interest immunity and the following arguments:
  - That therapists owe a duty of confidence to children and families who access their service.
  - That the therapeutic work therapists undertake with children and families is, by its nature, confidential.
  - That therapists do not believe that it is in the public interest for confidential files to be disclosed.
  - That, if such records were liable to be disclosed, clients would be discouraged from being open and frank, and this would have a detrimental effect on the effectiveness of therapeutic work with both children and their families, who may not feel that they can trust therapists.
  - That it may be harmful to the 'victim' to have their files disclosed to the defence and, thereby, possibly, to the perpetrator.

When making a decision about a practitioner's case notes, the judge has to achieve a balance between the rights of the defendant to a fair trial and the public interest in maintaining confidentiality. In addition to the national protocol, which may be read in full on the CPS website (www.cps.gov.uk), it is useful to know the local protocols for the police and local authorities. A useful summary of the implications of legislation and case law regarding therapy notes is provided by Jakobi and Pratt (2002).

Having discussed a number of implications of child protection legislation and policies we now turn to the concept of protection as understood and developed within TA, before concluding the chapter with some reflections on ethical decision-making.

Child protection and TA

In 1966 Crossman wrote a short article published in the *Transactional Analysis Bulletin* about 'Permission and protection' in which she argues that protection is part of 'good enough' mothering and, later, parenting. However, in a situation where parents are parenting children based on their own archaic needs (Child) or from introjected, unintegrated aspects of their own personalities (Parent), then protection can become and can be experienced as conditional, for instance, "I'll look after you as long as you . . ." This conditionality is, in TA terms, the source of over-adaptation and a self-limiting life story or script. We may say, echoing Bozarth's (1998) point about Rogers' theory, that conditionality is the bedrock of *any* theory of pathology.

Thinking about the effect of abuse in terms of script formation, a child will form beliefs about themself, others and the world, typically:

- About self: I am bad. I am unlovable. Bad things happen to me because I'm just not good enough. If only I can be better or try harder things will be better.
- About others: People are not to be trusted. They hurt you, and you have to guard against them.
- About the world: The world's a horrible place where bad things happen.

These beliefs will be reinforced by observed inauthentic behaviour, certain reported internal experiences, and fantasies; and by reinforcing memories and emotional memories – the whole forming the client's closed script system (Erskine and Moursund, 1988). The therapist has a chance to confront the client's script system by being different from other adult and parent figures in their life, and by doing things differently from the client's parents or carers.

Crossman makes the point that, if the therapist is offering a client permission to resist or counteract their script, then the therapist also needs to know the dynamics and effect of this conditional protection. Furthermore:

> The therapist is giving permission to the patient's Child to disobey the instructions of his Parent, and this is only possible if the patient's Child sees the therapist as better, stronger and more effective. So when a therapist gives permission he is implying protection.
>
> (Crossman, 1966: 153)

For Steiner (1968: 64) 'Both permission and protection involve behaviour on the part of the therapist which is best characterized by the word *potency*.' As he puts it (Steiner (1971: 181) this refers to 'the therapist's capacity to bring about a speedy cure. The Potency of the therapist has to be commensurate with the potency of the injunction laid down by the parents of the

patient'. The addition of Steiner's contribution to Crossman's work is commonly referred to in TA literature and training as the '3Ps' of therapy. In both his publications Steiner extends Crossman's view of protection to that afforded by the therapist between sessions, for instance, over the phone, as a kind of temporary holding transaction in order to carry the client's temporary state of panic and existential burden or vacuum. This is the origin, in our view, of the emphasis in TA on protecting the client and, specifically, on protecting the client's archaic Child ego state. Thus, the therapist or practitioner, as part of their role, offers, in this case, protection to the child's Child.

This is conceptualised in different ways. As Crossman (1966: 154) puts it: 'the therapist may appear to be coming from Adult, but in fact he will be heard by the patient's Child as Parent.' Steiner sees – and still sees – protection as a function of the Parent ego state. In his trilog theory Rissman (1975) argues that the Parent protects first; and Boyd (1976) argues that, by processing the therapist's input in Adult, the client forms the self-protection they need in Parent (P_2). Another strand of thinking about ego states in TA views such transactions differently, for a summary of which see Tudor (2003). In this sense, the therapist's here-and-now 'protection' is viewed as an example of an Adult-Adult empathic transaction – which may also be experienced (or 'heard') and construed as protective by the client's archaic Child.

Just as TA has been explicit about the importance of protection, so it has also offered a critique of 'overprotection'. Schiff and Schiff (1971) argue that overprotection is an example of a disturbance in the normal or healthy symbiotic relationship between mother and child and, specifically a disturbance in the differentiation of the child from the mother. English (1972) views overprotectiveness as an example of racket or inauthentic behaviour and feelings, often expressed as excessive helpfulness, sweetness, and devotion. To these we would add the overprotectiveness of rigid and often legalistic 'health and safety' responses to the complexities of life, one example of which is the nonsense of prohibiting parents taking pictures of their children engaging in school activities – out of a paranoid fear that the photos might end up on pornographic internet websites. Steiner (1971) gives an example of advising an alcoholic client what to do in order to avoid relapsing and drinking between sessions. By doing so, he is creating an albeit temporary dependency on himself as the therapist. Whilst this may be appropriate in terms of gaining social control or even a transference cure, we are cautious about creating, or co-creating such dependency. Within the broader context of a permissive, protective and potent therapeutic relationship, it may be more important for a client to experience and 'work through' their anxiety. It *is* too late to have a happy childhood – even for some children. In this sense we think that there is a danger of therapists and other practitioners working with children making an elision between protecting the client's Child and protecting the child client.

Of course, there is a danger in being unprotective of the child client. In a situation in which a child has clearly described suffering abuse or neglect, and the therapist is clear about this and the necessity of taking action, then not to take action or to refer to the appropriate authorities or agencies, would be problematic for a number of reasons:

- From a *clinical* perspective, non action could have the effect of reinforcing the defences of the Child ego state and the child's introjected Parental beliefs that the abuse must be their fault, precisely because nobody does anything about it. In terms of a (second-order) structural ego state analysis, P_1 and C_1 become completely overwhelmed by abuse, a process which can lead to dissociation, arrested development and trauma. Non action on the part of the therapist may reinforce the negative beliefs the child has about themselves ("I'm worthless"), significant others ("Adults can't be trusted") and the world ("Nobody can save me"). In this context, the action the therapist takes to protect the child client may offer a powerful (potent) and reparative experience to the child of being protected by someone who is not scared to stand up to the abuser – both the external abuser as well as the internalised abuser (P_1) – and to begin the process of integrating those cut off and defended parts so that the child can stand a chance of living an ordinary life. Whether the therapist reports and refers or does not, the therapeutic issue is whether the here-and-now therapeutic relationship can withstand any rupture caused by the decision the therapist makes.
- On a *professional* level, non action may breach codes or frameworks of professional practice,

although this needs to be mediated by consideration of other issues such as discussed in the second part of this chapter (see pp. 63).
- *Ethics* and ethical decision-making are so vital in child protection that it is important to distinguish whether a concern is an ethical one or something else. As supervisors, we are aware that often what is presented as 'an ethical dilemma' turns out to be neither particularly to do with ethics, nor is a dilemma! Tudor and Worrall (2005) discuss the nature of a dilemma, and offer a framework which distinguishes a number of distinct domains of influence on theory and practice which help in locating issues and dilemmas and in decision-making – with which we are framing our current discussion (see Figure 5.1).
- In the *personal* domain, non action on the part of the therapist may represent some level of passivity or passive behaviour. This piece of TA theory (Schiff et al., 1975) is useful in identifying a range of passive behaviour beyond the obvious:
  – Doing nothing – not taking action when action is required.
  – Over-adaptation – taking action without thinking because someone says so.
  – Agitation – taking a lot of action.
  – Incapacitation – being overwhelmed by concerns, issues or dilemmas (see above).

Supervision, personal therapy, and continuing professional development can all help the therapist to work out and work through issues which block their clear thinking, such as transferential and co-transferential process that may cloud Integrating Adult decision-making:

- We discuss issues in the *legal* domain (pp. 49–52 above).
- The *social* and *cultural* domains refer to wider perspectives on the issue of child protection. By referring to them we are acknowledging that the other domains of influence do not exist outside social and cultural contexts, and that these are constructed and change over time.

Ethical decision-making

In the first two parts of this chapter we summarise and discuss relevant legislation and some parameters of professional practice in response to child protection. In the third part we

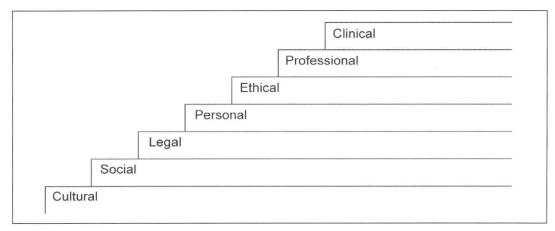

Figure 5.1   Domains of influence (Tudor and Worrall, 2004)

discuss the concept of protection within TA. In this final part we draw these various parameters and discussions together and, with specific reference to therapists in independent, private practice, we offer some ideas about and frameworks for ethical decision-making.

Ethics, sometimes referred to as the science of morals, is a complex subject which attempts to help people make sense of and bring some moral principles to bear on the complexity of and conflicts in life and, in this context, therapeutic practice with children and young people. Moreover, there are a number of dimensions to ethics: professional, theoretical, clinical, virtue, social and cultural (see Tjeltveit, 1999). Making ethical decisions is never easy and cannot be undertaken simply or in isolation. Just as the individual child whose confidence may be breached needs lots of support, so too does their therapist. That support usually comes from colleagues, supervisors, managers, child protection specialists and, though perhaps more unusually, ethicists. Indeed, Tjeltveit writes about the psychotherapist as ethicist.

Ethical decision-making is viewed as relatively straightforward, and based on agreed principles, especially where the law is concerned and involved. In reality and practice, this is more often not the case, and especially so for the therapist working in independent, private practice.

Cassie, aged 15, was referred by her GP to a therapist working in independent, private practice. Cassie had gone to her GP with 'exam nerves'. Initially she talked about her fear of failure and about

feeling let down by some of her friends. Gradually, she began to tell the therapist about the situation at home. Cassie was the eldest of three, with a sister aged 13 and a brother of 11. Both her parents had previous marriages and both had other, older children. Her mother, who was the dominant partner and very forceful, had a personality disorder, whilst her father was generally absent. On occasions they were violent both to each other and to Cassie and her younger siblings. Both parents were also neglectful, often leaving the children to fend for themselves. The family were known to the local social services department and, at a child protection case conference, had been put on the at risk register on the grounds of physical abuse. However, both parents consistently refused professional help, and Cassie's mother alternated between being very convincing and maintaining what Cassie referred to as a 'nice, well-dressed middle-class façade', and being aggressive and abusive to the professionals involved, most of whom appeared to be scared of the parents. Supported by her GP, Cassie continued to see the therapist, much against her parents' wishes, especially her mother, who wanted the family to 'close ranks'. At this stage Cassie told her therapist that 'there's more', but that she couldn't and wouldn't say what. She also reported that her younger sister had said that if she, Cassie, 'told', then she would not say anything and would deny anything Cassie said. Her mother had told all the children that if they said anything to anyone outside the family that she would have a heart attack and die. There followed a difficult period of therapy in which Cassie questioned the value of professional help. Apart from the therapist she didn't trust anyone, and was angry about the lack of help from social services. One day she had gone to school and was so upset that she couldn't attend lessons. She was sobbing in the secretary's office. The school 'phoned social services but, despite reassurances, no one came. In another incident, following an overdose, the hospital had 'phoned Cassie's mother, who went to the hospital, was abusive to the staff, and, having taken Cassie home, subsequently attacked her. Later, talking to her therapist, Cassie said she wished that the GP hadn't reported the original abuse and got social services involved, as that had only made things worse. The therapy continued. After some months Cassie did 'tell'. For some time her mother had been 'chatting' on the internet, offering Cassie and her sister as prostitutes, as a result of which both of them had received text messages from men responding to this pimping. She told the therapist that her step-sisters had previously been prostituted. Having told her therapist all this, Cassie also said that she didn't want her to report any of it, as things would only get worse. Whilst she wanted to get out of the home, and away from her mother, she didn't want to leave her younger sister and brother.

Given the context of her work, the therapist had two supervisors, one managerial and the other clinical. Whilst this worked in most cases, with regard to her work with Cassie, the therapist experienced a tension, represented by her two supervisors, between the therapeutic and the managerial/organisational spheres or domains. After much discussion with Cassie, her supervisors and colleagues in the field, and against Cassie's wishes, the therapist decided to report this situation to social services. At first the social worker didn't believe Cassie's story, as reported by the therapist, and was reluctant to respond. The therapist had to be quite persistent to get social services to take any action. Eventually, they did, but appeared to draw out the investigative process. Again, Cassie's mother was very convincing, and one social worker hinted that the investigation would be dropped in a few months, once Cassie was 16, and stated that, in any case, there were no local authority resources, such as foster carers, available for Cassie. The therapist challenged this and eventually a case conference was called. This confirmed the decision of the previous case conference and, in an almost unanimous decision, determined that there was not enough evidence to register on the grounds of emotional abuse! When the therapist had reported her disclosure, Cassie had stopped seeing her but, later, during the investigation, had maintained some contact. However, following the decision of the case conference, Cassie had terminated therapy. She remained at home.

This case study highlights a number of issues:

- Failures in the system, including:
  – A lack of joined-up or integrated working between agencies. Neither the abuse in both previous families nor in the extended family was connected to the present situation and referral.
  – Disbelief on the part of some of the professionals involved regarding the nature, extent, degree and continuity of abuse.
  – A lack of resources – or apparent resources.
  – Some cynicism on the part of some of the professionals involved both in terms of delaying the investigation, and of attempting to bargain with Cassie's parents (regarding the status of risk and prosecution) in order to encourage their engagement with professional help.

- The nature of therapy. In this kind of situation the task of therapy and the role of the therapist inevitably changes from a therapeutic one to a protective one, in which the therapist is often sharing the client's dilemma. Once statutory agencies are involved, the therapist is caught up in a number of dilemmas (which we have highlighted throughout the chapter). Also, in this case, the therapist took an active advocacy role regarding child protection, but one which, ultimately, sacrificed her therapeutic one.

The therapist's ethical decision-making is more likely to be consistent if their values, based on personal philosophy, are congruent or fit with the values and principles which underpin their chosen theoretical orientation and practice (see Tudor, 2002). Below we elaborate three parameters which can help the independent practitioner in their ethical decision-making.

Philosophy, values and principles

What is referred to as the 'basic philosophy' of TA is expressed in three statements:

- People are OK.
- Everyone has the capacity to think.
- People decide their own destiny – and these decisions can be changed.

Together these promote personal responsibility which, along with dignity and autonomy, forms a tripartite value basis for including the client as much as possible (in terms of 'Fraser competence') in decisions about them. Working with children as clients clearly this involves achieving some balance between promoting the client's autonomy; fulfilling a duty of care; causing no harm (one of Berne's 1966 therapeutic slogans); promoting the greatest good; and acting justly – all of which reflect general ethical principles. One of the dilemmas experienced by Cassie's therapist was the tension she experienced between respecting Cassie's autonomy and competence to make a decision, that is, not to report her parent's abuse and neglect, and her own view as a therapist about failing in her duty of care had she not reported the systematic and systemic abuse.

Theory

TA is based on the contractual method and open communication. As the EATA (1998) guidelines state it (Clause E): 'The ethical practice of transactional analysis involves entering into an informed contractual relationship with clients'. Thus, with regard to ethical decision-making, the TA practitioner is mindful of the contract, including their and the client's understanding of confidentiality, client confidence and its limits. In Cassie's case, the therapist ultimately decided to breach her client's confidence, a decision which jeopardised the therapeutic relationship and, in the event, precipitated its termination. Reflecting on the therapy with Cassie the therapist thought that, in her contracting with Cassie, she might have made the limits of confidentiality more explicit, and that she might have given more attention to the therapeutic relationship and Cassie's process immediately before her disclosure – which may have meant that Cassie would not have disclosed, or that she would have disclosed and that the therapist would have respected her confidence. Bollas and Sundelson (1995: 55) address this point robustly, arguing that 'proponents of the reporting laws place the legal system's hunger for information before the aims of psychotherapy and the confidentiality that makes it possible to achieve them'. In their work on children's rights, confidentiality and the law Daniels and Jenkins (2000) elaborate this view with reference to statutory legislation and common law decisions which bear on the child's right to therapy.

Practice

The third, practical parameter involves the therapist's – and the client's – assessment of risk, including, again, balancing the risk of current and further abuse in the present situation, with the disruption to the therapy caused by reporting,

and the risk of non action on the part of the statutory services – as in Cassie's case. Hayman (1965/2002) reports her own principled stand in defence of maintaining absolute client confidentiality.

Finally, in terms of ethical decision-making, it is useful to subject any proposed course of action to a test. Stadler (1986a, 1986b) proposes three such tests:

- Universality – that is, could your chosen course of action be recommended to others, and would you condone it if it was done by someone else?
- Publicity – could you explain your course of action to other therapists, and would you be willing to have your actions and rationale exposed to public scrutiny?
- Justice – would you do the same for other clients in a similar position, or if they were well known or influential?

To these we would add:

- Personal, equity – would you do it if another therapist were to do the same with regard to your child?

Raising children is no easy task. Protecting children in a complex and conflicted world is no less difficult, and there are no easy solutions or absolute safeguards against risk – nor, arguably, should there be (see Furedi, 1997, 2001, 2003). For some, how we as a society protect our children is a mark of our civilisation; for others 'child protection' has become an industry, which neglects and, at worst, abuses the very children it seeks to protect. In this chapter we have sought to offer a critical guide to the legislative context of child protection in order to help the practitioner to reflect on the implications of child protection for her or his practice and ethical decision-making.

Legal references

Table of cases

Bolam vs. Friern HMC [1957] 1 WLR 835, 2 All E 118
Gillick vs. West Norfolk and Wisbech Area Health Authority [1986] AC 112

Table of statutes

Adoption and Children Act 2002. London: The Stationery Office.

Children Act 1989. London: HMSO.

Children Act 2004. London: The Stationery Office.

Data Protection Act 1998. London: HMSO.

Education Act 2002. London: The Stationery Office.

Human Rights Act 1998. London: The Stationery Office.

Protection of Children Act 1999. The Stationery Office.

Sex Offenders Act 1997. London: The Stationery Office.

Sexual Offences Act 2003. London: The Stationery Office.

References

Bainham, A. (2005) (Ed.) *International Survey of Family Law*. Bristol: Jordans.

Bell-Boulé, A. and Roche, T. (2002) Legal Issues in Therapeutic Work with Adult Survivors of Sexual Abuse. In Jenkins, P. (Ed.) *Legal Issues in Counselling and Psychotherapy*. London: Sage.

Berne, E. (1966) *Principles of Group Treatment*. New York: Grove Press.

Bollas, C. and Sundelson, D. (1995) *The New Informants*. New York: Jason Aronson Inc.

Boyd, H.S. (1976) The Structure and Sequence of Psychotherapy. *Transactional Analysis Bulletin*, 6: 2, 180–3.

Bozarth, J. (1998) Unconditional Positive Regard. In Bozarth, J.D. *Person-Centered Therapy: A Revolutionary Paradigm*. Llangarron: PCCS Books.

Clarkson, P. (1996) *The Bystander*. London: Wiley.

Crossman, P. (1966) Permission and Protection. *Transactional Analysis Bulletin*, 5: 19, 152–4.

Crown Prosecution Service. (2003) *Investigation And Prosecution Of Child Abuse Cases*. Protocol. London: CPS. Also available online at: www.cps.gov.uk/publications/agencies/protocolletter.html

Daniels, D. and Jenkins, P. (2000) *Therapy with Children: Children's Rights, Confidentiality and the Law*. London: Sage.

Department for Education and Science (2005) *What To Do If You're Worried a Child is Being Abused*. London: HMSO. Also available online at: www.teachernet.gov.uk/publications

Department for Education and Skills (2003) *Every Child Matters*. London: HMSO.

English, F. (1975) The Three-cornered Contract. *Transactional Analysis Journal*, 5: 4, 383–4.

Erskine, R. and Moursund, J. (1988) *Integrative Psychotherapy in Action*. Newbury Park, CA: Sage.

European Association for Transactional Analysis (1998) Ethics Guidelines. In *Training and Examination Handbook*. Nottingham: EATA.

Featherston, B. and Evans, H. (2004) *Children Experiencing Maltreatment: Who Do They Turn To?* London: NSPCC.

Furedi, F. (1997) *Culture of Fear: Risk-Taking and the Morality of Low Expectation*. London: Cassell.

Furedi, F. (2001) *Paranoid Parenting: Abandon Your Fears and Be a Great Parent*. London: Allen Lane.

Furedi, F. (2003) *Therapy Culture: Cultivating Vulnerability in an Uncertain Age*. London: Routledge.

Hayman, A. (2002) Psychoanalyst Subpoenaed. In Jenkins, P. (Ed.) *Legal Issues in Counselling and Psychotherapy*. London: Sage. (Original work published 1965)

Home Office, Department of Health and Crown Prosecution Service (2001) *Practice Guidance on the Provision of Therapy for Witnesses Prior to a Criminal Trial*. London: HMSO.

Jakobi, S. and Pratt, D. (2002) Therapy Notes and the Law. In Jenkins, P. (Ed.) *Legal Issues in Counselling and Psychotherapy*. London: Sage.

Jenkins, P. (1997) *Counselling, Psychotherapy and the Law*. London: Sage.

Jenkins, P. (2002a) Introduction. In Jenkins, P. (Ed.) *Legal Issues in Counselling and Psychotherapy*. London: Sage.

Jenkins, P. (Ed.) (2002b) *Legal Issues in Counselling and Psychotherapy*. London: Sage.

Laming, H. (2003) *The Victoria Climbié Inquiry: Report of an Inquiry by Lord Laming*. London: The Stationery Office.

Lyon, C. with Cobley, C., Petrie, S. and Reid, C. (2003) *Child Abuse*. (3rd edn). Bristol: Jordan.

Mental Health Foundation. (2003) Every Child Matters document (2003)

National Society for the Protection of Cruelty to Children (2005) Inform: An Introduction to Child Protection Legislation in the UK www.nspcc.org.uk/inform

Palmer, S. (2002) Confidentiality: A Case Study. In Jenkins, P. (Ed.) *Legal Issues in Counselling and Psychotherapy*. London: Sage.

Rissman, A.H. (1975) Trilog. *Transactional Analysis Bulletin*, 5: 2, 170–7.

Schiff, A.W. and Schiff, J.L. (1971) Passivity. *Transactional Analysis Bulletin*, 1: 1, 71–8.

Schiff, J.L. et al. (1975) *Cathexis Reader: Transactional Analysis Treatment of Psychosis*. New York: Harper and Row.

Sills, C. (Ed.) (2006) *Contracts in Counselling.* (2nd Edn.) London: Sage.

Stadler, H. (1986a) *Confidentiality: The Professional's Dilemma – Participant Manual.* Alexandria, VA: American Association for Counseling and Development.

Stadler, H. (1986b) Making Hard Choices: Clarifying Controversial Ethical Issues. *Counselling and Human Development*, 19: 1, 1–10

Steiner, C. (1968) Transactional Analysis as a Treatment Philosophy. *Transactional Analysis Bulletin*, 7: 27, 61–4.

Steiner, C. (1971) *Games Alcoholics Play.* New York: Ballantine Books.

Steiner, C. and Cassidy, W. (1967) Therapeutic Contracts in Group Treatment. *Transactional Analysis Bulletin*, 62: 1, 29–31.

Tjeltveit, A.C. (1999) *Ethics and Values in Psychotherapy.* London: Routledge.

Tudor, K. (2002) Transactional Analysis Supervision or Supervision Analyzed Transactionally? *Transactional Analysis Journal*, 32: 1, 39–55.

Tudor, K. (2003) The Neopsyche: The Integrating Adult Ego State. In Sills, C. and Hargaden, H. (Eds.) *Ego States.* London: Worth Reading.

Tudor, K. and Worrall, M. (2004) Issues, Questions, Dilemmas and Domains in Supervision. In Tudor, K. and Worrall, M. (Eds.) *Freedom to Practise: Person-Centred Approaches to Supervision.* Llangarron: PCCS Books.

United Kingdom Council for Psychotherapy (2003) *Psychotherapy with Children: Principles, Aims and Guidelines for Training.* London: UKCP.

United Kingdom Council for Psychotherapy (2007, in press) *Code of Ethics for Working Psychotherapeutically with Children and Young People.* London: UKCP.

United Nations (1992) *Convention on the Rights of the Child 1989.* London: HMSO.

CHAPTER 6

Milieu Therapy: The Development of Transactional Analysis with the Young People and Staff of a Social Services Establishment

Anita Mountain

To Anyone Who'll Listen
  I feel empty tonight
  I'm not excited about things like my mates are
  I don't want to be alone.
  I won't think about anything but really I'll think
    about everything,
  I've got stomach pains
  and I want to cry, but I can't cry
  Because I feel empty tonight.
  As if I've been used too much
  Scratched and worn and no good to anyone any
    more,
  A nuisance, someone in the way,
  'Go tidy your bedroom'
  Do you have to dream all day?'
  'Can't you do something instead of just sitting there?'
  Tired and empty lone and afraid
  Not knowing what to do next
  Whirling around in a world of confusion
  Then stop
  And tell people how I feel
  But shan't I'll leave that to others
  Because I feel empty tonight
                              (Faith, aged 14 years)

This chapter is based on ten years' work, undertaken between 1990 and 2000. It outlines the establishment of a Transactional Analysis programme within a Social Services Department (TASS). This unique example of innovative work, with adolescents and staff, prompted other sections of the same department to consider training and support for staff using TA in their work.

The Warner Report *Choosing Care* (1993) highlighted the need for a specialised system of support to young people in residential homes and those working with them. To assist young people in making their own decisions about themselves and their lives, one social services department adopted an open participative approach using Transactional Analysis (TA) as the underlying philosophy of one long-stay home. This process began with a colleague, Gwyneth Phelps, at that time a Transactional Analysis trainee, who

contacted the Head of Children's Services. He saw the benefits of the approach and commissioned Gwyneth to work in a particular children's home. She then brought me in, and for one year we worked together until she left. For the remainder of the next ten years, I worked mostly on my own.

In order to develop a therapeutic environment I needed to use of a range of concepts. These included Clarkson and Fish's (1988) model of overlapping sub-systems, and my own 'Concepts for thriving' (2004), based on Roberts' (1992) work which provided an overview. The complex network of relationships involved in working in a Social Services establishment can be explained through an extension of English's (1975) three-handed contract. I also needed to consider a range of other issues including attachment and drew on the work of Bowlby (1973/1980) Ainsworth et al. (1978) and, latterly, Hobbes (1996, 1997).

The programme lasted for ten years. During that time many of the young people coming into the care establishment had borderline personality structures and many had conduct disorder. Although care needs to be taken with diagnosis of those under 18 years of age, there were sufficient criteria to indicate that our interventions needed to keep this in mind (American Psychiatric Association, 1994). Work with those young people with borderline structure was influenced by Woods and Woods (1982) and Masterson (1985). The approach adopted by Woods (1980) and also by Samenow (1980) greatly influenced the programme's work with those with conduct disorder. Trieschman (1969) emphasises the need to work within the social milieu with young people in residential care. Being both an individual and group psychotherapy, as well as a social psychology with an organisational application, Transactional Analysis is particularly well placed to respond to this need.

Within this chapter I explore the development of a therapeutic environment, including contracting and theoretical considerations. I have also covered organisational aspects of working in this context as these are crucial to the efficacy of the programme. Working within a Social Services context is also discussed, before moving on to the exploration of future developments.

TA has a crucial place to play within the statutory sector, encouraging empowerment at all levels through developing confidence, awareness and knowledge in order that young people can be better supported.

The context

The staff at the home were very caring people with a lot of skill and experience. The young people were, therefore, already receiving good support and care before I went to the home. The TASS programme heightened the staff's awareness, raised their own self-esteem and confidence, and gave them a tool-kit and a structure in which to work. It also offered the young people an opportunity to learn some of the basic TA concepts through the staff so that they all learnt together in different ways. This chapter is written with the aim of accounting for the staff's experience and expertise prior to the TASS programme, as well as for their determination and willingness to learn new concepts and skills to further develop the service of care to young people.

The TASS programme first began in a children's home known as the Intensive Support Unit (ISU) based on a campus on a residential estate. The campus included two other residential units (Reception and Short Stay), a school, administrative offices, a communal laundry, and kitchens. Staff from one section would, at any time, walk between sections using a pass-key. Today the long-stay unit, then the ISU, is housed in two small, modern, semi-detached houses on the edge of this campus. To promote positive identification the unit is now called by the road name rather than by its function. Boundaries have been established to ensure respect for the establishment as a home.

Work with the individual young person took place in a number of different ways, and changed and developed throughout the programme. Latterly I undertook the initial assessment and, with the Attached Workers, wrote a treatment

plan. I also provided staff support, through consultations, on ways to work with each young person. This process was designed to empower staff, enhance their relationships with young people and encourage their Adult ego state thinking.

Developing a therapeutic environment

Therapy within a young people's home needs to be undertaken within an environment that is therapeutic. When considering the most appropriate therapeutic interventions to use Clarkson and Fish (1988: 123) consider three sub-systems:

- the individual child
- the family system
- the socio-cultural system

This is in keeping with the work of Trieschman et al. (1969), who promotes the use of the milieu as a therapeutic tool. His notion is that the actions of adults with children, and the adults' control of the environment, can be coordinated to improve the children's lives. His major concern is the 23 hours outside the psychotherapy session, 'because that is when and where most of the milieu is' (1969: 1). Hence one of the major components and priorities of the TASS programme was training the staff as their work with residents is key to the development of these young people. When I started no one within the establishment was undertaking groupwork with the residents. Given the importance of the milieu, one important area of training needed to be groupwork process. When a group was set up a staff member shadowed and assisted me as I undertook groupwork with the young people. In this way the staff member acted like an apprentice, developing the skills and confidence alongside me. I then withdrew, and the person assisting me became the group facilitator with another staff member assisting. This process was designed to rotate every six months with the assistant becoming the facilitator and so on.

To take account of the different sub-systems which impact on the lives of young people in care I applied Clarkson and Fish's (1988) model (see Chapter 1), thus, the 'family system' became the children's home or unit, including the staff. In this context the staff act in place of the parents, setting boundaries and offering nurturing.

Training, and continued support for staff is required to ensure the use of appropriate parenting interventions and the provision of opportunities for the young people to introject new, positive Parent ego states. The 'sociocultural milieu' of Clarkson and Fish's (1988) model comprises the residential campus. The predominant frame of reference seemed to be that young people in care do not deserve privacy nor do their boundaries need to be respected by adults. Yet, at the same time, young people were expected to respect each other and to respect adults' boundaries. Considerable changes within each sub-system were required to create a safe environment. Decontamination work with staff was also required to enable them to be free of the organisational cultural scripting which maintained the aforementioned frames of reference.

An environment was therefore required where young people felt safe enough to express their pain rather than defend against it through acting-out. 'Cure' cannot take place within an unsafe environment. Roberts' (1992) 'hierarchy of functionality', with emotional safety as its foundation, was used to enable staff to understand the rationale for some of the changes made. I amended and re-titled this model 'concepts for thriving' (Mountain, 2004) and taught it in a training session to the staff.

During the model's exposition the staff experienced relief as they started to understand why they sometimes felt under pressure (see Figure 6.1). They felt that the social services department wanted them to be at the 'productive activity' level with young people, whereas they were working at the 'emotional safety' level. For example, a young person might need to sit and talk with a staff member about what was going on for them at a particular time, and how they felt about this. Whereas the social services department's priority was for residents to become independent and to undertake training in order to develop their confidence on buses, in domestic work etc. The 'concepts for thriving' model enabled staff to understand their own as well young people's resistance to some of the activities. It gave them permission to work at the appropriate stage for each young person. The understanding of this process empowered the staff as it gave them to tools to explain their practice in a coherent way (see Box 6.1).

Coleman (1987) outlines three tasks for the adult: to provide a setting where young people

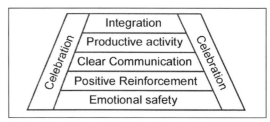

Figure 6.1   Concepts for thriving

can experiment within limits and in safety; to provide continual definitions of what the limits are, and to provide a living demonstration of survival in the face of continuous attempts to transgress those limits. Functionally, these positive Parent modes are ones which young people in residential settings have rarely experienced from their biological parents. Inevitably Residential Social Workers (RSWs) need to offer good parenting in order that the young people develop positive Controlling Parent and Nurturing Parent modes of their own (Temple, 1999, refers to modes instead of ego states). Training on parenting styles took place as well as regular consultations for staff members who may have been struggling with one or more young person. In this way staff received support and were then more able to support the young people.

Initially, staff unwittingly reinforced negative behaviour by giving it a great deal of attention, whilst giving positive behaviour little attention. Acting-out behaviour fell within this area, and I needed to support the staff in developing an understanding of the role that acting-out behaviour plays. For example, all the time a young person was receiving strokes for being angry, then their underlying pain and hurt was unlikely to be addressed. After all, we never get enough of what we don't need. Staff eventually learnt to create emotional safety through positive reinforcement and the celebration of the individual.

Training and debriefing sessions were a really important part of the programme. During these sessions I encouraged the staff to think through situations and develop their awareness of their own processes. Regular consultancy sessions accounted their ideas and reinforced their A_2 structural ego state functioning. As a result, staff are more often in Accounting Adult and therefore able to choose the appropriate behavioural mode.

Emotional Safety (This includes physical, intellectual, emotional, and spiritual dimensions)	When I have this, my primary needs are taken care of, and I am comfortable with myself, and boundaries are maintained. I am celebrated and welcomed into the world.
Positive Reinforcement	I am given positive strokes and there is mutual exchange. I continue to be accepted and celebrated, and I reciprocate.
Clear Communication	I know I *am* being heard, and I am therefore more willing to hear others. I experience being valued and value others.
Productive Activity	I have script free behaviour. I collaboratively problem solve. I recognise, and am recognised, for my competency, and have a sense of who I am. I am able to balance giving and receiving.
Integration	I can be spontaneous, I make positive things happen in my life. I recognise my achievements. I enjoy who I am and what I do. I have learnt from my past experiences and use these in my everyday life.
Celebration (This runs through every stage and includes a spiritual dimension)	I am celebrated for who I am and I celebrate who I am.

Box 6.1   Concepts for thriving: Definitions (developed from Roberts, 1992)

The professional contract

The aims of the TASS Programme were:

To provide a therapeutic environment for the young people in care. To enable the staff to provide a coherent approach to work with young people through the use of Transactional Analysis, in order that they offer a more effective and supportive service to them.

Providing a therapeutic environment for the young people required a range of different contracts for each individual. I considered elements of Clarkson and Fish's (1988) model of overlapping sub-systems and incorporated ideas from English's (1975) three handed contract into a multi-faceted contracting matrix (Figure 6.2).

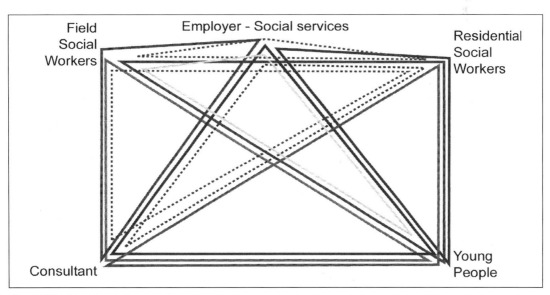

Figure 6.2   Multi-faceted contracting matrix

Steiner's (1974) four requirements for effective contracting – mutual consent, consideration, competency and lawful object – were also incorporated and taught to the staff so that they could contract with each party as necessary. This then allowed for the development of administrative, professional and psychological contracts.

Individual and group psychotherapy

Theoretical considerations

Adolescence is a difficult enough time anyway without having to cope with issues surrounding being in care. Erikson (1950) considers it the age of 'Identity vs. Identity Diffusion', whilst Levin (1974) talks about the need to recycle all the previous stages and separate out and work through previously unresolved problems. Berkowitz (1987: 18) puts it well:

> For the adolescent who is severely disturbed, the developmental task of individuation is made even more problematic by intense issues of aloneness and abandonment anxiety as well as heightened impulsivity and lack of control, lower level defences, low frustration tolerance and deep mistrust.

Often these young people have not yet learnt the rules by which they can live with others (Illsley Clarke 1978), and have missed getting their developmental needs met at almost every stage (see also Chapter 10). Clarkson (1992: 20) notes that psychophysiological disturbance can happen in at least three major ways:

1. *Through affective and cognitive interference in the functioning of the integrated ego (confusion model).*
2. *Through the existence of internal conflict between different parts of the ego (conflict model).*
3. *Through developmental deficits and inadequate parenting (deficit model) for extended periods at the time of trauma.*

This is in keeping with Friedrich (1995: 98) who explores the biochemical components of trauma:

> Traumatic life experiences can have an impact on the development of the brain, specifically on those portions of the brain involved with mediating the stress response . . . When stress is prolonged (as would be the case with recurrent abuse, a chaotic home environment, or frequent disruption) there is increasing chance that a more abnor-

mal and persisting pattern results, particularly if prolonged stress occurs during critical and sensitive periods of development.

Many of those who come into care have been physically, emotionally or sexually abused. Those who have been sexually abused experience betrayal, stigmatization, powerlessness, and inappropriate early sexualisation. Each of these factors has a powerful impact on their psychological processes. The young people often present with low self-esteem and have difficulty in tolerating frustration.

The level of motivation for changing their destructive behaviour is affected by the types of stroking the young people have received within their family of origin; their existential life position; the way they structure their time; the feelings they substitute for ones which were not allowed in their families (racket or substitute feelings) and the repetitive patterns of behaviour they have developed which have familiar unsatisfactory outcomes (games).

Another significant consideration is that of attachment. Where abuse occurs, attachment difficulties are usually present. When a child is secure this security will have been developed in relation to an adult figure in their life. A case vignette illustrates this point:

> After some months of being in care a teenager, Mary, was showing signs of stability. She heard that her mother was coming out of prison and wanted Mary to visit her at home. At this time Mary became unreasonable in her manner and actions to all those with whom she came into contact. This behaviour suggested ambivalence about proximity and was indicative of her insecure attachment to her mother.

Bowlby's (1973) attachment theory highlights that the basis of personality is derived from the repetitive experiences of two processes:

- The child's role in relationships: 'Am I good enough and worth supporting?'
- The caretaker's role in the relationship: 'Can I count on this person being available and caring?'

Many young people in the care system would answer these questions negatively.

Ainsworth et al. (1978) explore and evaluate the child's responses to an attachment figure. Three distinct patterns were noted:

- *Secure* – those who express their anxiety, seek reassurance and then experience security.
- *Insecure avoidant* – those who ignore their need for reassurance irrespective of their stress levels.
- *Insecure ambivalent* – those who cling to the attachment figure but resist reassurance at the same time.

Later a fourth pattern was identified:

- *Insecure disorganised* – those who rapidly alternate between avoidant and resistant.

Hobbes (1996, 1997) explores the link between life positions and attachment theory, which is in keeping with Bowlby's view that the basis of personality originates in the process of attachment. The child can develop a broad range of interaction styles or become inhibited or exaggerated, both of which fit within the TA concept of adaptation.

'One of the most impressive characteristics of abused children is their need to deny the trauma' (Clarkson, 1988: 87). This denial will lead to one of the following existential life positions being decided upon by the child, dependent upon their reaction to the abuse. Below I summarise Clarkson's description of the abused child's existential life positions, which I have then applied, giving examples within the TASS programme:

- *The rescuing fantasy* – I'm not OK, You're OK (It's all my fault). The child's desire is to protect the abusing parent. This was experienced with one young woman who owned what had happened to her but said that it was not her dad's fault and that he loved her even though she was bad.
- *The victim's sanction* – I'm not OK, You're not OK (A dog that didn't deserve to be a child. [Bloch, 1979]). Hostile urges which threaten to erupt against the external object are turned against the self. In the home, when some of the young people were distressed they would barricade themselves in their bedrooms and self-harm.
- *Identification with the abuser* – I'm OK, You're not OK ("Corporal punishment made me the man I am!"). The child internalises an abusing parent. For example, one young man could be extremely threatening to female staff in the same way as his father was toward women and also toward him.

Bowlby (1980) suggests that the child constructs two models of the self for each relationship: one cognitive, one affective. Later, Bretherton and Waters (1986) suggested a third, behavioural model. This is in keeping with Ware (1983: 18) who explores the process of adaptation to the environment and the development of six basic patterns which individuals assume: 'Each personality typically invests energy in either thinking, feeling or behaviour, and to facilitate change the therapist must understand these patterns'.

Attachment theory is crucial in working with young people in care. Many of them have never experienced a secure, loving family and they can become extremely uncomfortable in a surrogate setting. The warmth of an intimate foster family situation often recreates the pain of their own, contrasting family. The foster family's therapeutic qualities are often too intense for the youngster and in order to maintain the homeostasis (Erskine, 1993) they resist and make hurtful responses. Such behaviour often becomes uncontainable in the family setting and a move into a residential establishment is precipitated. Here they can be offered more 'emotional space'. Within this residential setting they need to receive a consistent approach which takes account of their individual therapeutic needs.

When training the staff I included consideration of the needs of the young people with primary attachment difficulties, as these are often hard to meet. I needed to support the staff to be patient as it often takes time to develop a close relationship with a young person and sometimes the staff felt themselves to be inadequate as they sometimes took one step forward and two back. Once a relationship was established then the development of a 'working alliance' and making a contract for change could occur. Influencing the length of residence, so that the young people stay long enough to attach, then individuate, was an important factor in the creation of a therapeutic environment. The social services department's frame of reference was that attachment and dependency (which they perceived as harmful) were considered to be synonymous. The staff and I challenged this perception so that Field Social Workers (FSWs) placing residents, eventually considered the home a long term provision and, as a result, are now more likely to undertake consultations with the home, rather than make decisions about a young person without the staff's involvement.

Assessment and treatment planning

I needed to encourage staff to consider ways to neutralise the negative programming of the parental injunctions and encourage them when progress was slow or even seemed to be non-existent. This took a great deal of awareness and understanding on the part of the staff. Clarity of assessment and clear treatment planning was imperative as a means of empowering the staff to undertake the difficult 24 hours of being with young people who exhibit extremely challenging behaviour.

Young people rarely go into care with a positive view of personal development and personal change. Contact with professionals often leaves them feeling analysed and alienated. They are used to everything being written down and circulated to Field and Residential Social Workers, so nothing is private. This was true for those coming into this particular home. The philosophy of TA, including its commitment to open communication, helped to develop trust. The completion of bi-monthly 'TA sheets' by staff with young people, offers a method of assessment both short and long term (see Appendix 4). Structurally, this develops the young person's Adult ego state, raises their awareness of their process and offers them time which is designed to develop attachment with a staff member. This process reinforces the teaching and application of TA with young people.

Assessment

Prior to residence a young person was offered an induction period. During this time a staff member and I would meet separately with the young person. An assessment was undertaken and the appropriateness of the placement considered. During this time a range of information was assessed:

- Their socio-economic context.
- The family context, size, history, nature of the relationships and interactions, and ways of dealing with conflict.
- Any major family life events, including birth of siblings, separations.
- The young person's views of their life circumstances, their views about coming into care.
- Expectations about future plans, from FSWs, parents, and the young person's perspective.

This early assessment period included the completion of TA sheets by staff (see Appendix 4). Later, as young people learnt about TA they too were involved in completing the sheets. This served to create a structure for the young person and their key worker within which they could establish their relationship. It also offered a means of evaluation and assessment over time.

Assessment of young people in this context can be difficult as their vocabulary is often limited and they have few permissions to express their internal process. Turner's (1988) 'Drawing task' provides a useful projective method of assessing ego states and, to a limited extent, scripting. It involves drawing three figures on a sheet of paper: one who looks like a parent, one who looks like an adult, and one who looks like a child. The relationship between these figures provides a visual-spatial representation of a client's ego states. I have included one of the drawings that a 14-year-old young man did during his assessment (Figure 6.3).

Clarkson and Fish (1988) highlight six categories for describing children's difficulties. Here I take their categories and apply these to the work undertaken within the TASS programme, giving a case example for each.

1. A blocked developmental process

The developmental process is hampered through, amongst other things, inadequate parental support for the child's developing capacities. When this happens the child can stay stuck at the unresolved stage or can by-pass a stage and move onto the next.

Case example: Jack, 14 years old, originally entered the care system when he was one year old. The assessment period in TASS highlighted that he had difficulty expressing his feelings, particularly fear, tending to use the substitute or racket feeling of anger instead. Within the care system a child is likely to see angry feelings being expressed and given attention, thereby stroking and reinforcing them. On admission to the home Jack's developmental age was between 18 months and three years. The characteristics of this are:

- A sense of separateness and feeling enraged.
- An oppositional, negative stance.
- Grieving over loss of structure and no longer being the centre of the universe.

Figure 6.3 Projective drawing task of 14-year-old male

Jack's behaviour first became cause for concern when his foster parents had a child of their own and Jack had to share them.

As a young adult the characteristics include:

- Using anger to mask other feelings.
- Being negative and wanting control.

Jack had been very violent toward staff and had been threatened with a placement out of borough. Recent bail conditions imposed on him showed that he could keep himself and others safe as he had not shown violence to others or smashed up property for two weeks. On coming to the programme a social control contract was made with him. During this process he discovered that he was violent to others when he wanted to hurt himself.

The contract established with him drew on the concept of non-contracting (Kouwenhoven, 1984). Kouwenhoven outlines a non-contract as outlining what the therapist and the client will not do – for example, instead of drinking the client will ask for contact, and the therapist will

not prematurely stop seeing them because they are drunk. Using Kouwenhoven's formula, Jack and I worked out what he needed to do, and what he wanted staff to do when he started to agitate. Thereafter he was willing to talk about his scare, as well as the other feelings he had just prior to his agitated behaviour. With the staff's help Jack worked out what he needed just before he would usually agitate. The staff agreed to support him in meeting this need e.g. he would come to them and let them know what he was concerned about and they would talk with him and explore what he could do instead of agitate. This enabled Jack to move from passive to proactive behaviour and learn to problem solve. This is in keeping with the notion of confronting passive behaviours. Schiff and Schiff (1971) identified four such behaviours: doing nothing, overadaptation, agitation, incapacitiation or violence. The Schiffs' view is that there is more thinking in the overadaptation stage, and this is consistent with the fact that Jack was an intelligent young man and very able to converse. The work with Jack was defined by the contract I

Contract

Jack
16 December 1996

General:

I agree to see my attached workers for an hour a week.

I agree to attend group once a week.

I will continue to go to school every day.

Personal:

I will learn to control my temper. I will learn to express my feelings in an appropriate and safe way.

I lose my temper after being silly. For example, I push things off seats that aren't mine. I start to do this if I am scared. I get scared that I want to hurt myself I then go and hurt someone else. Or I might want to hurt myself after I'd hurt someone and I regret it.

When I feel bad, scared or angry or some other feeling where I might be unsafe or make someone else unsafe I will talk to staff. If staff see me with the 'silly' grin on my face and doing 'stupid' things I would like the staff to come and talk to me, remind me of my contract, and ask me about my day, go and make a cup of tea with me or something. A member of staff could go to my room with me and talk about good things.

I could stop myself with this contract by losing my temper and putting people down instead of expressing what I am feeling in a safe way. When I get angry and scared I feel worse than other people.

Even when I am feeling bad I will keep other people safe and keep myself safe.

Other people will know when I've done this when they feel safe living with me and I feel safe living with them.

I want staff to check this contract with me daily for 10 minutes. I do not want them to go on and on, just take 10 minutes.

Box 6.2   Jack's contract

made with him (see Box 6.2) and my treatment plan (Box 6.3) both of which are reproduced with his permission.

Having contracted with Jack my task would be to write up a treatment plan in order that staff could obtain support and direction for working with him. Regular case conferences were also held on each young person. These case conferences consisted of the key staff involved, who would then pass information on to the others, and also included regular monthly meetings with all the staff.

2. The effects of trauma, (chronic or acute)

In order to maintain the parents' love, the child makes decisions about how to survive their family, which can cause the Child ego state to be fixated.

Case example: Anne, a 15 year old, developed a Please Others driver as a way to survive the multiple abuse she received from her family. She decided that there must be something wrong with her (Erskine, 1993) and that she wouldn't

grow up, as it was too scary. Not having been protected from the incestuous abuse she was made a victim. She maintained this later in life through not knowing she had a right to put in the boundary, or how to do it, as she had never had the experience herself. Further, by being in Victim she could keep trying (unsuccessfully) to get the healing for her Child from external adults.

In the residential home Anne kept coming to staff for protection from a bullying and abusive young male resident. Initially staff insisted she learn to protect herself and would send her off. I suggested that they give her the protection she required until she could do it for herself. The staff did this and six months later, when threatened by the bully again, she successfully defended herself and stopped the process.

The initial commission was for the transactional analysts to undertake therapy with the young people. Thus, while the staff was working in the social milieu, I and the other therapist were working one hour a week with each young person. On one occasion my colleague could not attend and I saw her young

Jack – Treatment Plan

Jack requires a sense of safety. He needs to feel 'held'. By 'holding' in this sense I mean that an adult or adults are able to ensure that the boundaries are set. These boundaries need to include agreements from Parent, with himself, that he will keep himself safe. He will not be able to hold to these agreements long term. In his contract he asks that staff review this with him daily for no more than 10 minutes. If daily 'safety' agreements are experienced as covering too long a period I suggest that the time period be half a day or less. **It will be very important to re-contract with him at the given end of contract time**. Not to do so lets the 'Little Professor' or A_1 think 'Ah ha, I can go ahead and hurt someone now as the time is up'. Remember though that this will not be in awareness.

In Jack's contract he asks for staff intervention when it seems he is starting to agitate. **It is important that staff take note of this.** This is why I have asked for three people to be on duty so that there is someone to take time with him when it looks like he might be moving into agitation.

One of Jack's trigger points is other people talking about him. Given the other young people in the home it is likely that they will attempt to set him up. Work will need to be undertaken with them about this prior to Jack coming. Adult to Adult discussions concerning Jack and them are necessary, enabling them to think through how they will manage their relationships. This of course leads on to a wider discussion about their inter-relationships and the influence they have on one another, which is worth exploring. It will be important to undertake this from Adult and get them to do some of the thinking; if you go into Parent ego state they are likely to go into Rebellious Child.

Underneath Jack's violent behaviour there is a great deal of scare. He often wants to harm himself and because this is a frightening thought he acts out and harms someone else instead. We need to help him to explore these thoughts and feelings about self-harm. These protective behaviour statements are important: "We all have the right to feel safe all of the time (and that includes others from you)" and "Nothing is too awful that we can't talk to someone about it." However, without exploration they are just statements and will mean nothing. We need to help him put meaning to them.

He needs to know that all his feelings are fine and that we take his feelings seriously. When he is scared about self-harm we need to support him to talk about this with staff **as soon as** he is aware of these thoughts, rather than doing nothing. You can think about this with reference to the four passive behaviours. It is likely he will *do nothing* first, then swiftly move to *agitation*. You may see very little *overadaptation,* and then he may move quickly to *violence*. Jack is clearly asking in his contract for help when he is starting to agitate. Please read this contract and support him by trying it. It will be important to debrief with him about what was going on, encouraging him to think about what he was feeling, when he has more Adult ego state available. This should not be left too long however, and certainly not ignored. He needs to learn to recognise the body sensation, thoughts and feelings he has before he starts to agitate so that he can decide to do something different next time.

Jack's developmental age is 18 months to 3 years. The characteristics of this are a sense of separateness and feeling enraged, grieving over loss of structure and no longer being centre of the universe, with an oppositional, negative and resistant stance. As a young adult the characteristics are discounting of solutions: "I can't", "I won't", "You can't make me", together with discounting others' feelings; using anger to mask other feelings; and being negative, oppositional, and wanting control.

Jack requires a social control contract, which is what I have drawn up with him and which is checked regularly. He needs permission to be negative and oppositional with no harm to self or others; also permission to be separate, to think and feel at the same time, to be potent, and to be sure of what he needs to get from others. Expect him to take others into account. Confront not OK behaviour with logical consequences. Separate anger from other feelings.

Jack has very little Free Child ego state. We will need to help him develop this; however, this is much later in the treatment plan. We currently need to focus on social control and permission to talk about his thoughts and feelings of self-harm if and when this arises.

In conjunction with this treatment plan everyone needs to read the contract which was made with Jack's social worker.

Anita Mountain, TA Consultant   December 1996

Box 6.3   Treatment plan for Jack

people. During the first session with me Anne came into the room, saying she wanted to work with puppets. She gave me one puppet, saying it was her, and picked up one for herself, which was her father. Anne spontaneously proceeded to enact the abuse with the male puppet attacking the female one on my hand. During the process her voice changed to a menacing evil tone. I gave protection to the Anne puppet, using positive Controlling Parent mode and offering spot reparenting (Osnes, 1974). Having received the protection, Anne came out of the enactment and stated "I wish someone had been there at the time." She then returned to the drama using her mother in the process until, with additional spot reparenting for the traumas during her childhood, she was able to make a script redecision which was that she was good enough, and deserved to be protected.

This work was all on tape and Anne agreed that staff hold the tape for safety and return it to her when she wanted to listen to it in private. This reinforced the healing in the Child ego state so that she could move on from the previous fixation.

3. *Systemic pathology within the family*

When undertaking the parental or caretaking role within the family the child's detrimental behaviour can mask difficulties experienced by other members of the family system.

Case example: 13-year-old Fritz, had looked after his mother who had parented him from her P₁ ego state. His father had been violent and Fritz had attempted to protect his mother until his father left. Fritz's behaviour had deteriorated to stealing and driving cars and setting fires. When he came to the home he had a highly developed Adapted (Rebellious) Child mode and showed very little sign of Natural, Spontaneous Child. Once the boundaries had been set that I was in control of the session and not him, he visibly relaxed, although he often tested the boundaries to check I would maintain them.

I used board games and football as a way of teaching and maintaining the boundaries, gradually allowing him to negotiate the rules for the football, which I ensured were maintained. On leaving the home the Deputy Team Leader asked him what he had got from the therapy sessions and Fritz responded: "She learned me how to play."

4. *Changes in the constellation of the family system*

Children and young people frequently have to adjust to changes in the family constellation. This requires an adjustment in the family-group imago and if the child is not supported in the expression of their ensuing thoughts and feelings, difficulties can result. Whilst this may well have occurred in the young peoples' original families it was being repeated within the TASS programme. At first there was a high turn over of young people and occasional changes in staffing. Because the residents had attachment difficulties they tended to act out rather than express their feelings appropriately.

Case example: A new resident, Jack (the same as in the case example above pp. 72) was due to come into the home from the Short Stay Unit. The other young people expressed their dislike of him. Jack's personality adaptation was obsessive-compulsive which was completely different to the other young people. He took pride in his appearance and his room had to be impeccably neat, even office like. Jack's violent behaviour was also of concern to other residents.

When Jack arrived he was on the outside of the group. On one occasion a staff member was informed by Jack that two residents had told him that Milly, a female resident, was going to 'get' him. When this was checked out with Milly she was angry as it was untrue and this threat had been made as a way for the other residents to get at Jack. Milly called a Resident's Meeting and took control of the process, informing the two residents responsible that she would not be used in this way to frighten Jack. The staff noted that Milly was appropriately angry on her own behalf and resolved the problem without resorting to violence. Her actions had impact on the group and helped the two responsible to realise that their actions had impact on Milly as well as Jack, and that there were consequences to their behaviour. This action also had the effect of bringing the group closer together, and offered Jack and the other residents a new experience and way of responding to changes in the 'family'/group constellation.

5. *Socio-cultural based problems*

One of the influences on the child is the culture in which they live as well as that handed down through the family, and that of the educational system. If the different cultures are in conflict then a way needs to be found to develop understanding and, where appropriate, mediation.

Case example: Ali was of dual heritage: his father was Asian, from Pakistan, and his mother was white British. Ali was prejudiced against Pakistanis. A staff member, also of dual heritage, was attempting to undertake some positive identification work with Ali. However, Ali rejected this assistance as he over-identified with Jim, a Black staff member of Afro-Caribbean origin. During this process Ali became more rejecting and disparaging to other Asian staff as well as to Asians in general.

Jim's assistance was recruited to use the positive aspects of his and Ali's relationship to encourage the positive transference to the other colleague in order that the identification about being of dual heritage could continue.

6. *Adjustment to injuries or events ('Acts of God' or 'Fate')*

Clarkson and Fish added this category to allow for difficulties in children due to non-psychogenic illnesses, intellectual or physical handicap, and the effects of catastrophic events such as war or earthquakes.

Case example: Jane had always had difficulty in school attendance when, aged 15, it was discovered that she was dyslexic. With extra tuition and through the RSW's gathering information about dyslexia Jane began attending school on a regular basis and eventually became a prefect.

Further considerations in diagnosis and treatment

Many of the young people in TASS had developed borderline personality structure and many have conduct disorder (American Psychiatric Association, 1994). Naturally, diagnosis of an adolescent needs to be undertaken with caution as it is a time of change. However the actions and levels of contamination evidenced in many of the young people who come into the home have led to the consideration of these two diagnoses more than any other.

Conduct disorder

Through his work with those with anti-social behaviour Woods (1980: 243) developed the theoretical understanding of the Child ego state structure (C_2) as follows: 'The positive side of the C_2 structure operates as one constellation and the negative side of the C_2 operates as another constellation' (see Figure 6.4).

When working with young people with this structure it has been important to use a game-free approach rather than adopt the use of 'attack therapy'. The reasons for this are numerous and include: the nature of the accommodation; the staffing of the home; the evidence that 'the game' does not work (see Woods, 1980) but, most importantly they are young people, not adults, and the approach needs to be different.

Samenow (1980) discusses how he tells anti-social clients about themselves. He controls the interview at the initial session in order to facilitate the client's examination of him. Samenow proceeds to paint a negative picture of the client. He establishes that they have wrapped themselves in a mantle of secrecy and sought excitement at the expense of others. They have no concept of trust, friendship, love or loyalty, regarding the world as theirs to deal with as they choose and appropriate whatever they want.

Case example: Colin, 16 years old, was physically and sexually aggressive. He previously disclosed abuse at an out-of-borough children's home where no action had been taken due to 'lack of evidence'. In the first assessment session with me Colin was uncommunicative and defiant. He lay on the couch with no eye contact. After a while I started telling Colin about himself. I did so in a positive, respectful, I + U + way. The aim was to enlist Colin's co-operation rather than attack or inflame him. My style was probably more gentle than Samenow's would have been, given that I was working with an adolescent. Gradually, as Colin felt more and more understood by what I was saying about him, who he was, and why he did what he did, he began to sit up and be more responsive.

In addition to the work undertaken with Colin at individual level, I supported the staff through the development of a treatment plan that emphasised fairness and the speedy resolution of disagreements, alongside confronting Colin when they experienced contradictions in his behaviour. For example, if Colin said that people were against him staff would need to sketch out a picture of Colin as a young person who has thrown away opportunities, giving specific examples. This would hopefully enable him to see that he was part of the damaging situation.

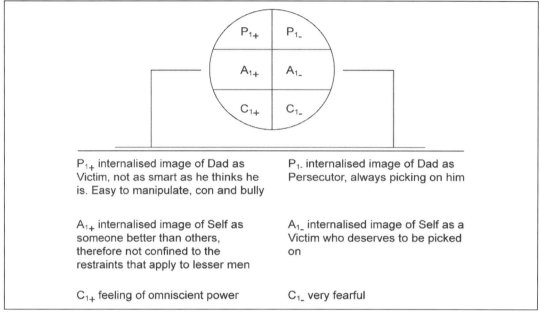

P_{1+} internalised image of Dad as Victim, not as smart as he thinks he is. Easy to manipulate, con and bully

P_{1-} internalised image of Dad as Persecutor, always picking on him

A_{1+} internalised image of Self as someone better than others, therefore not confined to the restraints that apply to lesser men

A_{1-} internalised image of Self as a Victim who deserves to be picked on

C_{1+} feeling of omniscient power

C_{1-} very fearful

Figure 6.4   Child ego state model (C_2) (Woods, 1980)

They also stroked Colin's good points whilst, at the same time, letting him know that these can be overshadowed by the suffering he caused others. When undertaking this type of work the staff communicated from Accounting Adult mode, as the use of the Criticising Parent mode was likely to reinforce either the negative or the positive side of the constellation described by Woods (1980).

Borderline structure

Many of the young people who came to the home had borderline structure. Masterson (1985) notes that the fundamental causes of borderline structure are abandonment depression and narcissistic, oral fixation. This is in keeping with Woods and Woods (1982: 289) who state that:

> . . . the dynamics of the borderline condition are based on the arrest-in-development at the symbiotic stage. There-fore, utilization of a treatment approach that is based on the primacy of the original mother-child dyad, that focuses on the issues of Attachment, Symbiosis and Separation-Individuation is indicated.

This also links with Clarkson and Fish's (1988) category of 'blocked developmental process' (see pp. 72–74 above).

The treatment approach outlined by Woods and Woods (1982) is difficult within a social services residential setting. With no training to enable them to understand the processes of concordant and complimentary identification, the staff used to get hooked into a good/bad split. The young person's need to control would often hook the Criticising Parent mode of the staff as an attempt to dominate the situation and to feel safe. After a particularly difficult or dangerous situation had dissipated there would often be a shift to Negative Nurturing Parent mode. As Woods and Woods (1982: 290) note: 'If the therapist (staff) wins, the client's condition will deteriorate. If the client wins, the therapist's condition will deteriorate'. As I enabled staff to develop an understanding of themselves, the young people, and the conceptual framework, they were able to remain in the I+U+ position and stay in Accounting Adult mode.

The social milieu

The social milieu is of great importance when working in this setting. Initially, whilst the staff were constantly involved in the dynamics of the residents' interactions, no specific work was being undertaken with the residents as a group and a community. A weekly group was established to enable this group of teenagers to communicate and attach to each other. Initially I facilitated the group with a staff member apprentice; later, it was facilitated totally by staff who were supervised by me. Since the group's inception the young people are increasingly giving and receiving feedback to each other and taking more responsibility for their actions (see case example under 4 above, p. 76). The group workers also learnt to contract with each other and debrief after each session so that they could learn from the process.

In addition to this group a three-day residential weekend was set up with an outward-bound centre. This programme was based on the concept of self-reparenting (James, 1974) and was facilitated by staff. Having planned the programme with the staff I then attended to support them with the process. After each session with the young people the staff and I met to debrief the process.

This work was inspired by Gayol's (1995) work with young offenders in Mexico. Gayol demonstrates that, as well as being applicable to therapeutic work with middle-class adults, the technique of self-reparenting is also useful in promoting change in young people with challenging behaviour. Some of the process of self-reparenting was changed to take account of the age and the reasons for the accommodation of the residents. For example, 'Historical diagnosis of Parent figures' was likely to be misinterpreted by these young teenagers as a criticism of their parents. Therefore, rather than exploring the actions of their own parents, they role-played different styles.

Staff shared TA concepts including parenting styles and recognition of the inner Child. Young people were involved in experiential exercises including, for example, writing a letter from their Child ego state to the Parent ego state, and vice versa. The outward-bound activities gave the staff the opportunity to explore with the young people when they had needed to take care of themselves and when they needed to be taken care of. The staff gave permission to the young people to express their feelings through workshop exercises, debriefing the activities, and by sharing their own fears about taking part in some of the outward bound activities. Back at the home the young people were encouraged to continue to reparent themselves and keep themselves safe, instead of engaging in self-destructive actions.

Organisational considerations

In order to develop a consistent approach the TASS programme required a range of interventions at the organisational level. These included the following work in the following areas:

Staff training and support

At the end of the pilot phase of the programme my colleague and I drew up the following chart (Box 6.4) and undertook a one-day consultation process with staff where we worked through it, and took on board their comments and suggestions.

Psychological distance

Following the pilot programme we needed to consider the issue of 'psychological distance' (Micholt, 1992). Micholt developed English's (1975) concept of the three-handed contract and considered this with regard to the potential for game playing. Micholt notes that, ideally, the emotional or psychological distance between those involved in the contract should be equidistant. In social services, the Field Social Workers (FSWs) are the case holders and initially saw it as their job to inform the Residential Social Workers (RSWs) how they should undertake the work with the young people, and thus discounted the staff and their work. The RSWs experienced themselves as distant from the Social Services Management – the 'Great Powers' in English's (1975) model – and from the FSWs.

Further, the way in which management imposed transactional analysis on the unit initially disempowered the staff and alienated the consultants. Other departments, such as the General Support Team (GST) and the Adolescent Placement Team (APT) also wanted to dictate what should happen to young people, and experienced the transactional analysts as threatening their position. This perspective put the analyst closer to the RSWs and GST, and the APT closer to the FSWs. Conflict ensued about who would 'call the shots', resulting in a competitive Parent-Parent ego state process.

Some of the various dynamics, and the psychological distance between the various groups are outlined below:

1. The transactional analysts were brought in by management who, as it turned out, had not

Change required	Management implications	Specific behaviour from: Workers	Young people	Therapists/Trainers
Boundary setting	Have a restricted smoking rule Have an appropriate dining area Review catering including food for vegetarians, Asian menu, etc. Young people to make own supper Change home's name – 'unit' not appropriate Clarify role expectations, role boundaries and responsibilities	Smoking to be restricted Establish a 'home' dining area Supervision of, and involvement of young people of supper preparation Respect structure agreed once agreed	Smoking restrictions – times/areas (this was prior to the current guidelines for such establishments) To respect the dining area To be involved with making supper	Support Support
Positive stroking	Hold an end of day group for young people – home time Ensure staff receive strokes	To lead end of day groups To agree methods of recognition (stroking) for colleagues and young people. To teach young people about strokes	To agree tasks, contract and attend end of day group To be aware of their, and others, need for positive strokes	Set up end of day group – structure etc Support workers to facilitate group Training
Initiate responsibility	To ensure young people have some control in the organisation For the team leader to have greater influence in the organisation	To agree a tasks list To complete daily task sheet for young people Shift leaders structure to be initiated	To agree task contract To complete daily task sheet for self and rest of group – e.g. serve dinner; fill paper towel dispensers; organise preparation of supper	
Structure for workers	To review domestic staff duties – e.g. young people to vacuum own room weekly	Encourage young people to do tasks All staff to work on Fridays	To contract and carry out tasks	
Team leader	To offer staff regular supervision To have financial control of clothes allowance, pocket money, petty cash	Workers leave planned 6 months to year ahead Cover to be provided for training Discussion to take place on young people's reports Weekly support session to be held with centre manager Weekly support session to be held with shifts		Support concentrated through key worker meetings

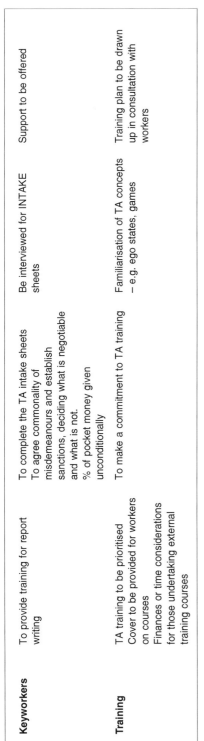

| **Keyworkers** | To provide training for report writing | To complete the TA intake sheets
To agree commonality of misdemeanours and establish sanctions, deciding what is negotiable and what is not.
% of pocket money given unconditionally | Be interviewed for INTAKE sheets | Support to be offered |
| **Training** | TA training to be prioritised
Cover to be provided for workers on courses
Finances or time considerations for those undertaking external training courses | To make a commitment to TA training | Familiarisation of TA concepts – e.g. ego states, games | Training plan to be drawn up in consultation with workers |

Box 6.4 Summary of consultation process

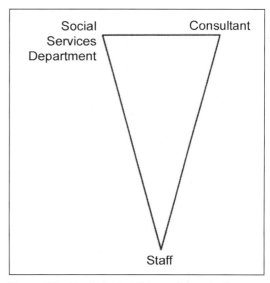

Figure 6.5 Psychological distance (example 1)

contracted with staff about this. Staff distrusted the consultants and their motives as they were experienced as being close to management (see Figure 6.5).

2. Eventually the group manager had less involvement with the home, which began to exercise greater control of its own functioning (see Figure 6.6).

Within a few years the home eventually received respect and credibility for the work being undertaken. This meant that the FSWs were willing to work more closely with the staff. Today the psychological distance between the RSW's, FSW's and young people is more equidistant (see Figure 6.7)

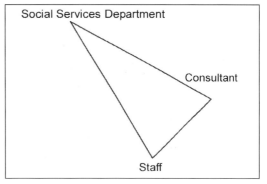

Figure 6.6 Psychological distance (example 2)

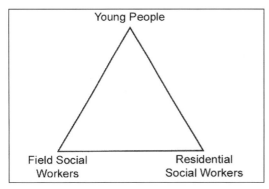

Figure 6.7   Psychological distance (example 3)

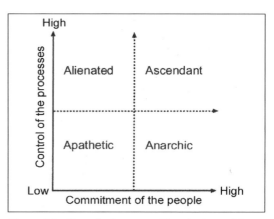

Figure 6.8   Organisation types: The simple model (Wickens, 1995)

The Ascendant Organisation

When conflict arose the staff would often operate with external organisations or departments from the Victim position (Karpman, 1968). As staff did not believe they had any power to state their position and set boundaries, they were often passive in their process (see Schiff et al., 1975). This belief of powerlessness meant that staff felt vulnerable. This, in turn, gave rise to internal strife and splitting between staff, which mirrored the splitting which many of the young people did, both intrapsychically and in their transactions with staff. It became clear that work would need to occur on every level within the home in order for the therapy with young people to be effective.

Wickens (1995) has developed the concept of an 'Ascendant Organisation', a concept which I believe fits well with the OK Corral (Ernst, 1971). Wickens noted four types of organisation: Ascendant, Anarchic, Apathetic and Alienated, and placed these on a grid in relation to how much control there is of the processes and how far the employees are committed (see Figure 6.8).

For Wickens the Ascendant organisation is the one in which there is most prosperity, power and happiness.

The Anarchic quadrant has high levels of individual commitment but little control. People do what they think is right individually for the organisation or themselves, without much thought for any corporate objectives. This is within the 'I'm OK, You're not OK' (I + U-) quadrant on the OK corral (see Figure 6.9).

The Alienated organisation utilizes top-down imposition of rules and procedures, with no attempt to involve people or get their co-operation, except by edict. Low-calibre management experience being alienated and become autocratic, placing emphasis on results. This fits with the 'I'm not OK, You're OK' position (I-U +).

With the Apathetic organisation there is neither commitment nor control; no centrally respected authority, nor any attempt to involve the workforce. People broadly do what they want, without any shared objectives or sense of direction. This is within the 'I'm not OK, You're not OK' position (I-U-).

Within the children's home the staff had high levels of commitment but little control. People did what they thought was right individually without much thought for either the rest of the team, or what the goal was they were trying to achieve together. This fitted with the Anarchic position on Wickens' grid, and 'I'm OK, You're not OK' (or I + U-) on the OK Corral.

In order to enable the staff to provide a coherent approach to their work they would need to move to the Ascendant (I + U +). Using Clarkson and Fish's (1988) model, the focus would need to be on the family systems sub-system.

The goals of an ascendant organisation are prosperity, power and happiness, together with product development – in this case the 'product' being staff who are able to work effectively together to support young people in their development. Long and short term goals would enable the staff to do this.

Short term goals include:

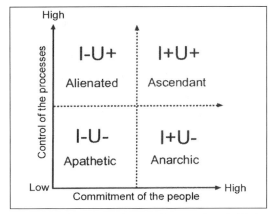

Figure 6.9 The ascendant quadrant overlayed with the OK corral

- To create a therapeutic environment.
- To develop an understanding of TA and how it would assist them in their work and in their relationships as a team.
- To establish rapport with the staff and develop trust.
- To establish emotional safety.
- To provide therapy for young people.

Long term goals include developing an ascendant organisation, characterised by:

- Mutual respect and trust between all those involved in the contract.
- Rapport and development of trust between staff and consultants.
- Increased competence and a confident staff team.
- Empowered staff thinking for themselves, both individually and as a team and taking positive, problem solving action.
- Celebration of staff achievements, and the ability to learn from their mistakes.

Throughout the programme, staff consultations and training were given a high priority. I gave regular monthly workshops where I taught TA concepts and then encouraged the staff to apply what they had learnt to their work with the young people. This developed into a regular slot being devoted to case conferences on each young person in which the theory could be applied in the second half of the afternoon of the training event. This had a range of positive outcomes:

- The staff increased their ability to discuss and relate to each other.

- This, in turn, developed a greater team spirit.
- Staff developed their confidence in thinking through the concepts and their application to a young person.
- As different staff felt more able to work with different concepts they were able to build on each other's ideas through discussion, and to develop coherent ways of working with a young person.

The training workshops included an introductory TA '101' course and a one year Foundation Course in TA. I also facilitated applied workshops in TA, which included:

- Parenting skills
- Child development
- Making the most of support and supervision
- Managing challenging behaviour
- Working with those who have been abused
- Making the relating work with adolescents
- Stress management
- Transference and counter-transference
- Understanding groups
- Listening skills

I also undertook regular team development days with the staff where they learnt to use the TA concepts for themselves, not just with the young people.

Conclusion

Work within a social services context meant working with all the systems incorporated in Clarkson and Fish's (1988) model. In addition, concepts of leadership and power needed to be considered. I needed to keep reviewing and evaluating the process and, as previously mentioned, decided that the dual role of staff consultant and psychotherapist to the young people was detrimental to both the staff and young people. The staff experienced me as 'expert' and, as I was initially working with the same young people as they were, this tended to undermine their own skills and experience. Further, undertaking both therapy with the young people, and training and consultations with the staff, reflected the often incestuous and boundaryless relationships the young people were in. Therefore we were working within a negative parallel process (Searles, 1955). I decided to change my role to a purely consultative one and, as I did so, moved from coaching to a participative style of leadership as the work progressed (see Krausz, 1986).

In summary the constraints and difficulties of working in the social services department included:

- Working within a frame of reference that believed that attachment leads to long-term dependency.
- Working in a politically controlled system which is service rather than user-led.
- The need to develop and negotiate a wide range of contacts and contracts with associated departments.
- The lack of choice for young people about residency, which made contracting difficult.
- The different status between field and residential staff and the associated need to develop positive existential life positions in order that residential staff used the influential power they did have.
- Field social workers, family and the courts can all have a bearing on the length of residency for a young person, which can thereby interrupt treatment planning.
- My one-day a week contract meant that my availability was limited.

The work nonetheless proved invaluable to all those concerned. One year there was an independent evaluation report on the management of stress by the TASS programme team and a Juvenile Justice Team in the Borough. The latter was apparently struggling. There were underlying difficulties between staff which were never addressed, and which created further stress. The TASS team, trained in TA across a wide range of areas, were found to be in charge of their stress, supporting each other and able to function well.

Considering Clarkson and Fish's (1988) model of sub-systems, alongside the process of contracting and the development of congruent treatment plans for young people in residential care facilitated the development of a potent therapeutic environment. None of this could have occurred, however, without the development of trust between myself, as the transactional analyst consultant, and the staff members. My previous experience working in residential settings established my credibility, and the staff's enthusiasm and commitment to the young people made progress possible.

My only role, in terms of direct contact with the young people, was during the assessment process when I would be part of the team who would assess and meet up to discuss our thoughts on each young person. By this time the staff were confident in their own thoughts and processes and I could support them to become confident in applying what they were learning in the training sessions. Once I had changed my role, the staff progressed in terms of their understanding and application of TA, and the team went from strength to strength.

On my departure it was originally envisaged that those staff more experienced in TA would support those who were new to the home. Monthly case conferencing about each young person could then have been held with a qualified TA trainer and supervisor, who could also supervise individuals enabling them to apply their learning. This would have accounted the years of training the staff had undertaken with the TASS programme and would have empowered them. Unfortunately budget cuts, alongside a change in management, meant that this development did not occur. However, a transactional analyst is involved and continues to positively influence the work with young people.

Those staff who were involved with the TASS programme have benefited both professionally and personally. They state that the programme positively changed the way they work and changed how they view themselves and others. The level of training and consultation they experienced has influenced them long term and this will have benefit for the young people with whom they come into contact.

The development of this work has hopefully led to fewer young people writing poems like that of Faith's:

Tired and empty lone and afraid
Not knowing what to do next
Whirling around in a world of confusion
Then stop
And tell people how I feel
But shan't. I'll leave that to others
Because I feel empty tonight.

Young people deserve to be heard and to have their Inner Child healed so that they can become independent and interdependent through the process of attachment. The use of TA as a coherent and consistent approach enables this to happen.

References

American Psychiatric Association (1995) *Diagnostic and Statistical Manual of Mental Disorders.* (4th Edn.) Washington, DC: APA.

Ainsworth, M.D.S. (1978) *Patterns of Attachment.* New Jersey: Erlbaum.

Berkowitz, D.A. (1987) Adolescent Individuation and Family Therapy. In Coleman, J.C. (Ed.) *Working with Troubled Adolescents.* London: Academic Press.

Bloch, D. (1979) *So The Witch Won't Eat Me.* London: Burnett Books.

Bowlby, J. (1973) *Separation, Anxiety and Anger.* London: Penguin Books.

Bowlby, J. (1980) *Loss, Sadness and Depression.* London: Hogarth.

Bretherton, I. and Waters, E. (1986) Growing Points of Attachment Theory and Research. *Monographs of the Society for Research in Child Development,* 50, 1–290.

Clarkson, P. (1988) Ego State Dilemmas of Abused Children. *Transactional Analysis Journal,* 18: 2, 85–93.

Clarkson, P. (1992) *Transactional Analysis Psychotherapy: An Integrated Approach.* London: Tavistock/Routledge.

Clarkson, P. and Fish, S. (1988) Systemic Assessment and Treatment Considerations in TA Child Psychotherapy. *Transactional Analysis Journal,* 8: 2, 123–31.

Coleman, J. (1987) *Working with Troubled Adolescents.* London: Academic Press.

English, F. (1975) The Three Cornered Contract, *Transactional Analysis Journal,* 5: 4, 383–4.

Erikson, E. (1950) *Childhood and Society.* London: Penguin.

Ernst, F.H. (1971) The OK Corral: The Grid for 'Get-on-With'. *Transactional Analysis Journal,* 1: 4, 33–42.

Erskine, R. (1993) *Integrative Psychotherapy: Enquiry Attainment and Involvement. A Theory of Methodology.* Workshop (6–8 July) Iron Mill Institute, Exeter, Devon.

Friedrich, W.N. (1995) *Psychotherapy with Sexually Abused Boys.* Thousand Oaks, CA: Sage.

Gayol, G.N. (1995) Self-reparenting With Female Delinquents in Jail. *Transactional Analysis Journal,* 25: 3, 208–10.

Hobbes, R. (1996) Attachment Theory and Transactional Analysis. *ITA News,* 46, 37–40.

Hobbes, R. (1997) Attachment Theory and Transactional Analysis. *ITA News,* 47, 33–8.

James, M. (1974) Self-reparenting: Theory and Process. *Transactional Analysis Journal,* 4: 3, 32–9.

Illsley Clarke, J. (1978) *Self-Esteem: A Family Affair.* New York: Harper & Row.

Karpman, S. (1968) Fairy Tales and Script Drama Analysis. *Transactional Analysis Bulletin,* 7: 26, 51–5.

Kouwenhoven, M. (1984) Problem Solving Sanctions. In Stern, E. (Ed.) *TA the State of the Art.* Dordrecht: Foris.

Krausz, R. (1986) Power and Leadership in Organizations. *Transactional Analysis Journal,* 16: 2, 85–94.

Levin, P. (1982) The Cycle of Development. *Transactional Analysis Journal,* 18: 2, 129–39.

Masterson, J.F. (1985) *Treatment of the Borderline Adolescent.* New York: Brunner/Mazel.

Micholt, N. (1992) Psychological Distance and Group Interventions. *Transactional Analysis Journal,* 22: 4, 228–33.

Mountain, A. (2004) *The Space Between: Bridging the Gap between Workers and Young People.* Lyme Regis: Russell House Publishing.

Osnes, R. (1974) Spot Reparenting. *Transactional Analysis Journal,* 4: 3, 40–6.

Roberts, D. (1992) *Hierarchy of Functionality.* Workshop notes. TA Conference, New Zealand.

Samenow, S.E. (1980) Treating the Anti-social: Confrontation or Provocation? *Transactional Analysis Journal,* 10: 3, 247–51.

Schiff, J.L. et al. (1975) *Cathexis Reader.* New York: Harper & Row.

Schiff, A.W. and Schiff, J.L. (1971) Passivity. *Transactional Analysis Journal,* 1: 1, 71–8.

Searles, H.F. (1955) The Informational Value of The Supervisor's Emotional Experiences. In *Collected Papers on Schizophrenia and Related Subjects.* London: Hogarth Press.

Steiner, C. (1974) *Scripts People Live.* New York: Bantam Books.

Temple, S. (1999) Functional Fluency for Educational Transactional Analysts. *Transactional Analysis Journal,* 29: 3, 164–74.

Trieschman, A.E., Whittacker, J. and Bredtro, L. (1969) *The Other 23 Hours.* Chicago, IL: Aldine.

Turner, R.J. (1988) Parent-Adult-Child Projective Drawing Task: A Therapeutic Tool in TA. *Transactional Analysis Journal,* 18: 1, 60–7.

Ware, P. (1983) Personality Adaptations: Doors to Therapy. *Transactional Analysis Journal,* 13: 1, 11–9.

Warner, N. (1993) *Choosing Care*. London: HMSO.

Wickens, P. (1995) *The Ascendant Organisation*. London: Macmillan.

Woods, K. (1980) Moving Away From Attack Therapy. *Transactional Analysis Journal*, 10: 3, 241–6.

Woods, K. and Woods, M. (1982) Treatment of Borderline Conditions. *Transactional Analysis Journal*, 12: 4, 288–300.

PART TWO

Therapeutic Practice with Children and Young People

CHAPTER 7

Transactional Analysis Psychotherapy with the Individual Child

Keith Tudor

This chapter considers a number of concepts and theories which frame transactional analysis (TA) psychotherapeutic practice with reference to working with the individual child. I discuss the initial contact and assessment; contracts and contracting, and some professional and ethical considerations; diagnosis; and, within the context of the therapy itself, the therapeutic medium of play (which forms a focus of Chapter 13), and primary prevention (Campos, 1986) and protection (Campos, 1988). In presenting this application I draw on TA literature, and on my experience of working as a psychotherapist in private practice with individual children, and especially one child, 'Tom', with whom I worked over a period of two years (from when he was four to when he was seven years old). The chapter begins with a brief introduction that acknowledges the significance of children in the history and development of psychotherapy.

Children and psychotherapy

The history of psychotherapy cannot be understood without appreciating the contribution of children and young people to its development. In his excellent history of psychoanalysis in Europe and America, Schwartz (1999) makes the point that it was Freud's early (adult) clients who contributed much to what we know today: 'Anna O' introduced Josef Breuer and Sigmund Freud to the importance of listening; and 'Cäcilie M' taught Freud to make sense of what he was hearing, which led him to develop the technique of interpretation. So too clients who were children: Breuer and Freud's (1895/1974) work on hysteria was informed by one of Breuer's early cases, a 12–year-old boy (Breuer, 1895/1974). Some years later Freud (1909/1977) treated a five-year-old boy, 'Little Hans', through working with his father, thereby offering perhaps the first example of a parenting class – a systemic intervention which was echoed some twenty years later by Melanie Klein when she consulted

Katherine Jokl Jones, Ernest Jones' second wife, for her 'parenting anxieties' (see Schwartz, 1999). The psychoanalysis and observation of children has been crucial in the development of psychotherapeutic theory and practice, notably through the work of three pioneers: Melanie Klein (1882–1960) Anna Freud (1895–1982) and Donald Winnicott (1896–1971) whose work is still influential and is referred to in this present work. More recently, many of the breakthroughs in self-psychology and developmental psychology have come about through reflections based on infant and child observation (see, for example, Stern, 1971, 1985, 2004).

Children have been not only the subject and object of our thirst for knowledge, but have also been the early beneficiaries of analysis and education, treatment and therapy – and, in this sense, psychotherapy has contributed to the development and growth of children. This applies across a number of theoretical orientations:

- Alfred Adler, an early colleague of Freud's, before they split over the question of human agency, founded the first free child guidance clinics in Vienna in the 1920s. One of the most important contributions to the later development of Adlerian psychology is Dreikurs' psycho-educational approach to child guidance, classroom counselling (Dreikurs, 1968) and family counselling (Dreikurs, 1972).
- Jacob Moreno, the founder of psychodrama, also began his career working with children, firstly in hospital, then in an internment village, and later in child guidance clinics. His early ideas about psychodrama came from watching children play; he then formed groups of children for impromptu play which, in turn, developed into the Theatre of Spontaneity (see Moreno, 1946/1977). Psychodramatists since Moreno have developed his ideas about child development work and therapeutic work with children, notably Bannister (1997, 2003, 2007).

- Carl Rogers also began his career as a counsellor working in a child guidance clinic; his PhD thesis was based on research he conducted into personality adjustment in children (Rogers, 1931) and his first published book was on the subject of *The Clinical Treatment of the Problem Child* (Rogers, 1939). Rogers describes Virginia Axline, the play therapist, as a close colleague. Later (in 1964) Axline wrote a groundbreaking and now famous book on her work with 'an emotionally lost child' *Dibs: In Search of Self*. Rogers' person-centred approach has been widely influential on therapeutic work with children (see, for instance, West, 1992) and has influenced a number of parenting programmes (see Gordon, 1975), and approaches to working with parents and children (see Embleton Tudor et al., 2004).
- Gestalt therapists and theorists have also contributed their perspective to our understanding of child development (Mackewn, 1991; Crocker, 1992; Wheeler, 2002); of attachment theory (Harris, 1996) and of working with children (Oaklander, 1969/1988, 1982; Wheeler and McConville, 2002).

Having acknowledged the significance of children in the history of psychotherapy, I now turn to exploring the impact of TA psychotherapy on the individual child.

Contact and assessment

This usually begins with a telephone conversation with a parent, a term I use in this chapter to stand for the person in the parenting or caring role, and usually legally responsible for the child. In my experience, this initial contact is usually made by the mother who wants me to see her child, to whom I refer at this stage as the 'notional client'. This is important in holding the child/client in mind whilst listening to the parent who, at least at this stage and in terms of being a customer and purchaser of a service, is also a client. This is the beginning of a three-handed contract (English, 1975) and a systemic assessment (Clarkson and Fish, 1988b) (see Chapter 1).

As human beings we cannot be understood outside of our environmental and social context, even if we live, work and love alone. This is more obviously the case for children who are born dependent and who remain socially dependent

on parents or carers for much of their early life, and thus enmeshed in several systems: family, school, clubs and so on. The therapist who works with children cannot work effectively or ethically without taking account of systems: systems theory, systemic therapy and systemic assessment. Minuchin (1974: 3) compares a therapist working within the framework of systemic family therapy to 'a technician with a zoom lens. He can zoom in for a close-up whenever he wishes to study the intrapsychic field, but he can also observe with a broader focus'. Clarkson and Fish (1988b) provide a representation which accounts for systems, based on three overlapping and interlocking sub-systems: the individual child, the family system, and the socio-cultural system, (thereby giving seven vectors for encompassing systemic work), and all located within a wider, universal system of 'life' or, as Angyal (1941) puts it, the biosphere.

One advantage of this model is that it locates the child within their immediate (family) context as well as their wider social context (family, culture, class). The therapist using this systemic model of assessment inevitably takes a wider perspective on any presenting 'problem', and has at least seven options for responding. This is especially useful if a child within a family is being presented as 'the problem' or as carrying the 'sick role'. The therapist may decide to work with the child but, equally, may decide to work with the parents and not the child. Indeed, I know of one therapist who refuses to work directly with children and only, in this context, works with the parent or parents. This perspective has a distinguished history. Freud never analysed a child directly but, in the case of 'Little Hans' (Freud, 1909/1977), 'treated' a five year old through working with his father. This is also the approach of 'filial therapy' (see Guerney, 1964) in which the parent becomes the child's primary therapeutic agent.

Using this model of assessment, I saw Tom, his mother and her partner for an initial assessment interview as a result of which the following systemic assessment and 'treatment' considerations were discussed and agreed:

- Child and school system: *Tom to be in contact with the educational psychologist at school (an existing arrangement).*
- Family and school systems: *The two mothers to be in contact with school and education authorities (current and ongoing).*

- Family systems interventions: *Tom and his mothers each in individual psychotherapy (existing arrangements); mother and partner to have couples therapy (subsequently arranged).*
- Individual psychotherapy with child: *Tom to have individual psychotherapy (subsequently arranged).*
- Child/parents' dyad: *Conjoint family work (to be considered – and, in this event, not relevant).*

Whilst the systemic assessment model implies that each option needs to be considered, there is no requirement to plan seven interventions; indeed, in most cases, such a response would not only be unrealistic in terms of therapeutic and financial resources, it would be too much for the family system to bear.

There are a number of advantages and disadvantages in choosing to work with a child individually. Advantages include the establishment, development and demonstration of a one-to-one, trusting relationship, and the experience for the child of direct, focused and undisturbed attention. Having organised therapy for the child, the parent/s may then seek help for themselves or as a family. The disadvantages of working with an individual child include the possibility of confirming and reinforcing them as 'the problem', that is, the identified 'sick role' in family systems theory and, ultimately, of pathologising them. Also, the therapist working therapeutically with the individual child may take – or be seen to be taking – undue responsibility for resolving 'the problem' and, thereby, may undermine the parents in parenting the child.

The initial meeting

Given the number of parties involved and the potential complexity of expectations and focus, I have often found it useful to offer some structure for initial mutual assessment meeting. In my experience, this meeting tends to fall into three parts:

1. Firstly, some initial time with both the child and parents together.
2. Then some time with the child on their own.
3. Lastly, some time with the parents, including some time without the child, to discuss the initial contract.

There is a danger that this process may confirm the parent's or parents' individualising frame of reference that, as it is the child who could benefit from therapy, it is them who are the problem. On the other hand, this structure also gives the child an opportunity to voice their views without their parents present. Notwithstanding the outcome of the decision of who the client is, I have found this 'rolling' structure to the initial session a useful one in developing a working relationship with all parties, and in demonstrating both a clarity about boundaries and a flexibility of working. In my experience this flexibility often prefigures the nature of the therapeutic relationship.

James (1969) suggests three questions that provide a framework for an initial session of TA with children:

1. Who is in your family now?
2. What do you think are the hurt points in your family? According to James both these questions are directed at the child's Adult but also elicit their Parent ego state.
3. What do you like doing? – A question designed to engage the child's Child ego state.

James also suggests drawing a structural ego state diagram, contracting, and giving an initial homework assignment. Although I think this structure may be used with a child, even with the parent present, I find it too rigid. In my experience, the process of contracting takes longer. Chapter 8 discusses the initial meeting in further depth.

Contracts and contracting

The contractual method lies at the heart of TA; indeed, it defines TA. The classic definition of a contract in TA is: 'an explicit bilateral agreement to a well-defined course of action' (Berne, 1966: 362). However, all therapeutic work with children below the threshold of 'Fraser competence' (Gillick versus West Norfolk and Wisbech Area Health Authority, 1986) necessarily involves at least *three* parties: the child, the therapist *and* the parent or parents. This can become more complex when the parents are separated and when other parties such as grandparents, or other authorities such as the social services or police, are involved.

Following the assessment with Tom, his mother and her partner, I considered the elements of the three-handed contract (Figure 7.1). The double-headed arrows represent the bilateral nature of the respective contracts.

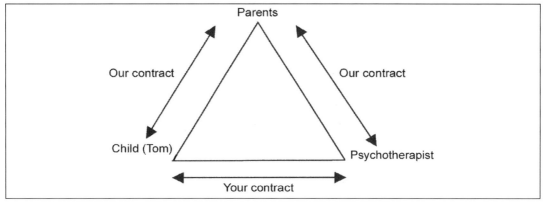

Figure 7.1   Three-handed contract between child, parents and psychotherapist (based on English, 1975)

In the same work Berne (1966: 227) makes several points about the nature of communication. His third rule of communication states that 'the behavioural outcome of an ulterior transaction is determined at the psychological level and not at the social level.' Thus contracts have both an explicit social level, that is, what is stated, *and* an implicit psychological level, that is, what is not stated, but often wished. Putting together these considerations of the (three) parties involved in the contract, the bilateral nature of contracts (between two people) and the social and psychological levels of communication (two), we can consider that in any three handed contract there are twelve possible elements of communication influencing the contractual relationship. This is significant, not least, in that the therapist may require additional time in order to clarify the contract and, in particular, to have a sense of the ulterior transactions and psychological level communication.

Following two meetings involving both Tom and his mothers, I clarified the following contracts relevant to my therapeutic work with Tom:
Parents – Child – Social level: We will bring you to see Keith and pay for it.
Parents – Child (Psychological level): (We want you to be 'cured', i.e. to be controllable.)
Parents – Psychotherapist – Social level: We want you to see Tom, to assess his developmental needs and to meet them, and to act as his advocate.
Parents – Psychotherapist (Psychological level): (We want you to act as a father-figure for Tom.)
Psychotherapist – Parents: I will see Tom for six weekly meetings, renewable by re-negotiation, and respond to what he brings. I will respond to his developmental needs as appropriate within a therapeutic relationship.

Child – Psychotherapist – Social level: I want to come and see you and play.
Child – Psychotherapist (Psychological level): (I want you to be my Dad.)
Psychotherapist – Child: I will play with you, and talk to you about what you do and how you feel and think. I will be your 'therapy friend'; I won't be your Dad.

Clear psychotherapeutic contracts should reflect clear, explicit Adult transactions, at least on the part of the psychotherapist. The administrative contract – about time, place, fees and other arrangements – then acts as a container for the therapy. Other, psychological level transactions then become part of what Berne (1966: 20) refers to as the 'therapeutic struggle'.

One example of this affected my initial therapeutic work with Matt, aged six. At a relatively early point in the therapy, after the initial contracting, Matt's mother began to pass me notes as he came into the room. For several sessions I accepted these whilst holding a certain amount of discomfort about this process. A few sessions later Matt, who did a lot of drawing, pointed to a female figure he had drawn and said: "Tell her off. Ask her 'Why?' Talk to her. Ask her to play and draw". I realised that I had a lot to learn from this particular client. Reflecting on Matt's statements and the whole process, I realised that not only was his mother influencing the agenda of the sessions, but also that she was 'speaking for' Matt, and hence he did not have to speak for himself. Subsequently I spoke to Matt's mother, listened to her anxieties, and agreed with her that, at this point, I needed to maintain the boundary and integrity of the therapeutic environment/space/session for Matt. Following this, and more explicit communication between Matt, his mother and me, Matt's play became more animated and his speech more fluent and consistent. Interestingly, Mahler, Pine and Bergman (1975: 7) view renounced, distorted or delayed speech as 'attempts to preserve the delusion of the unconditionally omnipotent symbiotic unity.'

Within TA, in recent years, many practitioners have focused more on contracting, the verb which describes the activity and process of making a contract, than on the contract (noun). This is reflected in the concept of process contracts (Lee, 1997: 94) which are defined as those contracts 'that are made moment by moment during the counselling session as part of the interpersonal process in the here and now.'

At one phase in his therapy, over several sessions, Tom would want me to make a house out of cushions:

Tom: Make me a long house.
Therapist: You want me to make you a long house?
Tom: Yeah.
Therapist: OK.

This exchange demonstrates the transactions involved in contracting: a request – in this case in the form of an instruction! – an offer and an acceptance of the offer. We continued in the same vein:

Tom: Give me that blanket. Make me a door too. I got the blanket wrong.
Therapist: You got the blanket wrong?
Tom: Yeah. I'll show yer. Wait a minute. That isn't a long house.
Therapist: How long do you want it to be?
Tom: That . . . no, make it over there.
Therapist: Make it over here?
Tom: No, here.
Therapist: . . . and here. Shall we make it this long?
Tom: Yeah.
Therapist: OK. How wide do you want it?
Tom: Oh. It's night time.
Therapist: It's night time?
Tom: Yeah.
Therapist: . . . in your house.
Tom: The wind's starting to blow my hair. What's this (examining a small cushion)?
Therapist: What do you want it to be?
Tom: There.
Therapist: There you go. Do you want the roof on? Do you want the roof on?
Tom: You got to go, go make me another one (cushion) there.
Therapist: I've got to make you another one there. That's the door.
Tom: That isn't a door.
Therapist: Where's the door?
Tom: Here.
Therapist: The door's up there?
Tom: It goes up there.
Therapist: Oh, OK. Well, let me put the roof on first. I think I'll have to make it a bit shorter

'cos I haven't got enough cushions. There we are.
Tom: Make me a door.
Therapist: That's the, that's the chimney. That's the roof for the chimney. And that's the door.
Tom: That's . . . not like that.
Therapist: Ah, but I've got another bit of the roof coming on. Another bit of the roof coming on. That's another bit of the side. And the last bit of the roof. There you are.

This exchange literally laid the foundation for subsequent work in which Tom gradually took more responsibility for building his own house of cushions. Discussing this extract in supervision I realised that, in saying that I hadn't got enough cushions, I may have conveyed a sense of scarcity to Tom. It didn't seem to affect him or the therapy, but it was a useful reflection and reminder of the potential significance of such a statement.

Working with children challenges the therapist not only to be creative (see Chapter 13) but also to be flexible. This may be reflected in the ongoing process of contracting regarding both the therapy itself in terms of content and process, and the practical, administrative or business arrangements. In my experience children in individual therapy tend to come and go, a process that reflects the importance for a child to be able to regulate access to their therapist. Winnicott (1977/1989), for instance, saw 'The Piggle' for over two and a half years in 16 sessions. The first six meetings were at regular monthly intervals, followed by meetings at intervals of between two and four months, including, occasionally, further monthly meetings. In my experience this is not an unusual pattern. In order to support such self-regulation, it is important, as Steiner (1971a: 134) puts it in the context of his discussion of competence as one of four requirements of a contract, that this 'is adequately dealt with by an agreement with the parents that the child will not discontinue treatment unless both he and the guardians consent to it.'

Professional and ethical considerations

Before agreeing to undertake therapeutic work with a child, there are a number of professional and ethical issues to consider which are additional to those associated with working with adults (see also Chapter 12).

In the ethics guidelines of the European Association for Transactional Analysis (EATA), there are four clauses which are relevant to the practitioner working with children, with regard to:

- Identifying protective responsibility (clause C).
- Competence (E).
- Responsibility for providing a suitable environment for the client (J).
- Demonstration of commitment to keep up-to-date in the relevant field of application (M).

(EATA, 1993)

Expanding these, respectively, in relation to psychotherapeutic work with children, I suggest that practitioners have professional and ethical responsibilities to consider the following:

- To arrange consultancy with and/or access to a child and family psychologist and/or a psychiatrist and to make themselves known to their local Social Services Department as working in this field (protection).
- To undertake some further specialist training in working with children, which may also involve personal therapeutic work (competence) (see Chapter 12 and Appendix 6).
- To ensure that the premises in which they practice are suitable for the work with children they are offering. This involves a considerable investment in materials: a variety of age-appropriate toys (animals, cars, etc.); a number of large soft cushions; crayons, chalk paint and paper; facilities for sand or water play; age-appropriate books; etc. (see West, 1992 and Chapters 12 and 13) (suitable environment).
- To arrange specialist TA supervision from a supervisor with experience of working with children and generally to keep abreast of writing and developments in the field of child psychotherapy (keeping up-to-date).

There is a second ethical consideration that centres on the value TA places on the therapeutic goal of autonomy. Berne (1964/1968: 158) defines the attainment of autonomy as 'the release or recovery of three capacities: awareness, spontaneity and intimacy.' However, whilst practitioners may be working on this basis, and a child may welcome this, explicitly or implicitly,

the child's parents may prefer an outcome of social control. Holloway's (1974) distinction between 'autonomy contracts' and 'social control contracts' is useful in this regard. In this situation the therapist's dilemma is that the parties involved in a child's therapy may have different desired outcomes (see discussion of this in Chapter 9). This is not uncommon (see 'Contracts and Contracting' above) and is of particular relevance in clinical practice when, for instance, the child's autonomy is contradicted by the parents' injunctions e.g. 'Don't think', 'Don't be you'. These instances highlight the need for valid consideration of the child's protection, and for clear contracting. The contracting which took place between Tom's two mothers and myself over the issue of assessing and meeting his developmental needs is a case in point. On the one hand it gave me as the therapist the task of supporting Tom's aspirations and autonomy and to do necessary anti-injunctive work (Campos, 1988). On the other hand, in terms of the family dynamics, Tom's increasing autonomy created, at least in the early months of the therapy, increasing difficulties at home. Also, in terms of the parents' role and, in this case, their developing parenting skills, as well as my own philosophical, ethical and professional principles, it was important that I did not undermine his parents' parenting, or create an unhealthy dependence in the psychotherapeutic setting (see Winnicott, 1963/1965).

A final professional and ethical concern is one of responsibility. During the session, and in any case if the parent/s leave the child at the clinic or consulting room, the therapist is, in effect, 'in loco parentis', a role which carries additional responsibilities for safety and protection beyond those usually accorded to adult clients (for further discussion of which see Chapter 12).

Diagnosis

There are two strands of thinking within TA with regard to diagnosis. The first, from Berne, himself a doctor and psychiatrist, follows a medical model and, indeed, has developed a plethora of diagnostic models and a 'technology' of diagnosis and assessment. The second, which derives from a radical, even anti- psychiatry perspective, views that 'everything diagnosed psychiatrically, unless *clearly* organic in origin, is a form of alienation' (Steiner, 1971b: 5). Steiner's assertion is no less radical today, and may be taken as a challenge to practitioners to think about the implications and consequences of diagnosis. In my experience, most practitioners working with children are acutely aware of the social consequences for a child of being diagnosed or misdiagnosed within the medical/psychiatric model and system, and of the potential that he may carry that 'label' for a significant part of his life. By contrast, most adults, with a social, functioning, integrating Adult, are in a better position to counter the iatrogenic effects of diagnosis.

The word diagnosis comes from the Greek *diagnôsis* meaning discernment that, in turn, derives from *diagignôskein*, to distinguish (*dia-*, apart; + *gignôskein*, to come to know, discern). There is nothing wrong in diagnosis *per se*, that is, in wanting to discern or to know; the problem comes along with the power of the person doing the discerning. From a client or person-centred perspective, Rogers (1951) has two objections to diagnosis: firstly, the fact that it places the locus of evaluation in the hands of experts leads to clients developing a dependency on those external experts with the result that 'there is a degree of loss of personhood as the individual acquires the belief that only the expert can accurately evaluate him, and that therefore the measure of his personal worth lies in the hands of another' (ibid: 224). Secondly, for Rogers and others, diagnosis has undesirable social and philosophical implications, such as the loss of control and, ultimately, liberty. Rogers (ibid: 223–4) concludes his questioning of the traditional medical/psychiatric model of diagnosis with a series of statements which assert the therapeutic value of a client-centred approach to diagnosis:

Therapy is basically the experiencing of the inadequacies in old ways of perceiving, the experiencing of new and more accurate perceptions, and the recognition of significant relationships between perceptions.

In a very meaningful and accurate sense, therapy is diagnosis, and this diagnosis is a process which goes on in the experience of the client, rather than the intellect of the clinician.

I have cited Rogers here as, apart from Steiner's early critique, there is relatively little in TA literature that advances or develops a critical view of diagnosis, which, as I have argued, is especially important in working with children.

This said, I now turn to two diagnostic models in TA which focus on the child's development and on developmental needs.

The script matrix – and the development of script

Script theory was first developed by Berne and Steiner in the mid 1960s. Berne's (1972/1975: 445) definition of 'script' is: 'A life plan based on a decision made in childhood, reinforced by the parents, justified by subsequent events, and culminating in a chosen alternative.' Steiner's original script matrix (1966) is a diagram that may be used to illustrate the directives which are handed down from parents and grandparents to the present generation. Figure 7.2 shows Tom's script matrix which, given his age (then four) is necessarily partial (see Campos, 1988). This is consistent with Steiner's (1966: 134) observation that 'the script is determined by P_1 and the counterscript by P_2. The script is pre-Oedipal, non-verbal, preconscious, visceral (gut level) while the counterscript is post-Oedipal, verbal, conscious; and the former pre-empts the latter'.

In this figure the dotted lines around P_1 and P_2 reflect the fact that, according to one strand of thinking about ego states in TA, these ego states have not yet developed. The argument goes: that the pre-Oedipal script is formed through the significant adults' injunctions whilst the verbal counterscript is already being presented to Tom, although he has not yet developed his P_2 receptor. The visual representation of such a partial script matrix has a powerful impact: it represents the scripting environment in which the unformed child is growing up. Furthermore, this particular combination of injunctions and counterscript messages – Please Others, Try Hard or Hurry Up, together with 'Don't be important' and 'Don't think' – add up to what might be referred to as a 'predictive' hysterical (or histrionic) personality adaptation (Ware, 1983). One value of drawing up this partial form of the script matrix is in order to identify the particular focus of anti-injunctive and anti-counterscript psychotherapeutic work with parents or significant others. I discuss the therapeutic implications of this below.

However, since Steiner's original work on the script matrix thirty years ago, script theory has moved on and there are a number of criticisms of this model and the theory it represents.

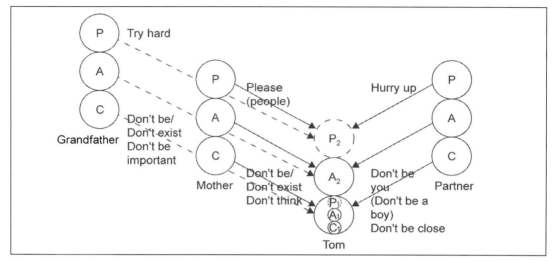

Figure 7.2   Partial script matrix of 'Tom', aged four, including second order structural analysis compatible with his development (based on Steiner, 1966; Campos, 1988)

Elsewhere, Summers and I have made a number of critiques of traditional script theory:

- Traditional, linear, stage theories of (child) development have been challenged by writers such as Stern (1985: 256): 'it, therefore, cannot be known, in advance, on theoretical grounds, at what point in life a particular traditional clinical-developmental issue will receive its pathogenic origin'.
- Scripts are co-created – Cornell (1988) refers to the current developmental research that suggests that infants influence and shape their parents as much as they are shaped by their parents.
- Injunctions, programs and drivers/counter injunctions are, equally, co-created and decided, and only become part of a person's script if accepted and 'fixed' as such.
- Despite the concept of cultural scripting (White and White, 1975) the script, in one of its most popular and most used manifestations – the script matrix – in its reference only to the heterosexual nuclear family, is deeply culturally-determined.
- A postmodern script theory suggests that we can have several stories about our lives running in parallel – and that we can choose between them. Allen and Allen (1995: 329) state that 'each person is entitled to more than one story'. The stories we write may be based on motives combining survival, compliance,

rebellion, resilience, aspiration, self-assertion, loyalty, revenge and love. (Summers and Tudor: 32)

Cornell (1988) made some changes to Steiner's original script matrix. Summers and I took Cornell's perspective further and developed a co-creative script matrix. Figure 7.3 shows this, again applied to Tom.

This script matrix is also partial, in the sense of being necessarily incomplete, as it does not attempt to map all the messages Tom has received or makes sense of. It is more sensitive to Tom's particular family system which comprised his mother and her female partner and hence two mothers. It also highlights the co-created nature of scripts and shows that injunctions, programmes and drivers cut both ways. Tom's response to his grandfather to 'Go away' was a response to his grandfather's injunction, *and* may, in turn, be conveying a 'Don't exist' injunction. Of course the relative impact on the parent or grandparent who, predominantly, has more power than the child, will vary according to his or her own development, history, experiences, pathology and present support. Similarly, the driver messages are equally mutual: Tom's counter-injunction to please was matched by his message to his mothers to please (him), which, in turn, formed part of their own histrionic adaptations (see Ware, 1983; Joines and Stewart, 2002).

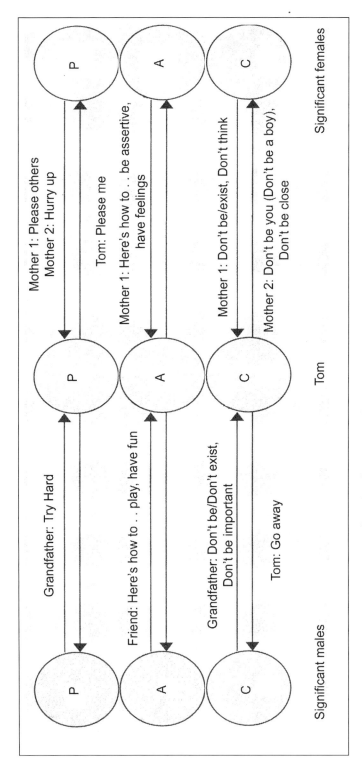

Figure 7.3 Tom's partial co-creative script matrix (based on Summers and Tudor, 2000)

Developmental needs – and developmental theory

Within TA a number of authors have written about child development, accounting for the child's age and stage of development in terms of personality and ego states (Schiff et al., 1975) and identifying specific developmental needs and affirmations (Levin, 1988a, 1988b). Almost all are based on the view that we develop ego states and subsets of ego states – the second order structural analysis which encompasses the concept of the Child in the Child (C_1), the Adult in the Child (A_1), and the Parent in the Child (P_1) (see Chapter 1). Thus, Schiff et al. (1975) view the neonate (0–6 months) as dealing with existence and discern this as developing C_1. Following this, they suggest that between 6–18 months the baby is concerned with what they can do (C_1); between 1–3 years old, with what others do (A_2), and so on.

However, such a schema is based on a conflation and confusion of metaphors (Tudor, 2003: 204) between:

> . . . on the one hand, ego states as an image and representation of the structure of personality and, on the other, ego states as a metaphor for stages of development. Assertions that the Adult ego state (A_2) does not begin to develop until 12 months . . . 18 months . . . or 'a later stage of cognitive development'. . . are not based on a structural definition of ego states.

Berne (1961/75a: 76) defines the Adult ego state as 'characterised by an autonomous set of feelings, attitudes, and behaviour patterns which are adapted to the current reality'. That reality and adaptation to the environment exist from conception onwards and, in this sense, a person is conceived 'Adult' or, more accurately (ibid: 204) 'the foetus, developing autonomous sets of feelings, attitudes and behaviour patterns, adapting to its reality *in utero*, may be thought of as having a neopsyche or an Adult ego state.'

In this schema, the metaphors of Child and Parent ego states are reserved for, respectively, those archaic experiences, thoughts, feelings and behaviours which, due to misattunement, trauma, abuse or other interruption, remain unresolved and fixated; and, those thoughts, feelings and behaviours which are introjected from parents and parent figures which remain undigested or unintegrated.

It is critical to distinguish between these two strands of thinking as they lead to different conclusions about therapy and its practice. Theorists and practitioners advocating a stage theory view of the development of ego states believe in 'growing' the Child (the stuff of ubiquitous 'Inner Child' workshops) and in reparenting the Parent. Those representing the second strand of thinking focus on the 'development' of an Integrated or Integrating Adult (see Tudor, 2003 for an elaboration of these differences).

In my work with Tom, a number of themes emerged which reflected some developmental deficits: that he didn't believe he could do things, and hence his part in the psychological game of 'Do me something'. He also believed that he was not important, that he got things wrong and that he was too much, also that he was unlovable and even that he was bad. It is helpful to distinguish these beliefs, and TA has useful ways of doing so, for instance, viewing the first three of these beliefs as introjects which Tom maintained (Parent ego state) and had maintained within his immediate familial and social context; and the last two as the sense Tom himself made of these introjects and how he experienced himself (Child ego state), again in the context of his environment. The purpose and process of the psychotherapy was to help him work through these beliefs and feelings, and the experiences, memories and fantasies (and phantasies) which supported and reinforced them. The work included identifying developmental needs and being affirmative, saying in effect and sometimes in actuality: "You have a right to be here", "It's OK to explore", "It's OK to test out", "It's OK to let me know how you feel". Consistent with the second strand of thinking in TA about ego states, I view this work as expanding Tom's Adult; in effect, helping him to develop an autonomous set of feelings, attitudes, and behaviour patterns which are a response to his current reality.

Therapeutic work

It is now commonplace to assert the importance of the therapeutic relationship in therapy and in determining therapeutic outcome. For discussion of this within TA see Berne (1966) Clarkson (1992) Tudor (1999) and Hargaden and Sills (2002). We also know, from communication studies, that as much as 90 per cent of communication between people is non-verbal (see Fromkin and Rodman, 1983). With children, communication takes place principally through play.

Play, interpretation – and reality

It was Klein (1932/1975) who first saw that play could replace adults' free association as a medium of communication. However, it was Winnicott (1971, 1977/1989) who elaborated this aspect of working with children, seeing play taking place in the area between the child's inner and outer reality, and expressed through 'transitional phenomena' or 'transitional object'. As regards play therapy, Winnicott emphasises the importance of play *in itself* and not for any interpretive value it may have for the therapist.

The main attributes and, in my view, requirements of the child psychotherapist are: an ability to be contactful, to play and to be creative, and to be real and flexible. This is the inspiration and challenge I take from reading Winnicott. His (1960/1965) paper on *String: A Technique of Communication*, for instance, in which he describes the line or 'squiggle' he draws on some paper and then invites the child to draw, engages my creativity as a therapist. Alongside play is interpretation, also one of Berne's (1966) eight therapeutic operations, which Hargaden and Sills (2002) have reformulated as empathic transactions. Interpretation or empathic understanding is a necessary form of communication in order to help both child and therapist translate non verbal communication, precisely because the child is communicating a reality, or an area between realities, which is often hard for an adult or the therapist to grasp. One way of making sense of this is through reflective practice in therapy and in supervision.

> With regard to my work with Tom, in supervision, I began to make sense of his regular request of me to build him a house, 'a long house' out of cushions, as possibly being to do with his birth, a Caesarean section, and his subsequent need both to feel constricted and to push against and out of this – which he did a lot in therapy. I am not suggesting that this is the only interpretation or reality, or that the 'house' did not have any other significance, which it did. I am arguing that the therapist needs time and space to reflect on his or her practice in order to consider the possible meanings that transactions and interactions carry. With regard to my work with Tom, for instance, it was only in reviewing one session in supervision that I realised that, in play time, we had played through a day and a night:

> Tom: What we got in it? (unzipping a cushion cover)
> Therapist: What we got in it?

Tom: That's got a baby dinosaur.
Therapist: It's got a baby dinosaur?
Tom: This is . . . (zips up the cushion). Oh.
Therapist: It's got a baby cushion.
Tom: You missed another bit there.
Therapist: That was for the chimney.
Tom: We must put it on a bit.
Therapist: Oh. Are you going to put the last bit in?
Tom: I'm going in my house.
Therapist: You're going to go in your house.
Tom: I don't like you. You better shut my door. I'm going in my house.
Therapist: O.K.
Tom: (From inside the 'house') Shut my door. That's my, that's my . . . I got my pillow.
Therapist: You haven't got your pillow?
Tom: Yes . . .
Therapist: You better shut your door to keep all the things you don't like outside.
Tom   :Yeah. Shut my door.
Therapist: Do you want me to shut your door? You shut your door.
Tom: I can't.
Therapist: Yes you can.
Tom: Oh, I can't.
Therapist: I bet you can.
Tom: No. I can't . . . I'm not (my) a big man.
Therapist: You're not . . . ?
Tom: Not (my) a big man.
Therapist: You're not a big man yet but you're a big boy and you can close the door.
Tom: No.
Therapist: Do you want to know how to close the door?
Tom: Oh. Yeah.
Therapist: Put your hand out. Grab the pillow and pull. Pull, pull, pull, pull.
Tom: (Tom pulls cushion/door) Now put it on the top.
Therapist: There you are: you put it on the top.
Tom: I been waking, Keith. (Opens the cushion/door) Good morning Keith.
Therapist: Good morning, Tom.

Primary prevention and protection

Having identified the child's script in formation, and depending on the contract, TA psychotherapy with children may involve the primary prevention of script formation. Writing about redecision therapy with children, Campos (1986) identifies a number of intervention principles in this kind of prevention work including:

- 'If it's not broken don't fix it'.
- The importance of encouraging active play which, when freely chosen, serves as a permission structure.

- The key role of protection e.g. 'I won't let you hurt me or yourself'.
- Potency: 'children must perceive the therapist as potent or more potent than their own parents so they feel adequately protected when they get permission to behave counter to the script that is forming.'

(ibid: 20)

In a subsequent article, Campos (1988) focuses on protection, identifying four sources of healthy protection:

- That provided by parents.
- That provided by a safe environment.
- That provided by children's own healthy self-protection.
- That provided by therapeutic intervention – through the therapy room itself and through play.

As regards my work with Tom, these sources were mixed. His mother, her partner and his grandfather all used to hit him, although, by the time they had referred him and themselves, his mother and her partner had realised that this was not OK. As they recognised this, they were making the home a safer environment for Tom by agreeing not to hit him, and to explore other, positive parenting strategies (see Crary, 1993); to spend more time with Tom; and to supervise the time he spent with his grandfather. When I first met Tom, when he was four years old, he was not protecting himself in that he hit himself and called himself names. He also hit me on a couple of occasions when he was too quick for me. I was challenged by this behaviour and, in order to understand it, drew on my knowledge of this as a 'normal' or (I prefer) 'usual' developmental phase. I also turned to the TA literature on hitting and applied it to my work with Tom. Goulding and Goulding (1979) view physical abuse as a non-verbal way in which a 'Don't exist' injunction is given by the parents to the child and, indeed, this was so in Tom's case. In addition to decontamination work with Tom about hitting, I did some anti-injunctive work with Tom's parents to stop any continuing message that it was OK to hit, and to minimise the impact of the erstwhile injunction. Chapters 11 and 18 present further examples of therapeutic work with children and their parents. With Tom himself I said at several points in the therapy "I won't let you hit me – or yourself", thereby offering him some interim protection (Campos, 1986). I say 'interim' as, from an existential viewpoint, I do not believe that it is possible to deliver or guarantee protection or to make therapy – or life – safe.

On this theme, a large part of the protection Tom experienced in therapy was, in my view, co-created by him. I think of the therapy room as a temenos, a

boundaried 'space set aside from common purposes' (see Tudor and Embleton Tudor, 1999). However, it was Tom who defined the boundaries of this space by spending much of the beginning of each of the initial sessions running around on the foam seating at the side of the room, as if marking his territory. He sought and received protection through play by initially asking me to build him and later building himself a house out of cushions.

The logic of primary prevention work is also to work with the parents. Since, according to Campos (1988: 139) 'parents hold the injunctive power . . . such [family] intervention is necessary to interrupt any injunctions in formation. Parental injunctive power can be effectively weakened by working directly with the enjoining parent.' In this sense, all psychotherapy is family therapy, as any therapeutic work with one part of a family system is bound to affect the whole family – and, indeed, this may support the logic of not working directly with children and only working with the parent/s or carer/s. However, from a co-creative perspective, it is important to identify and work the co-created dynamic whether directly in an interpersonal relationship (child and parent, child and therapist) or whether with the client's intrapersonal or intrapsychic experience of this.

One mechanism by which the injunctive power of the parent is maintained is symbiosis. As in nature, symbiosis between a parent and a child can be healthy and, given that human babies, unlike some other mammals, are born before they are independent, is a necessity. As Winnicott famously put it: 'There's no such thing as a baby; only a mother and baby.' A symbiosis becomes unhealthy and pathological when it interferes with the development of a child's capacities for, in TA terms, spontaneity, intimacy and awareness. In therapy, unhealthy symbiosis can be understood in terms of Child-Parent or Parent-Child transactions between client and therapist. It is important to distinguish these transactions from Adult-Adult transactions which can promote the 'we'-ness of the therapeutic relationship (Saner, 1989). Traditionally, transactional analysts have been discouraged from using 'we' language, for fear of inviting or perpetuating symbiosis. However, more recent constructivist, co-creative and relational perspectives are challenging the individualism of this and others aspects of TA. One example of unhealthy symbiosis is the parent who does not let go of a child and/or is dependent on a part of him for her satisfaction or fulfilment in life. In this symbiotic system the child discounts his own needs in order to make things OK for his mother. Schiff et al. (1975: 6) give the example of a 'smothering mother' who constantly showers the infant with affection:

> *Spontaneity is interfered with because the infant does not have an opportunity to initiate affection. Intimacy is interfered with because offers of affection and acceptance of it are not bilateral. Awareness is interfered with because the infant does not have time and motivation to explore the world.*

From a neuroscientific standpoint, this suggests an over-attunement on the part of the primary carer which results in: the impediment of vitality affect and self-agency (see Stern, 1985, 2000) a distortion of the reality of how many people there are in the relationship, and of the developing child's capacity for empathy; and a lack of space in which the infant can learn about their frustration and anxiety. Invitations to symbiosis are common in therapy.

Tom: *What's your name?*
Therapist: *Keith.*
Tom: *Keith?*
Therapist: *Keith.*
Tom: *Keith?*
Therapist: *Keith.*
Tom: *Keith.*
Therapist: *That's right.*
Tom: *Your name's Keith.*
Therapist: *That's right . . . and your name's Tom.*
Tom: *Oh, my name's Tom.*
Therapist: *Yes. Tom.*
Tom: *Tom James George.*
Therapist: *Tom James George. Are those all your names?*
Tom: *You're Keith is . . . Your name is Keith James George.*
Therapist: *No, my name's Keith Tudor.*
Tom: *Keith Tudor. (Goes and hides.)*

This exchange may be understood in a number of ways. On one level it shows the therapist confronting a possible symbiotic invitation (that he has the same names as the client). The fact that Tom responds by hiding could indicate that he felt ashamed, as if he'd done something wrong. Given Tom's history, there was a danger that he may have experienced the therapist's 'No' as a rejection ('Don't be close', 'Go away'). This interaction came towards the end of the main phase of the therapy, and my thinking at the time was that it was important to support Tom's separate, self-identity. In the event, he recovered (uncovered)

quickly, came back and re-engaged in a way which suggested that he could accept and take in a difference and feel good about himself and the other and act positively – and, indeed, this stands as a summary of the outcome of Tom's therapy.

References

Allen, J.R. and Allen, B.A. (1997) A New Type of Transactional Analysis and One Version of Script Work with a Constructivist Sensibility. *Transactional Analysis Journal*, 27: 2, 89–98.

Angyal, A. (1941) *Foundations for a Science of Personality*. New York: Commonwealth Fund.

Axline, V. (1972) *Dibs: In Search of Self*. Harmondsworth: Penguin. (Original work published 1964)

Bannister, A. (1997) *The Healing Drama: Psychodrama and Dramatherapy with Abused Children*. London: Free Association Books.

Bannister, A. (2003) *Creative Therapies with Traumatized Children*. London: Jessica Kingsley.

Bannister, A. (2007) Psychodrama and Child Development. In Baim, C., Burmeister, J. and Maciel, M. (Eds.) *Psychodrama: Advances in Theory and Practice*. London: Routledge.

Berne, E. (1966) *Principles of Group Treatment*. New York: Grove Press.

Berne, E. (1968) *Games People Play*. Harmondsworth: Penguin. (Original work published 1964)

Berne, E. (1973) *Sex in Human Loving*. Harmondsworth: Penguin.

Berne, E. (1975a) *Transactional Analysis in Psychotherapy*. London: Souvenir Press. (Original work published 1961)

Berne, E. (1975b) *What Do You Say After You Say Hello?* London: Corgi. (Original work published 1972)

Breuer, J. and Freud, S. (1974) Studies on Hysteria. In Strachey, J. Strachey, A. and Richards, A. (Eds.) *The Pelican Freud Library. Vol. 3: Studies of Hysteria*. (trans Strachey, J. and A.). Harmondsworth: Penguin. (Original work published 1895)

Campos, L. (1986) Empowering Children: Primary Prevention of Script Formation. *Transactional Analysis Journal*, 16, 16–23.

Campos, L. (1988) Empowering Children II: Integrating Protection into Script Prevention Work. *Transactional Analysis Journal*, 18, 137–40.

Clarkson, P. (1992a) A Multiplicity of Therapeutic Relationship as a Principle of Integration. In Clarkson, P. *Transactional Analysis*

Psychotherapy – An Integrative Approach.
London: Routledge.

Clarkson, P. (1992b) *Transactional Analysis Psychotherapy – An Integrative Approach.*
London: Routledge.

Clarkson, P. and Fish, S. (1988a) Rechilding: Creating a New Past in the Present as a Support for the Future. *Transactional Analysis Journal*, 18, 51–9.

Clarkson, P. and Fish, S. (1988b) Systemic Assessment and Treatment Considerations in TA Child Psychotherapy. *Transactional Analysis Journal*, 18, 123–32.

Cornell, W.F. (1988) Life Script Theory: A Critical Review from a Developmental Perspective. *Transactional Analysis Journal*, 18: 4, 270–82.

Crary, E. (1993) *Without Spoiling or Spanking.* (2nd edn) Seattle, WA: Parenting Press.

Crocker, S. (1992) *A Philosophical Framework for Understanding Developmental Issues.* Paper prepared for The Gestalt Journal's Annual Conference, Boston, MA.

Dreikurs, R. (1968) *Psychology in the Classroom.* New York: Harper & Row.

Dreikurs, R. (1972) Family Counselling: A Demonstration. *Journal of Individual Psychology*, 28, 207–22.

Embleton Tudor, L., Keemar, K., Tudor, K., Valentine, J. and Worrall, M. (2004) *The Person-Centred Approach: A Contemporary Introduction.* Basingstoke: Palgrave.

English, F. (1975) The Three-Cornered Contract. *Transactional Analysis Journal*, 5: 383–4.

European Association of Transactional Analysis (1993) *Ethics and Professional Practice Guidelines.* Les Diablerets, Switzerland: EATA

Freud, S. (1909) Analysis of a Phobia in a Five-year-old Boy ('Little Hans'). In Strachey, J., Strachey, A. and Richards, A. (Eds.) *The Pelican Freud Library. Vol. 1: Case Histories I.* (trans Strachey, A. and J.). Harmondsworth: Penguin. (Original work published 1895)

Fromkin, V. and Rodman, J. (1983) *An Introduction to Language.* New York: CBS College Publishing.

Gordon, T. (1975) P.E.T. Parent Effectiveness Training. New York: P.H. Wyden.

Goulding, M.M. and Goulding, R.L. (1979) *Changing Lives Through Redecision Therapy.* New York: Grove Press.

Guerney, B.G. Jr. (1964) Filial Therapy: Description and Rationale. *Journal of Consulting Psychology*, 28: 4, 303–10.

Hargaden, H. and Sills, C. (2002) *Transactional Analysis: A Relational Perspective.* London: Brunner-Routledge.

Harris, N. (1996) Attachment Theory: Some Implications for Gestalt Therapy. *British Gestalt Journal*, 5, 103–12.

Holloway, W.H. (1974) Beyond Permission. *Transactional Analysis Journal*, 4, 15–6.

James, M. (1969) Transactional Analysis with Children: The Initial Session. *Transactional Analysis Bulletin*, 8: 29, 1–2.

James, M. (1977) *Techniques in Transactional Analysis.* Reading, MA: Addison-Wesley.

Joines, V. and Stewart, I. (2002) *Personality Adaptations: A New Guide to Human Understanding in Psychotherapy and Counselling.* Nottingham: Lifespace.

Klein, M. (1975) *The Psycho-Analysis of Children.* London: Hogarth Press. (Original work published 1932)

Lee, A. (1997) Process Contracts. In Sills, C. (Ed.) *Contracts in Counselling.* London: Sage.

Levin, P. (1988a) *Becoming the Way we Are.* (3rd edn.) Deerfield Beach, FL: Health Communications.

Levin, P. (1988b) *Cycles of Power.* Hollywood, CA: Health Communications.

Mackewn, J. (1991) *Child Development in Early Gestalt literature.* Unpublished paper.

Mahler, M.S., Pine, F. and Bergman, A. (1975) *The Psychological Birth of the Human Infant.* London: Hutchinson.

Minuchin, S. (1974) *Families and Family Therapy.* London: Tavistock.

Moreno, J.L. (1977) *Psychodrama. Vol.1.* Beacon, NY: Beacon House. (Original work published 1946)

Oaklander, V. (1982) The Relationship of Gestalt Therapy to Children. *The Gestalt Journal*, 5, 64–74.

Oaklander, V. (1988) *Windows to our Children: A Gestalt Approach to Children and Adolescents.* Highland, NY: The Centre for Gestalt Development. (Original work published 1969)

Rogers, C.R. (1931) *Measuring Personality Adjustment in Children Nine to Thirteen.* New York: Teachers College, Columbia University, Bureau of Publications.

Rogers, C.R. (1939) *The Clinical Treatment of the Problem Child.* Boston: Houghton Mifflin.

Rogers, C.R. (1951) *Client-Centered Therapy.* London: Constable.

Saner, R. (1989) Culture Bias of Gestalt Therapy: Made-in-USA. *The Gestalt Journal*, 12: 2, 57–73.

Schiff, J.L. et al. (1975) *Cathexis Reader*. New York: Harper & Row.

Schwartz, J. (1999) *Cassandra's Daughter: A History of Psychoanalysis in Europe and America*. London: Allen Lane.

Steiner, C.M. (1966) Script and Counterscript. *Transactional Analysis Bulletin*, 5: 18, 133–5.

Steiner, C.M. (1971a) *Games Alcoholics Play*. New York: Grove Press.

Steiner, C.M. (1971b) Radical Psychiatry: Principles. In Agel, J. *The Radical Therapist*. Harmondsworth: Penguin.

Stern, D.N. (1971) A Micro-analysis of Mother-infant Interaction: Behaviours Regulating Social Contact Between a Mother and her Three-and-a-half month-old Twins. *Journal of American Academy of Child Psychiatry*, 13, 402–21.

Stern, D.N. (1985) *The Interpersonal World of the Infant*. New York: Basic Books.

Stern, D.N. (2000) *The Interpersonal World of the Infant*. Rev. edn. New York: Basic Books.

Stern, D.N. (2004) *The Present Moment in Psychotherapy and Everyday Life*. New York: W.W. Norton & Co.

Summers, G. and Tudor, K. (2000) Co-creative Transactional Analysis. *Transactional Analysis Journal*, 30: 1, 23–40.

Tudor, K. (1996) TA Intragration: A Meta-theoretical Analysis for Practice. *Transactional Analysis Journal*, 26, 329–40.

Tudor, K. (1999) 'I'm OK, You're OK – and They're OK': Therapeutic Relationships in Transactional Analysis. In Feltham, C. (Ed.) *Understanding the Counselling Relationship*. London: Sage.

Tudor, K. (2003) The Neopsyche: The Integrating Adult Ego State. In Sills, C. and Hargaden, H. (Eds.) *Ego States*. London: Worth Reading.

Tudor, K. and Embleton Tudor, L. (1999) The Philosophy of Temenos. *Self & Society*, 27: 2, 32–7.

Ware, P. (1983) Personality Adaptations (Doors to Therapy). *Transactional Analysis Journal*, 13, 11–9.

West, J. (1992) *Child-Centred Play Therapy*. London: Edward Arnold.

Wheeler, G. (2002) The Developing Field: Toward a Gestalt Developmental Model. In Wheeler, G. and McConville, M. (Eds.) *The Heart of Development: Gestalt Approaches to Working with Children, Adolescents and Their Worlds*. Hillsdale, NJ: Gestalt Press/The Analytic Press.

Wheeler, G. and McConville, M. (Eds.) (2002) *The Heart of Development: Gestalt Approaches to Working with Children, Adolescents and Their Worlds*. Hillsdale, NJ: Gestalt Press/The Analytic Press.

White, J.D. and White, T. (1975) Cultural Scripting. *Transactional Analysis Journal*, 5: 1, 12–23.

Winnicott, D.W. (1965a) Dependence in Infant-care, in Child-care and in the Psycho-analytic Setting. In Khan, M.M.R. (Ed.). *The Maturational Processes and the Facilitating Environment*. London: Hogarth Press. (Original work published 1963)

Winnicott, D.W. (1965b) String: A Technique of Communication. In Khan, M.M.R. (Ed.) *The Maturational Processes and the Facilitating Environment*. London: Hogarth Press. (Original work published 1960)

Winnicott, D.W. (1971) *Playing and Reality*. Harmondworth: Penguin.

Winnicott, D.W. (1989) *The Piggle*. Harmondsworth: Penguin. (Original work published 1977)

CHAPTER 8

The First Meeting*

Dolores Munari Poda

The first tête-à-tête

Whenever we speak of children and 'meetings with children', irrespective of their reason or purpose, whether informative, medical, diagnostic, clinical, or simple conversation, it is as well never to lose sight of the fact that children are just what they are: little people with sophisticated and, at the same time, highly vulnerable mechanisms. Children look around, observe and sense their environment, perceive its atmosphere, warm or cold, moist or dry, welcoming or rejecting, attentive or distracted, organised or functionless (James, 1974). Day by day they piece together fragments of the world around them from which to draw conclusions, plan their survival (English, 1977) and define their first script decisions (Goulding and Goulding, 1979). This amazing wealth of interior activity, however, goes hand in hand with a very circumscribed power to change their surroundings. Not even a carat's weight is accorded to a child's opinions about routine matters, while their contacts with events of great moment (deaths, losses, the breaking up of families and homes) are obscured by the provision of meagre, incomplete, inappropriate, insufficient, or even frankly distorted information. It need hardly be said that they are not the one who chooses the place and time of their first tête-à-tête with a psychologist nor indeed is the latter. The child arrives at the point of the globe desired by their family, indicated, proposed or imposed by their parents or by others, such as the grandparents. In Italy, grandparents are a mighty force to be reckoned with, as children are often parked with them for the entire day. Their judgements are anxiously awaited.

A child thus arrives at a place of therapy whose attributes are extolled as magical – 'a lovely place', a strawberry patch à la Bergman; described and sometimes publicised as a kind of toyshop or games centre – 'a place with ever so many games to play'; and inhabited by strange and somewhat know-all creatures who play with children, talk things over with grown-ups, and are there for the express purpose of 'listening to other people's problems'. Embarrassment often worms its way into the decision made by the parents ("How can it be that an outsider is needed to play with, talk to and try to understand our child? Where have we gone wrong?"). A child knows exactly which way the wind is blowing. From the depths of what is half said and half unsaid, they understand that something new is on the horizon. Circumspect or clamorous, they set out to know more, ask questions, and sharpen their mind. If the answers they receive are not much help, usually neither convincing nor given with conviction, and in any event far from comprehensive, they resort to their imagination, summon up the characters they have met in cartoons, films and books or during lessons at school, and build their own personal picture of the 'mysterious place'. Successful introduction of a child into this mysterious place thus requires many qualities from the adult who dwells therein: fine-tuned sensitivity; healthy curiosity; open-mindedness acquired through experience; a visible wish to explore the world; the ability to be kind and firm, affective and containing; and, above all, an awareness of the unique nature of each consultation with its wealth of constantly interacting major and minor themes. As Binswanger (1970/1995: 148) so splendidly described it:

> The entire story of the inner life of an individual, irrespective of whether it runs a linear, consequential or a tortuous, intermittent course, is nothing other than the development of a single, yet in itself inexhaustible theme composed of multiform and equally inexhaustible major themes, themselves consisting of countless minor themes . . . Psychotherapeutic treatment is not just a psychological activity conducted by two persons around a common

*The author wishes to thank the publishers Upsel Domeneghini Editore, Padua for permission to translate some passages from her article 'Il primo colloquio con il bambino' (The first meeting with the child) which appeared in *Il Colloquio Psicologico* (The Psychological Meeting) edited by V. Calvo and D. Rocco (2003). This chapter has been translated from the Italian by John Iliffe. All quotations have been translated from the Italian, including those taken from works originally written in English (see References).

subject and a common task. It is not just a service or a contribution, but also an uninterrupted, reciprocal communicative contact, a continual interaction ... An interaction, a new interhuman relationship understood as a genuine being together (miteinander sein).

Great care must therefore be devoted to this special approach, particularly when the other party is a child.

In the period preceding what Romanini (1999) calls 'The first visit', the person young in years we are called upon to encounter has very likely gone through days when their intimacy was abused, their hours distressed and fragmented. They may have suffered frustration and disappointment, and experienced few of the splendours and many of the miseries of existence. Now this child is here with us because their way of being in the world presumably constitutes a problem for someone: parents, teachers, paediatricians, instructors. In all probability, therefore, we shall be approaching a disturbed creature, prematurely wounded by life. Our task will be to welcome them, watch them, look at them, understand them, and help them to express that which is oppressing their vital energy (English, 1988) to discover their resources and to restore options for the future (Bollas, 1989).

The therapist will need to possess a broad spectrum of capabilities and tolerance to establish a truly maieutic dialogic structure (Attanasio, 1992). They must be able to listen, ask questions, remain silent, play and be a spectator (Winnicott, 1971a) and, above all, to restore to every child the voice to which they are entitled (Salinas, 1933/1979) by letting it flow out in whatever way they choose for expressing the ideas that fill their life: games, drawings, words, looks, moments of silence.

If the first tête-à-tête is to be a true meeting (*Begegnung*), it must be free from prevarication, artifice, excess or affectation. It will be honest, simple, clear and direct, as in Winnicott's masterly description (1971a) of his meeting with the five-year-old Diana. It will also be an adventure with the risks this entails, since getting to know oneself always involves a risk (Resnik, 1990). The meeting with Diana is quoted below because it is a particular narrative style:

It was Diana who took the initiative right from the start. When I opened the door to let her mother in, I was faced by an impatient little girl thrusting out a small teddy bear. I did not look at the mother, nor at Diana, but turned

straight to the bear. 'Well, what's his name?' 'Just Teddy Bear,' she replied. In this way a strong relationship between Diana and myself was quickly established.

(Winnicott, 1971a: 88)

A meeting may also reach moments of extraordinary intimacy.

Diana took her little bear and shoved it into the breast pocket of my jacket. She tried to see how far inside it would go, examined the lining and then went on to look at the other pockets and observe that they were separate from each other.

In the game Diana and I played together, a timeless game, I felt free to be playful. Children play more readily when the other person is ready to be playful. I suddenly put my ear against the bear in my pocket and said: 'I heard him say something.' Diana was very interested. 'I think he wants someone to play with.'

(Winnicott, 1971a: 89)

If we allow intimacy to flow gently through us like a light breeze (Minkowski, 1954/2000) then the first tête-à-tête with a child will be immediately therapeutic in the true sense, since the original Greek word *therapeia* comprises the notions of attention, care and devoted attendance.

Many grown-ups: one child

The reasons why a child is brought to a psychologist are both many and varied. A consultation is sometimes suggested by a family's paediatrician, though a meeting is more frequently arranged because a kindergarten or primary school points out the need for consultation, stresses its desirability and to some extent turns it into a necessity. The reasons for such a step range from sleeping and feeding disturbances in early infancy to fear, anxiety and obsessive-compulsive disorders, adjustment and somatoform disorders, conduct and emotional disorders, depression and global alteration of psychological development (Fava Vizziello, 2003). These difficulties are often emphasised when the child comes into contact with a school class, a sport or a boy scout group. The decision to consult a psychologist rarely stems from the parents alone.

This does not change the position of the child. They are always accompanied or 'brought' to the therapist. Children never turn to a psychologist. The choice is that of their parents, who, of course, always decide 'with the best intentions' (Bergman, 1991, 1994).

Those who work with minors must thus be ready to plunge into a wide and complicated network of family relationships and interrelations whose serenity has been at least transiently deranged. A meeting with a child, in fact, involves their private and social life, their roots, the traditions of their environment, ancient secrets, and their conclusions about survival and those of the group to which they belong (Cottle, 1980; Byng-Hall, 1995). Each child constitutes a group (Munari Poda, 1999) and it is with this group that the therapist must be engaged, whether directly (parents, grandparents, babysitters) or indirectly (teachers, physicians, instructors). This is a complex relational system, strong and important for the child and established before the therapist enters the scene, a vital system in which they have discovered and experienced the good and the bad facets of their ways and means of existence. It is against this background that the therapist will be careful to translate requests, contextualise references, map out a diagnostic or therapeutic path and establish its timetable and methods (Sichem, 1991). If the way in which the parents wish to contribute to the well-being of their child is not planned and made clear from the start, if a good contract is not concluded (English, 1975; Sichem, 1991) then once again the child will be the victim and scapegoat of the entire process.

Careful exploration of the situation requires patient separation and decodification of the fancies, expectations, anxieties and frustrations of the father and the mother, and their own families, in order to shed light on the gap between unreal hopes and day-to-day reality, between the 'imagined child' and the 'actual child'.

Meeting a child

The therapist and the child are together at last. Previously there will have been a session with their parents or extended family, during which many voices will have spoken about them. I always arrange one or more preliminary meetings with parents to learn their convictions, to find out how they bring up their family, and to help them from the start to transform a 'problem child', viewed solely with the problems in mind, into a 'child to be discovered' through his unexpressed qualities so that an exploratory lode can be tapped, along with hope. Fuller understanding of parents results in more functional treatment planning for the work with

the child. As Clarkson and Fish (1988) have suggested, various ways of working within the child's system can be envisaged in order to respond to different situations. Now the concert is for a single voice, though the 'words for saying it' (Cardinal, 1975/1994: 30) for relating sufferings and thoughts, are not always ready to hand.

Interviewing children is a complicated affair. Asking the questions needed to obtain worthwhile information, while taking account of the ethical limits and the one-sidedness of the relationship, is a really hard task (Romanini, 1999). Guidelines help to show the way to go and also provide support. Yet the paths that lead to a child, apart from words, may well prove to be the most unpredictable and the most deeply coloured, the roughest and the least codified. Therapists naturally elaborate their personal styles.

In both the first tête-à-tête and during all the subsequent meetings, the prime concern is the maximum respect for the child's intimacy, free from any desire to find out at all costs, from challenges, from insistence, from rigidity. A consultation with a child is like the performance of a musical composition. It must be listened to over and over again. Every note must be examined to establish its significance within the child's history, to detect the specific points in his existence, the privileged messages, the deep-rooted injunctions. Meetings must thus be recorded and replayed many times until the manner of expression of each player become familiar, as in a favourite concerto. When is a breath taken? How is the melody shaped and which are its most important notes? Why? Would it be possible to reframe the melody? What alternatives exist? Space must be left for each sentence, each pause, and especially for the *pianissimi*, the overlaps, the *legati*, when the child and therapist chance to say the same word together while talking about everyday things or looking at a drawing as it grows. Every child teaches therapists a new way of listening to themselves: that child with that therapist, in that room, in that moment.

Like adults, children as patients would agree with Margaret Little's account of her analysis with Winnicott:

He was not infallible, but often spoke in suppositions or wondered: "I think that" "I wonder whether . . ." "It seems that . . ." This gave me the chance to feel and determine the content of what he was saying and thus be free to accept or reject it.

(Little, 1990: 48)

It was Horowitz who declared 'Seek out what is behind the notes. Behind the notes.' (Schonberg, 1992: 192). Every meeting is an adventurous journey among and behind the notes, among the words and the signs, beyond the problems, in the search for one's creative potential, this, of course, being different for the two players, freely expressed and respectfully heeded. As Romanini (1999: 443) says: 'I do not believe intimacy can exist, whatever the relationship between the partners, in the absence of a just right to withdraw. In this way alone are each player's freedom and need for trust respected.'

In the first tête-à-tête each player makes their 'voice' heard in their own way. Signs, colours, movements, rhythms and stories are all forms of 'speech'. A creativeness that had perhaps dried up is regained. Expression is given to the emotion aroused by the discovery of a new and different way of being listened to. Light is thrown on glimpses of unfamiliar settings and perhaps the door of hope becomes ajar (Milner, 1987; Bollas, 1989).

The squiggle game

Winnicott (1971a) introduced a wonderful way of conducting a tête-à-tête with a child, one that is not easy, nor spontaneous, but is open to infinite variations and ensures that a child's dignity is fully protected. Winnicott (1971b: 18) understands and stresses that 'a child's symptoms reflect a pathological state of one or both of their parents or their social environment'. It is unusual for there not to be contributory or in some way ancillary causes of a child's distress. He goes on to add: 'these are the very factors that require the maximum attention. Furthermore it is often the child himself who shows us the main deficiency of his environment'. The child points it out and the therapist's vigilant attention is needed to understand and evaluate it.

Winnicott uses what he calls the squiggle game as a form of communication in his meetings with children: 'I'm going to close my eyes and draw a line on a sheet of paper. You can turn it into anything you like. Then it will be your turn to do the same and I will make your line become what I like' (Winnicott, 1971b: 24). The words 'I'm going to close my eyes' usually have a profound effect on children. Their immediate message is that it is all right to be confident. When the therapist closes

his eyes, children often exclaim: 'So you are confident!' in a mixture of incredulity and longing to be the same. The first tête-à-tête, therefore, may well give rise to what a child once called 'a two-piece' drawing, something that the child and the grown-up work out together, that facilitates the beginning of their relationship and nourishes an underlying trust.

Winnicott also adds a sort of manifesto of the respect that must be shown towards children. It is worth quoting in full because it provides a clear picture of the meaning of meetings with children in difficulty. Therapists naturally express comments on the drawings produced and set out to interpret them:

Whenever I come out with an interpretation and the child does not agree, or does not answer, I am ready to immediately retract what I have said. My interpretation in such cases is often wrong and the child is able to correct me. On other occasions, there may be resistance, which means that my interpretation is correct, but denied. Its non-acceptance means I have presented it at the wrong moment or incorrectly, and so I withdraw it unconditionally. Even if it is correct, I have evidently been mistaken in presenting its contents at that moment and in that way. Dogmatic interpretation faces a child with only two choices: acceptance of what I have said as propaganda, or rejection of not only the interpretation, but also myself and the whole system. I think and hope that in the relationship they establish with me children feel entitled to reject what I say or the way in which I interpret things. I firmly believe that these meetings are dominated by the child, not by me.

(Winnicott, 1971b)

By 'dominated' Winnicott intends that the child must be respected as a feeling and thinking interlocutor, protected by the therapist who, for their part, must always remember that when their life crosses that of a child, they become a permanent feature of the child's script, and vice versa. They become a witness of passions, perhaps 'a saving witness' in accordance with Miller's felicitous definition (Miller, 1988/1993).

An appropriate emotional atmosphere, therefore, is essential for the attainment of a successful meeting: an uncontaminated state of expectation, not overshadowed by the wishes of parents nor the proposals of teachers, a time for understanding and not for judging. A generous readiness to listen to the *voce sola* (the single voice).

Here is an account of my first tête-à-têtes with four children: Cosimo and Luca, who drew and

Illustration 8.1 A scattered rainbow

made up stories, and Lanfranco and Eugenio, who played and made up stories.

Speaking through drawings

I am a painter (Cosimo)

Cosimo is six and a half, strong and powerful. He realises his difficulties, but does not like to talk about them. We know that children do not need to use words right away to reveal what is torturing them. Sometimes it is not even possible. Pain is speechless, beyond the reach of words. It is useless in cases of this kind to resort to conventional methods, to interrogate. Children communicate their emotions in their own way. Cosimo says: "I'm a painter". He speaks, in fact, with colours. He takes a big handful and holds them tight. He starts off with the greens, then moves to the yellows, the pinks, orange and lastly red. Red is spread out in a deep blotch through a tangle of boldly drawn signs. There are few blue lines, and so much violet that the green and orange almost disappear. "It's a rainbow", he assures me, though "a scattered rainbow".

"It's come out as a scattered rainbow, but lovely. For me, it's even more lovely. I don't know about you". Cosimo is familiar with battles, conflictinng opinions, cutting and disparaging remarks. He prefers to express a cautious and slightly defensive appreciation that correctly

leaves everyone free to make up their own minds. It is his way of approaching things. He sees how the land lies. It is up to the therapist to understand. The therapist looks at the scattered rainbow and declares her opinion aloud, weighing her words to make sure they are not too many and do not result in other injuries. Remembering Winnicott, she ventures a comment: "So many colours filled with light. Rather like some of the lovely things we have that are sometimes scattered and fall to pieces. The pieces are beautiful all the same, though it's hard to remember what the whole things looked like."

Cosimo gets the message, but does not take it up. He repeats: "I'm a painter. I can also do complete and scattered tassels. Rainbows, too, I do whole and scattered." He is stressing his skills and boasting of his technical capabilities. He says: "Look at the black. Can you see what it's like? The blue's a bit calmer, but the red is fire. It breaks everything. It burns everything." His voice drops to a whisper. At the time of the Talmud, the philosopher Martin Buber (1995: 10) reminds us, the mystic doctrine was still a secret that could only be confided to a Master of the Whispers. In front of his provocative palette, Cosimo whispers that he has a horrible secret. "It's a nasty secret." It is making life hard for him, but he clearly does not want to talk about it.

He takes up the felt-tip pens again and draws a house with no foundations that rises from the

Illustration 8.2   A house

paper, a fragile affair on two blue, flamingo-legged walls. So much lightness, or perhaps so much recognised fragility seems to get across to him, to move him. He looks at the house and says: "Now I'll paint the roof water-green, it's the colour I like best." The moving softness of the roof of a house that will no longer be able to protect those who live in it: this is the countertransferential feeling of the therapist. Above, at the edge of the sheet, a piece of sky, also in the form of a roof, the last boundary and extreme cover. Cosimo continues: "The door, look, it's emerald green, that goes well with blue." His voice becomes laboured: "Now I can draw a rider on a galloping horse. They are going to rest in the house. They go up the stairs, but cannot find the bed. Then they find it. It had been hidden by a horseman who came to burn the house down because he was wicked. He was born wicked. Look here. This black mark in the centre of the house is the bed. Now I'll light the fire. The fire is burning the bed and setting the whole house on fire." (This is followed by a long silence. The pencil goes back and forth over the place of the bed.)

Then, once again in a whisper: "The horseman was born wicked. But I knew people who were born good. There's you, my mother, my brother, my girl friend Vale and then my father. He is fire and flame and sometimes I'm a bit scared."

Cosimo's pictures are also fire and flame: in plain colours, violent and disruptive. They are a concentrated story, as drawings always are, especially those produced in a child's first tête-à-tête. An endless tale of emotions that compresses within a special palette the burdens and disturbances of the past, the nights without stars, beloved faces suddenly transformed into incomprehensible masks, heart-rending tearings apart, separations, weepings, fires, the central story of every child (Balbo, 1990; Munari Poda, 2003). Yet they also comprise hope. If Hillman (1995) is right in saying that black smothers the old colours to allow new colours to appear, then new life will be born from the ashes of a world destroyed. Cosimo has summarised his short taste of existence, his six and half years of passions, in signs and colours. He has synopsised dramatic happenings and expressed his point of view. Cosimo is alive, active, convinced. His alliance with the therapist is established simply, directly and confidently. His creations are dispensed with a lavish hand. Finally he says: "Now I'll do another rainbow because the storm is over. I need a huge rainbow." He takes two sheets, glues them together and draws a mighty rainbow.

This rainbow, generated within or perhaps from his relationship with the therapist, is entrusted with the hope that a harmony will be

Illustration 8.3   A rainbow

recomposed in his life and that the colours will regain their true space in the sky and recreate what Turoldo (1991: 487) refers to as 'the beauty of that moment':

> The beauty of that moment when the rain
> drummed on the roof of the farmhouse
> and you were at peace with the world
> remembering friends and times gone by,
> the hopes and the loves
> that adorned the windowsills!
> Then the joy of the thunder
> that shed light again on the fields
> and the whole crown of the neighbouring hills.

That's me in the balloon! (Luca)

Luca is, according to his parents, lazy: he does not 'render' enough. Children today are seen as a costly investment from which a return is expected. A child must therefore 'render' in the form of success at school, since this will make his parents the subject of gratifying compliments on their qualities as educators and rearers. On the kids' 'kerb market', however, Luca is a 'no trade', frozen stock. At school, he does not pay much attention, does not really participate, does not make his presence felt. Luca, in short, is 'not up to much'.

His face is broad, open, sterile and resigned. His sober introduction of himself is revealing:

"I'm ten and in the fourth class. *I'm not all that good* at school. I play football, but *I'm not all that good* in the football class, I go to the religious lessons, but *I'm not all that good.*" The therapist listens and takes note of a life downtrodden, the embarrassment that accompanies its telling, the unease aroused by the feeling of being examined, the deprival of strokes (Steiner, 1971; Romanini, 1999). Strokes provide the therapist with a powerful, yet very delicate therapeutic tool. Re-establishment of a correct economy of strokes requires calmness, patience, and accuracy. For a person unaccustomed to being recognised as such, the risk lies in refusing, barring the entry, or underrating the attention of the other person (Steiner, 1971).

"Do you like drawing?" The answer is just what one would expect from a good boy who has adjusted to his situation: "Yes, but *I'm not all that good.*" The therapist answers on the rebound: "Neither am I." Silence. What did Alice Miller say? 'By demanding performance, they kill a child's creativity' (Miller, 1988: 70). Luca's fingers slowly rove over the felt-tip pens. He picks one up and colours a sky-blue rectangle, then an aeroplane, a balloon, a fox and a bush. He tells the story as he goes on drawing. "The aeroplane has hit the man. Before he succumbs, the man fires at the cockpit. He strikes, too. He hits the cockpit of the aeroplane. The plane falls on the

Illustration 8.4   The war of the Germans

man. And the man dies. There's a fox looking on. Since this is a desert, you can only see a bush. The balloon is coming here to catch the fox. It is carrying a German who wants to capture the fox. He regards it as sacred because it has eaten one of his friends. The fox lay in wait for him and ate him, and so he is no more. The man in the balloon has a transmitter. He catches the fox and takes it away. Later it, too, will be eaten". The title of the drawing is: *The war of the Germans.*

The therapist follows the construction of the picture. First the intensely sky-blue rectangle (a desire for peace?), then the thin strip of ground (a very slender, unsure base), a red figure holding a pistol, the bush, the fox and, lastly, the balloon topped by a helmet with a swastika. Next, attention is paid to the way the tale is told with the use of uncommon words, such as 'succumb', and associations (the 'sacred' fox). The therapist is at a loss and examines the final picture very carefully. Luca also studies it and then adds the little figure in the previously empty basket of the balloon. The therapist says: "This is a complicated drawing, like the story. I find it very interesting." The initial portion of genuine strokes thus directly delivered gives Luca, so convinced of his little worth, a new awareness of his potential, respect for his fantasy and a celebration of the moment (Bollas, 1989).

"I'm very interested", says the therapist. "Now suppose, just for fun, we were to give faces you know to the persons you've drawn. A family, for example, who would be who?" Lacklustre Luca, according to the label he has been saddled with, comes fully alive. He invents, creates with a more certain hand and seems at ease. He starts with himself. "That's me in the balloon! The pilot sees everything from up there. He gets by because he eats the fox and becomes crafty. Do you know they say that anyone who eats a fox acquires its cunning? Dad's the pilot of the 'plane, Mum's the one on the ground, wounded. My mother, d'you know? She's pregnant, I'm afraid she may die. The fox is my cat Mitzi." This is the distracted, inconclusive Luca: the one that is out of order and does not do well at school. As in so many of my first tête-à-têtes, the first drawing relates that which could never be uttered with the spoken word.

A plane is diving diagonally across the centre of this terrible *War*. It is carrying some bombs (shown as vermilion blotches) and spewing others against the red figure lying on the ground who retaliates and hits the plane. The pilot dies and so does the figure on the ground. The destruction thus declared is complete. Luca portrays his parents as a couple engaged in a reciprocal, fiercely aggressive combat from which there is no escape, a bloody interpretation of a death-bringing, amorous encounter. The wide-open eyes of the thin, fragile figure in the basket below the balloon stare down at the scene. The balloon is tethered by faded green ropes. "Sometimes I feel at the end of my tether", Luca admits. The brilliant green bush is the only sign of life in the desert. In the eyes of

Illustration 8.5   The dinosaur and his house

the therapist, it is an unmistakeable sign of survival.

Yet there are some resources to hand. Luca reveals them in the thick green foliage of the little bush. Green in a child's drawings is often regarded as a sign for hope and growth (Balbo, 1990). The balloon offers a means of being not too close and not too far, and can be interpreted in several ways. A place where children who do not know where they are, who live suspended, rising and falling, can feel at home, or perhaps a desire for detachment akin to that which underlies the three-year-old's walkie-talkie period (English, 1977). On the threshold of adolescence, too, children like to be both 'close' and 'apart', within earshot, perhaps, but out of reach. Because everything generated in the room where the meetings take place has a meaning within the relationship that is beginning to form, the therapist thinks that the metaphor of the balloon could also serve as an elegant illustration of the 'nearness' the child could feel good with also within the therapeutic relationship: not too close, yet not to distant.

Talking through playing

I am a little green dinosaur (Lanfranco)

Lanfranco is almost seven. He is solemn, inscrutable, remote. He is holding a little green dinosaur. He says nothing. The therapist knows he lives in a part of Piedmont called the Langhe, and to put him at his ease asks him to say something about his town. But this scares him. Every question upsets him. He believes the therapist is trying to find out his address. He is agitated and unable to think clearly (Schiff and Schiff, 1971). Almost breathlessly, he blurts out: "I haven't got the address, I haven't got it, I don't know, I don't know." The therapist thinks that he is a 'missing' child and remembers Christa Wolf's phrase: 'Where I am not: it is there that happiness lies' (Wolf, 1979/1984: 10).

The therapist looks for a firm footing and sticks to reality. 'I see you've got a dinosaur there.' "Yes", says Lanfranco. A long silence follows. He continues to clutch the dinosaur. The therapist considers the importance of this object, but says nothing, like Lanfranco. Then Lanfranco starts to move the dinosaur a little. Therapist: "Let's play a game. Let's put him on this sheet of paper and see if we can manage to draw his outlines because I'm not all that good at doing dinosaurs." "Neither am I", says Lanfranco in a neutral, uninterested tone. The therapist continues: "I'll give you a sheet of paper. Which colour would you like?" "White." The therapist is encouraged by this first sign of a decision. Lanfranco lays the dinosaur gently on the sheet of paper and traces its outlines. It seems to be set on four paws with wheels like a mechanical toy. Its outlines are lightly drawn, soft, uncertain. The very gentle expression on its little snout makes it seem a member of a new, rare and somewhat fragile species. Lanfranco adds a sun that strangely rolls from left to right. If we accept the notion that the sun is the symbol of the father figure, we should have a ruffled, but very luminous idea of this large, warm halo turning in the wrong direction. Lanfranco carries on in his own way and adds a slightly tilted yellow farmhouse with a red roof, glowering black eyes dripping eyeshadow, a little brown door, and a thin meadow base.

At last Lanfranco sighs with satisfaction and says "It's the dinosaur's house". The therapist wonders: "Can the dinosaur fit into the house?" "It's not really a house", Lanfranco replies, "but a kennel with a little door." "How does he get in?" the therapists asks. "He puts his head down". To show what he means Lanfranco measures the house with the dinosaur in his hand. The therapist thinks about 'putting his head down' as the metaphor for the state of existence of this adapted, silent child. Then Lanfranco starts on the landscape. He seems to like moving the dinosaur and drawing. "Here I've put the mountains." He never lets go of the dinosaur. "This was when I did my tables well." The therapist does not understand and asks: "Can you tell me what you mean?" "Yes, the schoolmistress has just given me the dinosaur because I knew my multiplication tables well." Lanfranco comes alive. The recollection of his successes kindles his enthusiasm. He shifts the dinosaur around and plays with it. He talks to himself: "Look, look, now he's going to do a somersault." He takes a light transparent sheet of paper and draws a double bed on the left edge. "Here is the bed. He has to be careful when he does his somersaults otherwise he could hurt himself on the railing. Now I'll do the dinosaur. Can you find me a paler colour for his tummy? That's the most delicate part of dinosaurs. He's here. Mum and Dad are on the other pillow. My brother has a little bed near the door."

The dinosaur goes up and down and whirls around. It is alive. The first tête-à-tête draws to a close. A little smile goes along with the arrangement of the next meeting. Lanfranco has spoken about himself through his small, transitional object, the reward for success at school in a world full of hardships and frustrations. Regarded as 'unsuited to' the world, inadequate, 'strange', cold and distant, he spoke through his little green dinosaur which, as he

Illustration 8.6   The dinosaur and his bed

very clearly explained, needs a little meadow, a kennel-house, a sun, albeit ruffled, a large bed on which to do somersaults without hitting the railing – and a little love and warm acceptance.

I'm afraid the world is going to come to an end (Eugenio)

The life of the four-year-old Eugenio is well guided by his mother. His father is in a place he cannot leave. Eugenio regularly visits this place with his mother. Our tête-à-tête came about because Eugenio's sleep has recently been troubled by nightmares. He is afraid at night. "I don't know what of", he tells his mother. We meet, therefore, to play and perhaps make the acquaintance of these obscure phantoms.

Eugenio is a lovely child, trusting and ready to talk about his days, a somewhat picaresque tale of hunting a mole in a field near his home, of hens and cockerels, of squirrel's tails, and tortoise eggs eaten by horrid sewer rats. He is convincing – if you make allowance for the grandiosity spontaneously generated by his crop of four full

Figure 8.1   Wooden figures 1

years. The starting point of our tête-à-tête is the therapist's big box of little wooden animals, which immediately unleashed fantasies and emotions. Eugenio likes to play. He picks up the animals, feels them all over, looks at them and begins his tale. "Once, you know, I caught a little blue mole with my hands and put it in a basin." A mild, harmless story, immediately followed, however, by a gruesome account of hens, all killed, and the cockerel, too, its head chopped off, and a gnawed squirrel's tail found in the garden. "And the squirrel was dead". He speaks about

two tortoises and their eggs, and remembers they did not hatch the last time. "The little tortoises died, suffocated, I think." The shadow of death floods over animals and fables alike. Eugenio himself is taken aback. But he pulls himself together and says: "I'll take the toy cars. All the little vehicles are going to visit the animals."

The animals, however, are none too pleased to see them and trouble breaks out. The rhinoceros charges a country bus and the cow tips it over on its back. The horses attack a large open tourer. The cars fly through the air and crash on the

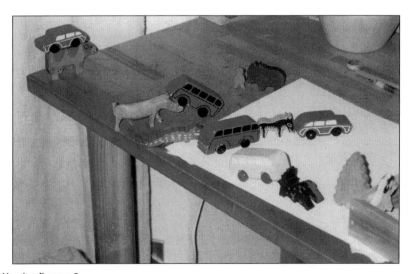

Figure 8.2   Wooden figures 2

Figure 8.3   Wooden figures 3

table. Eugenio comments: ''They're tossed in the air, I tell you. All these toy cars can be catapulted. There's only one way to stop being thrown into the air. The owners of the park come and do something to the animals, such as taking a whip and beating them. But the men will die, all of them, because the crocodile swallows cars and people in a single gulp.''

Eugenio is in the throes of a sort of death-bringing headiness. The therapist tries to speak: ''What world is . . .'' but Eugenio cuts her short and interrupts: ''Here is a world of fear. If I've put in a tree or two, that doesn't matter. It's a world of fear all the same.'' Eugenio gets up from the carpet and makes a few karate passes. He says: ''We protect ourselves with karate. We've got to be a bit strong. Look at this one here eating a baby, what a way to go on!''

Therapist:	How frightening!
Eugenio:	Frightening?
Therapist:	Frightening. Are you afraid sometimes?
Eugenio:	Nooo!

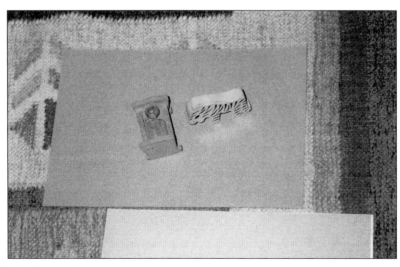

Figure 8.4   Wooden figures 4

Therapist:	Well, I am.
Eugenio (yielding):	If I come to think of it, I'm afraid of the dark. But look at that. The cars have deliberately driven into a lot of animals.
Therapist:	Why deliberately?
Eugenio (ignoring the question):	They're defending themselves. The baby's squashed. He's squashed, I'm telling you. Look. They won't be all that happy. The cars slaughtered them. In the end, the cars died, all of them. Lots of reinforcements are needed. Wait till I get some more animals. Here everyone has died. I'm afraid the world is going to come to an end. They've even massacred that strange animal. All dead. Let's go. Let's get away.

Eugenio has finished his game, cast out his distressful drama. He is very tired. He leaves the room. When he was small, there was an old piano in the waiting room. Eugenio sits on the stool and runs his fingers over the keys. He strums a kind of blues, very softly. He bends over the keys to listen to the notes more clearly. He calls his mother over and they play four-handed. He says: "The music is lovelier when played by four hands". He also asks the therapist to join them. He says: "With so many hands you hear the concert." Eugenio has used terrible voices to express his fear of life and death. He also tells us how you can replenish yourself with hope: by playing the piano, but together, in concert. Six hands on the piano keyboard are indeed a happy foretaste of the nascent therapeutic alliance.

Conclusion

During their first tête-à-tête every child uses their own very personal language, be it graphic, narrative, musical or in the form of play, to illustrate their way of being in the world and offer glimpses of their emotions and unconscious fantasies and the ups and downs of their inner heart. Several challenges must be faced by the therapist in this first tête-à-tête. They must know how to be worthy of trust and how to take in a child's central story by focusing on the problem that forms its core, as well as on the child's potential resources. They must be able to remain 'with' the child and not bureaucratically 'in front' of them. These requirements constitute the meaning of every subsequent meeting. Lastly, it must never be forgotten that 'the healing process is not just an art and a craft. It is also a mystery' (Clarkson, 1989: 202).

References

Attanasio, S. (1992) Il Dialogo Maieutico (The Maieutic Dialogue). *Rivista Italiana di Analisi Transazionale e Metodologie Terapeutiche*, 7: 23, 7–12.

Balbo, G. (1990) Aliamet. *La Psychanalyse de l' Enfant*, 8, 9–28.

Bergman, I. (1994) *Con le Migliori Intenzioni* (With the Best Intentions, C.G. Cima, trans). Milano: Garzanti. (Original work published in Swedish 1991)

Binswanger, L. (1995) *Per Una Antropologia Fenomenologica* (Towards a Phenomenological Anthropology, E. Filippini, trans). Milano: Feltrinelli, (Original work published in German 1970)

Bollas, C. (1989) *Forces of Destiny*. London: Free Association Books.

Buber, M. (1995) *Le Storie di Rabbi Nachman* (The Stories of Rabbi Nachman). (Original work published in German)

Byng-Hall, J. (1995) *Rewriting Family Scripts*. London: Tavistock Publications.

Cardinal, M . (1994) *Le Parole per Dirlo* (The Words to Say, N. Banas, trans). Milano: Bompiani. (Original work published in French 1975)

Clarkson, P. and Fish, S. (1988) Systemic Assessment and Treatment Considerations in TA Child Psychotheraphy. *Transactional Analysis Journal*, 18: 2, 123–32.

Clarkson, P. (1989) *Gestalt Counselling in Action*. London: Sage.

Cottle,T.J. (1980) *Children's Secrets*. New York: Anchor Press.

English, F. (1975) The Three-Cornered Contract. *Transactional Analysis Journal*, 5, 383–4.

English, F. (1977) What Shall I do Tomorrow? In Barnes, G. (Ed.) *Transactional Analysis After Eric Berne*. NewYork: Harper's College Press.

English, F. (1988) Whither Scripts? *Transactional Analysis Journal*, 18: 4, 194–303.

Fava Vizziello, G. (2003) *Psicopatologia dello sviluppo* (The Psychopathology of Development). Bologna: Il Mulino.

Goulding, M.M. and Goulding, R.L. (1979) *Changing Lives Through Redecision Therapy*. New York: Brunner/Mazel.

Hillman, J. (1995, August) Il Colore 'Non-colore'. (The Colour of Non-colour). Interview. *La Stampa*.

James, M. (1974) Self Reparenting: Theory and Process. *Transactional Analysis Journal*, 4: 3, 32–9.

Little, M. (1990) *Psychotic Anxieties and Containment*. New York: Jason Aronson.

Miller, A. (1993) *La Chiave Accantonata* (The Untouched Key). Milano: Garzanti. (Original work published in German 1988)

Milner, M. (1987) *The Suppressed Madness of Sane Men*. London: Institute of Psycho-Analysis.

Minkowski, E. (2000) Espace, Intimitè, Habitat (Space, Intimacy, Habitat). In Leoni, F. (Ed. and trans) *Cosmologia e Follia*. Napoli: Guida. (Original work published in German 1954)

Munari Poda, D. (1999) Ogni Bambino è un Gruppo (Every Child is a Group). *Rivista Italiana di Analisi Transazionale e Metodologie Terapeutiche*, 37, 30–8.

Munari Poda, D. (2003) *La Storia Centrale* (The Central Story). Milano: La Vita Felice.

Resnik, S. (1990) *Mental Space*. Torino: Bollato Boringhieri.

Romanini, M.T. (1999) *Costruirsi Persona* (Building Oneself as a Person). Milano: La Vita Felice.

Salinas, P. (1979) *La Voce a Te Dovuta* (The Voice You Deserve, E. Scoles, trans) Torino: Einaudi. (Original work published in Spanish 1933)

Schiff, A.W. and Schiff, J.L. (1971) Passivity. *Transactional Analysis Journal*, 1, 71–8.

Schonberg, H.C. (1992) *Horowitz*. New York: Simon and Schuster.

Sichem, V. (1991) Le Multicontrat en Therapie d'Enfants (Multicontracts in Child Therapy). *Actualitès en Analyse Transactionelle*, 60, 147–51.

Steiner, C. (1971) The Stroke Economy. *Transactional Analysis Journal*, 1, 9–15.

Turoldo, D. M. (1991) *O Sensi Miei . . . Poesie 1948–1988* (O My Senses . . . Poems 1948–1988). Milano: Rizzoli.

Winnicott, D.W. (1971a) *Playing and Reality*. London: Tavistock Publications.

Winnicott, D.W. (1971b) *Therapeutic Consultations in Child Psychiatry*. London: Hogarth Press.

Wolf, C. (1984) *Nessun Luogo. Da Nessuna Parte* (No Place. From Nowhere) Cocconi, M.G. and Sobottka, J.M. Milano: Rizzoli. (Original work published in German 1979)

CHAPTER 9

Attachment, Separation and Loss

Kath Dentith and Jean Lancashire

And a woman who held a babe against her bosom
said, Speak to us of Children.
And he said:
Your children are not your children.
They are the sons and daughters of Life's longing for
itself.
They come through you but not from you.
And though they are with you yet they belong not to
you.
You may give them your love but not your thoughts,
For they have their own thoughts.
You may house their bodies but not their souls,
For their souls dwell in the house of tomorrow,
Which you cannot visit, not even in your dreams.
You may strive to be like them, but seek not to make
them like you.
For life goes not backward nor tarries with yesterday.
Kahlil Gibran (1926: 22)

This chapter considers the theory of attachment
when working therapeutically with children and
young people. The authors show how attachment
patterns develop as a result of ruptures to early
relationships. Through the integration of
attachment theory and transactional analysis we
will demonstrate how the disruption of the
arousal/relaxation cycle can lead children to
form script beliefs about self, others and the
world. The main focus of this chapter is on the
development and quality of the attachment
between a child and his caregivers. Separation
and loss represent ruptures in attachment, and as
such, are dealt with in only brief detail. The
nature of attachments within different cultures
and ethnic groups, whilst relevant, are not within
the scope of this particular chapter. Using case
studies, we demonstrate how we work with each
of the attachment patterns using concepts from
transactional analysis (TA) theory.

The concept of 'attachment theory' as
developed by John Bowlby (1951) has enabled
professionals to understand why children need to
develop close relationships with their caregivers.
Bowlby's theory, and that of others, has provided
a platform for understanding what happens to
the psychological, emotional and behavioural
development of children who have not
experienced satisfactory relationships. Secure
attachments in infancy are a good predictor of
later emotional and social adjustment and
eventually help the child develop
self-responsibility.

According to the International Transactional
Analysis Association, TA is a 'theory of
personality and systematic psychotherapy for
personal growth and personal change'. Eric
Berne, the founder of TA, recognised the
importance of early and ongoing attachments.
Healthy development cannot take place unless
the child is supported and socialised in a secure
relationship. Many children who have
experienced loss, due to divorce, rejection, death,
adoption, fostering, domestic violence, abuse or
neglect, show signs of underlying emotional
problems that usually involve a lack of
attachment and emotional developmental delay.
These then contribute to behavioural difficulties.

History of attachment

John Bowlby (1951), child psychiatrist and
psychoanalyst, developed his theory of
attachment and loss in the 1950s. Bowlby (1969:
371) defined attachment as a child being 'strongly
disposed to seek proximity to and contact with a
specific figure and to do so in certain situations,
notably when he is frightened, tired or ill'. He
drew on the work of Konrad Lorenz (1935) an
ethnologist who studied the interaction of genetic
and social forces on animals. Lorenz observed
'imprinting', a special form of learning akin to
instinct that occurs in some species of birds. Soon
after birth, the chicks would quickly notice their
mother and instinctively follow her around
despite the absence of food. Bowlby further
observed that animals from the same species
usually remain in close proximity to their mother.
He suggested that this attachment behaviour is
genetically predetermined; the purpose being
survival and preservation of the species. His
interest in the study of animal behaviour
subsequently led to his theory that children need
a caregiver who is a source of protection, safety
and comfort.

Bowlby (1951) in his research, studied children in hospital who were separated from their parents for at least a week. At that time, mothers were not allowed to visit their children in hospital as it was thought that this contact would distress the child. Although Bowlby's research focused on mothers as the caregiver, the authors wish to note that fathers and other caregivers may also be main carers. Bowlby observed emotional reactions in the infants during the period of separation. He identified three stages to these reactions. At first, the child would *protest* at their mother's absence by crying, being angry, and searching for her. After a few days, the child would appear to experience *despair*, whereby they became withdrawn and refused comfort, play and food. Finally, after a few days, the child would *detach* from relationships and become further withdrawn, making few or no demands for comfort or attachment.

According to Bowlby, a child's mental health is dependant upon the child experiencing a warm intimate and continuous relationship with their mother, in which both find satisfaction and enjoyment. Attachment begins prenatally on a neurological and emotional level, and is dependant both, on how the mother takes care of herself, as well as her feelings towards the baby during pregnancy. Ainsworth (1978) a researcher who worked with Bowlby in the 1950s, used the term 'bonding' for the mother's relationship towards her baby, and 'attachment' for the baby's relationship towards their mother.

Human hungers

Berne (1970: 189) identified a range of 'human hungers'. These are basic psychological needs that, when met, enable infants to maintain physical, mental and emotional well-being. He wrote 'Just as the human body has a hunger for food and vitamins and will waste away without them, so the nervous system has a hunger for sensations and will fall apart if they are taken away'. Smith (2001: 10) summarised Berne's theory of human hungers and identified stimulus hunger as, 'a need for physical, emotional and intellectual contact with others'; recognition hunger as, 'a need to have one's existence as an individual recognised'; and structure hunger as, 'a need to structure one's time to meet the need for strokes'.

Berne (1970) defined a stroke as a unit of recognition. He used this term as the child initially receives recognition by touch from the primary caregiver. Steiner (1974: 58) supported Berne's notion that strokes are as indispensable as food and restated that 'strokes are as necessary to human life as other primary biologically needs such as food, water, and shelter – needs which if not satisfied will lead to death'. He identified different types of strokes, for example, positive strokes that are pleasant to receive and negative strokes that feel unpleasant. Strokes can be verbal or non verbal. Steiner also considered that it is the need for strokes that motivates people to behave in certain ways in relationships and this can be seen in the cycles below (see Figures 9.1 and 9.4).

Figure 9.1   Positive arousal relaxation cycle (Fahlberg, 1991) with example

Healthy attachment cycle

In order to survive, a newborn infant is totally dependent upon the response of the caregiver. The attachment and bonding between the caregiver and infant is a result of their interactions with each other. The infant initiates interaction with their caregiver by using attachment behaviours such as crying and the caregiver relieves the infant's tension through unconditional positive strokes. These are conveyed by physical touch, holding close eye contact, and smiling, all of which satisfy the infant and enable them to trust that the caregiver will meet their needs. This is called the 'arousal relaxation cycle'; Figure 9.1 illustrates a successful arousal-relaxation cycle between caregiver and child. For the child, successful repetition of this cycle builds a sense of trust, security and attachment with the caregiver.

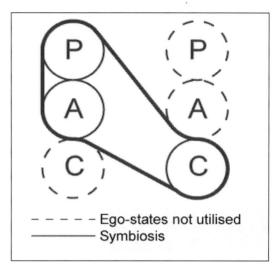

- - - - - Ego-states not utilised
———— Symbiosis

Figure 9.2   First order symbiosis

> *Lucy, for example, was aged eight months when removed from her mother's care due to the neglect she experienced. Lucy's attachment needs were unmet and she learnt not to make demands on her caregiver. Lucy was later placed with a foster carer who responded to her cues and met her needs consistently. Lucy is now 18 months old and is developing a secure attachment to her carers. This is evidenced by the way she clings appropriately to her caregiver when a stranger enters the room.*

Symbiosis

Attachment, therefore, is an emotional bond with a specific caregiver and is demonstrated by the need for physical closeness and dependency between infant and the mother. Schiff et al. (1975) recognised the importance of the early relationship between the infant and the main caregiver in the concept of 'healthy symbiosis'. Symbiosis is a relationship in which, 'two or more individuals behave as though between them they form a whole person' (ibid.). This means that neither person will cathect their full complement of ego states in the relationship. One person will cathect Parent and Adult and exclude Child and the other will cathect Child and exclude Parent and Adult (see Figure 9.2). They will operate as though they have only three ego states between them.

Schiff et al. (1975: 5) stated that: 'Symbiosis is a natural occurrence between parents and children' which develops as a result of the oral stage of development where there is 'a merging or

sharing' of their needs, thus forming a 'healthy' symbiosis. The caregiver's role in this symbiosis is to tune into the infant's communication and to respond to the distressed child, both physically and emotionally. Woollams and Huige (1977) however, viewed that 'normal dependency' is a more appropriate term because there is no discounting of ego states as the infant has not developed a functioning Parent and Adult (see Figure 9.3).

The parents draw on their own Parent and Adult ego states in order to care for, and protect the child (Stewart, 1987), this 'aims at eventual autonomy for the maturing youngster' (Woollams and Brown, 1978: 109). This will be a careful balance between the parents' offering 'permissions' in relation to the child's growing developmental needs.

In a normal dependency the mother senses the child's needs and meets this whatever she is feeling. When the arousal cycle (see Figure 9.1) is positive and consistent in this way, the infant learns how to self-regulate affect. This means that although a child may not always get what they want, the caregiver will help the child to regulate their feelings through attunement. Stern (1985) described this as the possibility of sharing emotional states where the caregiver acts as a container for the child's affective expressions. Secure attachments enable a child to increase their feelings of self worth and age appropriate self-reliance.

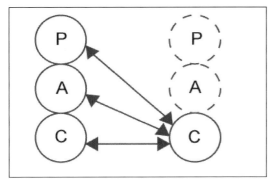

Figure 9.3 Normal dependency (Woollams and Huige, 1977)

Negative attachment cycle

Attachment can be affected by various circumstances, which impact upon the interaction between the child, their caregiver and their environment. Children who are born with conditions such as stimulation and sensory difficulties or learning disabilities sometimes experience difficulty developing an attachment, even though they have experienced parenting that promotes healthy attachments. Equally, if a carer is not attuned to the child's need for nurturing, protection and safety, the child may internalise their distress and, as a result, be unable to develop trust in the carer (see Figure 9.4).

When a child has a negative arousal cycle they experience inconsistency, unpredictability and do not learn how to self-regulate affect. Instead, they learn to regulate their feelings in an ineffective way, thus making decisions which perpetuate their negative view of life, and in TA terms, confirming their script or life plan. Berne (1972: 445) defined a script as a 'A life plan based on a decision made in childhood, reinforced by the parents, justified by subsequent events, and culminating in a chosen alternative.'

Within the negative cycle, a child accepts or experiences negative strokes from his caregivers whose style of parenting lacks attunement. Their parenting may be insensitive, inconsistent, or frightening. Although these strokes are unpleasant, this lack of attunement is familiar to the child, who may actively seek negative strokes as the only recognition available. A lack of positive strokes may cause a child to be underdeveloped. Clarkson and Fish (1992) stated that this developmental difficulty may be irreversible. Children, who have experienced intermittent neglect, or abuse, are generally more likely to exhibit difficulties in their ability to attach and relate to others. Such children frequently experience emotional, psychological, and behavioural problems alongside developmental delay (Fahlberg, 1991).

For example, Adam, aged 11, was referred for therapy after sexually abusing other children. Both his parents had physically, emotionally and sexually abused him from a young age. He suffered significant trauma, which resulted in an irreversible developmental delay and a lack of conscience. Adam

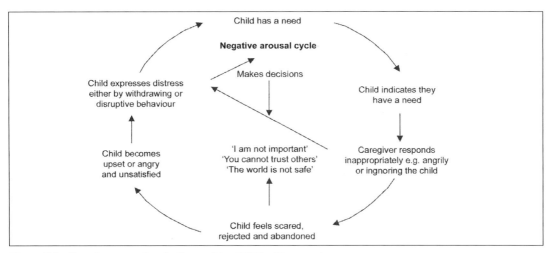

Figure 9.4 Negative arousal cycle (Lancashire, 2002) with example

presented as being unable to attach to his foster carers and functioned as a three-year-old child in terms of his thinking, feeling and behaviour. Adam was unable to accept any responsibility for his offences, and sadly, is not allowed to socialise with other children due to the sexual risk he poses to them.

Another aspect of the negative cycle is that a child may start to look after the caregiver by not expressing their needs. This unhealthy dependency develops as the child takes care of the caregiver's emotional needs and may become a life-long pattern known as second order symbiosis. The caregiver appears to take care of the child on a social level, whilst the child cares for the parent on a psychological level (see Figure 9.5). We find the concept of second order symbiosis a useful way to describe the psychological situation when children experience varying degrees of loss in their childhood as their needs for dependency are unmet.

Separation and loss

Children may experience separation and loss in a wide variety of situations. The attachment process may be disrupted by a single incident such as separation from a parent, the death of a parent, or by a series of incidents that impact on the family, such as, illness, substance abuse or

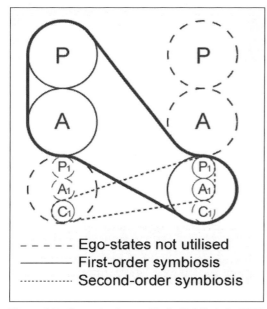

– – – – – Ego-states not utilised
————— First-order symbiosis
·············· Second-order symbiosis

Figure 9.5   Second order symbiosis (Schiff et al., 1975)

other life events. Separation and loss are part of the natural process of life alongside building relationships, growing as a family, and maturing. However, when children are separated from their main caregiver, temporary or permanent, they experience an acute sense of loss. Winnicott (1984: 19) stated that:

> *. . . the pain of separation from those we love is for all of us a devastating experience, but for a dependant child the whole of his or her world collapses and everything loses meaning. The worst thing that can happen is that the trauma can be so great and the child feels so helpless in the face of it that all feelings are clamped down on, leading to deadness and depression.*

Children do not usually develop the emotional mechanisms to be able to cope with loss when they have not experienced a positive attachment. Bowlby (1969:13) referred to the 'emotional mechanism' as the 'internal working model', which is discussed in more detail below. When children experience further separation and loss their difficulties are exacerbated. There are several factors that influence a child's reaction to loss. These are the strength of the relationship being severed, the abruptness of the separation, and the child's developmental stage. Professionals, and society in general, may tend to discount the impact of separation and loss in children, particularly when this occurs during infancy. Bowlby's (1951) work identified that children do grieve, although they may process their grief differently to adults. For example, a child may not have the cognitive ability to process and understand their loss and grief, which may be linked to the stage of development. The effects of separation or loss are not lesser or greater at any stage of the child's development, simply different (Fahlberg, 1991).

One way of thinking about a child's development is in terms of the developmental tasks that need to be accomplished. Children tend to master developmental tasks sequentially; therefore, any ruptures to their significant relationships at any development stage may interfere with progression up the developmental ladder. This may lead to regression in terms of the skills that they have most recently required. Rutter (1981) considered that children aged between six months and four years are the most significantly impacted by separation. This is particularly relevant for toddlers as separation interferes with the balance between dependency and autonomy. The child may become either too clingy, or self-reliant. Underlying both of these reactions is a loss of trust. A pre-school child may use magical thinking to make sense of his loss, which is a normal stage of child development. They may, for instance, believe that they are responsible for their loss.

> *Nick, aged 14, was self-harming when referred to the therapist. When he discussed this he realised that he was internalising the anger he felt towards his foster father. Further exploration revealed that Nick, when aged four, had been angry with his father shortly before his death. Nick told the therapist that he believed his anger had killed his father. Nick subsequently became aware that he was afraid to express anger towards his foster father in case he killed him.*

Children frequently experience difficulty in attaching to foster carers. Such children may believe that in accepting care from their foster carers, and becoming emotionally close to them, they are being disloyal to their family of origin. Unresolved separation issues may thus interfere with the development of new attachments in foster placements and contribute to their instability. When foster children experience several placements, their ability to develop trust in others is limited and they express their distress via inappropriate behaviours, which frequently invite negative strokes from those around them.

> *Jodie aged four, was placed into local authority care due to the neglect she experienced from her mother's erratic parenting and drug abuse. As a result of this neglect, Jodie did not learn to regulate her feelings and behaved in an impulsive and unpredictable manner. Foster carers were unable to manage her chaotic behaviour and, consequently, from the age of four to nine years old she lived with 14 foster families and experienced nine changes of primary school. Jodie never formed an attachment and was later diagnosed with a reactive attachment disorder (see below pp. 124).*

Individuals may also have attachments to an object as well as a person, for example, animals, belongings, homes, schools, toys. When a person or object is unexpectedly withdrawn, an individual may experience an emotional state of loss, and subsequently the range of feelings known as grief. Usually the grief initiates a period of mourning. Kübler-Ross (1969) identified a five-stage sequence to loss: denial, anger, bargaining, depression and acceptance.

She postulates that a person passes through this sequence in order to let go of their attachment and recover from the loss. Klass et al. (1996) however, introduced the notion of a continuing bond. They suggested that individuals maintain their attachment to loved ones, and manage their loss throughout their life cycle, rather than 'letting them go'.

Some children may also need to go through the grieving process for a parent-child relationship that never occurred. Their grief involves not having a parent who was able to love and care for them in a consistent way. This form of grieving carries just as much emotional pain. Frequently however there is less understanding and support from the adults caring for children during this type of grief process.

> *Hannah was adopted when she was an infant due to her mother's alcoholism. When Hannah was 14 years old her adoptive parents told her that her mother had chosen to abuse alcohol rather than take care of her. Hannah was distraught when she heard this and experienced immense grief. Hannah was unsupported by her adoptive parents who did not understand her grief, given she had been abandoned by her mother 13 years earlier.*

Internal working models

As a result of their experiences of attachment, separation and loss, a child develops mental representations, or internal working models of self, others and the world (Bowlby, 1969). The child's relationship with their caregiver influences the quality of the child's internal psychology; therefore, the self will be experienced either positively or negatively (Howe, 1999). A child bases their sense of importance and self-worth on whether their caregiver is 'available' and predictable, and has the willingness and ability to provide care and protection for them. A child who is successful at gaining comfort develops a positive internal working model of themselves and others. However, if a child experiences rejection rather than being soothed, they will develop a negative internal working model. As a result, they may believe they are worthless, unsafe and ineffective and see their caregiver/s as unpredictable, inconsistent, unresponsive, threatening and even dangerous. Consequently, this child does not develop healthy attachments and internalises a negative frame of reference about self, others and the world. Erskine and Zalcman (1975) developed the 'racket system', now referred to as 'script system', as a way of working with this internal structure (see below p. 128).

Bretherton and Waters (1985: 94) stated that the child perpetuates a negative or self-limiting internal working model by sifting out any information which conflicts with their accepted model by means of 'perceptual and behavioural control mechanisms'. Main et al. (1985) however, claimed that the internal working models are actively created and can be restructured. This view supports the three central philosophical assumptions which underpin TA. They are:

- That people are OK.
- That everybody has the capacity to think.
- That people can decide their own destiny and that these decisions can be changed.

Tudor (1999: 94) stated that these philosophical assumptions have 'implications for the counsellor's attitude to the therapeutic relationship'. The counsellor's adherence to these assumptions results in positive and mutual respect towards the client and a belief in personal responsibility and autonomy. This contributes towards establishing a therapeutic relationship, which is the foundation for effective work. We consider that attachment patterns are also an important consideration when working with children as these provide information and assist in building a therapeutic relationship.

Attachment patterns

Ainsworth (1973) distinguished between infants who are securely and insecurely attached and observed that the main difference between the mothers of such infants is their sensitivity to their child. By this Ainsworth means the extent to which a mother detects her infant's signals, interprets them correctly, and responds promptly and appropriately (see Figure 9.1). Ainsworth et al. (1978) carried out research which they called *Patterns of Attachment: The Strange Situation*. She and her colleagues observed infants' reactions when their mothers were present, when they departed, and when they returned. Upon the mothers' return, particular note was taken of the infants' exploration of their environment. The research identified three patterns of attachment:

- *Secure attachment*
  Securely attached children show some distress on the departure of a parent. When reunited, they positively greet the parent, seek acknowledgement, and return to their play. The parent is responsive to the child's needs.
- *Insecure and avoidant attachment*
  Insecure and avoidant attached children show few signs of distress at separation. When reunited, they ignore the parent, will not seek physical contact and their play is inhibited. The parenting style is insensitive to the needs of the child.
- *Insecure and ambivalent or resistant attachments*
  Children who are insecure and who have ambivalent or resistant attachment are very distressed at separation and difficult to calm when reunited. They are resistant to being pacified but will run after the parent if they walk away. Ambivalent children will, at the same time, demand and angrily resist attention and are reluctant to return to play. Parental care is inconsistent.

In 1991, Main identified and added a fourth type known as:

- *Insecure and disorganised attachment*
  Children with insecure disorganised attachment demonstrate both avoidant and ambivalent kinds of attachment behaviour, which is indicative of extreme insecurity. Upon reunion with their caregiver, they appear apathetic, disorganised and confused. The parents can be the source of the children's anxiety as they often experience them as frightened or frightening.

Reactive attachment disorder (RAD) is a reaction to a severe insecure attachment. This is recognised as a mental disorder and is associated with the failure by the child and caretaker to bond in infancy (APA, 1994). This disorder starts in the first five years of life and probably occurs as a direct result of severe parental neglect, abuse or serious mishandling. Children who are diagnosed with RAD are so neurologically disrupted that they cannot go through the normal developmental processes, nor establish positive relationships with other people. They are often incorrectly diagnosed with severe emotional and behavioural difficulties. Many of these children may have been incorrectly diagnosed as having mental disorders such as attention-deficit

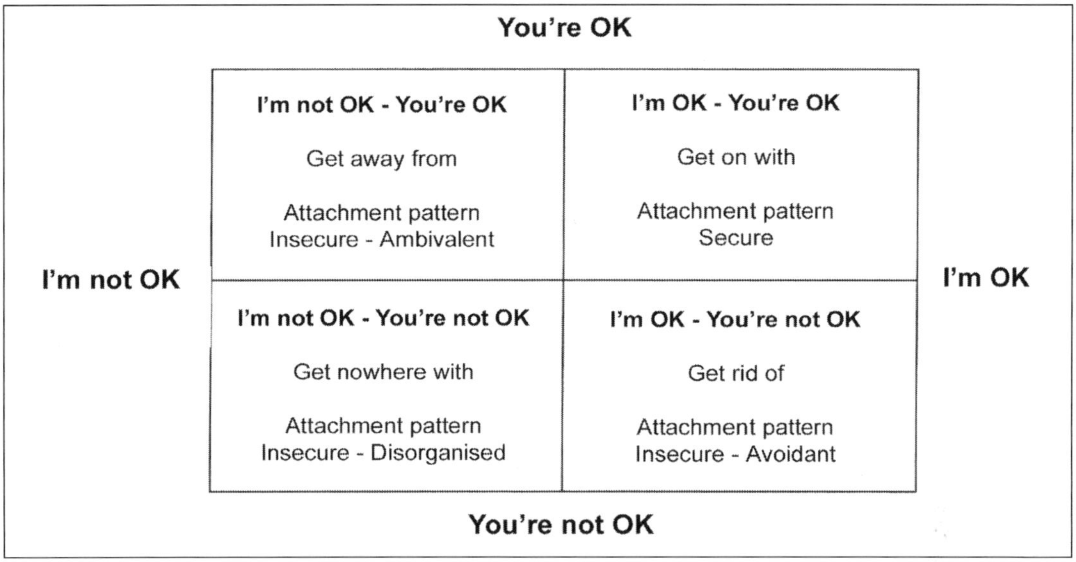
You're OK
I'm not OK - You're OK
Get away from
Attachment pattern
Insecure - Ambivalent
I'm OK - You're OK
Get on with
Attachment pattern
Secure
I'm not OK
I'm OK
I'm not OK - You're not OK
Get nowhere with
Attachment pattern
Insecure - Disorganised
I'm OK - You're not OK
Get rid of
Attachment pattern
Insecure - Avoidant
You're not OK

Figure 9.6 The OK corral with attachment patterns (Hobbes, 1990)

hyperactivity disorder (ADHD) Asperger's syndrome or autism. They may be prescribed unnecessary medication in response to such diagnoses.

Hobbes (1990) has integrated the work of attachment theorists with TA and illustrated the similarities between attachment patterns (Ainsworth, 1973) and life positions (Berne, 1962) by placing them within the OK Corral (Ernst, 1971). According to Berne there are four basic life positions that people adopt (see Figure 9.6). A life position is a person's basic belief about self, others and the world, and each position represents an outlook which has a profound effect on the way they live their life. Hobbes (1990) states that 'four patterns of security seeking behaviour emerge that correspond exactly with the Life Positions as outlined by Berne' (p. 34).

Case studies

In this part we offer three case studies, which illustrate the use of TA whilst working therapeutically with each of the insecure attachment patterns.

Daniel

Daniel had an insecure-avoidant attachment pattern and his script decision was 'I have to look after myself because everyone leaves me.' Daniel's birth father left the family home soon after he was born, leaving his birth mother as the sole carer. Daniel was placed on a care order due to his mother's substance abuse and frequent indifference to his needs. He was subsequently placed for adoption. As a result of these ruptures to his early attachments, Daniel became compulsively self-reliant and distant. This was evident as Daniel cared for himself rather than being reliant on his adoptive parents, or other adults. He made contact with the world by being hurtful and rebellious, with an attitude of 'I'll fight you' and 'You can't make me'. Daniel's adoptive parents struggled to manage his disruptive and oppositional behaviour and placed him in local authority care when he was 12 years old. He was referred for therapy at this stage. Daniel had a life position of 'I'm OK -You're not OK'.

The main focus of the therapeutic intervention with Daniel, given his attachment pattern and life position, was establishing a therapeutic relationship using permission and protection (Crossman, 1966). This provided a protective and consistent environment allowing Daniel to have a different attachment experience. In the first session, the therapist explained her role, the limitations of confidentiality, and safety issues. She also explored with Daniel what he wanted from therapy. This practice established a clear structure for therapy and highlighted Daniel's potency as he mutually agreed the boundaries. The therapist modelled potency and permission by giving Daniel a pro-active choice about what he wanted to discuss.

Throughout therapy, Daniel had several foster carers who found his oppositional and aggressive behaviour difficult to cope with. However, it was always Daniel's choice to move placements. Daniel would 'Get rid of' his foster carers before they got rid of him by asking his social worker to move him on (see Figure 9.6). He did this by absconding from school and refusing to go home. At each move he showed no signs of insecurity or vulnerability. After three foster homes Daniel was eventually placed in a residential home where the therapy sessions were held. The therapist's potency during the above transitions was to maintain the therapeutic relationship by accepting Daniel unconditionally and being available to him on a regular basis.

Fourteen months into therapy, Daniel told the therapist that he had been arrested for shoplifting and that his adoptive mother had been supportive of him in the police station. The therapist asked him how he had experienced being supported. He started to cry and appeared to cover this with 'racket' or inauthentic anger (English, 1971, 1972). Daniel told the therapist that she could not help him and that she was "a waste of fucking time". He stormed out of the room and told her that he was never going to talk to her again. The therapist was aware that Daniel had shown his vulnerability and had 'Got rid of' her by storming out of the room. In doing this he was maintaining his emotional distance, which was his survival strategy. The therapist recognised that she had gone ahead of Daniel rather than working at his pace. This lack of attunement ruptured the therapeutic relationship.

Although Daniel refused to see the therapist for 12 weeks, the fact that she was consistently there at the same time each week was an important part of the attachment, and indeed, the therapeutic process. On each visit, the residential staff informed Daniel that she was available to see him if he changed his mind. By doing this, the therapist conveyed to him that she was available, and that he did not have the power to 'Get rid of' her. On the twelfth of these sessions, Daniel appeared at the door and asked the therapist "Why do you keep coming back when I've told you I don't want to see you". The therapist explained that she cared about what happened to him and that this was something he could not control or change. The therapist then invited him to think about what he could control in the present situation. This intervention was designed to help him discover that he only had power and control over himself, and not others. Daniel chose to come into the session. At a later date, when the therapist asked him why he had decided to make contact with her at that particular time, he replied "Well, you kept coming back." The therapist recognised the importance of stroking Daniel's strategy of staying away. She told him that whilst this strategy had been useful for him in the past, he could now choose different options and stay in the relationship with her.

The relationship was further strengthened by the therapist acknowledging to Daniel that she had made

a mistake by going ahead of him and not working at his pace. This indicated the therapist's intention to work with him in a respectful and protective manner and reflected the 'I'm OK - You're OK' position. The therapist was the only significant adult with whom Daniel did not fight all the time. The attachment with Daniel started to develop through this process, however, he still did not feel secure enough to acknowledge and communicate his painful feelings. This was consistent with his avoidant pattern of attachment. The therapy continues and Daniel will need to feel safe and supported in his placement before he is able to heal his primal wound of abandonment as a result of the separation from his birth mother (Newton Verrier, 1993).

Ben

Ben had an insecure-ambivalent/resistant attachment pattern and his script decision was 'I have to take care of you so you don't leave me.' When he was three years old, Ben experienced the sudden death of his father. Following this his mother had a nervous breakdown. This resulted in her parenting being insensitive and inconsistent. Aged 14, Ben's teacher referred him for therapy as he had poor school attendance and was under-achieving. His educational history showed that he had experienced extreme anxiety on being separated from his mother when he started school at the age of five. From the age of seven, Ben cared for his mother on a physical level by doing all the household chores and shopping, and on a psychological level Ben was his mother's main source of emotional support. This was an indication that Ben had moved into a second order symbiosis, by psychologically caring for his mother's early Child ego state (C_1) from his early Parent and Adult ego states (P_1 and A_1) leaving his own early Child ego state (C_1) unsupported (see Figure 9.5). This was evident because, whilst Ben wanted to be with his mother, he resented the fact that she was dependant on him. This prevented him socialising with his peers. Ben had a life position of 'I'm not OK – You're OK'.

It was evident from information about Ben's family background that his emotional and psychological growth had been impeded at a critical stage of his development. He had experienced 'abandonment' due to the sudden death of his father, and the emotional unavailability of his mother. As a result, Ben did not have the relational support to be separate and was therefore prevented from adequately developing the capacity to trust, explore new experiences and develop self-reliance. Toddlers usually learn to separate and individuate from their carers, which is a vital stage in developing trust and self-reliance in their own abilities (Mahler et al., 1975). Levin (1988) supported this view and stated that children are ready to become independent individuals in their own right in stage three of this cycle. At this stage they also develop their power of thinking.

Ben presented in therapy as a young person who experienced self-doubt. He believed he was stupid and unable to understand or do his work in class. Ben described several occasions when he believed teachers had humiliated him, and he experienced shame. On further exploration, Ben recalled feeling shamed on a number of occasions by his mother. She would criticise and humiliate him in front of his siblings and friends when he wet himself. On such occasions, Ben felt blamed and shamed by his mother, and was scared she would abandon him. According to Stern (1985) the development of shame is a natural part of child development that occurs between the ages of 12 months and three years. When the parent is responsive to the child's emotional needs, shame can help a child learn how to manage criticism and develop a conscience (Hughes, 1998). The parent's role is to attune to the child and help them integrate and regulate shameful experiences, and to convey through touch, looks and tone of voice, what they want the child to do. However, if a parent is not attuned, as in Ben's case, then shame is denied and not integrated into the child's emotional repertoire. Ben's mother, like many other parents, used shame as a form of social control. English (1975: 26) argues that if a child experiences shame as blame, then out of awareness, they make script decisions about themselves. 'Shame messages are internalized in P$_1$ (the Spooky Child) and they operate in addition to and in combination with injunctions and attributions'.

Shame messages represent cultural scripting, and operate more forcefully because they are internalized so early in life and get absorbed within the child's whole physiology. As a result, Ben's experience of shame was carried through to adolescence and led to physical panic when he felt shamed by his teacher. As English (1975: 26) stated 'If a person has had shaming as a child, then later, when he is grown up, his Child ego state will respond with physical panic to overt or covert shaming in here and now transactions'.

A significant change in Ben's therapy occurred when, with the therapist's support, he explored a specific incident in the classroom. Through sensitive inquiry, Ben was able to identify his script belief as "Something is wrong with me". The therapist's attunement was essential as, through this process, he uncovered shame as his racket feeling (English, 1971, 1972). The therapist helped Ben to recognise that his feelings of shame had become his habitual defence against taking risks, which he feared would expose his 'vulnerable self' to criticism and humiliation if he made mistakes in the classroom. Erskine (1997) stated that shame arises out of this script belief to provide a defence to the loss of a relationship when the critical needs for physical and emotional contact are not met.

Another important stage in Ben's therapy was when he contracted for change. He identified as a behavioural marker that he would take risks in the classroom, for example, he would answer questions when he was not certain of the answers; he would read out loud in front of others; he would take part in discussions. Ben's confidence grew as he learnt to takes risks. He learnt to stay in the here-and-now when he made mistakes by using 'grounding techniques'. The therapist had encouraged him to monitor his breathing and use his fives senses, that is, touch, taste, sight, sound and smell. This enabled Ben to develop self-reliance and trust his abilities. He was able to attend school regularly and choose his examination options.

Sue

Sue had an insecure-disorganised attachment pattern and her script decision was 'I can exist as long as I don't show my feelings and pretend I'm fine.' Sue, aged 10, lived with foster carers. Her mother had a mental illness and was ineffective and helpless. Sue experienced her mother as frightening because she had physically and sexually abused her. Sue had also witnessed domestic violence between her parents. When taken into local authority care, Sue idealised her parents and was confused as to why she was removed from their care. She was unable to trust any adults to care for her because of her early experiences of neglect and abuse. The therapist assessed that Sue had an insecure-disorganised attachment and a life position of 'I'm not OK – You're not OK'. Main (1991) suggested that someone fitting this pattern wants to attach but is afraid to do so. Sue transferred her disorganised pattern of attachment onto her foster parents and showed this by being physically present, whilst at the same time emotionally withdrawn.

For the first time ever, Sue experienced a secure and loving environment whilst living with foster parents. The contrast between the foster family and her birth family led her to question why her birth parents had treated her in an abusive way. Sue believed the abuse she experienced must have been her fault and that she was 'bad'. Due to this she developed a negative internal working model and one of her script beliefs was that adults could not be trusted.

The racket system as devised by Erskine and Zalcman (1979) demonstrated how a person supports and carries out their script beliefs in day-to-day life. The system of thoughts, feelings and behaviour develop out of script beliefs, and is maintained by the individual as a self-reinforcing mechanism. The racket system has three inter-related and interdependent components: script beliefs and feelings, rackety displays, and reinforcing memories (see Figure 9.7).

Script beliefs and feelings are based upon a person's beliefs about self, others and the quality of life. The system demonstrates how an intra-psychic process takes place whereby a person re-experiences script beliefs and feelings and they reinforce and

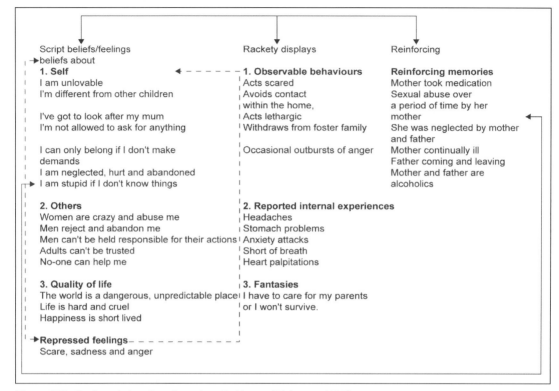

Script beliefs/feelings	Rackety displays	Reinforcing
→beliefs about		
1. Self ◀ – – – – –	**1. Observable behaviours**	**Reinforcing memories**
I am unlovable	Acts scared	Mother took medication
I'm different from other children	Avoids contact	Sexual abuse over
	within the home,	a period of time by her
I've got to look after my mum	Acts lethargic	mother
I'm not allowed to ask for anything	Withdraws from foster family	She was neglected by mother
		and father
I can only belong if I don't make	Occasional outbursts of anger	Mother continually ill
demands		Father coming and leaving
I am neglected, hurt and abandoned		Mother and father are
→I am stupid if I don't know things		alcoholics
2. Others	**2. Reported internal experiences**	
Women are crazy and abuse me	Headaches	
Men reject and abandon me	Stomach problems	
Men can't be held responsible for their actions	Anxiety attacks	
Adults can't be trusted	Short of breath	
No-one can help me	Heart palpitations	
3. Quality of life	**3. Fantasies**	
The world is a dangerous, unpredictable place	I have to care for my parents	
Life is hard and cruel	or I won't survive.	
Happiness is short lived		
→**Repressed feelings** – – – – – – – – –		
Scare, sadness and anger		

Figure 9.7   Sue's racket system (based on Erskine and Zalcman, 1975)

maintain their script decisions. At the same time, their authentic feelings are repressed and substituted with unauthentic feelings, which English (1971, 1972) described as racket feelings.

Rackety displays are observable behaviours, for example, language, futile tone of voice; agitation, emotional expressions and statements such as 'Nobody cares about me anyway', and are a direct result of the intra-psychic process. Individuals may report internal experiences such as headaches, stomach problems, anxiety attacks, muscle tension or psychosomatic ailments. These internal experiences help an individual replay their script beliefs and maintain their script.

Reinforcing memories in the racket system provide justification and evidence that serve as a feedback loop to script beliefs. Erskine and Zalcman (1979: 163) stated that 'Any therapeutic intervention that interrupts the flow in the racket system will be an effective step in the persons changing his or her racket system and therefore his and her script'.

The following work illustrates how the therapist intervened in Sue's racket system.

Sue's foster carers reported to the therapist that Sue acted scared and extremely withdrawn after contact meetings with her parents. The therapist

explored this with Sue and it transpired that, during contact sessions, her parents had threatened not to see her again if she continued to live with her foster parents. Sue experienced racket feelings of confusion and terror because of her irresolvable conflict, given that she was on a full care order, and did not have a choice about who she lived with. This meant that her parents had again failed to recognise her right to be appropriately cared for, and reinforced her belief that adults could not be trusted.

The therapist explored with Sue her racket feelings of confusion and terror, and her associated rackety displays. Sue's 'observable behaviours', such as withdrawing to her bedroom and becoming lethargic, had alerted Sue's foster carers to the distress she seemed to experience after the contact meetings with her parents. The therapist subsequently enabled Sue to identify her 'reported internal experiences' which she described as her heart racing, feeling sick and becoming short of breath in the contact with her parents. It later transpired that her 'fantasy' was that she would die if her parents rejected her.

Sue's parents' threat of rejection during the contact session had reinforced her belief that adults could not be trusted which, in turn, activated a recycling of confusion. Sue had covered her authentic feelings of scare, sadness and anger with racket feelings of terror, guilt and confusion. This 'recycling' reinforced her beliefs and feelings from early childhood and created another reinforcing memory. This acted as a feedback loop to her script beliefs and ensured the flow of her racket system. This also reinforced her attachment pattern of being frightened to attach to her foster carers because she feared her birth parents would reject her if she did.

Sue was clear that she wanted to continue the contact with her parents despite recognising that they were unable to meet her needs. She subsequently identified, however, that she wanted to leave the meeting if she felt threatened by them. Sue's understanding of her reported internal experiences enabled her to recognise when she did feel threatened. She contracted to learn grounding techniques as a way of managing her distress. Sue cathected Adult by focusing her energy on the here-and-now by using her five senses and regulating her breathing. This helped her to manage her anxiety. The therapist also encouraged Sue to make a 'reality check' by asking the adults around her whether she would really die if her parents rejected her.

The therapist used the therapeutic relationship to challenge Sue's script belief that adults cannot be trusted. This was mainly achieved by the therapist communicating to Sue that her needs and safety were important. Through this process, Sue gradually learnt that some adults could be trusted. Berne (1972: 355–6) discussed how individuals who lack an effective parent in early life need to have this 'vacuum filled by someone who will 'be there' before any other kind of treatment will be effective'. By 'being there' he meant that the patient knows there is somewhere they can go; someone they can talk to; someone who provides cookies. The support the therapist gave Sue by 'being there', and the interest she showed her on a consistent basis, began to address her developmental deficit around trust to give her a corrective emotional experience.

Stewart and Joines (1989) stated that permanent escape from the racket system requires the client to do two things, that is, update their script beliefs and resolve the script feelings that accompany them. The work described above enabled Sue to break the feedback loop in her racket system, restructure her internal working model, and attach to her foster carers.

Conclusion

Attachment theory focuses on the predisposition of all individuals to make affectional bonds to significant others. Ruptures to attachments give rise to insecure attachment patterns and the different responses children, and adults, make in their relationships with others. Emotional distress, including anxiety, fear, anger, depression, and grief occur if there is a failure to make an attachment, or an unwilling separation and loss. A child's experience of attachment, separation and loss will contribute to the decisions they make about how they see themselves, others and the world and will determine how they live out their script.

In the case studies, we demonstrated how we integrate attachment theory and TA into our practice. In addition, when working with children and families, we undertake a systemic assessment (Clarkson and Fish, 1988) of the family history, and current situation. This highlights the family patterns of interaction and aids the formulation of a TA diagnosis. This leads to an appropriate contract and treatment direction (Guichard, 1987). We find the contracting process particularly pertinent when working with children as this provides protection and permission as well as embracing the philosophical assumptions of I'm OK, You're OK. Furthermore, the mutuality of contracting offers children the opportunity to develop negotiation skills and address the power imbalance that is often present in the child and adult relationship. This process strengthens the therapeutic alliance and contributes to a secure environment where children can get to know themselves, sort out their confusions and develop their sense of self with someone who will listen (Winnicott, 1984).

References

Ainsworth, M.D.S. (1973) The Development of Infant-Mother Attachment. In Caldwell, B.M. and Ricciutti, H.N. (Eds.) *Review of Child Development Research. Vol. 3*. Chicago, IL: University of Chicago Press.

Ainsworth, M.D.S., Blehar, M., Aters, E. and Wall, S. (1978) *Patterns of Attachment: A Psychological Study of the Strange Situation*. Hillsdale, NJ: Laurence Erlbaum.

Berne, E. (1961) *Transactional Analysis in Psychotherapy*. New York: Grove Press.

Berne, E. (1962) Classification of Positions. *Transactional Analysis Bulletin*, 1: 3, 23.

Berne, E. (1970) *Sex in Human Loving*. New York: Viking Penguin Inc.

Berne, E. (1971) *A Layman's Guide to Psychiatry and Psychoanalysis*. New York: Grove Press. (Original work published 1947)

Berne, E. (1972) *What Do You Say After You Say Hello?* New York: Grove Press.

Bretherton, I. and Waters, E. (1985) *Growing Points of Attachment Theory and Research*. Chicago, IL: University of Chicago Press for the Society for Research in Child Development.

Bowlby, J. (1951) *Maternal Care and Mental Health*. World Health Organisation Monograph (Serial No.2). Geneva: WHO.

Bowlby, J. (1969) *Attachment and Loss. Volume I: Attachment*. London: Hogarth Press.

Clarkson, P. and Fish, S. (1988) Systemic Assessment and Treatment Considerations in TA Child Psychotherapy. *Transactional Analysis Journal*, 18: 2, 123–32.

Clarkson, P. and Fish, S. (1992) *Systemic assessment and TA Psychotherapy with Children*. In Clarkson, P. *Transactional Analysis Psychotherapy: An Integrated Approach*. (pp. 229–56). London: Routledge.

Crossman, P. (1966) Permission and Protection. *Transactional Analysis Bulletin*, 5: 19,152–4.

English, F. (1971) The Substitution Factor: Rackets and Real Feelings. Part I. *Transactional Analysis Journal*, 1: 4, 225–30.

English, F. (1972) Rackets and Real Feelings. Part II. *Transactional Analysis Journal*, 2: 1, 23–5.

English, F. (1975) Shame and Social Control. *Transactional Analysis Journal*, 5, 24–8.

Ernst, F.H. (1971) The OK Corral: The Grid for Get-on-with. *Transactional Analysis Journal*, 1: 4, 231–40.

Erskine, R. (1997) *Theories and Method of an Integrative Transactional Analysis: A Volume of Selected Articles*. San Francisco, CA: TA Press.

Erskine, R. and Zalcman, M. (1975) The Racket System: A Model For Racket Analysis. *Transactional Analysis Journal*, 9: 1, 51–9.

Fahlberg, V. (1991) *A Child's Journey Through Placement*. London: BAAF.

Kubler-Ross, E. (1969) *On Death and Dying*. London: Routledge.

Gibran, L. (1926) Children. In *The Prophet*. New York: Alfred A. Knopp.

Guichard, M. (1987) *Writing the Long Case Study*. Workshop, EATA Conference, Chamonix.

Hobbes, R. (1990) Attachment Theory and Transactional Analysis. Part Two -Developing Security. *ITA News*, 47, 33–7.

Howe, D. (1995) *Attachment Theory for Social Workers*. London: Macmillan Press.

Hughes, D. (1998) *Building the Bonds of Attachment*. Northvale, NJ: Jason Aronson.

Klass, D., Silverman, P. and Nickman, S. (Eds.) (1996) *Continuing Bonds: New Understandings of Grief*. Washington, DC: Taylor and Frances.

Lancashire, J. (2002) *Unpublished CTA Exam Case Study*. European Association for Transactional Analysis.

Levin, P. (1988) *Cycles of Power*. Deerfield Beech, CA: Health Communications.

Lorenz, K.Z. (1957) *Instinctive Behaviour*. Schiller, C.H. (Ed.) New York: International Universities Press. (Original work published 1935)

Main, M., Kaplan, N. and Cassidy, J. (1985) Security in Infancy, Childhood and Adulthood: A Move to the Level of Representation. In Bretherton, I. and Waters, E. (Eds.) *Growing Points of Attachment Theory and Research*. Chicago, IL: University of Chicago Press.

Mahler, M., Pine, F. and Bergman, A. (1975) *The Psychological Birth of the Human Infant: Symbiosis and Individuation*. New York: Basic Books.

Newton Verrier, N. (1993) *The Primal Wound: Understanding the Adoptive Child*. Baltimore, MA: Gateway Press.

Rutter, M. (1981) *Maternal Deprivation Reassessed*. London: Penguin Books.

Schiff, A. and Schiff, J. (1971) Passivity. *Transactional Analysis Journal*, 1: 1, 71–8.

Schiff, J. et al. (1975) *The Cathexis Reader: Transactional Analysis Treatment of Psychosis*. London: Harper and Row.

Smith, J.K. (2001) *Transactional Analysis: A Pictorial Reference to the Basic Concepts of TA*. EduGraphics.

Steiner, C. (1974) *Scripts People Live*. New York: Grove Press.

Stern, D. (1985) *The Interpersonal World of the Infant: A View from Psychoanalysis and Developmental Psychology*. New York: Basic Books.

Stewart, I. and Joines, V. (1987) *TA Today*. Nottingham: Lifespace Publishing.

Tudor, K. (1999) 'I'm OK, You're OK – and They're OK': Therapeutic Relationships in Transactional Analysis. In Feltham, C. (Ed.) *Understanding the Counselling Relationship*. London: Sage.

Winnicott, C. (1984) 'Face to Face with Children.' *In Touch with Children (Work Book)*. London: BAAF.

Woollams, S. and Brown, M. (1978) *Transactional Analysis*. London: Prentice-Hall.
Woollams, S. and Huige, K. (1977) Normal Dependency and Symbiosis. *Transactional Analysis Journal*, 7: 3, 212–20.

CHAPTER 10

Working with Adolescents

Mark Widdowson

What is going on with young people? The experience of teenagers themselves, and their parents, carers and therapists, as well as research studies all suggests that there is a crisis concerning the mental health of today's adolescents. This also predicts troubled times ahead. According to a recent time trend study conducted by researchers at the Institute of Psychiatry at King's College, London, a number of themes are evident:

- *The mental health of teenagers has sharply declined in the last 25 years,* and the chances that 15 year-olds will have behavioural problems such as lying, stealing and being disobedient, have more than doubled.
- *The rate of emotional problems such as anxiety and depression has increased by 70 per cent amongst adolescents.*
- *Boys are more likely to exhibit behavioural problems, and girls are more likely to suffer emotional problems. This rate is higher for emotional problems, now running at one in five 15–year-old girls. The study found no increase in aggressive behaviour, such as fighting or bullying, and no increase in rates of hyperactivity.*
- *The increases cannot be explained by the rise in divorce and single parenthood. Comparable increases were found in all types of families. Nor can growing inequality over the 25 years explain the rise in problem teenage behaviours, due to the fact that rates of increase are comparable across all social classes. Mental health problems in adolescence correlate to the increased chances that young people will experience a range of poor outcomes as adults, such as homelessness, dependency on benefits, and redundancy, as well as poor mental and physical health. This indicates that the rise in problems is a real trend and cannot be attributed or explained away by an increased awareness or a greater likelihood to report such problems.*

(Collishaw et al., 2004)

Young people are blamed for many things: rising crime levels, overloaded welfare systems, poor housing (as opposed to poor management of housing estates) to name just a few examples. Young people are bombarded with 'information' about who or what they are (''You're so rude and ungrateful'') who or what they should be, about what they should and shouldn't wear, and how. The information may come via friendly tips in magazines which may have dubious selling undertones; by their peers who want them to conform, or at least to conform to non-conformity; by their parents who have aspirations about them, and who are likely to be unhappy about some aspect of their child's personality or behaviour; by their teachers who quite often just want them to sit down, shut up and get on with it; and by a government which constantly sets targets, and has high aims for young people which may or may not be in line with what is going on for them or which corresponds with their desires or aspirations. They are told that they are too young for some things, and yet are expected to behave in a mature and adult fashion. They have few rights, and are rarely consulted or really listened to. They find some of their developmentally normal behaviours and processes demonised and pathologised. What are they supposed to think? How are they supposed to behave?

In response to this bewildering situation, what on earth is a therapist, who will usually be trained in working with adults (often, motivated, middle class, articulate adult clients) supposed to do with them? To encourage their autonomy, and to run the risk of the young person upsetting every apple cart in their system, with the potential result that the therapist is hauled up on ethics charges by angry parents? Or, conversely, to push the adolescent to adapt and, thereby, potentially reinforce a limiting and possibly even damaging script. Understandably, many therapists are extremely reluctant to work with adolescents. Some therapists do work with adolescents and, of these, many are not specifically trained to do so, or do not receive adequate supervision to help them understand their work or develop it further. A further, possibly large number of therapists would like to work with adolescents but simply do not have any idea of where to start.

This chapter aims to offer something to therapists who identify with these professional questions and issues. It begins with some reflections on the 'Inner Adolescent'. This is followed by some initial considerations about working with adolescents from a contextual perspective, drawing on UK social legislation. The next five parts of the chapter focus on therapy: from contracting, establishing a working alliance, the initial meeting and developmental considerations, through to the process of therapy itself. The chapter concludes with a practical example of working with a group of adolescents from a psycho-educational perspective. The chapter is written from a practical viewpoint, and in a direct tone which parallels my approach to working with adolescent clients. In each part I make some links to TA theory and conclude with some questions for self supervision, both of which are designed to help you, the reader/practitioner, to develop your own thinking and model of working with adolescents.

The 'Inner Adolescent'

Many therapists working with children and young people find their work with this client group to be both rewarding and challenging, disturbing and stimulating. It is often evocative, even provocative. Perhaps more than working with adults, it requires the therapist to reflect on their own experience of being a child and young person. Therapists trained in humanistic forms of psychotherapy are often invited to 'meet the client on their turf' and to find creative ways of joining, and develop meaningful, co-created dialogic channels. How can this change of relational 'method' be successfully deployed with adolescent clients, when there is not only the usual power dynamic imbalance, but also a generational gap, and culturally different frames of reference interacting?

Self Supervision 1: Reflecting on the experience of adolescence

Take some time right now to think back to your own adolescence. What was it like? What did you look like? What were your thoughts about yourself, other people – of all ages including your peers, parents and family members? What ideas did you have about what the

world had to offer? What did you think you'd be doing when you were grown up and able to do what you wanted – or at least thought you might? What music did you listen to? What did you do with your spare time? Who were your best friends? Why did you associate with them? Are you still friends with them? What was good or bad about those relationships? How did you get on with your parents and siblings? What scrapes did you get into? How did you get out of them, or lie your way out of them? Who were good influences on you? Who were bad influences? How did you deal with the surge of hormones and the massive physiological changes you were experiencing? What helped you? What would have *really* helped you? What information do you have now and wish you did then? Put this book down and take some time to think about these questions – it may well be helpful to you later. Get in touch with your 'inner adolescent'.

You may wish to talk to family members and friends and ask them what they can remember about your adolescence. Take some time to observe adolescents, and find out about them. In what ways are they similar to you and your friends and in what ways are they different? What must it be like to be a teenager today, in our modern society?

Take time to develop this awareness. If possible, make notes, and allow yourself to write creatively and fluidly on your awareness.

Initial considerations in working with adolescents: the welfare checklist

Any therapist working in England and Wales with children and young people must be mindful of the relevance of *The Children Act 1990* and, specifically, the implications of the welfare checklist (also see below) which form the essence of the *Act*. Here I review the key points of the welfare checklist, and draw out some implications for the therapist:

- *The ascertainable wishes and feelings of the child concerned – considered in the light of their age and understanding.*
  This means that the therapist needs to actually consider the wishes of the young person, specifically in relation to whether they engage in therapy or not. The young person's wishes, however, do need to be considered in light of their developmental stage and thus the concept of 'Fraser competence' is relevant here. Can the young person effectively consent to therapeutic work, with a full awareness of the potential

impact of what they might be embarking upon? This concept is found in TA as one of Steiner's four criteria for effective contracting (Steiner, 1974). It also links clearly with another of Steiner's criteria, that of mutual (and informed) consent. In light of the client's competency to make a decision, do they actually know what therapy entails, and what will be required of them? It is possible for a therapist to make a 'soft' contract of 'exploration' to give the young person an opportunity to find out more about the therapist's style and what therapy involves before a therapeutic contract is achieved.

- *The child's physical, emotional and educational needs.*
  How will the therapy contribute to the young person's physical, emotional and educational needs? Often the answer to this is 'favourably'. Many young people who engage in therapy take better care of themselves physically, and often improve in educational terms. Will the therapy be the best opportunity for meeting their emotional needs? This is a relevant question, especially when faced with an adolescent who is 'sent' to therapy by a social worker or parent where clearly there are significant missing parts in the adolescent's home environment which do not adequately meet their emotional needs. Can the therapist provide what is missing? Would a more intensive multi-agency approach be better? Are there other services available which might be more relevant and appropriate for this particular young person? Whose emotional needs are met when the young person attends therapy?

- *The likely effect of any change in his circumstances.*
  Has the young person recently moved home, for example, have their parents recently split up? The adolescent may be experiencing an adjustment crisis. Therapy may be very helpful at this juncture, and many people have benefited greatly from therapeutic support in readjustment processes; however, the therapy can also be disrupting, especially when deep emotional problems are being addressed. Therapy can bring up too much 'material' for the young person to deal with and, in some cases, it may be best to postpone therapy until such a time as the young person is more settled. Attending therapy certainly counts as a change in circumstances, both directly in terms of practicalities such as times, frequency etc and also indirectly in terms of the weight and

significance that people such as family members, carers, and other professionals who may be involved with the young person attach to the therapy. A further consideration is the potential for the therapeutic journey of the young person resulting in the young person seeking change in their circumstances, which may or may not impact upon the various systems which the young person is part of.

- *The child's age, sex, background and any other relevant characteristics.*
  Cultural factors are significant here. The young person needs to be considered in a complex matrix of social and cultural factors. Maybe a different therapist may be best placed to work with a particular young person. Matching therapist to client, for example, in terms of ethnicity or gender, may be very relevant when working with a young person around identity issues. Young people are often acutely aware of and fascinated by differences. If you work with adolescents, you may be familiar with the experience of them explaining what their perceived similarities and differences to you are. How would such scrutiny impact upon you as a therapist? Some of this can be understood with the self-psychology concept of twinship transference, and the selfobject needs of the young person (Kohut, 1971). It would also seem that in adolescence twinship transference is a critical developmental relational need (Erskine and Trautmann, 1996) in the formation of the young person's sense of self.

- *Any harm which the child has suffered or is at risk of suffering.*
  Is there any indication of any previous abuse or current abuse? Is the young person self-harming or acting aggressively or violent towards others? What has been the impact of any harm? Does the therapist have the necessary skills for dealing with disclosure? Does the therapist have adequate referral procedures for dealing with disclosure, and is the young person aware of the therapist's policy regarding disclosures of harm?

- *How capable is each of the child's parents, and any other relevant person, in relation to meeting their needs.*
  Who has made the referral? Are they in a position to make a referral? Do they know what to expect? What are the expectations of the referring party? Are these expectations explicit, or implied? Are you as a therapist capable of dealing with *this* young person's needs?

The principles of taking into account the many factors which impact upon a young person's welfare espoused in the welfare checklist offer the therapist working with young people a good underpinning framework to inform the ethical commencement of a therapeutic relationship. The principles of 'beneficence' and 'non-malevolence' are especially relevant (Kitchener, 1984). The welfare checklist can also guide a therapist to choose their short and long term treatment strategy with a young person if the therapist notes that one particular aspect of the welfare checklist needs specific attention. The therapist may decide on reflection that it is best to not enter into a therapeutic relationship at this time with the young person, or may feel that a multi-disciplinary approach would be more fitting, and so the therapist may contact various agencies to set the referrals in motion.

Self Supervision 2: Welfare principles and practice

Reflect upon your work with an adolescent client in relation to the different points of the welfare checklist. Have all the points been addressed, either directly or indirectly? Do you need to revisit the contract (see below) in light of the welfare checklist? Do you need to view your client or the therapy differently in light of these principles?

Contracting: handling complexity

Therapy with adolescent clients usually involves some kind of three-handed contract (English, 1975) and needs to be handled and considered carefully before any kind of therapy begins. Therapy with a young person can effectively be sabotaged by insufficient attention being paid to the three-handed contract at the outset (Tudor, 1997).

When contemplating working with the young person the therapist needs to know who is making the referral. What is their motivation in making the referral? If the referrer simply wants the young person to acquiesce and adapt, then the therapy can be jeopardised from before the first meeting. If the therapist works within a school or organisation, the intention of the organisation in providing therapeutic support needs to be considered. These intentions and wishes may not be detrimental to the therapy, for instance, a school wanting its pupils to do well

academically may recognise the important role their students' mental health has in their ability to learn, and so may employ a counsellor. The implicit contract goal here is 'We want you to do well academically.' The therapy would be jeopardised, however, if the school withdrew the therapy on the grounds that, in the view of the school authorities, a particular (or several) young people were not behaving themselves sufficiently well. It is worthwhile exploring with referrers and organisations what their specific outcomes are. What do they want from the therapy for the young person? What do they want for themselves in the young person attending therapy? Careful, but sensitive attention to 'in whose interest is this referral' (the young person's or the referral person's need for an easier time) is well advised.

Another perhaps obvious, but frequently overlooked focus for questions about contracts and outcomes is the client themselves! What does the adolescent want out of the therapy? Ask, and they are likely to tell you. When they tell you, ask them if that is what they want for themselves, or for someone else. If their goal is, in effect, for someone else, will they get anything out of it? "Yeah, well, it'll keep my mum off my case, and that will make me feel better." Sometimes, if the young person has been 'sent' to therapy, they may not have a specific goal for themselves. This can be hard to work with. Seeking to tease out a goal from a young person who doesn't desire any change, or any change facilitated through therapy, or attempting to persuade your client to accept someone else's idea of what and how they should change (information they are likely to know, having been told many times before) and you are on a hiding to nothing. A soft contract for 'exploration' is probably best at this point (see below on engaging with the adolescent). Finally, what do you, the therapist want out of this work? Other than pay, and all the usual considerations, what do you want out of the therapy? Answering this question may raise issues for you to take to personal therapy or supervision. What do you want for the referrer, and for the adolescent client? Why do you want these outcomes? Why do you especially want to work with adolescents in the first place?

In thinking about the different parties to (or stakeholders in) this therapy, and about these questions regarding outcomes I have developed Stewart's (1998) outcome matrix, applying it to such three-handed contracts.

Outcome	Referrer/Organisation	Young person	Therapist
Referrer/organisation's outcome	For self	For young person	For therapist
Therapist's outcome	For referrer/organisation	For young person	For self
Young person's outcome	For referrer/organisation	For self	For therapist

Box 10.1   Three-handed outcome matrix (developed from Stewart, 1998)

Self Supervision 3: Contracting: accounting for complexity in the therapeutic relationship

Take some time to think about the different parties who are involved or who have a stake in your work with your adolescent clients. What is the influence of legislation and government policy upon your work? What do all the different parties involved, or connected with the young person, want from the therapy? How might their influence be felt? How might the influence of parties other than the young person support or sabotage the therapeutic work?

Drawing an 'authority diagram' (Berne, 1963) may be helpful. Account for the requirements of each part of the diagram hierarchy in relation to the therapy contract with this young person.

Chatting and beyond: engaging with the adolescent

Young people presenting for therapy fall into three broad categories:

1. Those actively seeking therapy, professional help or wanting 'someone to talk to'.
2. Those who reluctantly attend therapy, often at the urging of others.
3. Those who are 'sent' to therapy.

Some young people will be sceptical, and some downright hostile to the idea of therapy. However, even of those young people who are initially reluctant about or who are sent to therapy, some are glad of the opportunity to talk to a therapist. They may have heard positive reports about therapy from friends, or from reading articles about therapy in magazines. Many young people, regardless of their willingness to attend therapy are curious about the whole process of therapy, and may wonder what will happen. Ask about their expectations, what did they expect before they arrived, what do they expect once they have arrived and have

met you – you may be surprised, and perhaps even amused by some of the responses.

The relationship and rapport that the therapist establishes with the young person is of paramount importance and is probably the single most important factor in determining a positive outcome. Even if they are keen to talk, the young person may well be very suspicious of the therapist, and may be concerned that the therapist is some agent of social services, their school, or operating on behalf of their parents to coerce the young person into 'behaving', i.e. adapting. The boundaries of confidentiality need to be very clearly delineated very early in the process. It is helpful to use examples to illustrate the boundaries of confidentiality, and also to be clear that grey areas do exist. For example, should the therapist disclose a single, and relatively mild act of self-harm? It is important that the therapist makes explicit that, should a grey area surface, the options would be discussed and any disclosures would be done with the young person's full knowledge.

A young person attending therapy for the first time is likely to be sizing up the therapist. A therapist is a prime target for being considered 'weird'. However, bear in mind that to a young person, being thought of as weird may actually be a great bonus in their eyes! Your clothing, gestures and speech are likely to be under scrutiny. It is likely that the therapist may be viewed as being old fashioned and frumpy, freakish, or embarrassing. This is especially true for a therapist wearing items usually worn by young people. That said, comfortable casual clothes are often viewed positively. A young person is also likely to be very pleased if the therapist comments that they like the clothing and appearance of the young person – but only if it is true! (No marshmallowing or throwing of fake strokes please!) – and they will usually respond well to a therapist who takes an active interest in adolescent fashion. However, a young client hearing their therapist saying things like "I used to wear these years ago" is likely to find you embarrassing, and to view you with as much suspicion as they (may) regard their parents.

It is important that you remain congruent. Congruence acts as a powerful modelling of potency (Crossman, 1966) and will enhance the development of the trusting, empathically attuned relationship. Many young people are very astute at spotting incongruity, so the therapist needs to remain congruent, whilst still maintaining a position of curiosity. It is also important that they experience you as making an effort to understand their frame of reference and to appreciate their values and sub-cultural frames of reference.

Often, young people who have not previously met the therapist like to have someone with them for the first session. This may be a parent, foster carer, social worker, youth worker or, perhaps more challenging for the therapist, a friend (yes, this has happened to me on more than one occasion). Whoever the young person chooses should be accepted and brought into the first session. It is often useful to talk with the young person in this session about their relationship with the person who is supporting them. In the case of a 'supporter' being brought into the therapy session, the young person may want the supporter to do much of the talking. This is fine and can get things the young person may feel embarrassed about talking to a stranger about into the open, however, at every possible opportunity seek the young person's own opinion.

How the therapy is framed and offered to the young person is also of importance. Words such as psychotherapy and even counselling can be very frightening for young people. It is wise to be clear that your job is as a therapist, but the young person may prefer to come and see you 'for a chat'. The young person will not forget that you are a therapist, and will be mindful of your role. Many young people, especially young men with antisocial behaviours, find that 'life coaching' is desirable, whereas attending therapy is somehow seen as a failure (Phelps, 2004). It is perfectly acceptable to agree to see a young person for a chat. The young person will, in this instance, often feel less threatened by any standard therapeutic inquiry which, of course, should be similarly toned down – as the contract, at this stage, is for a 'chat' and not for therapy. Just as important conversations with children often take place when they're in the back of a car, during 'a chat', a young person is more likely to tell you about their problems, with the result that the therapist can gain useful information about their frame of reference. During this process, the young person is developing trust in the therapist. A working alliance can be established and cemented during a 'chat', and of course, issues raised in the 'chat' can give the therapist items for specific contracting ("Would you like me to help you with feeling a bit better about yourself in relation to this?"), thus deepening and refining the contract on a moment to moment process basis (Lee, 1997). In addition to gaining information, the therapist is learning how to attune to the young person (Erskine, 1993; Hargaden and Sills, 2002) and gently uncovering the young person's own specific 'edge' for attunement, their areas which are defended etc. As in any therapeutic work, the development of trust is crucial. With young people, it is vital that trust is developed early on in the therapy. A young person will simply not engage with a therapist who they do not hold even very basic levels of trust with. The therapist will possibly be viewed as being in cahoots with whomever the young person is in conflict with, and insufficient trust will not permit the formation of any kind of working alliance. Young people are often mistrustful (possibly, with good reason). In my professional experience, approaching this issue around trust is best done as it would be with an adult client with a mixture of antisocial and paranoid personality adaptations (Kahler, 1979; Ware, 1983; Joines and Stewart, 2002).

Self Supervision 4: Establishing a working alliance

Think about recent encounters you have had with adolescents. This may be in your personal or professional life.

Who were the young people? How did you spend your time with them? How did you engage with them? Did you feel a sense of 'connection' with the young person, and if so, for how long?

Take time to think about the 'making and breaking of contact' with adolescents. What enhanced interpersonal contact? What hindered or fractured contact? What gave you a signal that contact had been made? An intuitive sense? A visceral response? Eye contact? Candid conversations?

Contrast this with a recent moment of contact with an adult (client, friend, colleague, partner, relative). What were the significant similarities? What were the differences? Did you need to do anything differently, or change your perception of contact?

Spend a little while thinking about an adolescent's definition of trust. If you can, ask some young people how they define trust, and how they decide they can trust someone. If you work with teenage clients, ask them if they trust you, and if so, why. What would create a loss of trust?

Take time to think how you can facilitate contact and trust with adolescent clients, bearing in mind each one will be unique and have their own idiosyncratic needs, but that some general features can be identified.

Self Supervision 5: Examining motives: claiming your resources

Think about your work with young people. What motivates you to work with this client group? What experience do you have of working with adolescents? How might an adolescent client react to you? What might you need to change in your way of working to make your approach more friendly to young people? What resources do you need to help you relate more effectively to young people? Are there aspects of 'teen culture' you need to learn about? What and whom are the current (and do bear in mind this will change frequently and rapidly) cultural icons for adolescents?

The relational challenge

The effectiveness and depth of the therapeutic relationship, and consequently the therapy itself, is determined by the capacity of the therapist and client to create a new relational experience (Summers and Tudor, 2000; Hargaden and Sills, 2002). As in work with adult clients, therapy with young people can focus in turns on 'back then', 'out there', and 'in here' exploration of the young person's experiences of relationships (Jacobs, 1988). One way in which the therapeutic relationship can be a very different kind of experience for the young person is in relation to how the therapist views 'the problem' and task of therapy. Viewing the problem as one which is located in an interpersonal, rather than intrapsychic frame has a significant impact. If the young person in front of you is someone who has been referred due to behavioural problems or emotional difficulties then the problem is often seen as being something which is located within the client, rather than a problem which occurs in the interface between the client and the world. To

pursue the problem as being solely located as within the young person is a mistake and one which does not lead to a therapeutic outcome. Taking time to view how the problem is located in an interpersonal matrix, and, at root, has a positive intention, has a different impact to a problem that may be perceived as just the young person 'being difficult'. In my experience, such externalisation does not result in the adolescent either disavowing their own experience of the problem, or in them blaming the environment. Young people attending therapy may already be seeking to blame the rest of the world for their problems. Looking at their problems as being intrapersonal won't change that, and in my experience, often results in the opposite effect with the young person seeking to understand what it is that happens between them and the other people in their life. Sasson-Edgette (2006) presents some interesting ideas on a candid approach to working with young people whereby the therapist is judiciously self-disclosing about their reactions to the young person in the room with them in a way that is not preachy or corny. She proposes a method of therapeutic frankness, flavoured with congruence and immediacy, whilst being mindful of patterns in the young person's life, and the developmental issues young people may face.

Working relationally with adolescents is in some ways different from working relationally with adult clients. The transference is present and alive in the young person's expectations of you, their therapist, and may be plain for all to see, and yet, as with adult clients, there's often more. For example, open hostility may hide a deep, painful need to connect. Positive transferences can sometimes quickly result in the young person seeking to turn the therapist into an object of need gratification. It is not the role of the therapist to gratify the needs of the young person, and doing so may well be counterproductive. It is important to promote the young person's ability to self-soothe and to tolerate frustration, rather than that the therapist perpetuates the myth that one's mental well-being is entirely at the mercy of others gratifying one's needs immediately. Futhermore, it is helpful to explore the young person's experience of frustration; how they experience it and you, the therapist; and what their emotional and behavioural responses can be. The therapist's attitude to negative transference may also need to be different. In my experience the adolescent client may experience negative reactions as overwhelming, may not be able to tolerate them, and may vote with their feet and stop coming to therapy. In this context, it is important to invite your client gently and repetitively to come back to a discussion of what is happening between you, and how they react to your responses. What makes them feel safer and what makes them feel less safe? Like all people, young people use defences as a protection against some threat, often some kind of pain. The sensitive exploration of moment-to-moment reactions, moments of pain, how they withdraw or get hostile in response to you can often shed light on interpersonal patterns, which may be the main reason that the young person is in therapy in the first place (DeYoung, 2003). Drawing attention to your relationship, its dynamics and significance can be bewildering and, to some degree, may be amusing to many young people who, generally, are not invited into participating in a relationship in a mutually influencing way. It could be argued that the core of therapeutic transformation lies here, and that the careful establishing of a new relational experience *is* the therapy with the adolescent.

Starting out: the first session

Coming to therapy can be a frightening, bewildering and strange experience for many adolescents – and adult clients too! Usually the young person will have little or no idea of what to do, or what to expect, so it is useful to take charge of the session without monopolising it or imposing an agenda. In my work with adolescents I have found it useful to cover four basic areas in the initial session:

1. *Discuss the nature of the problem with the young person.*
   Explain to the young person very briefly what you know of their presenting problem, especially if they have been 'presented' by means of a referral. Check out with them that you have understood 'the problem' or issue correctly and invite them to elaborate. It is wise at this point not to probe too deeply. The purpose here is to get a sense of what the situation is for the young person and to begin to comprehend their meanings, develop a sense of their frame of reference and to establish an empathic understanding of them.

2. *Ask the young person what they do in their spare time.*
   Genuine questioning is often useful here, and enables the therapist to build a sense of the young person's social constellation, their interests, and what kind of things are likely to engage them. What are their hobbies and interests? The therapist can also use this information to begin to generate therapeutic metaphors which will appeal to the adolescent client. For example, an adolescent with a keen interest in computers will respond to, and readily understand metaphors of 'circuitry' and 'software problems' when talking about rackets. I have found young people who engage in sports can often be rapidly engaged in 'talking around' complex dynamics and family/ social constellations when using sports teams as metaphors. Parallels can be drawn, the adolescent client can be invited to reflect upon similarities and differences, and can even take on board the idea of 'changing how the team work together'. Working with metaphor also represents an empathic transaction as the young person has a sense of the therapist entering and understanding their frame of reference. In her framework for the initial session of TA with children, James (1969) suggests a framework which includes asking 'What do you like doing?' which, according to her, is designed to engage the child's Child ego state, and enhance the therapeutic relationship by showing genuine interest in your client, combined with willingness to prize what they value.

3. *Talk about school with the young person.*
   Ask them what their favourite subjects are, and which ones they don't like. Ask them whether it is the teacher or the subject they dislike – or both. Invite the young person to reflect on what they do and don't like. This encourages and promotes self-determination and, once again, allows the therapist an opportunity to formulate metaphors and to enhance their empathic understanding of the young person. This is a very simple but powerful intervention and, on more than one occasion, information gathered at this point has been immediately useful in making changes.

   For example, Imran had, until recently, always enjoyed mathematics lessons. It emerged that there was some personality clash between him and his teacher. He was brought to therapy by his education welfare officer, who had a word with the head of mathematics at Imran's school, and arranged for him to move classes. After a few weeks in therapy I checked this with Imran, who reported that he had begun to enjoy his maths classes again, and had caught up on work he had got behind with.

4. *Explain a little about how therapy works.*
The therapist needs to discuss and explain the boundaries of the therapeutic relationship, the nature and limitations of confidentiality, frequency of sessions and so forth. This is similar to the administrative and business contracts (Steiner, 1974) but needs to be done in a way which accounts for the young person's development and cognitive abilities. Adolescent clients are likely to be even more unfamiliar with the nature of therapy than an adult client, and so explaining how you see the sessions working for the young person, and discussing what they might expect to gain from therapy, and also what they might be expected to do is wise. This can often spontaneously lead into the young person generating their own therapeutic contract, and also paves the way for some procedures which the young person might find unusual. For example, you might tell a young person that you may invite them to engage in 'role play' with you in the sessions as a gentle way of introducing two-chair work. Liberally scatter explanations and illustrative examples throughout.

Self Supervision 6: Initial meeting

Reflect upon a recent first encounter with a teenager. How did you feel on meeting the young person? How did you feel during the encounter? How did you feel afterwards? What is your perception of how the young person was feeling immediately on meeting you, whilst talking to you, and after the meeting? What do you think you could have done differently to improve the level of contact between you? Was the pacing and depth of the work appropriate and well attuned? What skills do you already have in meeting people and making them feel comfortable? Think of three personality characteristics you possess which make you an easy person to be around and/or which mean that others view you positively?

Pacing

The pace and tempo of all therapy needs to be attuned to the individual rhythms of the client

(Erskine, Moursund and Trautmann, 1999). However, psychotherapy with young people requires that the therapist pays particular attention to the pacing of the therapy. Adolescence is a time of phenomenal neurological pruning and re-organisation, and as part of this process, teenagers operate with a different temporal sense to adults. Whilst adolescents commonly have a very rapid and jumping-from-theme-to-theme cognitive process, young people may also have a slower, more considered process, taking time to assimilate information, and it is not uncommon for young people to switch between rapidly shifting attention, to slower processes. The therapist needs to attune to the pace of the particular young person's process on a moment-to-moment basis. If the therapy is felt to be too slow by the young person, they are likely to lose interest and disengage. If the therapy is felt to be moving too quickly, the young person may well feel overwhelmed, and could potentially draw negative self-conclusions, for example, ''This is going over my head. I must be really stupid.'' It is often useful to vary the pace of sessions, partly to avoid a sense of predictability. An unpredictable pace can help to keep the young person curious and interested and would possibly be a neurologically attuned way of meeting the young person's stimulus hunger. Our needs for stimulus hunger changes throughout our life cycle, and different stages of development require different levels and intensities of stimulation. The changes taking place in an adolescent's pre-frontal cortex are possibly the cause of this need for more intense stimulation, and a need for higher incident hunger. Furthermore, the therapist changing the pace of the therapy and maintaining high levels of stimulation to keep pace with the adolescent client's rhythms is in keeping with the treatment approach used with clients with an antisocial adaptation (Joines and Stewart, 2002), a treatment approach often very suitable for use with adolescent clients.

A few words on empathy

In many ways empathy is the 'oil' which lubricates therapy. Many writers of different theoretical orientations have written eloquently about empathy and its centrality in the therapeutic encounter, so here I shall just focus on the utilisation of empathy in therapy with adolescent clients.

Empathic responding is not just about looking for the emotional flavour of what the client is saying, or even the flavour of what the client is *almost* saying. To me, empathy goes deeper and accounts for the *context* of the client, and the context both within and outside the therapy room of what they are saying in order that you as the therapist reach as full an understanding of your client as is realistically possible. Part of this context is the interpersonal (see previous section, The relational challenge), and I think it worthwhile to consider how our clients stay where they are because of what they believe about other people, and about other people's reactions to them and any change. Sasson-Edgette (2006) reminds us that many teenage clients are so painfully attached to the thought that they might lose face that change seems impossible without humiliating themselves in some way. If, as a therapist, you can consider this kind of dilemma, then you may achieve a more attuned, accounting, empathic response which will deepen the relationship. In my view it is such consideration of the emotional, interpersonal and social impact of change for the young person that deepens our empathic response to them, and creates options for further exploration.

Adolescent development: therapeutic implications

In engaging in therapy with adolescent clients, the therapist needs to be particularly sensitive to providing therapy which is in keeping with the young person's development.

Throughout the course of adolescence, young people are constantly re-writing their script. Traditionally within TA, script formation is considered to be complete by approximately ages 8–10. However, due to the plasticity of the brain and new developmental stages the adolescent is moving through, the original script can be re-written or confirmed. This has significant implications for therapists working with adolescents, as skilled intervention can 'put a new show on the road', and effectively transform the young person's script prospects.

Adolescence is primarily a time for formation of script in the context of self and others. In adolescence we are shaping our identity to create a sold sense of 'I', and more specifically 'I-in-relation-to-you'. Erikson (1950) described this stage as the phase of 'identity versus identity diffusion'. Both Sigmund and Anna Freud see the libido as being directed outwards, towards others at this stage (Freud, S., 1905; Freud, A., 1963). Specifically from within a TA framework, Levin (1974) describes adolescence as the stage of 'sex and separation', whereby the individual is learning how to be separate, and attached at the same time, and also developing ways of being in relation to others.

Throughout my career as a psychotherapist I have worked with many adult clients whose social difficulties and anxiety can be directly attributed to bullying that occurred during their adolescence. Young people who have injunctions such as 'Don't Be Important', 'Don't Belong', 'Don't Be You' and 'Don't Exist' are very likely to view the bullying as confirmation of these injunctions. It is possible that such young people may even be more susceptible to bullying in the first place, as they are very likely to feel a little awkward in social settings and have no sense of any right to act assertively and value their self.

The reactions of others to the bullying is also important. A young person who seeks help and does not get the help they need, or the 'help' is counterproductive or makes the situation worse due to lack of potency and clear thinking may well develop a despairing position and have significant problems with trusting others. Conversely, an effective and potent response to the bullying, combined with work to preserve the young person's self-esteem and develop their sense of 'OK-ness' is likely to result in an enhanced sense of trust in the world, a belief that they are important and are valued, and the young person may possibly introject new positive Parent ego states.

Social development is a central part of adolescence. Teenagers commonly spend hours on the phone to their friends, and spend increasing amounts of time socialising. Issues around belonging are in the forefront, and young people are in effect asking the question "Where do I fit in and with whom do I fit in?" Naturally, mistakes will be made along the way, however, a therapist working with a young person through such occasions can help reframe such disappointments and assist the young person to learn from them and not draw unhelpful inferences. The emergence of sexual relationships and sexuality is also of vital importance here. Many young people are preoccupied with thoughts about boyfriends and girlfriends, and may be sexually active. Obviously, the establishment of a strong therapeutic alliance where the young person trusts the therapist, and can disclose such things to the therapist without fear of being 'preached at' or 'moralized at' is highly desirable. It is important though that as a therapist, you work out what your position is on underage sex. If a client of say, thirteen years discloses that they are having sex, how would you react? What would you do? Would the age of their partner signify in your decision? How would taking any particular course of action be interpreted by the young person? It is my view that the therapist working with young people needs to be prepared to take on some educative tasks, particularly in relation to sex and sexual health (Smith and Widdowson, 2003). I would urge all therapists who either work with adolescents, or intend to work with adolescents to avail themselves of up-to-date sexual health information (and to keep updating) and find out about young people's sexual health services in their area.

The cognitive changes of development take a quantum leap in adolescence, and the therapist can effectively intervene and utilise the plasticity of the brain and cognitive changes to promote healthy development, and help reverse previous negative scripting. Significant changes in the way young people think are occurring, for instance it is during the teenage years that abstract and ethical thinking is developed (Piaget, 1966; Flavell, 1977; Kohlberg, 1984). Therapeutic methods for examining script and script beliefs can be very powerful tools in working with adolescents. One such example is the racket system (Erskine and Zalcman, 1979). The script beliefs about self, others and the quality of life which emerge during the course of therapy with your teenage clients can be effectively challenged and replaced with healthier, more positively adaptive beliefs which will be more helpful to the young person throughout their life. Adolescents commonly like to question things, and are developing the ability to think in abstract terms (Piaget, 1966; Flavell, 1977). In this respect, script beliefs are 'ripe for picking' as the therapist can facilitate the adolescent through imagining the potential long-term impact of a particular script belief. Of significance in the therapeutic arena are the developmental processes the young person is going through of emergence of thinking in terms of causal relationships, the examining of 'exceptions to the rule', and also of working out myriad possible outcomes. The development of such faculties can be positively utilised by the therapist to great effect. Gentle confrontation and reality testing or indeed any interventions which invite an Adult processing of available information, or ones which confront racket fantasies may need to be provided by the therapist in the case of abstract thinking going to unlikely extremes or outcomes which are not really based on reality (which of course can be a sign of the young persons developing creativity, but also can be linked to their lack of life experience).

The processes of adolescents can be likened to those of narcissistic and antisocial personalities. This is not to say that adolescents are narcissistic or antisocial *per se*, though, as a part of their normal development, they may appear to share many traits of these disorders. The healthy intention of such emergent processes is simply one of individuation and of developing one's own sense of self and value base. From a transactional perspective, it is helpful to think of this process in terms of anti-script, the idea of going against the script but from a rebellious position. The narcissistic or antisocial flavour to such processes can be considered from a wider social perspective that the young person is questioning norms and challenging cultural scripting. It is also common to come across young people who tell fantastically unreal stories about themselves, for instance, telling people that they are best friends with a pop star, when this is clearly not the case. It is not necessary to confront these fantasies; however, it might be useful to invite the young person to consider carefully who they tell such stories to, especially if they are experiencing problems with their peers. Young people are often prone to grandiosity or discounting and can often feel badly misunderstood ("You just don't understand!"). This can be gently and sensitively confronted, along with other forms and levels of discounting and redefining transactions.

Young people take great strides towards individuation and autonomy throughout adolescence. However, with little personal power and life experience, and the (ongoing) influence of their script and their family/social context, this process can be difficult, and often results in the young person defining their sense of self by employing their anti-script. Sensitive questioning and explanation by the therapist can be very useful to the adolescent in order for them to establish their individuation and autonomy, whilst both remain respectful to the need for some anti-script to be used as part of the process of the adolescent's individuation from their parents. Their emerging identity can be linked to the development of a constant and well-formed Adult ego state. Indeed, the promotion of a strong Adult ego state is clearly a crucial role for the therapist in working with adolescents, and the therapist can play an important part in encouraging the young person to develop their sense of self. Various TA authors associate different ego states as being the source of 'the self': Hargaden and Sills (2002) see the self as being located within A_1 (the Adult in the Child ego state), whilst Tudor (2003) sees the self as being located within the Integrating Adult (A_2). The therapist can work with either model of ego states, however adherence to one preferred model and consistency of application is vital to ensure continuity of therapeutic approach and of the therapy.

Teenagers are also often interested in the concept of fairness, and are able to think about other people, and other people's perspectives. Therapeutically speaking, this is useful when drawn out using circular questioning (see below). Also of therapeutic relevance is the development of a young person's social and moral conscience. The therapist may find that coaching the young person who begins to discuss matters of fairness in basic empathic skills greatly helpful. Learning how to empathise is in my view a skill which anyone would find useful, and seizing an opportunity to begin such learning is a valid therapeutic or psychoeducational strategy. My own experience has been that many adolescents enjoy learning such subtle interpersonal skills, and often apply them effectively and creatively in a wide range of situations.

Adolescents are undergoing phenomenal physical change, which has direct implications in terms of understanding their behaviour and their processes. Adjustment to such changes is not easy, given the rapidly moving vista the young person experiences on a daily basis. One way of considering this is that the young person by definition is experiencing a persistent state of adjustment crisis. A wise therapist accounts for the multiple changes, and multiply levelled changes occurring within and around the adolescent client.

We are all aware of the growth spurt which happens during adolescence, specifically, changes associated with puberty. The emerging sexuality, and physical sexual development and hormonal surges have implications in terms of genesis of sex-related shame, and sex-related script issues. Indeed, the potentiality for the foundations being laid for a future psychosexual problem seem to be immense. My clinical experience of working with adults with psychosexual problems has shown a general trend towards sex-related trauma, shaming or a negative sexual self-image commonly occurring during these critical adolescent years. The messages adolescents receive and internalise (or introject) during this phase of development can have a significant impact on their adult sexuality. Recently, some attention has been given to the messages young women are drawing from the fashion industry and popular culture. Images of thin young women with perfect hair and perfect teeth (which may, of course, be air brushed to wipe out blemishes) abound. Many people are critical of such imagery and are mindful of the potential effect routine exposure to such images may have on young women with fragile self-esteem. For young women who do not conform to such images, they may decide that they are unattractive, or may be ostracised socially. Young men are also more recently experiencing the influence of media images of gym-toned, tanned men and are also experiencing a surge in body image problems and eating disorders. Young people at school who either enter puberty very early or very late are often teased, which can result in poor self-esteem and unhelpful sexual scripting. The young person may need to internalise certain permissions and receive appropriate information during this period of sexuality development to inoculate against future pathology (see Levin, 1974).

The hormonal changes are only one part of a complex picture of adolescent development. Adolescence is a time of massive neurological reorganisation. The changes occurring within the adolescent brain are of such magnitude that they can be compared to the changes occurring in the brain of the new born infant – and as such, go a long way to explain the excessive sleepiness of adolescents! These changes have specific implications in terms of affective regulation. To simplify: young people do not necessarily have the neurological equipment to deal with strong emotions, or to contain their emotions. Witness the slammed doors and sudden outbursts. This is not intended to absolve adolescents of responsibility, but to draw to the therapist's attention that some types of affective regulation are simply not possible at various times during adolescence. The neurological changes also enable us to make sense of some of the risk taking that many teenagers engage in. Such risk-taking, however, needs to be understood in a complex matrix of factors, most notably peer relationships, and the types of risk-taking the young person engages in are likely to be influenced by the behaviours of their peers (see Strauch, 2003).

Self Supervision 7: Adolescent development

Spend some time exploring the different information available about adolescence and learning more about adolescent development. As you learn more, think about how each concept or process might impact upon the therapy. How might each of the developmental processes be manifest in the therapeutic relationship? What interventions might you use to promote developmental growth? How might each of these developmental processes either confirm, or contradict existing psychotherapeutic theory? How does this fit with your schema of therapy and your conceptualisation of psychotherapy?

Therapy with adolescents: process and tasks

Promote developmental growth

The therapist can play an important role in facilitating and promoting developmental growth with adolescent clients. This requires careful attention to the presenting developmental state of the adolescent client on a moment-to-moment basis. The therapist will need to employ varying modes of communicative matching as the adolescent client makes rapid shifts between age appropriate states or grown up modes of relating and thinking, and momentary regression into earlier, younger developmental states and modes of relating and thinking. Ideally, the therapist's interventions must invite the adolescent to increase their development, to make space for integration of developmental movement, or to prepare for later developmental progress. Repetitive regression is not necessarily an indicator of pathology, and indeed in many ways is very normal for teenagers.

Create a therapeutic environment for adolescent clients

It is worth spending some time in making your therapy rooms 'adolescent friendly'. Keeping a supply of soft drinks (be conscious of sugar levels and additives, especially if working with young people with ADHD) or fruit juice and snacks (fruit and crisps are popular and not laden with sugar and additives) will help make the young person feel comfortable. At the psychological level, the message hidden (implicit psychological level transaction) in the provision of such items gives the message "You are welcome here" and it is possible that your adolescent clients will also build a positive association between therapy and taking on board the sense of their physical needs being met, and that therapy is a space for them to feel nourished.

If you have a waiting area, offering a small selection of teenage magazines to read is a wise move. Be ready to replace these fairly regularly. It will very likely be noted and commented on if the magazines are out of date. Magazines for young people also contain articles of interest to young people and may, for instance, include articles on bullying or on sexual health and can provide a springboard into productive therapeutic work on those issues, especially if you have enquired about what the young person is reading. For example:

Therapist:	So what have you been reading about while you were waiting?
Client:	I was reading about skincare routines and there was this really stupid letter in the problem page by a girl who is having sex with her boyfriend and doesn't want to.
Therapist:	Yeah, I notice that you always pay attention and obviously take care of your appearance. What was daft about the letter?

This strokes the client's personal care and invites discussion about sexual health and issues of consent and assertiveness.

If a young person seems particularly interested in one of the magazines, it won't hurt to allow them to take it home to read (and possibly re-read) at their leisure and in privacy. Discussion of images contained in such magazines have also proved to be fruitful openers for evaluation of self-image in relation to prevalent media images.

It is also useful to keep a box or drawer with items of stationery and creative materials for young people to use. If you intend to use written exercises, homework or journalling with your clients as therapeutic tasks, giving the young person a nice notebook and a pen is a popular move. The notebook and pen may take on the significance of transitional objects for your clients, and may seek to act as a solid reminder of their therapy and their relationship with you. TA employs many diagrammatic representations of concepts and TA therapists often use diagrams to facilitate information gathering, for example, the racket system diagram (Erskine and Zalcman, 1975) (see Chapter 9) or, from outside TA, a family genogram diagram. Young people will often respond very positively to compiling such diagrams in the therapy session. Diagrams can be adorned with symbols and pictorial representations of issues presented, for instance, drawing sad faces etc. (see below for more on creative interventions with adolescents). I am reminded of one young man who spent much of his therapy making origami animals – and giving me many opportunities for stroking his creativity whilst also learning new skills myself! We would often then use the origami animals for psychodrama style enactments, or discussing the various attributes of animals, thus giving him an opportunity to work therapeutically on a metaphorical level and at a distance which felt safe for him.

Make and maintain therapeutic boundaries with young people

Attention needs to be paid to the boundaries of the therapeutic relationship. Boundaries which would normally be appropriate when working with adult clients are not necessarily appropriate or desirable in working with young people. One example of this is the relative fluidity of the role of therapist in working with adolescent clients. The therapist can effectively hold multiple roles simultaneously for the young person. The therapist may also act (in a lesser way) as a mentor, a role model, an advocate, a 'case coordinator' and many other possible roles at different stages of the therapy. Whilst protecting the integrity of the therapeutic space is paramount, therapeutic potency may require a willingness to expand the parameters of the therapeutic relationship. Any possibility that you might be invited to step outside of the usual boundaries, discussion of the proposed change

and the therapeutic benefits and potential pitfalls, all need to be carefully attended to in supervision.

It is often useful to consider each session with a young person as the whole of the therapy in itself. Adolescent clients may suddenly cease therapy without warning for a whole range of reasons; maybe they got what they wanted, or felt that the therapy was not right for them at that time. Informing the client at the outset of the work that they are free to end whenever they wish, and return whenever they wish (assuming there are no issues connected with funding etc) hands the control and power back to the young person and promotes their empowerment (and paradoxically, almost) is more likely to result in the young person attending regularly. Considering each session to be the last does not mean that all themes should be immediately attended to, and contracting to talk about a particular issue another time is fine, but do not be surprised if the client does not return for subsequent sessions, and ensure that the client leaves the session feeling relatively upbeat and positive. Such premature termination of the therapy is not, in my view, necessarily indicative of avoidance or resistance. From a humanistic perspective decisions to end therapy should always be respected and understood from the point of view that the young person has decided it is time to stop therapy. Where funding is not an issue, and a young person has abruptly ended what appeared to be useful therapy, the therapist can, if they see fit, contact the young person and invite them back for another session. I am increasingly finding that text messages are not only positively received but are a wise use of the currency of adolescence. I have made contact in this way several times with great positive effect and have usually had the response "Oh, I forgot the session and was scared you'd be angry with me, so didn't get in touch even though I wanted to." Of course, some young people may not want to resume contact, but as long as they know that that is OK with you, and that *they* are OK with you, the therapy can be considered to be ended, and concluded positively.

Specific interventions

I list here just a small selection of the myriad potential interventions a therapist may employ effectively with young people.

Questioning methods

The specific modes of inquiry the therapist employs with adult clients (Erskine, Moursund and Trautmann, 1999; Hargaden and Sills, 2002) need to be modified slightly to suit work with adolescent clients. Questioning needs to be done sensitively to avoid the therapy sessions deteriorating into question-and-answer sessions and to minimise any possibility that the young person may feel aggressively interrogated. An open style of questioning which reduces the chances of a one word answer being given are preferable, and ones which invite the young person to express their views, especially when this can be done 'at a distance', can be very helpful. The therapist can ask the adolescent client what their views are about a specific issue, for example contraception. The therapist needs to be cautious in having any specific agenda, as young people may well avoid any kinds of questioning which is likely to leave them feeling trapped, railroaded or caught out, and may also result in the young person terminating the therapy. A curious and open approach to questioning seems to provide the most consistently effective results.

As adolescents are often interested in the views and thoughts of others, circular questioning (a technique and tool of some forms of family and couples therapy) can be a very helpful method, especially when inviting a young person to consider alternative perspectives and different frames of reference. Circular questions are ones which invite the young person to express what they think others think or feel or how they think others would react in relation to a specific issue, for example: "So, what do you think your mum thinks about you and your brother fighting? . . . Ah, so she possibly feels really upset and angry about it . . . What do you think about you fighting upsets her most?" This is a safe method of questioning of young people, and often, after explaining what they think someone else might think, they will volunteer their own views.

Some of the questioning methods used in redecision therapy, both within TA and within neuro-linguistic programming, can be very helpful with young people. Questions which invite awareness of internal processes (psychological and physiological), as well as questions which heighten such awareness, can add significantly to the emotional literacy of a young person. Also, exaggerating questions such as "What's stopping all this from being a complete disaster?" can be useful.

Solution-focused approaches utilise 'finding the exception'. In this mode of questioning, 'the exception to the rule' is explored. This is useful when working with young people who claim something is always the case, such as "I always argue with my mum" or "The science teacher always shouts at me". The therapist can use a similar approach to invite the young person to draw distinctions between states or to account for the changeability of situations by using questions like "What times do you not feel so down?" or "When do you feel worse?"

Affirmations to change belief patterns

Generating a list of affirmations for the young person to use can often be useful. This method works best when the affirmations are co-created by therapist and client in direct response to the uncovering of specific limiting beliefs (Beck, 1979). Whilst compiling a racket system (Erskine and Zalcman, 1979) with the young person, the therapist can begin to formulate affirmations or reframed beliefs about self, others and the quality of life and the nature of the world, and at an appropriate time, introduce these into the therapy.

The affirmations can be drawn up on colourful paper, or written out with coloured ink. Some young people will often go home and redraw the affirmations list or type them out on a computer. Many young people will not repeat affirmations out loud – afraid of others hearing them or of generally feeling silly, so it is best not to push too hard for them to use their affirmations as a 'spoken out loud' exercise. Invite the young person to mentally repeat the affirmation, and as they do so, to determine how many per cent they actually believe the affirmation. They are then invited to repeat the process and see if there is any change to the percentage that the affirmation is believed. If a young person keeps a record of the percentages on a daily basis, the therapist can then explore with the young person what would be required for the percentage to rise. What other beliefs might they need to challenge? What could they actively do to increase their own attachment to positive beliefs? What events occurred to influence the change in percentage? If using this method, the therapist should pre-warn their client that the percentages can change from day to day, and that variations are to be expected, again, to prevent the young person drawing an unfavourable conclusion about themselves or a sense of shame.

Affirmations can also be given in the form of specific stroking. The therapist should ideally be liberally stroking with adolescent clients, positively commenting on achievements, however seemingly small. For example: "I think you dealt with that difficult situation really well". Remember: social relationships are important to adolescents, who define much of their sense of self from relationships, and positive strokes can be internalised with great positive effect for the young person.

Keeping a journal

Many young people like to keep diaries and journals. This, however, is a problem for young people who do not have sufficient privacy, and some young people are too scared to keep a frank, honest diary for fear of discovery. Indeed, many young people have experienced unpleasant and sometimes damaging reactions and responses from others when their diaries have been read. If the young person does have access to a safe place, or can leave their journal with someone they trust then this can be very facilitative. One young person asked me to look after a ring binder that they used as a journal; they wrote their entries on A4 paper, which they found relatively easy to hide, and then brought them to therapy. Writing a diary or journal can be an incredibly effective method for revealing patterns and emerging themes. The client can record and understand their own change process and develop a sense of mastery and ownership of their own narrative. Journals and specific journalling methods can help develop awareness of recurring problematic situations (which are then ripe for game analysis), promote the adolescent's reflective capacity, and enhance their emotional literacy and emotional differentiation.

If you intend to use journal writing with adolescent clients, you might wish to compile an information sheet (which you can amend as you find what works and what doesn't). Some suggestions include:

- What happened? What do I think about these events now?
- How did this event leave me feeling? How did I feel at the time/ how do I feel about these events now?

- What might I have done differently? What will I do in future in a similar situation? How will I help ensure I will react differently? Is there any specific support I need to help me do things differently next time?
- What I have learnt is . . .
- What I need to do next is . . .

Emotional literacy

I present here a simple emotional literacy exercise which I have repeatedly found to be popular and immensely helpful with the young people I have worked with. Quite simply, invite the young person to write the following headings on the top of a piece of paper, one sheet for each sentence. The young person is instructed to finish each sentence as many times as possible using their own endings, and to rate the intensity of the feeling relating to each feeling statement on a scale of one to one hundred:

- I am angry that . . .
- I am sad that . . .
- I am scared that . . .
- I am glad that . . .

Finishing the exercise on a positive note will help with generating positive associations with emotional literacy work. This exercise is helpful in enabling young people to differentiate their emotional states and become aware of the complexity of emotions they may feel at any one time or in response to any one situation. Practice in expressing emotions in many different ways can be very helpful in providing your adolescent clients with a basic vocabulary to express their feelings in therapy.

For further reading on tools for use with adolescent clients see Geldard and Geldard (1999).

Self Supervision 8: Interventions and techniques

Brainstorm some of the interventions and techniques you use with adult clients. How might these techniques be used with adolescent clients? Which might be more appropriate? Which would need careful introduction?

Psychoeducational approaches

TA offers many easily understood, readily applied and powerfully effective tools for psychoeducational work. Teaching basic TA concepts to young people can be thought of as providing the young person with tools which they can use for more effective living, and for promoting their autonomy. TA uses language which is easily understood (albeit somewhat dated) and can be explained and comprehended by people of varying abilities. In working with young people, it can be extremely profitable to share your thinking in relation to specific TA concepts as and when they arise in the therapy. Adolescent clients will often respond very positively to such invitations, especially if they think the material is likely to be fun or have a problem solving function or gives them some kind of social advantage.

Psychoeducational group work differs from normal group therapy, in that it is more structured and general. Of course, in such group work there is scope for individual change and small pieces of work, but in a psychoeducational group with young people, the principal therapeutic task is to facilitate the strengthening of the Adult ego state of the participants.

A psychoeducational group tackling bullying*

The group was established in a school, and met weekly after lessons had finished. The education welfare officers contacted each teacher and asked them to promote the group to all their classes as a group for tackling bullying in the school. Young people who were known to be bullied were also specifically targeted and encouraged to attend. Meetings lasted for just over an hour.

The model

The group met in a large room, usually used for drama classes. The first ten minutes were spent moving chairs into a circle. The young people were often rowdy, and we would engage them in various small tasks, or conversations until the group were settled down. Sessions then began with an exercise we called 'One good thing, one bad thing'. Participants would describe something from the previous week which was good, and something which was bad. This exercise offered an opportunity to stroke and celebrate achievements or situations handled well, and in the 'one bad thing' part, to discover

what was bothering the young people, and alert us to any specific problems. Any problems could then be picked up and dealt with by the education welfare officers, modelling potency and providing a swift and effective intervention to tackle the bullying. Several channels for reporting bullying and processes for tackling the bullying and the bullies were established with key members of staff in advance. The young people were also gently coached in active listening skills and as expected, over a period of weeks became much more open regarding their emotions.

We then started the group off with an exercise. Exercises introduced included:

- Stroking and stroking profiles – the young people were taught about strokes and the stroke economy (Steiner, 1974) (see Chapter 1) and were then invited to draw graphs relating to their own stroking profile. Exercises in giving and receiving positive strokes followed.
- The drama triangle (see Chapter 3) – a short clip of a popular soap opera was played and the young people were then invited to analyse the clip using the drama triangle.
- Exploring the racket system (see Chapter 9) – the group were invited to think of bad experiences from their past, and what negative conclusions they drew from these events about themselves and others.

After one of these exercises, which, bearing in mind the attention span of the young people, would take no more than 15 minutes, we would have a 10 minute break, where soft drinks and snacks were available. Often young people would come up to one of the workers and disclose something about a particular event, or some concern of theirs. The break finished with a five to ten minute physical game, one which ideally involved lots of noise and running around to burn off some of the energy. We found the group got very restless and some members would get disruptive after 30 minutes until we put in a physical game as part of the session plan.

The next part of the session was spent on interpersonal skills, such as assertiveness or basic counselling skills. One concept was taught for about five minutes and then the young people were split into small groups to practice the new skill.

The session concluded with a long check-out circle, and members were invited to reflect on

---

*I would like to acknowledge Donna Jones, Youth Worker, and Jo Daley and Wendy Crookes, Education Welfare Officers, for their invaluable contribution to this work.

their feelings. Each person concluded with a statement about:

- How they were feeling at the beginning of the session.
- How they were feeling at the end of the session.
- What helped to change how they felt.
- What they had learnt, about themselves or others, or something they found useful or interesting (good feedback for group leaders – we could modify our approach from this feedback).
- What they were going to do differently, or for the first time in the following week.
- What nice thing they were going to do for themselves over the next week.
- What nice thing they were going to do to help someone else feel good over the next week.

Over a period of a few weeks, some young people left the group, as it did not meet their needs, whilst others joined and were accepted and supported quickly. The young people, all of whom had been bullied and had often been very isolated developed their own friendship groups, and spent time together at breaks and lunchtime. These groups would often intervene in bullying if they saw it happening, and would support other students (often using the basic counselling skills they had learnt in the group) experiencing bullying. At the end of the year, the feedback from members was excellent, and many had grown and changed dramatically as a direct result of the positive experience they had in the group.

Psychotherapy with adolescents can be wonderfully stimulating, intensely rewarding and massively frustrating work. Therapists trained in methods most suited to working with articulate adult clients will need to revisit their approach to therapy, and modify their therapeutic methods accordingly. Specific attention paid to the therapeutic relationship and the need for different boundaries will provide a potent space in which the young person can re-evaluate their script safely and update accordingly.

References

Beck, A.T. (1979) *Cognitive Therapy and the Emotional Disorders*. Harmondsworth: Penguin.

Berne, E. (1963) *Games People Play*. New York: Grove Press.

Collishaw, S., Maughan, B., Goodman, R., and Pickles, A. (2004) Time Trends in Adolescent Mental Health. *Journal of Child Psychology and Psychiatry*, 45: 8, 1350–62.

Crossman, P. (1966) Permission and Protection. *Transactional Analysis Bulletin*, 5: 9, 152–4.

De Young, P. (2003) *Relational Psychotherapy: A Preview*. London: Routledge.

English, F. (1975) The Three-Cornered Contract. *Transactional Analysis Journal*, 5, 383–4.

Erikson, R. (1950) *Childhood and Society*. London: Penguin.

Erskine, R. (1993) *Interactive Psychotherapy: Enquiry, Attonement and Involvement. A Theory of Methodology*. Workshop (6–8 July). Iron Mill Institute, Exeter: Devon.

Erskine, R. and Trautmann, R. (1996) Methods of an Integrative Psychotherapy. *Transactional Analysis Journal*, 26, 316–28.

Erskine, R., Moursund, J. and Trautmann, R. (1999) *Beyond Empathy*. New York: Brunner-Routledge.

Erskine, R. and Zalcman, M. (1979) The Racket System: A Model for Racket Analysis. *Transactional Analysis Journal*, 9, 51–9.

Flavell, J. (1977) *Cognitive Development*. Englewood Cliffs, NJ: Prentice-Hall.

Freud, A. (1963) *The Ego and the Mechanisms of Defence* (rev. edn.). Madison, CT: International Universities Press.

Freud, S. (1905) Three Essays on the Theory of Sexuality. In Stevens, R. (1983) *Freud and Psychoanalysis*. Milton Keynes: Open University Press.

Geldard, K. and Geldard, D. (1999) *Counselling Adolescents*. London: Sage.

Hargaden, H. and Sills, C. (2002) *Transactional Analysis: A Relational Perspective*. London: Brunner-Routledge.

Jacobs, M. (1988) *Psychodynamic Counselling in Action*. London: Sage.

James, M. (1969) Transactional Analysis with Children: The Initial Session. *Transactional Analysis Bulletin*, 8: 29, 1–2.

Joines, V. and Stewart, I. (2002) *Personality Adaptations: A New Guide to Human Understanding in Psychotherapy and Counselling*. Nottingham: Lifespace.

Kahler, T. (1979) *Transactional Analysis Revisited*. Little Rock, AR: Human Delevopment Publications.

Kitchener, K.S. (1984) Intuition, Critical Evaluation and Ethical Principles: The

Foundation for Ethical Decisions in Counselling Psychology. *Counselling Psychologist*, 12, 43–55.

Kohlberg, L. (1984) *The Psychology of Moral Development: The Nature and Validity of Moral Stages*. San Francisco: Harper and Row.

Kohut, H. (1971) *The Analysis of the Self*. London: Hogarth.

Lee, A. (1997) Process contracts. In Sills, C. (Ed.) *Contracts in Counselling*. London: Sage.

Levin, P. (1974) *Becoming the Way We Are*. Menlo Park, CA: Trans. Pubs.

Piaget, J. (1966) *The Psychology of Intelligence*. New York: Harcourt.

Phelps, G. (2004) *Life Coaching as an Alternative to Psychotherapy with Antisocial Young Men*. Unpublished essay. Berne Institute, Kegworth.

Sasson-Edgette, J. (2006) *Adolescent Therapy That Really Works*. New York: Norton.

Smith, B. and Widdowson, M. (2003) Child-centred Counselling Practice. In Lago, C. and Smith, B. (Eds.) *Anti-discriminatory Councelling Practice*. London: Sage.

Steiner, C. (1974) *Scripts People Live: Transactional Analysis of Life Scripts*. New York: Grove Press.

Stewart, I (1997) Outcome-Focused Contracts. In Sills, C. (Ed.) *Contracts in Counselling*. London: Sage.

Stewart, I. (1998) *Developing Transactional Analysis Counselling*. London: Sage.

Strauch, B. (2003) *Why Are They so Weird? What's Really Going on in a Teenager's Brain*. London: Bloomsbury.

Summers, G. and Tudor, K. (2000) Cocreative Transactional Analysis. *Transactional Analysis Journal*, 30: 1, 23–40.

Tudor, K. (1997) A Complexity of Contracts. In Sills, C. (Ed.) *Contracts in Counselling*. London: Sage.

Tudor, K. (2003) The Neopsyche: The Integrating Adult Ego State. In Sills, C. and Hargaden, H. (Eds.) *Ego States*. London: Worth Publishing.

Ware, P. (1983) Personality Adaptations: Doors to Therapy. *Transactional Analysis Journal*, 13: 11–19.

CHAPTER 11

Therapeutic Work with Children and Parents

Diane Hoyer and Laura Hyatt

This chapter expands on the approach outlined in Chapter 3, using case examples. We demonstrate different ways we work for change with children, highlighting the diverse nature of our work with parents to complement the therapy with the child. This can range from minimal involvement such as six-weekly review meetings, through to weekly sessions which focus upon parenting education.

We present two case vignettes demonstrating our respective work with children and parents, which illustrate our use of the treatment triangle, and the two different theories regarding the impact of trauma (see Chapter 3). We also present a positive parenting strategy that enables parents to understand the needs of their child or children, and offer methods for enhancing attunement and improving attachment (the details of which form Appendix 5).

Katie (LH)

Katie, aged 12, demonstrated secure attachment to her mother, Tina, and had no experience of abuse before the age of seven when she was physically and sexually abused by her step-father. Katie's early life experiences may thus be viewed in terms of the developmental theory (1) (see Chapter 3) whereby abuse interrupts usual developmental processes and alters the usual developmental pathway.

Katie experienced a global and overwhelming feeling of scare which related to herself at the age at which she was abused. I assessed/diagnosed that in her Child ego state Katie was confused by the trauma she had suffered. When faced with a threat to her life if she disclosed the abuse, her survival instinct took over and she opted not to tell her mother. Therefore, she did not receive the protection and nurture she needed at that time. Nevertheless, this decision demonstrated her commitment to staying alive, which supported my assessment that the parenting she received in her early years had been a positive influence on her development of self. In making my assessment I also took account of the Adult ego state energy available to Katie that would help her to stay in the here-and-now whilst doing this therapeutic work. In my opinion, Katie had sufficient energy for therapy to be viable and to make a contract with me in which:

- *She would identify the qualities of a good parent, and then*
- *She would apply these to what she would have needed, aged seven.*

For my part, I agreed:

- *To help and support her in this.*
- *To provide information, as needed.*

My treatment plan was to assist Katie to reparent herself, having identified deficits in the parenting she received from around the time her step-father came into the family. The change in the family dynamic meant that Katie's mother was less available for Katie and meeting her emotional needs. Firstly, I asked Katie to define what a good enough parent was and does, and what kind of parenting she would have liked to have had at the time of her abuse. It was important to establish this in Adult awareness so that Katie could integrate these qualities into her own Parent ego state. As Katie enjoyed artwork, she drew herself at the age of seven and talked to 'Little Katie' as a nurturing and protective parent would do, giving herself specific messages about the abuse, such as: "I am keeping you safe." In this way, and reinforced by affirmations from me, she incorporated a Nurturing Parent ego state, a process which James (1974) refers to as 'self-reparenting'. Katie benefited from this work by being able to keep herself safe and soothe herself when she was feeling scared.

In self-reparenting the New Parent is planned by the client's Adult ego state in order to balance the introjected negative qualities of other parent figures in the Parent ego state, as shown in Figure 11.1.

In the process of reparenting, the therapist provides experiences of parenting to the client to deal with developmental deficits. For example, when a child has a deficit from the 'thinking stage' of development (between 18 months and three years) which shows itself in difficulty thinking for themselves and solving problems, I provide time and space for the child to organise their thinking, encourage 'cause and effect' thinking, and give praise for achievement. In this way the child learns how to be a separate person, which is a necessary development at this stage.

Deciding whether to encourage a client to reparent themselves or whether as a therapist to use reparenting techniques depends on the inner resourcefulness of the child. In deciding between the

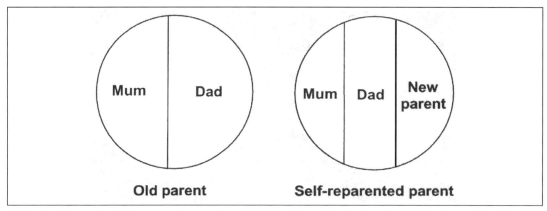

Figure 11.1   Parent ego states (James, 1974)

two, some the questions I ask myself include: "Does the child have a good foundation?" "Has the child introjected the resourcefulness of an OK parent?" and "Does the child have the cognitive capacity to do this work?" If the answers to these questions are "Yes" then I am more likely to encourage self-reparenting. Also, as we noted in Chapter 1, genetic influences, life experiences, and the quality of here-and-now relationships play a part in this assessment. Also, without the support of their parents/carers, children will have difficulty in changing their unhelpful beliefs and behaviour.

Within our work, Katie had wanted to tell her mother how sad and scared she was feeling and that she was worried that her abuser would return to harm her again, but was reluctant to do this. I explored with Katie her 'protection' of her mother by 'putting on a brave face' and pretending that she was OK. I reminded her that this was what she had done when she was seven and, at that time, was not able to get the support she needed. I considered that this was an opportunity for Katie to change how she related to her mother, with the added purpose of giving her mother a chance to support Katie and simultaneously meet her past and present unmet needs. Katie said that she was worried about her mother and "didn't want to put her through any more pain". I considered that Katie was 'parenting' her mother by taking responsibility for her mother's reactions and feelings. I told Katie that I was happy to facilitate a meeting between her and her mother to discuss this, and that I would support her. Katie agreed to this meeting. I had already met with Katie's mother, Tina, on her own and, as part of the contract for the work with Katie, Tina and I had agreed to contract further on work for her regarding any concerns that arose for her during the work with Katie.

I facilitated several sessions between Katie and Tina in which I used my knowledge of ego state theory and transactions to keep communication between them flowing and productive. This meant that I was

alert to any discounting, that is, someone ignoring information that could help in solving problems or issues. This could be ignoring the existence of a problem, the significance of it, any possibilities of changing it, and that someone could solve it if they wanted to (Mellor and Sigmund, 1975). As discounting takes place out of awareness it was useful and necessary to point out when this happened so that Katie or Tina could feel empowered to resolve any problems that arose for themselves or between them. I was also alert to any possible blaming.

Tina said that she felt scared and showed this in her facial expression and behaviour. At this time, I assessed that she was in contact with her Child ego state. I later learned from her that she had been sexually abused herself as a child and I realized that this conversation had stimulated her own memories and feelings of being a vulnerable child. As it was, Tina had been able to maintain her Adult awareness and responsiveness to the concerns being discussed. In one of these joint sessions, Katie 'regressed' to being around age six or seven which was evident by her 'little', whiny tone of voice and her bodily expressions; she even looked smaller as she had curled herself up into the chair. I explained to Katie and her mother what was happening to them in ego state terms and this helped them to stay in Adult and to calm themselves. What also helped Katie was when she had had her head down, I bent down and looked up at her in order to make and maintain eye contact. This action made her laugh, and helped her to stay in contact, in here-and-now Adult awareness.

At Katie's request, I explained to Tina Katie's reluctance to say how she felt and that she wanted to protect her mother from this. Tina then told Katie that she was the adult and the parent and it was her job to take care of and protect her. I gave Katie's mother positive strokes (Berne, 1964) to reinforce this behaviour. I later worked with Tina in individual sessions to help her with her feelings of guilt, and the *impact that her own abuse had had on her functioning as a person and a parent.*

Michelle (DH)

Michelle, aged nine, has learning disabilities that are consistent with neglectful parenting, in particular a lack of emotional warmth, poor stimulation, lack of effective separation, inconsistency, and unrealistic expectations (parentification). Her mother has mental health issues that significantly reduce her Adult functioning. Michelle was sexually abused by an adult male neighbour. Given her life experiences prior to abuse, Michelle had no sense of 'self' being different to 'other' and, therefore, found boundaries of privacy and personal space difficult. She had heavily discounted her own needs and feelings, having decided from an early age that she must take care of her mother in order to survive: 'I'm OK, if you're OK'. She therefore had little sense of anxiety, fear or mistrust. She craved emotional nourishment, and took on pseudo adult roles, including forms of dress and controlling bedtimes by delaying, refusing, and showing anger. This presentation meant that she fluctuated from Parent to Child ego state, with little available Adult. So, when she was targeted by an abuser, she had little awareness or resourcefulness to deal with the situation.

Michelle was vulnerable because of her lack of identity and of individuation (separation) her hunger for physical and emotional contact; her pseudo mature exterior; and her thrill-seeking behaviours. Being told "You should not . . ." was no inhibitor for Michelle. She clearly lacked a positive developmental foundation in her early years. This is consistent with the second developmental theory (see Chapter 3) which acknowledges that there is a developmental pathway that is already interrupted due to parenting deficits, and that this interruption makes the child more vulnerable which, in turn, compounds the developmental difficulty.

The therapeutic work with Michelle focused on establishing trust, recognising self and other, and developing Adult awareness of reality. This was done through non-directive play and intensive affirmations. My assessment/diagnosis identified personality adaptations of Critic and Sceptic (Kahler, 1979; Ware, 1983) with a powerful overlap of resistance to being close, feeling and trusting. In order to counter 'Don't Be Close' and 'Don't Feel' injunctions (Goulding and Goulding, 1979) I concentrated on three specific developmental issues: trust, sense of self, and awareness of others (decentring).

Trust

I established this through providing a predictable environment and materials, showing calm, soothing interactions, and clear expectations. Initially, Michelle found 'free play' difficult as she had no self-regulating ability, that is, she did not seem to trust herself, let alone me. In these early stages, it was therefore necessary to provide structured play and minimal materials.

I asked consistent, simple questions to counter Michelle's opt-out of "I don't know". Over time she was able to accept that she could think and feel independently of others. This required much encouragement, reinforcement and patience. At times I felt like I had no potency left to give. At such times it was important to give Michelle a sense of security and of my competence in managing my process and hers. This countered her script position of her 'OK-ness' being conditional on the 'OK-ness' of key adults.

Sense of self

I encouraged this by reflecting her posture and facial expressions to her along with my perception of her emotional state. This seemed to expand her descriptive repertoire and help her internalise links between her emotional state and behaviours or comments. Over time I was able to offer 'half-sentences' with gaps for her to finish e.g. "So when you . . . (throw) that doll, it shows others that you feel . . . (angry)." This reduced opportunities for discounting or grandiosity as well as providing a 'truth' for Michelle about her behaviours, and about how others see her. This has increased her ability to predict others' responses and to maintain awareness within relationships. During a catching game she asked me "How did you know I was looking over there?" This highlighted her sceptical thinking. She seemed unaware that I would know by her gaze pattern. This reminded me how far we still have to go in terms of her egocentric thinking limiting her awareness of the physical cues that we give to others.

Awareness of others (decentring)

I encouraged this by gently inviting Michelle to develop her Adult ego state. For example, by her being specific about her comments I was able to establish levels of discounting (Mellor and Sigmund, 1975), and then offer alternative perspectives on her degree of emotion or belief. This reduced her grandiosity, for example, "When you say 'really angry', others might see that as 'a bit annoyed.'"

I utilised process communication techniques (Kahler, 1978) in particular, linking Michelle's personality adaptations to the effective channels of communication, and play activities that promoted her development. Michelle's primary personality adaptations (Critic and Sceptic) demand different types of communication, ranging from emotive (Channel 5) which involved me expressing my emotions openly and

*bluntly; through requestive (Channel 3) in which
I asked Michelle to act, think or feel in a specific way;
to directive (Channel 2) whereby I issued a specific
instruction in a positively controlling fashion, usually in
response to potential danger in sessions.*

*Over 18 months, Michelle established an OK-ness
with her immediate surroundings. She is now
developing a sense of curiosity. It is interesting how
this timescale fits with expected child development in
the under twos.*

*Obviously such complex cases highlight unmet
need in parents. In Michelle's case there was a
psychologist working on attachment issues with her
mother, and a social worker involved to tackle issues
of neglect. My role therefore was to identify the
specific needs for Michelle and provide direct
strategies to both the social worker and psychologist
to promote changes in the parents' communication
with Michelle. The learning difficulties and mental
health issues of Michelle's parents precluded me from
taking a primary therapeutic role with them as it was
felt that introducing another worker for them to learn to
trust was beyond their current functioning. I therefore
provided a consultative role and met with parents
every six weeks at a Child in Need review. I was able
to influence issues such as communication,
congruence, and differing perspectives, as well as
promote goals for change.*

The Positive Parenting Strategy (DH)

Working with parents, I have developed a tool
called 'The Positive Parenting Strategy' (see Box
11.1 below) the guidance notes to which form
Appendix 5.

This strategy was initially developed as a
method for evaluating parental attitudes and
behaviour during my work with their children. It
was devised as a tool for discussion during
sessions or home visits, which could be recorded
and evaluated. The findings offered a
confirmation/comparison to the current process
for each child, for instance, in therapy sessions, at
home, or in school or nursery. These findings
could then be explored further in order to
highlight correlations, influences or triggers to
behaviour. Again the word parent is taken to
mean parents or carers.

I use this positive parenting strategy to explore
parents' knowledge and attitudes to their child's
development and behaviour. Usually, the
questions and subsequent exploration identifies
certain needs in the parents which, in turn, allow
their own development to progress. The positive
parenting strategy is reproduced as Appendix 5,
together with guidance notes for the therapist.

The sequence of the questions varies, but
generally I reflect firstly on the child, and then on
the parents, but always with the emphasis on
behaviour, this behaviour being the observable
and measurable detail. The questions focus the
parents on understanding the role of behaviour
and how, over time, behaviour, complemented by
language, cognition, and empathy, can create
healthy relationships. These questions have
proved to be a valuable tool for assessing
Parental and Adult ego state functioning, by
highlighting unmet Child need. They raise the
awareness of choice in the responses adults give
to children. However, awareness in itself does not
achieve long-term change. The following case
description summarises the process of change
that begins from the 'being' (awareness) level,
and progresses through 'doing' and 'thinking', at
a pace appropriate to the developmental needs of
the parents.

Using the strategy, in general, I have found two
particular themes which emerge in therapy:

1. Similarities in the language used by parents,
   and that of the children, for example, when
   parents use derogatory terms, their children
   also produce negative transactions.
2. Resistance by children to parental
   attitudes/behaviours/emotions.

These findings appear to link to research on
adaptation, i.e. the scale of accommodation and
assimilation the child makes to and with the
environment, originally described by Piaget
(1952) and utilised in play therapy theory by
Wilson, Kendrick and Ryan (1992). I was also
interested by the links between the ability of a
child to question or refuse parental 'rules', and
the therapeutic process. In short, children with
the ability to think beyond simply adapting to
parental boundaries demonstrated a greater
degree of change. This seems to have links with
the theory of early life decisions.

With these findings in mind, I devise methods
for encouraging appropriate levels of
encouragement, insistence, and negotiation for
parents, mindful of the individual needs of each
child. Parents seem to gain confidence because
they are given clear information about the needs
and capacities of their child. Once they begin to
see the behaviours of their child as serving a
purpose, they can begin to introduce new ways of
interacting with them. This leads to parents
viewing the child's needs holistically, and to

Positive Parenting Strategy Form

Child's name _____ DoB: ___/___/___ Date of completion: ___/___/___

First/subsequent review of Positive Parenting Strategy (PPS) (please circle)

List the top 5 'day to day' parenting issues:

1.

2.

3.

4.

5.

Pick a behaviour occurring at these times, and look at the cause/impact of it, using the following questions to guide your responses.

Behaviour:

Focus on the Child

Is this behaviour 'normal'?

Is it 'delay'?

Is it the sign of trauma?

(NB for therapist: Did you/they stop doing this in order to sort something else out?)

What does the behaviour signify?

What does the child need?

How do you know?

What messages/affirmations do you give – and how do you give them?

Consider 365 days worth of 'filing'* times the child's age. How do you gauge the current behaviour of the child (as we speak)?

Focus on the Adult

How do you decide if this behaviour is right or wrong in terms of:

• Culture?

• Experiences?

• Knowledge?

How does this awareness impact on your expectations?

How does this link to your own unmet needs/trauma?

What impacts upon your response to the child?

• Time, Day?

• Mood?

---

*I introduce the issue of how children learn, by using the analogy of a filing cabinet, drawing a simple rectangle with four squares within to represent drawers. I suggest that each time a child comes across a new experience or concept (a mental schema), it gets put in the cabinet. Along the 'usual' developmental pathway, from around the age of six years the child develops ways of organising information. I ask parents to guess what happens to the 365 days × six (years) of learning prior to the beginning of strategic memory (and the several years after, before they truly integrate it into their thinking) and assess their responses.

- Health, hormones?

- Relationship?

- Expectations of others?

- Faith?

- The needs of the child?

What strategies do you use for being positive, objective, and realistic when dealing with the behaviour of the child?

List 5 ways of meeting the needs of the child when they display this behaviour (Informed by filling in this form).

1.

2.

3.

4.

5.

Box 11.1   Positive parenting strategy form

them making links between physical, emotional, and social development, for example, the fact that diet and sleep impacts on concentration and sociability.

Parents/carers can begin to predict with authority the issues that underlie the behaviours of their child, and to intervene with confidence and skill. New expectations can be set relating to these interactions, for example, regarding consistency, tone of voice, and body language. As these new expectations are clear, they are measurable, so all parties can log progress which, in turn, releases energy for sustained change. The child experiences parents showing confidence, understanding, and being assertive, and they too gain a greater sense of security and knowledge in the form of positive introjects. This is particularly observable in play and social situations when children recall their world, through copying the phrases and actions of adults. These can then be positively reinforced and affirmed.

The Smiths

The Smiths comprise: Sue (34) (Mum) Allan (34) (Dad) both of whom have a degree of learning difficulty (and it is unclear whether this stems from biological, environmental, or relationship problems) and Toby (6), who has a developmental delay, functioning between 18 months and four years.

I had weekly play therapy sessions with Toby, exploring his understanding of the world within the

process of his play. Alongside this I saw his parents jointly, every other week.

The questions from the positive parenting strategy formed a predictable structure within which the parents consented to explore. We did not discuss their need for change, but jointly agreed that discussing these questions might help them understand Toby's life a little better. Whilst this was an imprecise contract, it acknowledged the parents' position, and the reason for their position, before offering new perspectives.

Over time I adjusted my questioning in response to the developmental changes within the parents themselves. For example, they began to ask 'why' questions such as "Why does he do it?" This seemed to signify their own unmet needs from the beginnings of 'verbal cognition', (3–5 years old) and a 'stuck' developmental issue for them, i.e. their inability to see another's perspective. At times I adjusted my questioning to account for possible transference/ countertransference between the parents ("When he does this I feel . . .") or to evaluate their growing child development knowledge. I explained, for instance, that for some children, learning happens in a predictable and orderly fashion, within stable relationships, with resourceful, 'aware' adults. In this context, the experiences the children are 'allowed' to have fall within their capacity to understand or manage. Examples include:

- *Realising that adults will meet their needs e.g. for food, safety, love.*
- *Realising that boundaries of space and behaviour are predictable.*
- *Accepting that adult and child roles are different.*
- *Understanding that reality and fantasy differ.*

When a child learns to 'trust' that, if he cries, the adult will come, then he has less need to follow the adult around. As he learns to recognise the 'grown-up' jobs, he learns to see himself as different and separate. As he experiences honest, consistent replies to his questions, he begins to develop a sense of reality. Through this teaching, Sue and Allan began to question their own actions, and to change their responses to Toby in relation to three key developmental needs: trust, separation, and defining reality.

The 'filing' metaphor (see footnote p. 155) has a further and more specific use for children who have experienced developmental disruptions. It helps both adults and children to understand what happens when the 'filing' doesn't get done, or when the child is expected to 'file' adult information. In Toby's case, this metaphor helped Sue and Allan reinforce his learning. I drew graphic and humorous pictures with them, depicting what happens when information enters a child's head. I used these to demonstrate that as a child develops, his understanding and capacity changes (more files within each drawer). The pictures illustrated what happens when children gain information that they do not yet have a file for – it gets put elsewhere. For most young children this is in the file marked 'behaviour', as this is the easiest one to find, and the one they know best. As far as Sue and Allan were concerned, at the beginning of the therapeutic work, Toby's 'filing system' had several problems:

- The adults (Sue and Allan) did not behave in a predictable fashion.
- The child (Toby) had experiences beyond his understanding, such as coping alone, caring for the grown-ups, and sexual relationships.
- The child's basic developmental tasks were not complete, such as developing trust, having a sense of self and of being separation, and establishing reality.

So the files labelled 0–6 were sometimes empty, sometimes overflowing, but disorderly, and not clearly labelled. Therefore retrieving information as required was a difficult task for Toby. This was compounded by the fact that his parents' own filing systems were similarly chaotic. Thus the work became 'developmental administration': compiling a profile of Toby based upon what the parents described, what I had observed in my play therapy with him, and providing factual information relating to the developmental needs and tasks of children. I explained developmental sequences, that is, what a child needs to know before it can do the next thing. Specific issues were around Toby developing a trust of others, and an understanding of himself. The issue of trust was a complex one to explore. His parents had a limited understanding of the word, instead focusing upon mistrust, as in deliberate deceit or harm. I

attempted to broaden this concept to include general reliance, truth, consistency, and prediction. Eventually they were able to link this to basic relationship skills such as acceptance, awareness, patience, respect and, in time, empathy. I used simple repeat questions such as "What have we trusted today?" to avoid them necessarily linking trust to behaviour and relationships.

Initially our discussions centred upon some basic 'rules' of our existence such as gravity, time, and the life cycle. I was then able to focus Sue and Allan on other 'givens' by which we live our life. The purpose of this was to explore their own understanding, and identify their assumptions about what their son would know at the age of 6 years. They came up with examples of hunger and tiredness. These became the vehicles for many future discussions. By talking about bodily awareness, some knowledge of nutrition and toxins, and how people behave when hungry or tired, they were able to see the limitations of their son's thinking. Initially they had presumed that Toby knew as much as they did. We explored how they had acquired their own knowledge, and mapped this onto a 'time-line'. Alongside this I introduced knowledge about child development to inform their new 'filing systems'. This led to discussions about the difficulties of keeping hold of good information whilst letting go of unhelpful information. They began to see the difficulties from their son's perspective, by asking questions like "If it's hard for us, how does he do it?" By exploring Toby's development, his parents found a safe and predictable space in which to explore their own needs, using techniques such as repetition, and guided learning. This minimised ridicule, embarrassment or criticism.

I then introduced them to the concept of ego states, using diagrams to appeal to their own developmental needs and abilities. They identified Parental introjects, and segregated the harmful messages. Eventually they began to recognise that Parental messages are separate from Adult reality, and that they have choices. This led to an increase in their own self-esteem as people and as parents, and their ability to offer resourceful responses to Toby's needs.

Sue and Allan later reflected that this had helped Toby to recognise things about himself, too. These techniques involved simple reflections (see below) and a method of 'balancing' reality by removing 'absolutes', critical tones, and other grandiosities. They noticed that discussing reality had become a 'ritual' for handling troublesome times, for instance, discussing the time of the day encouraged them to maintain routines such as bedtime and mealtimes, thereby minimising Toby's distress. Over time this awareness became broader, encompassing awareness of surroundings and emotions. At one point Sue commented "We sit and look at the sunset together, and notice how it changes things". Subconsciously, these rituals met many of Toby's *needs. Cuddles gave a sense of trust, attachment and consistency. The discussion itself acknowledged different perspectives, thus enhancing a tolerance of difference, and further separation and sense of identity. The awareness of these processes encouraged the development of the Adult ego state, and learning in an organised way. Such rituals clearly also had a positive outcome for parents.*

Within the play therapy Toby had little awareness of himself, so in my meetings with his parents I looked at how to 'reflect' awareness in general communications: "You seem tired", "Your eye lids are closer together now", "You're licking your lips", "Your fist is hard (when it hits me)." I explored these comments in their own context, such as raising awareness of the triggers to unacceptable behaviours, and as pointers to what Toby may need. Interestingly his parents began to develop confidence in recognising their own feelings, needs and responses, and appeared to prefer to focus upon these than on Toby's needs. This raised several issues relating to Toby being my 'primary client', whilst they as parents were also demonstrating their neediness for nurture and therapy. Contractually, the aim of the work was to aid Toby's recovery from abuse. Whilst encouraging his parents' abilities was clearly an important part of the work, their extreme need was jeopardising the quality of intervention with Toby. These dilemmas were not easily resolved, so I firmed up my boundaries through drawing attention to the aim of the work within Adult awareness. I did this by asking questions such as "Who will support you when you need to offload?" and "What can we most usefully talk about today?" I also set specific tasks or expectations such as praising Toby's accomplishments, and seeking medical help when necessary. Reminding the parents to separate their own needs from Toby's, enabled me to continue to work with both him and his parents.

We talked about the 'family heirloom', another filing cabinet made up of 'Things yer mother used to say, and other such nonsense' (the family's own words). This consolidated Sue and Allan's understanding of the ego state model, and offered affirmations and permissions around what to keep, what to let go of, who to listen to whom, and so on. I introduced written affirmations to facilitate this broadening of self-esteem and, at this stage, the parents actively encouraged each other to progress. This seemed to demonstrate a shift in their own development to that of collaboration, empathy, and strategic thinking. Whilst there remains a great deal to do with this family, I am now confident that the parents are ahead of Toby in the race to become a grown-up.

In summary, I chose techniques based upon the unmet needs of the parents and Toby. By working simultaneously with both sets of need, I was able to identify when these needs were in direct competition. Sue, Allan and I jointly developed strategies for recognising and meeting their own and Toby's

emotional and physical needs for food, rest and comfort. This improved parental communication and problem-solving abilities, and in turn, enhanced Toby's resilience by empowering him to seek help with difficulties that exist for all children within this age-group.

Conclusion

This chapter highlights the need for working with families to promote optimal outcomes for children in therapy. In the example of Katie, a unique opportunity was created that not only allowed for past deficits to be identified, but within the child's timescales, a new parental relationship was encouraged to develop. This enabled Katie to flourish through the essential parenting messages not only given to herself within *her* therapy, but given by her mother as a result of her mother's own new child development learning. This reduced the likelihood of Katie taking harmful introjects or negative beliefs in to her adult life and, potentially, into the next generation of children.

In the case of Michelle the work with parents was indirect, but nonetheless vital in encouraging the effective use of limited time, energy and understanding. The overview of personality adaptations, and process communications provided a treatment direction that was successful, rewarding and swift.

Katie's positive experiences of life prior to her abuse provided her with a resourcefulness that she was clearly able to draw upon. Michelle and Toby, by contrast, had limited resourcefulness, and teaching about resources formed an essential part of the therapy. However, once the therapist had effectively established permissions for being, doing, and thinking, the clients' resourcefulness flourished. The families became more cohesive and, thus, more able to deal with the developmental journey essential to each child.

References

Berne, E. (1964) *Games People Play: The Psychology of Human Relationships*. Harmondsworth: Penguin.

Goulding, M.M. and Goulding, R.L. (1979) *Changing Lives Through Redecision Therapy*. New York: Grove Press.

James, M. (1974) Self-reparenting: Theory and Process. *Transactional Analysis Journal*, 4: 3, 32–9.

Kahler, T. (1978) *Transactional Analysis Revisited.* Little Rock: AR: Human Development Publications.

Kahler, T. (1979) *Process Therapy in Brief.* Little Rock: Human Development Publications.

Levin, P. (1974) *Becoming the Way We Are.* Menlo Park, CA: Trans Pubs.

Mellor, K. and Sigmund, E. (1975) Discounting. *Transactional Analysis Journal*, 5: 3, 295–302.

Piaget, J. (1952) *The Origins of Intelligence in Children.* New York: Norton.

Piaget, J. (1959) *The Language and Thought of the Child* (M. Gabain and R. Gabain, trans.). London: Routledge and Kegan Paul.

Ware, P. (1983) Personality Adaptations: Doors to Therapy. *Transactional Analysis Journal*, 13: 1, 11–9.

Wilson, K., Kendrick, P. and Ryan, V. (1992) *Play Therapy.* London: Bailliere Tindall.

CHAPTER 12

On Becoming a Child Psychotherapist

Mica Douglas

In this chapter I discuss the transition from being an adult psychotherapist to working as a child psychotherapist and the implications for practice in the following areas:

- Making the change
- TA theory
- Further training

Making the change

As a psychotherapist working with adults, it is perhaps easy to assume that working with children would not be too difficult or too different. After all, the principles should be much the same, just with littler people who are brought to sessions by a parent or carer. Having held this view, which I subsequently realised represented magical thinking, meant that when I came to train as a child psychotherapist, I had to face a very steep learning curve about the myriad of differences that there are between working with children and working with adults – and how much more messy and involved it is being a child therapist.

Children are unpredictable and no less so when in therapy. Never in working with adults has there been a need to keep a stock of new underpants and knickers, in various sizes, just in case of an accident. Seldom, if ever are therapists invited to look at an adult's pooh in the toilet, or turned round to see an adult client sitting *in* the sand tray. Children are so immediate and embodied in their expressions that this alone can take some getting used to. Children in therapy don't come to talk, they come to play, to draw, to feel better. Unless the child is withdrawn, there is often spontaneity and an immediate invitation to share their imagination and their inner worlds. Unless they have been severely traumatised, children do not generally present such huge splits as adults do between mind and body, left brain/right brain, feelings and thinking. Children bring all of themselves into the therapy room.

The therapist's readiness and willingness to work with *all* that the child brings helps to provide a reparative and restorative experience. For example, working with a child with enuresis, who was being laughed at and bullied at school, provided an opportunity for the therapist to normalise his bodily reaction to the stress and embarrassment he was feeling. Working therapeutically with such a child can not only build their self esteem and resolve the problem, assuming it is an emotional rather than a physical, muscular problem, but can also offer an experience that is a non-judgemental acceptance of the child, and offers an antidote to previous shame-based responses. This illustrates the necessity of thinking through the practical implications of incorporating work with children and young people.

One basic consequence of working with children is to ensure that there are toilet facilities near to the therapy room. Children will sometimes want to leave a session to go to the toilet and only time will tell if it is a genuine need, anxiety based or a control issue. The issue leads to another question of how it is managed. Are you comfortable taking a child to the toilet? Is it different if you are a male therapist? Is there someone else who could accompany the child? There are no rights and wrongs about such situations, but as a therapist it is worthwhile thinking about and checking with the child and the parents or carers about what they would like you to do in those circumstances. Where possible, it is important that all involved have a clear agreement as to what needs to happen at these times. Are the parents or carers happy for you to accompany the child or do they want you to take the child to them so they can accompany them. What is clear is that if the child is at an age when they need help, it would be unethical to leave them to fend for themselves. It is the therapist's job to ensure that the child is supervised at all times until they are returned to another responsible adult. As a child therapist, for the duration of the session, you are *in loco parentis* and are responsible for the care and safety of the child. Working with children thus requires a more particular duty of care than arises in adult therapy.

Boundaries

Most children are not in the grown-up habit of sitting still for any length of time. This makes them quite active and lively clients, especially if they are nervous about being there. One little boy went running into the therapy room and instantly began throwing the sand out of the sand tray onto the floor and then bashing every available toy on the wall to see how tough they were. He was happy. It was the therapist who was in shreds wondering how she was going to survive each 50 minutes without becoming a complete anti-therapeutic control freak. As with adult clients, first sessions with children are important as they reveal the work that the child needs to do and offers clues about how to approach that work. As is often the case, this little boy calmed down in his second session and played excitedly for many weeks with the sand tray recreating internal conflicts through a recurring theme of goodies and baddies fighting, being buried and being rescued to live and fight another day. If children have a stimulating environment and they can find things to do that allow them free expression of their conscious and unconscious, the therapist's role becomes one of container and witness. Limits need to be set in order to preserve the worker and protect the room for other sessions. If the child's behaviour is too disruptive or destructive, the therapeutic work becomes lost in control battles. There needs to be a balance between boundaries that contain the child and freedom to explore and communicate within them. Every behaviour the child displays will be communicating something and, as fascinating as that may be, it cannot be an excuse for not setting limits that keep you, the child and the room protected and safe. As Moustakas (1959: 11) said '. . . limits define the boundaries of the relationship and tie it to reality'. It is scary for children to be totally free, particularly for children who can become violent and act out. The rules of the playroom need to be explained to the child from the outset of sessions in language that they will understand. Children need those limits to, not only to keep them safe, but so that they have something to push against in testing you and seeing how safe they really are. Talking about children locked in rage or hate who push boundaries, Sunderland (2004: 56) states:

For a child to feel contained when he goes into high arousal, you need to stay calm and strong. If you do, you

act as an emotional regulator for his highly overwhelmed state. This is containment . . . He will experience, on a deep visceral level, your kind firmness. He is also likely to be very moved by it.

The debate on limits is rich and wide ranging. Limits help to strengthen ego boundaries and help the child to learn how to contain socially unacceptable inner impulses. In *Therapeutic Use of Child's Play* Ginott (1976: 281) says of working with children with behaviour problems:

The aim of therapy with these children is not the relaxation of superego functions but the tightening of ego controls. By setting limits and invoking prohibitions the therapist becomes the external authority figure whose values, it is hoped, the child will absorb through identification and introjection. Without limits, therapy will only delay self-regulation, encourage narcissism, and lead to a false sense of omnipotence.

Communication

Therapists working with children cannot rely on a child engaging in talking. There has to be preparation for talking to be accompanied by doing. A whole new range of skills and equipment is needed for therapy with children: puppets, a dolls' house, art therapy equipment, a sand tray, clay, therapeutic stories, and other creative methods that allow the unsayable and the unconscious a means of expression. Talking is a very adult way of engaging in therapy and something that is quite a challenge for therapists trained to work with adults who then switch to working with children. A quick rule of thumb for me is: if I am asking too many questions I have the wrong approach with the child. Children do not have to talk directly about an issue such as abuse or their anger. Through unconscious communication in the sand tray or with clay, they can resolve the internal conflict by externalising the problem. Questions are usually about the therapist's need to know rather than the child's need to share.

Even very withdrawn children who may not want to speak about their hurts will often engage in other forms of communication that help them express internal conflicts and hurts. Working in media that the child enjoys requires flexibility and creativity in the therapist and some level of comfort and skill at using such interventions. Having a variety of play therapy equipment available in the therapy room allows the child to find their level and maybe revisit developmental stages if they have grown up too quickly. This is particularly true of children who have been abused; their anger and hurt is often expressed behaviourally at a much younger age, or at the age that they were abused. This may lead to attachment difficulties or behavioural difficulties that require interventions based on a developmental age rather than an actual age.

For example, a 15 year old who was very vulnerable and had been bullied and sexually assaulted, would not engage in talking therapy. She would answer questions monosyllabically, look bored and act as if she did not want to be in the room. Whenever she was asked if she wanted to continue with her sessions, she was always very adamant that she did and that she would like to keep coming forever. It was clear that she wanted to be at the sessions but she did not know how to use them or what to do. Thinking about her needs developmentally, it seemed that she needed to be seen and accepted in ways that would be recognised in a much younger child, and that called for a new strategy. The next time she attended her session, I invited her to choose an animal from the range of puppets in the room. She reluctantly chose an elephant because it was the first puppet she saw. At this stage she was not engaging and swinging her leg over the arm of a chair, chewing gum and trying to be 'cool'. Undeterred, I asked her to make herself comfortable because I was going to tell her a very special story and she needed to listen very carefully. The client looked a little unnerved and warily said: "Okay then". I made up a story about the baby elephant's life which described her happier childhood days and then her very troubled little life as she went to school and was bullied and chased by the other elephants. I went on to talk about the feelings the little elephant had about herself and about the people around her and how unloved she felt. Also, I very importantly, described how resourceful the little elephant was in seeking help and recovering from all the nasty things that had happened to her. I finished by talking about the future life of the elephant and how she had begun to grow strong and manage all her feelings – even her scary ones. When I reached the part that talked about the elephant's feelings, the client in the room sat enrapt with tears rolling down her cheeks. She had had an experience of empathy for little elephant and for herself, which enabled her to talk about how she felt and where she identified with little elephant.

It is unusual to offer so much definitive and assumptive information within adult therapy. Unlike adult therapy however, the child therapist sometimes needs to be willing to tell the child's story as a way of offering and teaching empathy. The story was a metaphor for the client's life with elements in it that were very close to incidents that had happened to the client. As Nichols, Lacher and May (2002: 27) state:

> *Use of third party narratives may decrease the possibility of resistance or dissociation to the reality of the child's experience. A narrative involving the child's favourite animal, television or cartoon character captivates the child's attention while simultaneously allowing processing of traumatic life events.*

This case example demonstrates the need to be responsive, creative and innovative to meet the child therapeutically through the use of varied methods that allow the child to express themselves. One implication for this way of working is that the look of your therapy room may change dramatically in switching to work with children. A child friendly room does need certain basic equipment (see Box 12.1) that will change the look of any 'standard' adult therapy room. This can have a positive impact on adult clients too as it gives them more permission to enjoy the child in them.

Basic equipment for working with children

- Sand tray/s and objects such as creepy crawlies, monsters, fantasy figures, shells, marbles, animals, fences, people, lighthouse, castle etc.
- Dolls' house, furniture and bendy dolls of different cultures
- Paper, paints, brushes, pencils, felt tips, pens, scissors
- Playdough or clay
- Puppets
- A collection of cuddly toys
- A blow up punch bag
- Slime
- Lego blocks and figures
- A table and chair
- Blankets
- A life-size baby doll, crib, nappies, feeding bottle
- Large cushions
- A collection of toys i.e. guns, swords, scary toys, animals, emergency vehicles, cars, houses and fences
- A waterproof table cloth or floor cloth

Box 12.1   Basic equipment for working with children

Practical differences

Working with children therapeutically presents different challenges to the therapist. The work is demanding and rewarding in ways that are hard to imagine before making the transition from adult work. There are many more differences than similarities in working with children and it is for that reason working with children needs special attention in terms of training and thinking through the issues. Many people may think it is easy to work with children; in reality the greater level of responsibility therapists have in working with children makes the work significantly more complex and demanding.

Some of the legal and ethical issues of working with children are more intricate than when dealing with adults, simply because children are dependents, and accountability is often not just to the client but also to a wider network of interested parties. This can mean that legal and ethical issues such as confidentiality, record keeping and child protection need extra thought and training around good practice. The main difference, and one that requires extra training, is the need to have a sound understanding of child protection procedures (see Chapter 5).

A number of practical differences exist between working with adults and working with children which are discussed below.

External pressure

There are enormous pressures on therapists to change the child to meet the norms of society, such as when a parent or school wants a child to change to meet *their* or *its* needs, a change which does not necessarily reflect the needs of the child. What can help to deal with the complexities of this pressure from third party referrals is very clear criteria for the children with whom you work or will work, and clear communication for the referrer about the process of therapy. For example, schools often refer children with behavioural problems that they want resolved. I would not want to assume that the identified behaviour was *the* problem as it may just be a symptom of an underlying issue. Therefore, I would not want to work with a child in a behavioural way, I would want to look at any underlying issues and trust that the behaviour would change once the issues were being addressed. The school would need to understand that about my approach and, by implication,

accept that, once the issues were being opened up, the behaviour may get worse before it gets better.

> For example, I worked with a 12-year-old boy who was on the verge of being excluded from school because he was having violent outbursts in the classroom and throwing chairs around. The school had already sent him to anger management classes, yet the behaviour had not abated but escalated. In therapy we went beneath the presenting symptoms to look at what was happening in the boy's internal world. It eventually transpired that his father had left the country and his grandfather was dying. Male teachers who were kind to him reminded him of what he did not have and they were the only people he felt he could be angry with because he wanted to protect his mum from his feelings.

In addition to being clear with third parties about how I work, I also want to ensure that the child wants to come to therapy and to work with me on any problems they may be experiencing. Just to get to the point of beginning work takes careful negotiation with parents and or carers, referrers and the child through clear contracting and managing everybody's expectations. Without that contracting in place, problems can be generated when a child is referred for therapy as part of someone else's agenda.

It is another dimension to working with children that there will always be a minimum of a three-cornered contract (English, 1975). It would be very rare indeed to work with a child and not have at least a three-cornered contract with a parent and/or carer or other agency, unless the Fraser competence applied and the young person could refer themselves without reference to anyone else.

Responsibility

In working with children, therapists often feel a weight of responsibility for the child's feelings. Therapists are often dealing with difficult feelings around the failure of society to provide adequate care, protection and psychotherapeutic support for vulnerable children. There are also unique pressures on therapists to perform, as their work with children is scrutinised in a way that does not happen with their work with adults. It is a bit like working in a fishbowl when a mother, who brings her son in every week, is asking: ''How are things going? He doesn't seem to be any better at home yet''. Of course, you think, she should be remembering your conversation at the initial assessment where you told her that these things take time and change does not happen overnight. Instead you smile sweetly and say: "We will all get a chance to discuss how it is going when we have a review session in eight weeks time".

Built-in reviews with carers or parents are a way of sharing information about how it is going, and gleaning information about home from the primary carers. Reviews hold parents or carers to their responsibility to parent and care for their child. This may include changing some key areas of their behaviour to support the work with the child. Reviews also help the therapist to get a bigger picture of the child's life and issues, and give him a chance to say things to parents or carers in the presence of the therapist. They offer an opportunity to build bonds and trust as the child experiences the boundaries of confidentiality being held, for example, about the content of the session, and sharing with the parents or carers only the things that you and the child have agreed.

Autonomy

By virtue of the fact that children are dependents, there is a limit to their ability to be in control of their therapy, particularly around referral, fees, timing, termination, consent and confidentiality. Children can be prematurely pulled out of sessions or have their therapy terminated because a parent may not understand the process or may feel threatened in some way by the child's enjoyment of therapy or attachment to you. If this happens it may be down to lack of communication between the therapist and the parent about the process; equally it may be something over which you simply have no control. When this happens it can be devastating for both child and therapist and clearly demonstrates how little power children have sometimes. An example of this was when a teenager, who was nearing the end of three years of therapy and had bravely dealt with issues of severe sexual abuse from a very early age, decided to tell her aunt about some of the post traumatic symptoms she had suffered after being abused. The aunt, who probably became scared because she had not known about the abuse or the therapy, stopped listening to her niece, persuaded the child's father to pull her out of therapy, and then paid privately for a psychiatrist to medicate her niece and take her through 20 sessions of cognitive behavioural therapy. It wasn't what the child wanted but it was what the aunt thought was best for her. Needless to say the counter-transference issues of the therapist and, in this case, me as the supervisor were huge: powerlessness, frustration, impotence, and feeling unheard.

Balance of rights

Balancing the child's right to self-determination with the complementary right to care and protection, and the parents' or carers' rights with regard to therapeutic decisions about their child is a difficult juggling act. The clear contracting principles of TA support therapists to achieve that balance, as the contract provides a framework for the extent and limits of confidentiality, reviews, recording and data protection.

Often therapists will find themselves working within systems that provide education, care and protection for children. Referring and liaising with other professionals and managing appropriately the different relationships and roles they may undertake at any given time, requires a high degree of flexibility and alertness to possible conflicts of interest. For instance, it may be useful to attend a professional meeting regarding the child with whom you are working, such as a case conference. However, in such meetings there are issues concerning the management of boundaries, especially that of confidentiality, as well as expectations of other professionals that you will contribute your views about the child. The United Kingdom Council for Psychotherapy publication on *Psychotherapy with Children* (UKCP, 2003, see Appendix 6) offers guidance on consulting with parents or caregivers and negotiating contracts with all parties concerned. Other considerations include the type of referrals you take, the kind of agency you may work for and what their guidance is for balancing children's rights with their protection.

Touch

This is an area that needs to be treated with great care. Whilst for some practitioners it will seem unethical and inhumane not to touch a child, for others it will seem unethical to do so. Therefore, if touch is in any way integral to the work or your style, it needs to be discussed with parents, carers and or relevant professionals within the setting in which the work is taking place. There needs to be a clear contract with the child, and age appropriate information related to complaints. Daniel Hughes of Family Futures explains touch to parents or carers by taking them through a consent form that gives reasons for why he may want to touch the child in the course of therapy, such as, holding a child's hand to help them relax. In the contract he says that whenever he touches or holds a child the parent or carer will be present and, if at any time, they do not think it is appropriate he asks them to say so (Hughes, 2005). Not every therapist works with the parent or carer present and, in those circumstances, it is important to have thought through your own stance on touch and therapeutic rationale. As a psychotherapist it will also be necessary to be informed and aware of the spectrum of debate on this subject. A Department of Education and Employment Circular (1998) quotes part of the *Education Act 1996* (S.550A) which states that holding is allowed when a child is in danger of hurting himself, others or property.

Of course there are many ways of communicating with children to convey understanding, empathy and to help regulate emotions that do not involve touch. Margot Sunderland (2004) talks about the following ways of regulating emotions in working with children, of which the first four do not involve touch:

- Attunement – attuning to the intensity of what the child is feeling through tone and facial expression.
- Validating – validating the child's experience through 'finding the right words', so the child can feel deeply understood and truly recognised in you finding the words for what they are feeling or experiencing.
- Containment – containing the child's feelings through being 'psychologically strong enough, kind enough and calm enough to be able to stay with the child's emotional roller coasters without withdrawing, sidestepping, feeling overwhelmed, attacking or cutting off'. Sunderland (ibid.) goes on to say that containing is necessary because the pain and often unbearable intense arousal of rage, fear or separation distress, are beyond the child's emotional capacity to handle alone.
- Soothing – soothing through tone and words will help a child to come down from rage, fear or distress.
- Calm holding – the calm holding of a child experiencing intense feelings can help to 'melt'

defences. Sunderland (2003: 175) says that she adds a word of caution to therapists that the intention would have to be holding that brought to the child 'an experience of gentleness, care and concern that often he has never know before'.

Recent neurobiological research and empirical studies have demonstrated that there are situations where lack of touch can be psychologically damaging. For example, the use of touch in comforting a child who is in an acute state of distress has been proven to be beneficial:

> *Calm holding can bring about a major shift in the child's brain chemistry. Extremely powerful brain and body biochemistry is activated by touch within the context of a secure relationship. Calm holding will activate the release in the brain of two very important emotion chemicals – oxytocin and opioids. In times of rage, fear or distress it is these chemicals that bring damaging levels of stress chemicals back to base rate. The whole feel of the world changes when opiods and ocytocin are in dominance in the brain. The child will feel calm and safe in the world. He will know a deep sense of well-being.*
> (Sunderland, 2003: 60)

Therapists also need to raise their awareness of unnecessary uses of touch, such as, when touch may be used as an avoidance of the child's feelings or emotional pain, or as an impulsive act. The use of touch needs to be as a result of considerable thought and in the service of meeting the client's needs, not the therapist's, and negotiated. A good question always to ask is "Whose need am I meeting?" Therapists need to be able to make distinctions between touch that is invasive, confusing, traumatising or that could be experienced as erotic. Sometimes children do not know the difference between appropriate and inappropriate touch and therapists may need to teach the child body boundaries. Touch is a topic that will be discussed for many years to come in therapeutic training and supervision groups and it is useful to have thought through what your style will be in working with children.

Inappropriate referrals

Not all referrals are appropriate. A referral may not be appropriate if a child has severe learning difficulties or a childhood psychosis; is about to undergo a major change; or doesn't want to engage in therapy. As children are always part of a wider system, a referral may not be appropriate if the child's family is not prepared to co-operate or to accept help. It would also be inappropriate to accept a referral if the therapist is without adequate supervision, support or time. As with adults, TA therapists will normally ask themselves: "Has this person got enough Adult available to benefit from the work?" With children it is a similar process. Put simply: if they can make a contract, they can do the work. However, which children and which issues you work with depends very much on the age and stage of the child, and the clinical skills of the therapist. Working with adults many therapists use a developmental model. Children, however, have not developed beyond the age and stage they have reached – literally. For children, it is not only about going back over stages that may have been missed, it is also about tailoring interventions and work to their development stage. Some therapists do not feel comfortable, for example, working with children who are very young, or who are presenting as dissociated. Each therapist needs clarity about their limitations, and a network of colleagues from different allied professions with whom to consult, from whom to gain support, and to whom to refer.

TA theory

As TA is a theory that integrates behavioural, humanistic and object relations approaches, it provides a range of interventions and methodology that can be used with children for different issues. For example, working relationally with a child who has been abused at an early age with the goal of integrating split off parts of the Child ego state, would draw on more recent theoretical developments in TA. Whereas helping a child to overcome behavioural difficulties in school may require more cognitive behavioural methods to support decontamination and new behaviours. TA provides a solid theoretical base in contracting, diagnosis and treatment planning that helps the therapist to make sense of what might be going on for the child and negotiate the approach that will be most effective. TA therapists offer flexibility to children by being able to span the range of such an integrative theory. However, if a therapist is working only from one tradition, such as an object relations perspective, or from a cognitive-behavioural stance, then there will be theoretical and stylistic differences over what

transfers and how children are effectively worked with. For example, counselling may be appropriate for addressing a number of children's issues such as self-esteem, confidence, bullying, and the impact of abuse. Counselling would encourage the child to feel valued and build inner resources that helped them to feel more robust in the future. Recent research published by the British Association for Counselling and Psychotherapy (Harris and Pattison, 2004) showed that humanistic counselling is effective in reducing the risk of repeated suicide attempts in children and young people, but not effective in reducing delinquency, aggression or hyper-activity in boys.

Psychotherapy can go deeper and broader and may deal with issues of emotional and behavioural disturbance, for example, post traumatic symptoms, dissociation, severe attachment disorders and some mental health issues. In Harris and Pattison's research, psychotherapy was shown to be effective with behavioural and conduct problems in the 5–13 age range; it was also found to be effective in reducing anxiety in children and in reducing post traumatic stress disorder (PTSD) symptoms associated with sexual abuse. There was preliminary evidence that psychodynamic psychotherapy was not effective with children suffering from depression, and that it may be particularly ineffective with ethnic minority young people. Cognitive behavioural therapies (CBT) were researched as effective for behavioural and conduct problems, reducing symptoms of anxiety, depression and PTSD. There was some evidence that short-term positive effects of CBT are not sustained over time. Creative therapies such as art, drama, music and play proved positive in working with sexual abuse and school-related issues, such as children at risk of developing emotional behavioural problems.

TA therapists are trained to work in each of these ways because of the traditionally different approaches that form part of our cultural heritage. How we work with clients depends entirely on personal style and preferences for the Classical school, for example, or the relational TA of Hargaden and Sills (2002). The point is that we have choices which make us highly flexible, adaptable and 'a good fit' for most presenting issues, as long as we can diagnose accurately and do not limit ourselves only to our favourite bits of the theories.

TA has many theories that support how therapists think about assessment, diagnosis, contracts and contracting, and treatment planning with child clients and the impact on people around the child. Here I discuss some TA theory which I have found the most useful in making the transition between working therapeutically with adults and with children.

Assessment and diagnosis

Existential life positions

From birth children are very busy learning from their environment and from the people around them how to get on in the world and what the rules are. Survival is a very anxiety-provoking activity that is inconsistent and confusing. The child's quality of care, combined with their receptiveness, and perception of what they are experiencing, all help to create the foundations for existential life positions. In understanding the existential position of the child, the therapist can design interventions to support the child's emotional needs and to heal some of the hurts. For example, working with many children who have been fostered, it is evident that for most of them their existential life position is 'I'm not OK, You're not OK' (Berne, 1972). By and large, they believe that they are bad and unlovable, and will aim to prove that by behaving in ways that provoke foster carers into pushing them away. TA therapists would describe this as a foundation for a losing script (Steiner, 1974) in which the child is convinced that life is futile and full of despair. There is debate within TA about how soon a child forms their life position. Berne (1966) believed it was by the age of three to seven and was made in order to justify a decision based on early life experiences. Steiner (1971) believed it was much younger, that is, in the first few months of life, based on experiences of feeding between mother and baby. My view also is that life positions are formed in the first few months of life, but based on the baby's experience of attunement from primary carers (see Stern, 1985). In therapy, it is through affectively attuning to the child and providing a balance of care and firm boundaries that the child can receive a different experience of relating to another: an experience that is safe, consistent, warm and trustworthy.

Existential life positions were originally based on Klein and her views of infant development and defences and they offer a theoretical link between adult and child development and attachment theory. Working as a child therapist made me look differently at existential positions and gain a great deal more from them than when I just applied them to thinking about adults.

Injunctions and permissions

In therapy, the child has the potential to change the injunctions they received from their parents such as Don't exist, Don't be a child, Don't be important, Don't belong (Goulding and Goulding, 1979). Children automatically give a lot of power to adults around them and a therapist can become a very important ally who will have huge influence on helping to dismantle some of the injunctions. An exciting part of working with children is that as they are young, they have not had years and years of being entrenched in repetitive, driven behaviours, and in some sense, therefore, are more amenable to therapeutic work which challenges their injunctions. Children are very responsive to new permissions and will often happily take them on board. However, the therapist's job has to involve encouraging parents and carers to take the new permissions on board too so that they can reinforce the message with the child. Parents are often pleased to do this if a 'therapist' has asked them to and they can see the rationale behind it. Injunctions are often difficult to spot because they are conveyed non-verbally and the only clues that a child is bumping up against an injunction may be through their body language i.e. tension, sweaty palms. For a child to take permission to go against their Don't Get Close injunction they need to be able to trust the therapist and know that the therapist is a bigger 'parent' in some ways than the people they took the original negative message from. When a child sees their parents or carers taking on that message too that it is okay to hug your child and be close as a family, it is a very powerful experience.

Attributions

Building on the strengths and resources that each child has, and the positive messages that they have absorbed from each parent, is an important part of helping children to recognise all aspects of themselves. They are not just the part that is foremost in their lives at the moment. They are not only a child who has been abused, or a witness to domestic violence. That is one part of them; they are also lots of other things. Helping a child to integrate all of their qualities and characteristics, partly through reclaiming the positive attributions (Kahler and Capers, 1974) they got from their parents or primary carers, helps build a positive sense of self. This is important in adult work too but somehow seems much more immediate and obvious in helping children work out who there are. Children are often hearing attributes for the first time in therapy and do not feel patronised or suspicious of why you may be pointing out their qualities and virtues.

Drivers

Beginning therapy can be very stressful, especially when children do not know what is expected of them or what they are going to have to do. Drivers are the 'do' messages of how to be OK with Mum and Dad, and will be expressed also in relation to other adults in authority. Drivers are likely to be evident in the initial assessment sessions and begin to give therapists information about some of the unmet needs of the child. Because driver behaviour gives key insights into underlying defences they are a useful diagnostic tool with children that can give the therapist a clear steer on what has been reinforced by parents and how the child has adapted to the internal Parent in order to feel conditionally OK. If the behavioural clues of drivers can be read accurately by the therapist, there will be an opportunity to offer a different experience and maybe address some of the unmet needs through a reparative relationship. Once you as a child therapist see what works with young clients, there is an opportunity in review sessions to help the parents understand what they could do more of or less of to reduce the driven behaviour (see Box 12.1).

Scripts

In therapy the child will express their script, with all the attendant embedded messages, through therapeutic play.

For example, a nine-year-old boy I worked with who was referred because he was emotionally flat, had no friends and was having nightmares, would act out in the sand tray a scene from a favourite cartoon where a queen, was frozen in a block of ice deep under the ocean, and the heroes had only 18 hours to save her life. In the film and in the sand tray the woman was not rescued in time and there was great sadness in the

story and in the little boy. For a long time he did not have an alternative scenario for how he would like the story to end so the story was the same for many weeks. I puzzled over the metaphor and would wonder what the story meant to my young client. It later transpired that the child was adopted and he did not feel as if he belonged in his family. What is more, he could not have any contact with his birth mother, or know the circumstances of his adoption, until he was 18 years old. Gradually I began to realise that the story was his script. He was locked in to a life that would be 'frozen' for 18 years and for him there seemed to be no alternative to the harmartic. Using script theory as a hypothesis I could then work with this little boy with a theoretical frame of reference that informed my interventions.

Through bearing witness to the child acting out their script the therapist, as Munari Poda (2003: 91) states, can 'understand how each young person interprets his or her world, existential position and internal and external relationships'. Script work can also assess how much hopefulness the child retains about their own future. Stories, puppets and sand trays are tailor-made for working with life scripts because through play the child projects and acts out their internal world, their beliefs, perceptions, their creative self, their destructive self, their anxious defences and rehearse different endings.

Games – the drama triangle

Many children who come for therapy have been traumatised or abused in some way and, as Herman (2001: 136) states: 'their emotional response to any person in a position of authority have been deformed by the experience of terror'. What is brought into the room is the helplessness experienced during trauma, feelings of abandonment and the persecution and manipulation of the abuser. A potent mixture that can easily result in the drama triangle (Karpman, 1968) being played out with the therapist cast in the role of Rescuer. It is so easy to want to take the child home and protect them forever, or to rail at the authorities for not doing more to protect this child. Catching yourself in the pull to Rescue or Persecute is a familiar skill to TA therapists and one that will be in regular use working with children.

Contracts and contracting

Contracting is one of the basic tenets of TA theory and making a contract with a child can be a very

Drivers	Behavioural clues	Possible unmet needs
Be perfect	Fearful of making a mess Does not want to engage in messy play Looks to therapist for guidance and reassurance Anxious about keeping room tidy Speaks as if older than actual age Work is always tidy	Freedom to be messy or clumsy Space to explore and play Freedom to be themselves Self-determination in decision-making Feeling OK when with others To learn it is OK not to know
Be strong	Long silences Monosyllabic answers Discounting language e.g. 'just' and 'only' Often bored Low energy Expressionless Tension in body	Being vulnerable and feeling safe Being able to express feelings To be less defended Learning it is OK to have needs Being able to relax, laugh and play
Please others	Worries about getting it wrong Can't decide if parent or carer should stay in the session Asks lots of questions Wants to know how you feel or are	The experience of their needs being important too Being loved for who they are Unconditional positive strokes Permission to get it wrong
Try hard	Keeps checking they are doing it right Only the toy that has rolled under the cupboard will do Nothing they create is good enough Throws work away before completion Often high energy	Being valued and cherished To be accompanied through to completion Successful completion of several projects Being praised for their choices Autonomy through self-trust
Hurry up	Moves quickly from one activity to another Cannot stay focused Worries about working fast enough Do not allow themselves thinking time Finishing off sentences or stories Checking the clock	Permission to take their time Working through things at their own pace Being encouraged to think things through Having unhurried time to play creatively and explore Permission to 'be' rather than 'do'

Box 12.2   Driver behaviours as clues to unmet needs in the child

empowering experience for them. Contracts with a children can boost self-esteem through them feeling consulted and having a say in what is going to happen in the sessions. Sometimes the process of contracting may be the child's first experience of someone asking them what they think they need. Even if it is too difficult for a child to answer such questions, the process of consultation helps set the tone for how things are going to be: the child gets the message that they will be involved in planning and making decisions about their time and their therapy. After initial assessment I always make a contract with a child that includes:

- How the child wants to use the session time – which may be a process contract such as "To talk about how I feel", an outcome contract

such as "To work out why I am angry so I don't get excluded from school anymore", or a combination of both.

- Confidentiality and its limits – this is always framed in age appropriate and child friendly language, and includes who else will know what we talk about such as a supervisor.
- Respect – that the child will always be treated with respect and that the therapist will create a safe and trustworthy environment.
- Reviews – that there will be a review with Mum or carer present every eight weeks when the child can decide whether or not they want any more sessions.
- Recording and access to records – which lets the child know how recording is done and that they will be able to see what has been written about them.

Treatment

Here I refer briefly to four concepts in TA which I find useful in treatment planning or working with children in therapy.

Group imago

When working with a child, the therapist must deal, separately or jointly, with all the parental figures present in the attributions, drivers and injunctions the child uses in creating and enacting stories that are an integral part of their life. In this sense the therapist witnesses the workings of entire family groups. As Munari Poda (2004) puts it 'Every child is a group'.

Child therapy can be very exposing for the whole family, and parents can often be suspicious or even jealous of what may be happening with their child in the therapy sessions. As a child therapist it is crucial not to alienate or criticise the parents, and I find Berne's (1963) thinking about the power of fantasies and the concept of group imago useful in understanding and managing such fantasies. For example, I will hold a fantasy of the family group from information on the referral and the first meeting will inevitably involve a shedding of assumptions and some reality checking. I anticipate that the family will also have a fantasy about me and expectations of what I will be able to achieve, which also needs talking through so that their expectations can be managed. Parents or carers will often see the problem as the child and not think about how their behaviour is affecting the family system and what the child may be holding or acting out on behalf of all the family members. In the initial assessment when the family group are often together, there is a chance to see the group dynamics in action and 'creatively interfere' in the family's interactions with each other in ways that may be supportive and stimulating, for example, by naming some of the positive attributes and qualities I notice in individual family members or making process observations about how they interact or who does not speak. I may also make intuitive 'best guesses' about family life and ask the family to rate how accurate they are. This is always done respectfully, with a light touch and oodles of curiosity inflected in my tone. It is important for the therapist to hold the child, parent/s or carer/s positively. If a therapist judges their parents, the child may perceive that part of them

is being judged too because they belong to those parents. Therapy is most effective if the whole family can understand that the therapist is intervening to support all of them as a unit. Even if the therapist never sees them all together, holding the family in mind whilst working with a child helps them feel held, and supports the child in their relationships with family members. Seeing family values, culture and behaviour manifest through the actions and voice of the child, also gives tremendous insight into the pressures placed on the child by the family. When a therapist supports the family unit, whether literally or mentally, they are helping to avoid splitting and game-playing.

Strokes

Bearing in mind the stroke economy (Steiner, 1974) where cultural patterns encourage parents to create a stroke shortage for children, healthy stroking patterns need to be established as soon as the child walks through the door. Almost without fail, families consistently follow the first restrictive rule of: 'Don't give strokes when you have them to give.'

> *One example of this was a grandmother who brought her eight-year-old grandchild for therapy to recover from experiences she had had through her mum, who suffered from fabricated and induced illness, which is now considered to be a form of child abuse. Over the course of therapy, grandmother had seen her grandchild change from having nightmares every night to having them once a week and yet was completely focused on why she was still having them at all. In helping the grandmother to focus more positively on the progress being made and praising her grandchild for achieving that, the child began to feel safer at home and subsequently stopped having any nightmares. What the child needed was a responsive carer who gave strokes when she had them to give. This helped her thrive in the relationship and become more securely attached to grandmother.*

Children experience being valued and respected when their views are sought over little things such as being offered drinks, and big things such as contracts and what they want from therapy. It is empowering for children to feel consulted and listened to and to be dealt with kindly and firmly. A clear and kind environment is also one that helps children feel OK about themselves, and to take risks to be closer to people, to think for themselves, and to be spontaneous.

Unconscious processes and the Child ego state

Unconscious processes are an important component of child therapy and crucial to offering insights into what might be going on both for you the therapist and for the client. As children enter therapy they may project parental figures onto the therapist and treat you as if they are those figures. Working with the negative (P_{1-}) and the positive (P_{1+}) Parent in the Child ego state through this kind of transference (see Moiso, 1985) transforms hope for the lost and longed for relationship into the possibility of new and trusting relationships. Supervision needs to be used for thinking through transference and counter-transference to support understanding of unconscious communication and what that might mean for the client and for the therapist. Exploration of the many ways that therapists can work with children imaginatively through, for example, storytelling, art therapy, clay work provides an open doorway to the unconscious and internal conflicts that trouble their lives.

There is debate within TA about exactly when the Child ego state is formed (see Hine, 1997; Allen, 2000; Hargaden and Sills, 2002; Cornell, 2003). My own view is that the Child ego state develops before Parent and Adult ego states and, moreover, that it does not develop until the child is about 18 months old. As Cornell (2003: 34) states:

> *Seen from the perspective of current neuro-physiological and memory research, the psychological states of organisation that transactional analysts call the Child ego state does not develop until the middle of the second year of life. An immense amount of enduring learning is occurring in those first eighteen months of life and throughout the life span through avenues other than the functions of the ego.*

Many of the children I work with have experienced neglect from birth or have been sexually abused, some of them pre-verbally. They cannot talk about their experiences because their memories of what happened are somatic rather than explicit. As Allen (2004) says, it is about age three that children develop language ability and a new type of memory becomes active, which allows us to verbalise conscious, autobiographical stories, whilst having the sense we are remembering. Children in this position will be able to act out their experiences through unconscious communication in play. Allen (2000: 262) states:

> *All this is done outside of conscious awareness; that is implicit memory is of major importance in the re-experiencing and recreating of previous behaviours, inter-actions and experiences. It accounts for much that we 'know' but do not know that we know.*

In working with the child's unconscious communication it is worth bearing in mind that sometimes we only have our own feelings to go on, and how we feel being in a room with a client. We may only be able to make sense of what is happening by looking at transference and counter-transference in supervision. When we do that, we need to be aware that what we uncover may not necessarily be the truth, but as therapists we do not need to know the actual truth only the child's experience and perception.

Further training

Therapists who originally trained as adult psychotherapists and who subsequently want to work with children will find that they need some additional training to help them make the transition and to boost their conscious competency. Professionally and ethically anyone offering therapy needs to be personally prepared and competent to do the work and, in any case, in *Psychotherapy With Children*, the UKCP (2003) makes it clear that practitioners should be qualified in the form of therapeutic work carried out with children, and should be transparent and accountable both to their employees and to the children with whom they work. It states also that practitioners should have specialist knowledge in psychotherapy for working with children over and above their generic training. Some of the areas that require further training are:

- Child protection – training in child protection, over and above what is taught at the moment on courses aimed at working with adults, is vital (see Chapter 5).
- Child development – some understanding of ages and stages of normal child development and training on how to work with children of different ages.
- Infant observation – the chance to observe the development of a baby over the first year or two of their life is an invaluable experience in finely honing the skills of behavioural and emotional observation, and mother-baby attunement or misattunement.

- Attachment issues – in depth knowledge of attachment theory and the consequences for the child when the attachment is not healthy is essential for working with children. A course on attachment will not only give you a confidence about diagnosis and treatment it will also help you to understand how to work with attachment difficulties and support the parents or carers too (see Chapters 9 and 11).
- Childhood disorders and how to work with childhood mental health issues – this is also necessary unless you have knowledge from previous training or work experience, and, in any case, it is useful to have good relationship with the local Child and Adolescent Mental Health Service to which you could refer children or from whom you could seek consultancy.
- Abuse – not every child who comes into therapy has been abused but I would be very surprised if you never got any. Inform yourself through continuing professional development courses or the literature that is around. Speak to a specialist at the National Society for the Prevention of Cruelty to Children or to a therapist who does have in-depth knowledge of working with physical, emotional and sexual abuse.
- Creative therapies – training in how to work with children using creative arts also makes the transition much easier. It is one thing to be with a child in a well-equipped room, it is another not knowing what to do with the range of items in there. There are plenty of reading materials but also plenty of course on creative therapies. The Institute for Arts in Therapy and Education (IATE) in London, for instance, runs courses that range from one-day seminars to four year therapy trainings in creative arts.
- Supervision – finding an additional supervisor who is trained in child psychotherapy or who has many years of experience is also well worth the investment and, where possible, peer group support from colleagues who are also working with children. Personal motivations for working with children need to be explored in training, therapy or personal development groups and supervision as it examines the conscious and unconscious motivations we all have that may lead us to work with children from an unmet need in ourselves. Examining and working through these is the best gift we can offer the children with whom we work.

References

Allen, J. (2000) Biology and Transactional Analysis II: A Status Report on Neurodevelopment. *Transactional Analysis Journal*, 30: 4, 260–9.

Allen, J. (2004) The Rejected Baby Dinosaur. *Counselling and Psychotherapy Journal*, 15: 1, 13–6.

Berne, E. (1961) *Transactional Analysis in Psychotherapy*. New York: Grove Press.

Berne, E. (1963) *The Structure and Dynamics of Organisations and Groups*. New York: Grove Press.

Berne, E. (1966) *Principles of Group Treatment*. New York: Grove Press.

Berne, E. (1972) *What Do You Say After You Say Hello*. New York: Grove Press.

Cornell, W. (2003) Babies, Brains and Bodies: Somatic Foundation of the Child. In Sills, C. and Hargaden, H. (Eds.) *Ego States*. London: Worth Publishing.

English, F. (1975) The Three-Cornered Contract. *Transactional Analysis Journal*, 5: 4, 383–4.

Gillick v West Norfolk and Wisbech Area Health Authority (1986) AC 112, (1985) 3 All ER 402, (1985) 3 WLR 830 (1986) 1 FLR 224.

Ginott, H.G. (1976) Therapeutic Intervention in Child Treatment. In Schaefer, C. (Ed.) *Therapeutic Use of Child's Play*. New York: Jason Aronson.

Goulding, M. and Goulding, R. (1976) Injunctions, Decision and Redecisions. *Transactional Analysis Journal*, 6: 1, 41–8.

Hargaden, H. and Sills, C. (2002) *Transactional Analysis: A Relational Perspective*. London: Brummer-Routledge.

Harris, B. and Pattison, S. (2004) *Research on Counselling Children and Young People: A Systemic Scoping Review*. Rugby: British Association for Counselling and Psychotherapy.

Herman, J. (1992) *Trauma and Recovery: From Domestic Abuse to Political Terror*. London: Pandora.

Hine, J. (1997) Mind Structure and Ego States. *Transactional Analysis Journal*, 27: 4, 278–9.

Home Office, DoH, CPS (2001) *Provision of Therapy for Child Witnesses Prior to a Criminal Trial. Practice Guidance*. London: HMSO.

Hughes, D. (2005) *Parent/Guardian Consent Form Regarding Touch/Holding*. Handout from Seminar on Trauma and the Road to Recovery, Family Futures Consortium, London.

Kahler, T. and Capers, H. (1974) The Miniscript. *Transactional Analysis Journal*, 4: 1, 26–42.

Karpman, S. (1968) Fairy Tales and Script Drama Analysis. *Transational Analysis Bulletin*, 7: 26, 39–43.

Moiso, C. (1985) Ego States and Transference. *Transactional Analysis Journal*, 15: 3, 194–201.

Moustakas, C.E. (1959) *Psychotherapy with Children: The Living Relationship*. New York: Ballantine.

Munari Poda, D. (2003) A Letter to Parents About Child Therapy. *Transactional Analysis Journal*, 33: 1, 89–93.

Munari Poda, D. (2004) Every Child is a Group: The Girl of the Snakes. *Transactional Analysis Journal*, 34: 1, 52–68.

Nichols, M., Lacher, D. and May, J. (2002) *Parenting With Stories*. Deephaven, MN: Family Attachment Counselling Centre of Minnesota.

Steiner, C. (1974) *Scripts People Live*. New York: Grove Press.

Steiner, C. (1971) The Stroke Economy. *Transactional Analysis Journal*, 1: 3, 9–15.

Stern, D. (1985) *The Interpersonal World of the Infant*. New York: Basic Books.

Sunderland, M. (2003) *Helping Children Locked in Rage or Hate*. Bicester: Speechmark.

Sunderland, M. (2004) *The Impact of Abuse and Neglect on the Brain*. Lecture, Institute for Arts and Therapy in Education, London.

United Kingdom Council for Psychotherapy (2003) *Psychotherapy with Children, Principles, Aims and Guidelines for Training*. London: UKCP.

CHAPTER 13

Creative Play Therapy with Children and Young People*

Roger Day

From its earliest days transactional analysis (TA) has promoted creative approaches in working therapeutically with children and young people. Berne (1966/1994: 354) himself states that one of the first requirements for therapy with adolescents is 'authenticity on the part of the therapist' as a response to the young person's 'love of drama and fear of boredom'. Instead of providing therapy for the young person who has been sent by their parents, Berne suggests that the therapist 'offers to teach the patient transactional analysis, with the proviso that the patient can do as he pleases with what he learns' (ibid: 355). Contemporaries of Berne who also encouraged therapists to work creatively with children include Muriel James (1969) Alvyn Freed (1976, 1991) Claude Steiner (1977) and Jean Illsley Clarke (1982). For instance, in working creatively with children aged eight and over, James (1969: 1) talks about having different kinds of chairs in the therapy room that the client tries until 'the Child has been relaxed, been comforted in this brief process' and then the therapist is able to 'talk to their Adult ego state'.

This chapter presents some ideas for working therapeutically and creatively with children through discussions on play and play therapy and creative experimentation, within the context of the safety and protection of the child concerned (see Chapter 5). It draws on a range of creative approaches that I have used and developed over a number of years in working therapeutically with children and young people in private practice, in medical settings, in childcare agency work, and, more recently, working in Romania with children who have been deprived of a close relationship with an effective primary carer. Although I draw primarily on TA, I also incorporate ideas and

techniques from gestalt and person-centred approaches to therapy, as well as from the tradition and practice of play therapy in which I have recently completed a training.

Play and play therapy

Play is the child's main business in life; through play he learns the skills to survive and finds some patterns in the confusing world into which he was born. Through play he learns to control his body and develops balance and coordination of brain, eyes and limbs; through play he explores the material world, collects facts and learns to think; through play he works out his emotional problems and learns to control his primitive feelings; through play he learns to be a social being and to take his place in his community.

(Lee, 1969: 32)

In my work with children in Romania, I have discovered that play, like smiling, is a learned behaviour, rather than something that develops naturally in a child. Whilst our ability as humans to play is innate, it is only developed through interaction and encouragement. Thus, an essential aspect of all psychotherapeutic work with children is play. Based on her own extensive reading and experience West (1992: 11) summarises the importance of play:

Play allows opportunities for physical, emotional, cognitive and social growth, and is often pleasurable, spontaneous and creative. Play can reduce frightening and traumatic events; it may relieve anxiety and tension; it can aid relaxation, amusement, enjoyment. Through play, children learn about the world and relationships; it offers an opportunity for rehearsal, for reality testing, for exploring emotions and roles. Play enables children to express aggression and buried feelings, and can be a bridge between phantasy and reality.

In my own therapeutic work with children, I am increasingly using 'pure' play therapy, in which the child generally sets the direction in the play and I as the therapist follow. The therapeutic contract is introduced as something like: "You

---

*In developing some of the ideas in this chapter I am grateful for the valuable suggestions and input from other TA therapists who are equally creative in their work with children and young people, and especially to Kath Dentith, Jean Lancashire and Mark Widdowson.

can use the toys in the room in any way you need to solve your problems and I'll be here to support you. Does that sound OK with you?'' The child will nod or ask a question to clarify a point and the contract is established. My view is that a nonverbal agreement to the contract is sufficient within the context of play therapy with a small child. Although the child generally sets the direction of the play (the nondirective approach), as the need arises I will become more active (the directive approach). I might then structure play by dividing the hour into five or ten minute chunks, and to keep things moving. I use this time for such activities as therapeutic play, drawing, board games and experimentation.

Yasenik and Gardner (2005: 9–10) have developed a 'dimensions model' to assist in understanding this link between the nondirective and directive approaches. They write:

> Structuring a portion of the play interaction does not necessarily undermine the entire play therapy process. There are times when the child needs to choose and direct the play activity. However, there are also times when children become immobilised and look to the therapist to provide structure or direction.

They also point out that 'it has long been recognised that play, in itself, will not ordinarily produce changes in hurt or troubled children. Rather, it is the therapist's interventions and utilisations of the play that are critical' (p. 4).

Play therapy was born out of the work of the early pioneers of child psychotherapy, including Melanie Klein (1961), Anna Freud (1945), Margaret Lowenfield (1935), and Donald Winnicott (1971). In the 1940s Virginia Axline began to develop nondirective play therapy, the principles of which were based on Carl Rogers' client-centred therapy (1951). In her first published work Axline (1947/1989: 69–70) proposes eight basic principles of nondirective play therapy:

1. *The therapist must develop a warm, friendly relationship with the child, in which good rapport is established as soon as possible.*
2. *The therapist accepts the child exactly as he is.*
3. *The therapist establishes a feeling of permissiveness in the relationship so that the child feels free to express his feelings completely.*
4. *The therapist is alert to recognise the feelings the child is expressing and reflects those feelings back to him in such a manner that he gains insight into his behaviour.*
5. *The therapist maintains a deep respect for the child's ability to resolve his own problems if given an opportunity to do so. The responsibility to make choices and to institute changes is the child's.*
6. *The therapist does not attempt to direct the child's actions or conversation in any manner. The child leads the way; the therapist follows.*
7. *The therapist does not attempt to hurry the therapy along. It is a gradual process and is recognised as such by the therapist.*
8. *The therapist establishes only those limitations that are necessary to anchor the therapy to the world of reality and to make the child aware of his responsibility in the relationship.*

Axline demonstrates these principles in action in her most famous work *Dibs: In Search of Self* (1964/1990). In it, six year old Dibs finds the beginning of his healing as he expresses his anger towards his father by repeatedly knocking over a toy soldier representing his 'Papa'. At the end of the session one reason for Dibs's previous reluctance to express his feelings becomes clear when Papa comes to collect him. Dibs tries to engage his father in conversation about American Independence Day. Papa shoves Dibs out of the door, saying through clenched teeth: 'Can't you stop that senseless jabber?' (ibid: 70). In a later play therapy session Dibs puts Papa in the toy jail saying that 'there is no going back after you get put in jail' (ibid: 177). A few minutes later he releases Papa from jail and buries the jail in the sandbox. His feelings are being expressed and he can move on in his relationship with his father. Conning (1998) sees Axline's work as compatible with TA as 'Axline closely followed TA principles in that she operated from integrated Adult' (p. 341). In his own work with children aged three to nine, Conning's diagnosis and treatment planning are based on Steiner's (1974/1990) three script types: 'No love', 'No mind' and 'No joy'. Conning (1999) believes that three qualities are needed to use play therapy in a TA framework:

1. Knowledge of play therapy theory, practice and dynamics.
2. Awareness of how rackets and authentic behaviour manifest in play.
3. The ability to feedback the play dynamics in a way that enhances the therapy.

Therapy room

As I have made the transition from being a psychotherapist using play as a part of the process to becoming a play therapist using play as the prime medium, my therapy room has changed accordingly. Unlike some play therapists I often prepare the room after the initial session according to what I consider are the client's current needs. Thus, in the case of individual clients, at times there may be only a few items in the room. At other times the room is full of all the toys and items used in play therapy. In the case of groups, in which I generally use a directive approach, there may be very few items if the focus is on group games and interaction. Here I describe the room for an individual client as if all the items were present. Other therapists will, of course, choose different items according to their needs (see Chapter 12).

In the centre is a large sand tray on a mat, surrounded by a wide selection of small items that can be used either in the sand tray or for other purposes. They include: cars and other vehicles; farm and domestic animals; wild animals; balls and marbles; natural objects; semiprecious stones and similar beautiful objects; monsters, dinosaurs, crocodiles and ugly creatures (spiders, etc.) fences and trees; people (dolls, babies); figures that can be grouped into families; soldiers; superheroes from children's stories. Also on the mat are pots of water and a baby feeding bottle as well as empty yoghurt pots and other kinds of containers. In Romania, I am privileged to have a very large play therapy room, though it doesn't have a sink and hence the pots of water. Elsewhere in the room are piles of cushions, plenty of assorted soft toys and a beanbag chair. There are items for anger work such as a large punchbag, and cardboard boxes and old telephone directories that can be destroyed. There is also a selection of hand-and glove-puppets, mainly based on animals; a large crate of percussion and other easy-to-use musical instruments; a tea set (which is popular also in Romania); and materials for art and craft, including paper, coloured pens, play-dough (see below), sequins and stickers.

Permitting the child to use the room in the exact way they want facilitates them in working through the developmental stages and tasks of being, doing, thinking, identity, being skilful, regeneration and recycling (Levin-Landheer, 1982). A set of Russian dolls that the child can open up, layer by layer, often helps them explore their own 'senses of the self' (Stern, 1985). In addition to a Russian doll, I have one with a similar purpose. The doll has a flap on her front that opens to reveal an identical doll in miniature, enabling the client to explore her Child ego state at an earlier stage of development.

I have found it useful to have play on the agenda even before the client comes into the consulting room, and have a copy of *A Child's First Book About Play Therapy* (Nemiroff and Annunziata, 1990) in my waiting room. Its purpose is to explain in words and pictures the concept of play therapy to children aged between four and seven. It also suits slightly older children, helping them to demystify the process of play therapy, and to give them permission for releasing their problems through play.

I have chosen various soft toys for specific reasons. A cuddly bear on all fours, named 'Therapy Bear', is often held by clients, and provides comfort at times of sadness and distress. A gorilla, 'Banana Guy', has his eyes partly open and is looking out of the corner of them, tightly clutching his banana. For many young clients he represents their intuition – in TA terms their 'Little Professor' (or A_1). A few children find him scary and this provides a useful medium for differentiating between racket and authentic fear.

One creative tool I always have in my work with young people is a small basket containing rocks, semiprecious stones, bark and driftwood. I collect these wherever I travel, wash them and add them to the collection. These items have important uses. Some children enjoy putting them in water and seeing them change colour. Others find comfort in holding them or building with them. Young survivors may hold the items one by one, feeling their texture and temperature. This sensory perception is part of Adult decontamination work in Retief and Conroy's (1997) seven-stage treatment for using TA with survivors.

Another important tool is some form of modelling clay or play-dough. The client can create something in modelling clay that is symbolic. He might want to keep it or throw it or stamp on it afterwards. Slime and noise putty also have their place for creative play. Both can result in a release of uncensored laughter and joy for the client. Most young children love 'gloop' which can be rolled into balls and then 'melts' and slides through fingers. It can be shaped and it then loses its shape. With these forms of messy play it is important that the child wears an apron or other protective clothing.

Using play therapy in a TA context

Sand tray

Probably the most popular and effective form of play therapy with individuals is the use of a sandtray. Rabone (2003: 11) comments:

> Silence in sand play is usually pregnant with potential and with the permission for the client to gather in what they need, permissions to choose and to do whatever they wish with the sand and their selection of objects . . . In caressing the sand and holding the toys with love, clients for the first time often stroke aspects of themselves that have for a lifetime been denied comfort.

The idea for this began in the early 1900s when H.G. Wells observed his two sons playing on the floor with miniature figures and realised that they were working out their difficulties in relating to themselves and others. Twenty years later child psychiatrist Margaret Lowenfield added miniature figures to the shelves of her therapy playroom and the first child to see them took them to play in the sandbox. She later described this as the 'world technique' (Lowenfield, 1979). According to Kalff (1986: 2) who introduced the name 'sand play', the technique can enable a person to come closer to wholeness 'It becomes possible to break through the narrow perspective of our bogged-down conception and fears to find in play a new relationship to our own depth'. Purists reserve the term 'sand play' for Kalff's approach, referring to other therapeutic work involving sand as 'sand tray therapy'. The young client is invited to select toys and other objects, and to create something in the sand tray. Bradway (1999: 2) writes: 'The process of touching the sand, adding water, making the scenes, changing the scenes, seems to elicit the twin urges of healing and transformation which are goals of therapy'.

> For five-year-old Sebastian the touch of the sand was more important than putting items into it. This is a common experience in Romania, where sand for play is still relatively new. Sebastian is autistic and I was helping him with his communication skills. For several minutes he repeatedly picked up a handful of sand and allowed it to slip slowly through his fingers. I began to copy the process on the other side of the sand tray. I moved my hand closer to his, always checking his reaction to ensure that this is what he wanted (the nonverbal contract). Eventually, after nearly a whole session, we were letting the sand slip through our fingers on to each other's hands and soon

> Sebastian broke into uncontrollable laughter of delight. Communication had been established.
>
> Gabriela, four, had displayed behavioural problems since her little sister was born. In the sandtray she repeatedly created family groups from animals and people, burying the smallest member under the sand. By pointing out her angry expression as she did this she was able to acknowledge her true as opposed to her racket feeling. In her final session she created several family groups, each with the members cuddling up to each other.

Family work

> A sand tray is a useful medium in working with families. One family developed a sand tray that was effectively divided into four, representing the four members separated from each other. I asked: 'Do you want to change anything?' Spontaneously, they recreated it in a way that seemed to me to bring the family together. As I pointed out different elements I saw, they were amazed and excited about the beginnings of therapeutic change.

With the increased complexity of families due to separation and subsequent reconstitution, it is important to provide creative ways for the young person to tell the family story. I find building toys useful for this such as Lego people. The client is invited to talk about each member of the family and to place that member on a table in relation to other family members. Coloured pipe-cleaners provide a means of shaping the family member then joining members in the way the attachment is perceived by the child. This provides important information on: script formation and script matrices (Steiner, 1974/1990); appropriate and unhealthy symbiosis (Schiff et al., 1975) and attachments (Trewartha, 1999). Part of the process of therapy can be breaking unhealthy and unhelpful first- and second-order symbioses. The client may represent this visually during the therapy by gradually undoing the pipe-cleaners until they have become autonomous.

Family dynamics can also be explored with a young client using 'family constellations' (Hellinger, 2001). The public version of this involves inviting members of an audience to come forward to help reconstitute the client's family. Family members who have died (including unborn ones) are also represented by members of the audience. The family members are then invited to move around, and the client explores what the new positions are like. Hellinger (ibid: 3) summarises: 'In the end all in the family are equal. Nobody is better, nobody is worse. So at the end, we can be very humble and take our place in the family, and by taking our place in the family, we feel good and free'. Working with a young person in a therapy room the same result can be achieved with actual family members or by using sheets of paper with a pair of life-size feet and the name of a family member written on each. By moving the sheets around in relation to the client some important information and therapy often emerges. I find it especially effective in my work with adopted and abandoned young people who have been affected by 'reactive attachment disorder' (American Psychiatric Association, 1994).

Drawing

Part of my initial assessment of children involves asking the client to produce a 'house-tree-person' drawing. This was originally developed by John Buck as a way of assessing intellectual functioning. I use it to help me understand the child's perception of themselves and those around them. I give the child a piece of paper and ask them to draw a person, a house and a tree. If they stop part way through I repeat the words but make no other comments until they have finished.

I then look at the three elements, as well as anything else on the paper, in terms of possible script decisions the child has made. I do this by asking simple questions: "Tell me about the tree", etc. Children who have no sense of history, for instance, those who have been abandoned, almost always draw the three figures at the bottom of the page with no baseline. A drawing of an indistinct person often indicates a poor sense of self. A tree without fruit may indicate low self-image. A house with very faint lines often indicates someone who is very unhappy, perhaps depressed, within the family. Noilon (2003) writes:

The basic assumption is that we project things on to the drawings that tell us about us. Houses reflect our ideas about family, trees are part of us we have difficulty facing (since it is easy to project things on to a tree since it isn't like us) and people are parts of us we mostly feel OK to acknowledge.

When nine-year-old Alin finished his house-tree-person drawing (Figure 13.1) I asked him about the person. "I forgot it" he said, scribbling in an indistinct pencil sketch of a person floating in air. I asked him about the tree and he immediately drew a ladder and a man coming to steal the fruit. The house

without windows had become for him a place of darkness. The drawing, together with other information, indicated the need for some urgent child protection for this vulnerable little boy.

Drawing is natural and enjoyable for most children and they usually readily take part. It is a way for children of most ages to express their worries, feelings and unmet needs. It also provides some children both at home and at school with a ready supply of positive conditional strokes: "Oh, that's a lovely drawing." "I think you're very clever/good with colours." and so on. In the therapy room the therapist can give appropriate and carefully directed strokes, including unconditional ones, after checking with the young person what they want and need.

One form of unstructured drawing is known as the 'squiggle game', originally developed by Winnicott (1971: 7). He suggests that the squiggle game is a way of putting down on paper 'the current problem or the emotional conflict or the pattern of strain which obtains at this moment of the client's life.' The therapist draws a squiggle on a piece of paper and offers it to the client, who completes the 'drawing'. As Thurow (2003: 4) puts it:

This [first] squiggle, offered to the child by the therapist, begins the first step in the experience of play. The unformed, yet potentially meaningful, line can be seen as both a 'psychological event' and as a 'transitional object'. In either case it is also an invitation to 'play'. In order for the child to respond to the invitation, to turn the squiggle 'into something', it must be received inside the child.

The squiggle game continues, with the therapist, in turn, completing a squiggle offered by the client, in a form of co-creative exchange.

Art is sometimes seen as a window to the soul. Art in therapy can provide insight into unmet needs. I think of drawing as having two levels, similar to Berne's theory that transactions may be understood on two levels (social and psychological). In the same way that 'the behavioural outcome of an ulterior transaction is determined at the psychological and not at the social level' (Berne, 1966/1994: 227) so the picture's message at the psychological level is stronger than that at the more obvious visual level. A child's drawing at the visual level may be of rain and clouds. At a psychological level the child may be conveying the darkness and gloom they feel inside, but how can the therapist

Figure 13.1   Alin's house-tree-person drawing

interpret a child's drawing at the psychological level? I am cautious in jumping to hasty conclusions, preferring instead to seek the client's own interpretation. Also, if the child is allowed free range, they often take permission to develop their drawings rather than having to stop to discuss a particular one.

Figure 13.2 was one of several pictures drawn by a 10-year-old boy during our first session together. He described it as a picture of him crying beside his holiday caravan. Days later, while I looked through the drawings, I noticed the protuberance on the left. At a social level it was the coupling used to tow the caravan along. At another level I wondered whether there was a message in its phallic likeness. My first and worrying thought was that this could be an indication of sexual abuse. I realised that this was over-reaction and that if I raised the subject in this way I could be in inviting the so-called 'false memory syndrome' (see Retief and Conroy, 1997). At the next session I casually commented something about the shape of the coupling. The client sighed deeply and, through tears, told of his sexual play with another nine-year-old boy a year previously. He now felt guilty and ashamed. More recently he had fallen in love with a girl in his class and was worried because he seemed to get an erection whenever he thought of her. Far from being a child protection issue, what his drawing showed at the psychological level was a need for reassurance.

Figure 13.3 seems a straightforward picture of two people with a tree, a rainbow and a teddy. The sad

expression on the central character's face is a clue to the fact that this eight year-old was still working through a range of emotions about her older sister's near death in a car accident.

Figures 13.4 and 13.5 are more straightforward, showing, respectively, the extreme anger of a nine-year-old girl and a 12-year-old boy.

Creative games in groupwork

Another approach to therapy is using various games for creative play. These are ideal with groups of children, families and between client and therapist. Both board games and team games work well in the therapy room. Board games are a useful part of the therapist's creative toolkit. Although ordinary board games can be used, I prefer therapeutic ones geared to different age groups. These can help with learning time-structuring, building confidence and self-esteem and expressing authentic feelings. There is now a large selection of these available on the specialist market, most of them researched and developed by child psychologists. Of team games, Brandes and Phillips (1977/1990: 5) suggest that:

> *Games can sort out problems, the kind of problems found in interpersonal relationships. They can help social inadequacy by developing cooperation within groups; develop sensitivity to the problems of others through games needing trust; and promote interdependency as well as an independence of personal identity.*

Figure 13.2   Crying beside the caravan

Figure 13.3   Two people, a tree, a rainbow and a teddy bear

In the human chain game (Leben, 1993) the children form a circle and lie on the floor on their backs. Each child rests his head on another child's ankles until a human chain is formed. One child starts a make-believe story with "Once upon a time", then each child in turn continues the story. The therapist promotes the flow of the story and watches for any players feeling uncomfortable. The game's purpose is to experience appropriate touch, enhance communication skills and aid in diagnosis and assessment.

Another of Leben's game, the toilet paper game, promotes strokes and learning 'I'm OK, You're OK'. Each child is instructed to pull off a handful of paper from a new toilet roll. Each child's amount will vary. They then separate their toilet paper into a stack of individual squares. Now the children are instructed to say one nice

thing about themselves for each sheet of toilet paper. A hyperactive eight year-old in one of my play therapy groups ended up with over forty sheets of paper, and everyone helped him to find positive things to say about himself!

A keen sense of observation and cooperation is promoted through the yarn drawing game (Leben, 1993). Each child unravels a length of knitting wool, forms a picture in front of him, then passes the ball of wool to the next child. Once everyone in the group has had a turn, each child's picture is discussed, as is the whole picture made by the group. One group of children were thrilled that, unknowingly, they had made a perfect map of Australia.

In the last session of one group I produced a bag full of hand- and glove-puppets and invited the children to find creative ways for the puppets

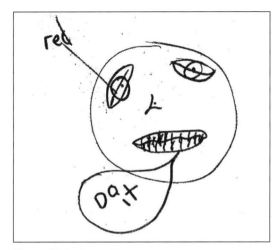

Figure 13.4   Anger (1)

whole group stands in a tight circle and the child falls in any direction and is propelled back to the upright position.

Experimentation

Creative experiment has an important place in TA therapy with children and young people. An experiment is something done to test a theory, a procedure adopted on the chance of its succeeding or for testing a hypothesis. The first reference to creative experiment in TA was made by Eric Berne, who published details of the 'intimacy experiment' (Berne, 1964). Two TA clients faced each other less than 20 inches apart, and within 15 to 20 minutes, experienced phenomena similar to those induced by prolonged isolation or LSD! Three years later Fritz Perls, founder of gestalt therapy, and Claude Steiner shared a platform in which Perls enacted experiments involving dreams or fantasies with two members of the audience (see Perls and Steiner, 1967). Experimentation was also propounded in TA by James and Jongeward (1971).

Later, the gestalt therapist Joseph Zinker (1978: 124) wrote that experiment 'transforms dreams, fantasies, memories, reminiscences and hopes into lively, ongoing, dynamic happenings between therapist and client'. It involves creative ways to help people to 'unstick their stuckness',

to say goodbye to each other. It was amazing to see puppets hugging, kissing and crying on each other's shoulders, none of which actions the children would have done with each other. It was part of the adjourning stage of groups (Tuckman and Jenson, 1977).

One of the most effective games for building trust and social skills is 'backward fall and catch' (see Brandes and Phillips, 1977/1990). The child stands in the middle, closes their eyes and falls backwards and forwards, to be gently held and propelled back to the upright position by two people acting as 'catchers'. In a group context the

Figure 13.5   Anger (2)

making script changes in a fresh, dynamic way. Although, in a sense, anything can happen with experiments, they are nevertheless contracted. While 'anything can happen', children need to know that the rules of safety will still be in place and that the therapist will be there for them whatever happens.

> *Many children love to experiment. I used it in my long-term work with a nine-year-old girl, Lucy, who presented with obsessional behaviour. Most children at some point avoid walking on paving cracks or something similar in case a monster will get them. Lucy's obsessions were more long term and severe. For her, it was essential to enter a room with her right foot and touch something initially with her right hand. 'Perfect' numbers (in her case multiples of 5) were acceptable while 'imperfect' numbers (4, 9, 14, and so on) left her feeling insecure. Illustration 13.6 shows how, when she had to write numbers at school, she managed subtly to change the 'imperfect' numbers of 4 and 19 into 5 and 20 respectively. I invited her to experiment in using her left foot or arm, and in writing 'imperfect' numbers. At first she found these tasks difficult. She would use her left foot, then quickly hop onto her right foot. She would write a number 4 but would put a tiny 5 in it or write 5 in the air with her other fingers. Eventually, through regular experiment, she reached the stage where she could use her left foot and write 'imperfect' numbers while remaining calm and relaxed.*

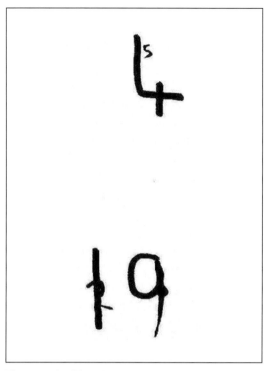

Figure 13.6   Changing numbers

Experiment can be highly creative. Extracts from significant films can be shown or music played as part of the therapy. The therapist and client can leave the therapy room for a time, ensuring that any carer is informed. Sometimes teenagers find it easier to walk and talk rather than being in a room. Drawing or writing an angry message on a piece of paper then setting it on fire in the garden, trampling on it afterwards, is another creative experiment. A similar approach, without leaving the room, is for the client to draw a face of someone he is angry with, screw up the paper and throw it in the bin or out of the window. Here I discuss two examples of using experiments to encourage strokes and to help children express their feelings.

Strokes

Berne (1964/1967: 15) defines a stroke as 'the fundamental unit of social action' and that 'An exchange of strokes constitutes a *transaction*, which is the unit of social intercourse.' He talks about the absolute necessity of strokes for all human beings, in satisfying a hunger for recognition which, in turn, is a form of 'stimulus-hunger'. He postulates a biological chain 'leading from emotional and sensory deprivation through apathy to degenerative changes and death. In this sense, stimulus-hunger has the same relationship to survival of the human organism as food-hunger' (ibid: 13).

I explain the importance of strokes to most young clients. Part of the creative experiment may be for the therapist to find ways to target strokes and for the client to experiment with accepting them. One way is to make the strokes so specific that the client finds it difficult or impossible to discount them. Another way is to invite the young person to paint a picture showing great things about themselves, and then to tell the therapist about the picture.

Many teenagers find it difficult initially to accept positive strokes. In such instances I have experimented with giving positive strokes wrapped in an apparent negative, such as: ''I don't expect you'll accept this, but I think you're an OK person'' (for more on which see Day, 2000). Another creative technique is to play some

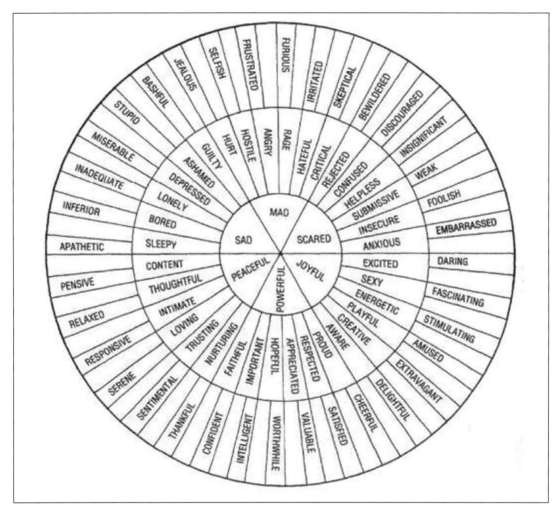

Figure 13.7   The feeling wheel (Willcox, 1982)

appropriate music that the client likes, and then to offer them a positive stroke. Most people find it difficult to reject such a stroke when finding pleasure in something else. I have also experimented with this by getting children to sit in the therapist's chair and to say things to an imaginary client who is like the child. The client sometimes finds that they are saying positive things about themselves before they know it!

Feelings

A child without feelings is like a car without an engine. When feelings are absent or greatly reduced, the child is emotionally unhealthy.

Children will often use racket or, what I refer to as 'cover-up' feelings (Day, 2004) instead of authentic or 'real' ones. I tell children: 'We have cover-up feelings, such as jealousy and loneliness, so we do not have to show or deal with how we really feel. Cover-up feelings leave us feeling bad or confused' (ibid.: 5). Of course, there may be good reasons why it wasn't or isn't safe for the child to show their real feelings, but they will need to relearn effective ways to express their appropriate feelings once those reasons are identified and it is safe to express authentic feelings once again. There are many experiments which enable a child to express the four authentic feelings of anger, sadness, scare and joy. Drawing feeling faces on paper plates is ideal. So is using symbolic representations to identify ego states in others (see Kleineweise, 1980). I enjoy using Willcox's (1982) 'feeling wheel' (see Figure 13.7) especially since three out of its six segments are about joy. Try, for instance, encouraging the client to close their eyes and drop a dart (or place a finger) on one of the enlarged sections of the wheel, and then describe the feeling. Pictures can provide lots of experimental ways to express feelings. Younger clients like to use stickers of cartoon characters showing different expressions – Donald Duck has some amazing expressions! I then get them to discuss the ones they choose.

Many young clients express various forms of inappropriate anger, lashing out at others and seeking to hurt friends or family. I encourage the expression of anger and the management of violence, as distinct from 'anger management' (K. Tudor, personal communication, 2000). This enables the client to take permission in expressing what they feel deep inside. I always keep old telephone directories and tear off sections that young people rip, with angry exclamations, as they think of situations where they are bullied or treated badly. Cardboard boxes can be kicked, jumped on or ripped up. Anger expression can take other forms. For instance, I contract for 'foot fights', even with my youngest clients. Both participants sit on the floor and, with shoe-to-shoe contact, they push against each other. It is amazing how strongly a small child with repressed anger can push with their feet. There are a number of toys which aid expression of anger including: stress balls (for squeezing); inflatable punch-bags and cushions (for hitting); and a spring-loaded device I use with older children, designed for strengthening hand muscles, but equally good for expressing anger.

Small children have more basic ways of anger expression. Spitting, for instance, is one of the most angry things small children can do. Interestingly, Sutherland and Engleheart (1993) encourage clients of all ages, not just the very young, to spit on a part of their 'Angry Page'. Spitting isn't the only basic instinct of angry small children, though certain others would never be acceptable in the therapy room. A mother told me about a six year-old boy who went home after a session, found a stone in the garden and drew on it a picture of an adult who had hurt him in a big way. His age-appropriate expression was then to urinate on the stone!

Conclusion

TA lends itself to a wide range of creativity in working therapeutically with children and young people. The examples given in this chapter are drawn mainly from my own extensive experience of working with young clients. There are many other possibilities. Each therapist has their own unique ways of working creatively. Read about other ideas, talk to therapists who use creativity, and above all, try things out with your own clients. Let your own creativity loose, and you will facilitate your own young clients to use creative means to solve their personal issues.

References

American Psychiatric Association (1994) *Diagnostic and Statistical Manual of Mental Disorders.* 4th edn. Washington, DC: APA.

Axline, V. (1989) *Play Therapy.* London: Churchill Livingstone. (Original work published 1947)

Axline, V. (1990) *Dibs: In Search of Self.* London: Penguin Books. (Original work published 1964)

Berne, E. (1964) The Intimacy Experiment. *Transactional Analysis Journal,* 9, 113.

Berne, E. (1967) *Games People Play: The Psychology of Human Relationships.* London: Penguin Books. (Original work published 1964)

Berne, E. (1994) *Principles of Group Treatment.* Menlo Park, CA: Shea Books. (Original work published 1966)

Bradway, K. (1999) Sandplay With Children. *Journal of Sandplay Therapy,* VIII: 2, 9–12.

Brandes, D. and Phillips, H. (1990) *Gamesters' Handbook.* Cheltenham: Stanley Thornes (Original work published 1977)

Clarke, J.I. (1982) Self-esteem: A Family Affair. *Transactional Analysis Journal,* 12: 4, 252–4.

Conning, E. (1998) Child Play Therapy From a TA Perspective. *Transactional Analysis Journal,* 28: 4, 341–6.

Conning, E. (1999) Integration of Play Therapy and TA. *Transactional Analysis Journal,* 29: 2, 139–40.

Day, R. (2000) Prickly Fuzzies: A Key to Reaching Teenagers. *ITA News,* 57, 11.

Day, R. (2004) *Being Mad, Being Glad.* London: Raintree Publishers.

Freed, A. (1976) *TA for Teens and Other Important People.* Carson, CA: Jalmar Press.

Freed, A. (1991) *TA for Tots and Other Prinzes.* Carson, CA: Jalmar Press

Freud, A. (1945) Indications for Child Analysis. *Psychanalitic Study of the Child*, 7: 127–49.

Hellinger, B. (2001) *Introduction to Family Constellations*. Paper available online at www.hellinger.com

James, M. (1969) Transactional Analysis With Children: The Initial Session. *Transactional Analysis Bulletin*, 29, 1–2.

James, M. and Jongeward, D. (1971) *Born to Win: Transactional Analysis with Gestalt Experiments*. Reading, MA: Addison-Wesley.

Kalff, D. (1986) *Introduction to Sandplay Therapy*. Paper available online at www.sandplay.org/whatis.html

Klein, M. (1932) *The Psychoanalysis of Children*. London: Hogarth Press.

Klein, M. (1961) *Narrative of a Child Analysis*. London: Hogarth Press.

Kleinewiese, E. (1980) TA With Children: Visual Representation Model of The Ego States. *Transactional Analysis Journal*, 10: 3, 1–2.

Leben, N. (1993) *Directive Group Play Therapy: 60 Structured Games for the Treatment of ADHD, Low Self-Esteem and Traumatised Children*. Pflugerville, TX: Morning Glory Treatment Center for Children.

Lee, C. (1969) *The Growth and Development of Children*. London: Longman.

Levin-Landheer (1982) The Cycle of Development. *Transactional Analysis Journal*, 12: 2, 129–40.

Lowenfield, M. (1935) *Play in Childhood*. London: MacKeith Press.

Lowenfield, M. (1979) *The World Technique*. London: Allen and Unwin.

Nemiroff, M. and Annunziata, J. (1990) *A Child's First Book about Play Therapy*. Washington, DC: American Psychological Association.

Noilon, R. (2003) *Notes on Protective Drawings*. Article available online at: www.psychpage.com/projective/proj_draw_notes.htm

Perls, F. and Steiner, C. (1967) Gestalt Therapy and TA. *Transactional Analysis Bulletin*, 24, 93–4.

Rabone, K. (2003) The Silent Therapy. *Counselling and Psychotherapy Journal*, 14: 7, 10–3.

Retief, Y. and Conroy, B. (1997) Conscious Empowerment Therapy: A Model For Counselling Adult Survivors of Childhood Abuse. *Transactional Analysis Journal*, 27: 1, 42–8.

Rogers, C. (1951) Significant Aspects of Client-centred Therapy. *American Psychotherapy*, 1: 415–22.

Schiff, J.L. et al. (1975) *Cathexis Reader: Transactional Analysis Treatment of Psychosis*. New York: Harper and Row.

Steiner, C. (1990) *Scripts People Live: Transactional Analysis of Life Scripts*. New York: Grove Press. (Original work published 1974)

Steiner, C. (1977) *A Warm Fuzzy Tale*. Rolling Hills Estate, CA: Jalmar Press.

Stern, D. (1985) *The Interpersonal World of the Infant: A View from Psychoanalysis and Developmental Psychology*. New York: Basic Books.

Sutherland, M. and Engleheart, P. (1993) *Draw on Your Emotions*. Bicester: Winslow Press.

Thurow, J. (2003) *Interactional Squiggle Drawings with Children*. Article available online at: www.focusing.org/chfc/articles/en/thurow-interaction-squiggle-total.htm

Trewartha, R. (1999) A Developmental Psychology and Transactional Analytic Perspective of the Role of Attachment in the Development of Social and Therapeutic Relationships. In Leach, K. (Ed.) *Conference Papers of the Annual Conference of the Institute of Transactional Analysis* (Paper 29). Edinburgh: ITA.

Tuckman, B. and Jenson, K. (1977) Stages of Small-Group Development Revisited. *Group and Organization Studies*, 2: 4, 419–27.

West, J. (1992) *Child-Centred Play Therapy*. London: Edward Arnold.

Willcox, G. (1982) The Feeling Wheel. *Transactional Analysis Journal*, 12: 4, 274–6.

Winnicott, D. (1971) *Therapeutic Consultations in Child Psychiatry*. New York: Basic Books.

Yasenik, L. and Gardner, K. (2005) An Introduction to the Play Therapy Dimensions Model. *Play for Life*, 5: 2, 3–12.

Zinker, J. (1978) *Creative Process in Gestalt Therapy*. New York: Vintage Books.

PART THREE

Theory and Research: Fields and Developments

. . . and They're OK

Chris Davidson

The concept of 'OKness' is probably familiar even to people who have not read much transactional analysis (TA). This concept is the core of transactional analysis, both in terms of its philosophy, and of its contribution to the understanding of people and their interactions: the analysis of transactions. This chapter explores the extension of the existing two dimensional 'OK Corral' (Ernst, 1971) and Berne's (1972/1975) elaboration of the third-handed position in his last book, published posthumously. The chapter presents ways in which this three-dimensional model furthers our understanding of individuals and relationships within a social context, with particular reference to working with children and young people.

OKness

OKness has been variously used to describe a philosophy of how we regard other people (Berne, 1972/1975), a frame of reference governing a person's whole outlook on life (op cit) and the minute-by-minute behavioural responses to what happens to us (Ernst, 1971). It was Ernst who developed the 'OK Corral' which shows the four basic positions we can occupy in terms of the way we view ourselves and others. We can be either *OK* or *not OK* with ourselves, and either *OK* or *not OK* with the other person (Figure 14.1).

If I am in the position of 'I'm OK, You're OK' then I will see both myself and 'you' in a positive and accepting way – which may or may not include agreeing with you. If this is my existential life position, it will represent my predominant way of being in the world. I am therefore likely to 'get on with' you in that moment, even though I may not like your behaviour. This is an important distinction, given the tendency for parents (and other caregivers) in white Western society to fuse children's personalities with their behaviour e.g. "You're a bad girl/boy" rather than something

I'm not OK You're OK *One-down position* Get away from Helpless	I'm OK You're OK *Healthy position* Get on with Happy
I'm not OK You're not OK *Hopeless position* Get nowhere with Hopeless	I'm OK You're not OK *One-up position* Get rid of Angry

Figure 14.1 The OK Corral: The grid to 'Get on With' (Ernst, 1971)

like 'What you have just done is unacceptable, and I am willing to stay in contact with you to talk about how you could do it differently next time.' Often, young people's behaviour and interactions invite caregivers to move away from this OK-OK position with the apparent aim of rejecting the young person. Staying in there, keeping oneself and the young person OK is, therefore, crucial to supporting them.

White (1994: 271) reports a personal communication from Ted Novey in which he defines OKness as: 'I am an acceptable human being with a right to live and meet my needs, and you are an acceptable human being with a right to live and get your needs met'. Stewart and Joines (1987: 6) describe OKness as meaning: 'You and I both have worth, value and dignity as people. I accept myself as me and I accept you as you. This is a statement of essence rather than behaviour'. Thus OKness can be seen as the way in which I value and feel comfortable with myself, you and, in the context of this chapter, others.

If I am in the 'I'm not OK, You're OK' position, I will see myself as less important or able than 'you', so that I am likely to give my power away to you, seek you to do things for me, for example, 'Because you are so much better at . . . than I am.' I am likely to want to 'get away from' 'you' in embarrassment or discomfort.

If I am in the 'I'm OK, You're not OK' position, then I place my self in a 'one up' position in relation to 'you'. This can take the form of two principal roles, in terms of the drama triangle (Karpman, 1968) that of Rescuer or Persecutor. In the former role, then I have a need to do things for you, with the implicit, and sometimes explicit, message that you don't have the ability to do these things for yourself. In this position I am also unlikely to check out with you whether you want these things doing anyway! In the Persecutor role, I will blame, berate, oppress or criticise you for all the things you supposedly get wrong. I may make you the cause of all my troubles: without you, my life would be so much better. This is an angry position, and ultimately leads to my wanting to 'get rid of' you.

The 'I'm not OK, You're not OK' position is 'hopeless'. If neither I nor you are OK, I can't blame you for things that happen: we are both 'not OK'. This is often the temporary place two people get to at the low point in an argument: where we have moved beyond blaming ourselves or the other person and reached a 'stalemate, a 'get nowhere' place.

It is important to distinguish between existential life positions, which are, in Berne's (1962:23) early definition, 'taken in early childhood (third to seventh year) in order to justify a decision based on early experience' and Ernst's model which is behavioural. The latter will be observable, whereas the existential life position represents an internal process, underlying behaviour and reactions over time.

I, you and others – in this schema 'They' – have a right to exist, to have needs and to set out to meet them. To dislike or disagree with someone is not necessarily synonymous with perceiving them as 'not OK'. It is possible to differ strongly from someone else, or to be unhappy with what they are doing, and still to hold them as being OK. This chapter examines some of the ways in which this 'ideal' situation of OKness can be out of balance in various ways.

Berne (1972/1975: 87–8) went on to discuss the adjectives which can be assigned to the different life positions, for example, rich and poor. These can be assigned to the four variants, dependent on parental attitudes:

(a) I am Rich (and therefore) OK, You are Poor (and therefore) not OK

(b) I am Rich (and therefore) not OK, You are Poor (and therefore) OK

(c) I am Poor (and therefore) OK, You are Rich (and therefore) not OK

(d) I am Poor (and therefore) not OK, You are Rich (and therefore) OK

Note that in this formulation 'I'm OK, You're OK' and 'I'm not OK, You're not OK' do not appear in this formulation.

The traditional Western view about wealth is that those who are rich either have innate superiority as members of the aristocracy, or have become rich because of their hard work. In contrast, according to this view, those without money are in the position they are because they are lazy, or not as 'worthwhile' human beings as their 'betters'. Wealthy people who accept this view would correspond to the position of (a) above. Conversely, those without money who take on this view would correspond to the position (d). Occasionally, someone of aristocratic birth rejects their socialised view of class and assumes position (b) possibly romanticising the realities of poverty. Finally the hard line socialist view of wealth would correspond to position (c).

Here we have an illustration of the subjective nature of the not OK positions. Arguably, if we believe in the innate value of all human beings, it is desirable to hold none of these four positions on wealth! Other examples of the assignment of adjectives in this way would be black-white, young-grown up, or male-female.

Three-dimensional OKness

No relationship exists in isolation. All of our interactions with one or more people take place in a variety of contexts: families, friendships, communities, teams, organisations, society at large and, increasingly, the global context. A young person is dealing with a complex web of relationships in their living situation, at school, in their local area, and in terms of the media. They may view themselves as 'OK' within their family, for instance, where they experience positive relationships. They may experience bullying at school, leading them to move to a 'not OK' position for at least the period they are in school, or on the way to and from school. They may see young people portrayed in general terms in a negative, uni-dimensional way in newspapers and on television, leading them to identify with and adopt an 'I'm not OK' position, because 'We're not OK' (a point also made in Chapter 10).

Berne (1972/1975) made brief reference to three handed OKness in which he referred to 'They' as the third hand complement to 'I' and 'You'. With the exception of the present author (Davidson, 1999) Tudor (1999) Summers and Tudor (2000) and, in a specific context, Jacobs (1987), the third position of this three-handed vision has been largely overlooked in the TA literature.

I have chosen the word 'dimensional' in preference to Berne's use of the words 'handed' or 'position' on two grounds. Firstly, it carries

something of the flavour of the difference, for instance, between seeing a scene in a two-dimensional way, and seeing the same scene in a three dimensional way, either by having a moving picture, or by being physically there. A photograph conveys a good deal of information, but this is incomplete when compared to being able to move around the space and see it from different perspectives. Secondly, I prefer the term dimension because it has the flexibility of allowing the positions to consist of either one person, or many persons.

In the familiar formulation 'I'm OK, You're OK', 'I' and 'You' represent two persons or positions. The third dimension of 'They' may represent an actual third person or, in different situations, the rest of a family, a group or gang, everyone else/the world, and so on. It could be argued that I may not know the relationship between 'You' and 'Them' or that it may be irrelevant (see White, 1994, 1995). However, as with two-sided OKness, we are dealing with subjective judgments: it represents an internal process. When a young person views 'You' or 'Them' as not OK, this does not mean that this is an objective fact! What is important is that it reflects the young person's perception of that relationship. Such judgments are, of course, influenced by the nature and quality of the social relationships in which we grow and develop.

The three-dimensional model

If we are to take account of the third hand of Berne's three-handed positions, the OK Corral needs to be extended in order to include a third person or persons (see Figure 14.2). It can be seen that each of the four original positions is related to two three-handed positions, where the third person or persons are either OK or not OK, as indicated by the arrows in the diagram.

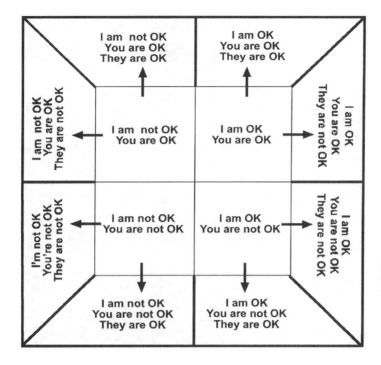

Figure 14.2   The three dimensional three-handed position

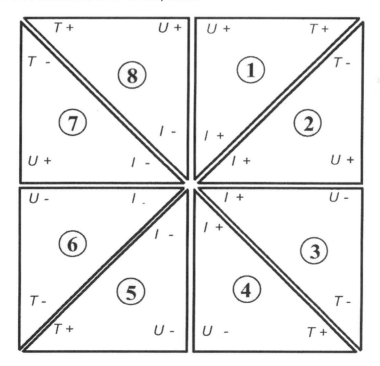

Figure 14.3   The OK square

Figure 14.3 shows a development of this model, which represents the eight different three-handed positions as related triangular wedges in an 'OK square'. The segments are numbered from 1 to 8, corresponding to the numbered descriptions which follow in this chapter. Each of the pairs of wedges (1 and 2, 3 and 4, etc.) represent the two options which emerge from the original OK Corral.

Here these eight different three dimensional positions are elaborated and illustrated from the standpoint of young people. In the figures I use the abbreviated versions: I for 'I'm', U for 'You're', T for 'They're', + for 'OK' and – (minus) for 'not OK'. Triangulating these relationships highlights the fact that although 'I' and 'You' can sometimes become 'We', there are other times when 'I' may feel isolated from both 'You' and 'They'.

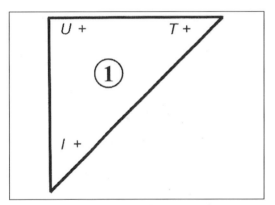

Figure 14.4   'I'm OK, You're OK, They're OK'

(1) Everyone's OK

There is balance here, in that a young person is not needing to place themselves in the one up or one down position either within their relationships, or in relation to anyone else outside those relationships. This is not to say that they will be in agreement with everyone in their sphere, simply that they treat people they relate to with respect, and expect others to treat them in the same way. Just as with the OK Corral, where 'I'm OK, You're OK' is regarded as the 'healthy' position, this is the only entirely healthy position of the eight.

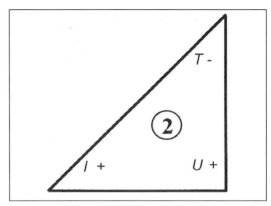

Figure 14.5   'I'm OK, You're OK, They're not OK'

(2) We're OK while we keep Them Not OK

Here the young person's relationships with others can only stay OK by making someone else not OK. These 'others' can be a whole range of people. The young person is also likely to shift who is not OK, depending on who they are with in the moment. A passage from Doyle's (1998: 181–2) novel *Paddy Clarke Ha Ha Ha* illustrates this well:

> It was great. Liam was finished now; Kevin and me wouldn't even talk to him any more. I was delighted. I didn't know why. I liked Liam. It seemed important though. If you were going to be best friends with anyone – Kevin – you had to hate a lot of other people, the two of you, together. It made you better friends. And now Liam was sitting beside Charles Leavy. There was just me and Kevin now, no one else.

This encapsulates the dynamics of this position which could be characterised as a symbiotic relationship relying on the demonising of a third person. This position is common at all levels of social relationships. It describes the dynamics between gangs, many political parties and most religions. It can be seen as the root of all discriminatory attitudes toward people of different race, gender, sexuality, class, intellectual or physical ability. This position also describes political relationships, for example, George Bush's dismissal of certain states as forming 'an Axis of Evil'.

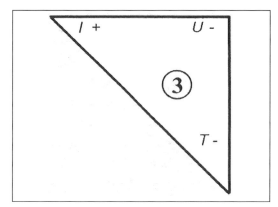

Figure 14.6   'I'm OK, You're not OK, They're not OK'

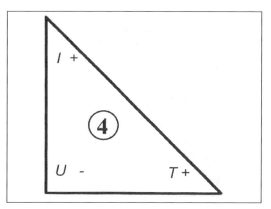

Figure 14.7   'I'm OK, You're not OK, They're OK'

(3) No one except me around here is OK

This is the antisocial position. The young person is consistent in treating everyone else as not OK. They are likely to be identified as a bully. Alternatively they may be someone who plays the psychological game 'Gotcha' on a regular basis: in other words, always catching people out with some aspect of themselves that is supposedly wrong. This position may also follow on from position 2. A young person may start a relationship with someone on a positive basis, styling them as 'different from all the others', only to move to the negative position of 'not-OKing' them: "You're no different after all. I knew I shouldn't have trusted you." At home Harry Potter is on the receiving end of this position: Harry's aunt and uncle and cousin Dudley, singly and collectively make Harry ('You') and everyone who has any connection with him ('They') (his parents, Hogwarts school) not OK.

(4) You're the only one around here who's not OK

This is a persecutor/blaming/scapegoating position. Here the young person may pick on one member of the group or gang, pointing out that everyone else is doing just fine. 'They' are not necessarily involved in this – they merely serve as the means to further the blaming process! This process could be going on within the gang when they are in their 'private' space, despite the fact that to outsiders, all the gang are 'OK' with each other and it is the rest of the world that is not OK. There is frequently a 'pecking order', with some members being bullied or picked upon. Families

can similarly present a united front to the world: "He's one of us (Bloggs). No one touches any of us and gets away with it."

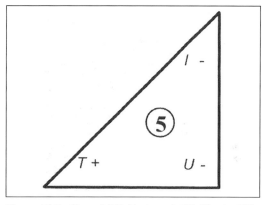

Figure 14.8   'I'm not OK, You're not OK, They're OK'

(5) They're the only ones around here who are OK

Here the young person might scapegoat a particular person, blaming them for some slight or problem. An alternative pattern is to scapegoat everyone within a group and making another group or gang OK, by elevating them in some way. From the viewpoint of a gang or other social grouping ('We') there is not necessarily the unity that may be seen from the outside. There is likely to be a pecking order (as in the previous position), with scapegoating being common. Moreover, the leader of the gang may be seen in a variety of OK and not OK ways by the individual members of the group (see 3 above).

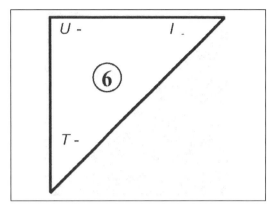

Figure 14.9 'I'm not OK, You're not OK, They're not OK'

(6) No one's OK

A 'hopeless' position from all sides. If this were to be more than a temporary position, it would reflect a severely dysfunctional young person who has lived, or is now living, in a dysfunctional situation. They would represent a high risk – since without the hope of self, others or the world being any different, the young person might well engage in violence to others (either 'You' or 'Them') or to themself. There is unlikely to be positive attachment here, since the combination of not OKness on all sides is unlikely to promote trust, or the motivation to get close to others (see Chapters 9 and 10).

(7) You're the only one around here who is OK

Here the young person could be idealising or idolising the person they are addressing ('You').

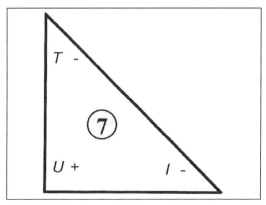

Figure 14.10 'I'm not OK, You're OK, They're not OK'

They might be saying something like "You're so clever. No one else here knows how to do it. I'd like you to show me how to do it." They are likely to see themselves as inferior to the other person, though other people are also seen as being not OK.

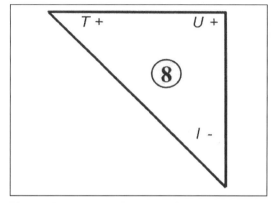

Figure 14.11 'I'm not OK, You're OK, They're OK'

(8) Everyone except me around here is OK

Here the young person may see themselves as a Victim in terms of the drama triangle (Karpman, 1968). They will be generally be isolated within the relationships and groups of which they are a part, for instance, a young person who feels less competent than other members of their peer group. They are likely to have very low self-esteem, and to compare themselves negatively with others, whether known or unknown to them. They may well have a 'Don't belong' injunction (Goulding and Goulding, 1976). They may switch from this position to position 3 (I'm the only one around here who's OK) which will feel less uncomfortable.

Conclusion

The extension of the two-handed 'I'm OK, You're OK' to include the third hand or dimension of 'They' offers a way to understand a young person's social context in a way that accounts for differences in their sense of their own and others' OKness. Whilst everyone may have their particular existential life position, this may not necessarily fit with the observable, social level of their interactions with others. This model can be used to work with a young person to assist them in understanding their transactions with others and to put words to some of their experiences. It can also be used from the perspective of a teacher, parent or other caregiver to help make sense of the young person's responses in relation to others.

This model has been successfully used in organisations with teams of individuals struggling to relate to each other in effective ways. In that context, once they recognise the patterns they perpetuate, individuals frequently make changes, or at least set out to make them.

References

Berne, E. (1962) Classification of Positions. *Transactional Analysis Bulletin*, 62: 3, 23.

Berne, E. (1975) *What Do You Say After You Say Hello*. London: Corgi. (Original work published 1972)

Davidson, C. (1999) I'm Polygonal, OK. *INTAND Newsletter*, 7: 1, 6–9.

Doyle, R. (1998) *Paddy Clarke Ha Ha Ha*. London: Vintage.

Ernst, F. (1971) OK Corral. The G to Get on With. *Transactional Analysis Journal*, 1: 4, 231–40.

Goulding, R. and Goulding, M. (1976) Injunctions, Decisions and Redecisions. *Transactional Analysis Journal*, 6: 1, 41–8.

Jacobs, A. (1987) Autocratic Power. *Transactional Analysis Journal*, 17: 3, 59–71.

Karpman, S. (1968) Fairy Tales and Script Drama Analysis. *Transactional Analysis Bulletin*, 7: 26, 39–44.

Stewart, I. and Joines, V. (1987) *TA Today*. Nottingham: Lifespace Publishing.

Summers, G. and Tudor, K. (2000) Cocreative Transactional Analysis. *Transactional Analysis Journal*, 30: 1, 23–40.

Tudor, K. (1999) 'I'm OK, You're OK – and They're OK': Therapeutic Relationships in Transactional Analysis. In Feltham, C. (Ed.) *Understanding the Counselling Relationship*. London: Sage.

White, T. (1994) Life Positions. *Transactional Analysis Journal*, 24: 4, 269–76.

White, T. (1995) I'm OK, You're OK. Further Considerations. *Transactional Analysis Journal*, 25: 3, 236–44.

On Being the Twelfth Fairy

Marie Naughton

The King and Queen sent out invitations to the Royal baby's christening party to the twelve good fairies of the land but, alas, they forgot to send one to the bad fairy . . .!

. . . and so the tale of the Sleeping Beauty unfolds: as a result of this parental oversight, the uninvited bad fairy gatecrashes the celebration, jumps the queue of fairies bestowing their gifts and spitefully puts a spell on the young princess, proclaiming that she will die when she pricks her finger on a spindle at the age of sixteen. So far, so bad, but at this point in the story, when it seems that all is lost, the twelfth invited fairy, who has not yet presented her gift to the baby, steps forward saying:

Take comfort, I have not the power to wholly undo what my elder has done, but instead of dying, the princess will fall into a deep and long sleep from which she will be woken after a hundred years by love's first kiss.

This is part of a familiar and treasured tale for many young Europeans to whom, from a very tender age, it will have been told and retold. Thanks to film and television, it has also reached a wider audience and forms a part of the narrative repertoire for children all around the world. But what is the relevance of the Twelfth Fairy for us nowadays as Transactional Analysts? What connection is there between an ancient fairytale and therapeutic relationships with adolescents in the 21st century?

In this chapter I draw a parallel between the role of the Twelfth Fairy in the life of the princess, and that of practitioners working with children and adolescents. Through this, I aim to highlight the transforming influence that adults can have in the lives of the young people with whom they come into contact, whether as counsellors or classroom assistants, as mentors or teachers, or in other contexts. I discuss the significance of stories and narrative as a functional part of human development, and review some of the main concepts from transactional analysis (TA) which provide the therapeutic structure in my work as a school counsellor.

Teachers, schools, counselling and young people

I am a qualified and registered psychotherapist running a counselling service in an inner-city high school for girls. The school has 1,800 students who come from a wide range of backgrounds. The clients I see are aged 11–18 and are referred to me for counselling either by their parents, teachers or school staff, or by the students themselves.

Before training as a therapist, I had many years of experience working as a teacher and lecturer in a variety of educational settings, and for ten years I taught statemented students with dyslexia. Through this work I became aware of the powerful impact that adults working in schools can have on the lives of students, and how willing most young people are to make strong attachments to these significant adults in this important area of their lives. This attachment does not go unnoticed in the public arena. Several years ago the Department for Education and Skills ran a successful teacher recruitment campaign under the banner: 'You'll always remember a good teacher'; national newspapers regularly feature columns in which well-known people describe their memories of a favourite teacher, or one who has had a powerful influence in their lives. Examining the links between educational failure of young people and future offending behaviour, Devlin (1995: 62) puts the question: 'what difference can a single teacher make to a child's life, anyway?'. She recounts the school experiences of many young offenders and, based upon their stories, passionately answers her own question: that they can make all the difference in the world.

Children and young people spend a large proportion of their time at school and, in the UK, recent debates about counselling for young people have acknowledged the significance of school as a support base in children's lives. Both the National Society for the Prevention of Cruelty to Children (NSPCC) (Stead, 2004) and the government Minister for Children, Margaret

Hodge (Doward, 2004) have made strong recommendations that counselling should be available to all children here in the place where they can access it most easily.

On completing psychotherapy training, I was aware that counselling provision was urgently needed in schools, and that by offering a counselling service in this setting, therapeutic input could make a significant difference in young people's lives. I decided to continue working with adolescents in school, but as a counsellor instead of as a teacher. My experience over the past few years is that counselling in school has been very well-received: students are enthusiastic about it and keen to make use of the service. Both they and their teachers are glad that their school provides it, and counselling has become an accepted and integrated part of the school culture.

Storytelling: the major part played by stories in children's psychological development

The Twelfth Fairy is a well-known character from children's literature, and I turn now to the importance of story-telling in child development, the crucial role that stories play in transmitting information to children about life and in enabling them to make sense of their world.

'I find out what I believe as I hear myself speak'. This statement summarises the essential experience of what it is to be a human being: we define who we are and what has happened to us by speaking about our experiences. As a result of telling our experience, and being listened to by other people, our sense of identity emerges and our self-esteem develops. Telling stories has been a central feature of most cultures around the world since time immemorial. Carter (1990: ix) writes:

> For most of human history, 'literature', both fiction and poetry, has been narrated, not written – heard, not read. So fairy tales, folk tales, stories from the oral tradition, are all of them the most vital connection we have with the imaginations of the ordinary men and women whose labour created our world.

We distil the world around us into the stories we tell and we do this from as soon as we begin to speak. We process our experiences through formulating language and an internal dialogue to describe to ourselves what we have been through;

our experience becomes somehow more real as we externalise it to another person who bears witness by listening to what we have to say. The little child just learning to talk gives running commentaries on what he is doing, telling those around him of both his internal world and his external experience in the form of a story which merges the two. Stern (1985: 174) describes the process thus:

> The advent of language ultimately brings about the ability to narrate one's own life story with all the potential that holds for changing how one views oneself. The making of a narrative is not the same as any other kind of thinking or talking. It appears to involve a different mode of thought from problem solving or pure description. It involves thinking in terms of persons who act as agents with intentions and goals that unfold in some causal sequence with a beginning, middle, and end. (Narrative-making may prove to be a universal human phenomenon reflecting the design of the human mind) . . . it is not clear yet how, why or when children construct (or co-construct with a parent) narratives that begin to form the autobiographical history that ultimately evolves into the life story a patient may first present to a therapist.

Although Stern says we do not fully understand how or why children construct narrative stories about their lives, what we are certain of is that they do it. Children's experiences in life, and the people with whom they come into contact, have a direct influence on their stories; these encounters serve to shape their perceptions of themselves, other people and the world. Children begin to define who they are in the stories they construct, and their character and personality emerge through the telling of the story; the one process intertwines with and supports the development of the other. As they tell their stories to others, children reveal clues about their unique view of the world; what they hear back from their listeners – both positive and negative – contributes to and is integrated into this view. In this way, the narrative that children weave is influenced by the stories they are told by others: both real-life experiences and the make-believe. All these strands are drawn together to form in the child a rich tapestry of self and life as perceived by them, and a pattern which the child uses to make meaning of their future experience. As Allen and Allen (1991: 14) remark:

> Our cultures, our subcultures, our families and our associations are a rich source of such stories. Indeed, in part, it is by their stories that they define themselves from

competing groupings, and learning these stories is part of a child's coming to understand what the world he lives in is about. It gives him a sense of identity and community, a way to understand things and to classify them, and a way to index and record his experiences.

Thus the characters encountered in stories play a part in how children begin to see themselves in the world. Based upon familiarity with the early stories told to them, they start to develop an understanding of how the world works, how people relate to each other and what they can expect of others. In identifying with the heroes and heroines of nursery tales, they start to see how society operates, how they can be helped and sometimes hindered on life's journey by the archetypal or stereotypical characters they meet. The Twelfth Fairy is one such stereotype.

The interpretations of fairytales

The story of the Sleeping Beauty has been interpreted, as have other fairytales, from a number of perspectives and, as I consider my professional work with young people, I find these analyses both engaging and informative.

Berne (1972: 40) uses fairytales 'to show the similarity between myths, fairytales and real people'. He describes how children identify with the colourful characters from their favourite tales of childhood, then later live out their own lives with the unconscious expectation that similar fates to their childhood heroes and heroines await them. Because of the scripted predictability of the stories when applied to real life, Berne's interpretation of fairytales is fundamentally negative. He uses the tale of the Sleeping Beauty to describe the script process which he labels 'Waiting for Rigor Mortis'. This process is characterised by the passive protagonist waiting for her life to get started through the arrival of someone else (the handsome prince), to break the spell that is paralysing her. In this interpretation, the Twelfth Fairy is not seen as a force for good who acts to save the princess's life. Instead, Berne refers to her as a 'witch' and he describes her intervention as a curse which is not much better than that of the bad fairy's. From this interpretation, Berne observes that part of the therapeutic process with this script pattern will focus upon the client's realisation that a handsome prince is not going to come, and that the client's magical thinking is holding her back.

He maintains that the princess/client needs to stop waiting around, wake up and get on with her life.

Bettelheim's (1976) interpretation of fairytales again focuses on the subconscious messages conveyed to children. However, he contends that through their symbolic meanings, and the subtle presentation of universally understood experiences, albeit in a magical setting, fairytales assist children in learning about the nature of life and what it is to be a human being. They lend models whose underlying messages imply that the trials and tribulations encountered by children and adolescents can be overcome. Moreover, Bettelheim underlines the stories' power to soothe and reassure children that, despite their fears and anxiety as they go through the natural stages of growing up, all is well with the world. His focus is upon how children use the tales creatively and positively. In his analysis of the Sleeping Beauty, he makes only passing reference to the role of the fairies. Instead, he compares the long sleep of the princess and the prince's tough struggle through the thorny hedge with the periods of protracted lethargy and intense activity which characterise the nature of adolescence. He comments that young listeners are intuitively aware that the tasks of the prince and princess are interchangeable, that both girls and boys will experience highs and lows in energy levels, and that achievement is a natural feature of this phase. The fairytale offers comfort and the wisdom of experience of previous generations to young people dealing with uncertainty. Bettelheim (1976: 19) comments:

Fairytale motifs are not neurotic symptoms, something one is better off understanding so one can rid oneself of them. Such motifs are experienced as wondrous because the child feels understood and appreciated deep down in his feelings, hopes and anxieties, without these all having to be dragged up and investigated in the harsh light of a rationality that is still beyond him. Fairytales enrich the child's life and give it an enchanted quality just because he does not quite know how the stories have worked their wonder on him.

From a social perspective, Le Guernic (2004) focuses upon the instructive and beneficial impact of fairytales upon children. She remarks that 'The Education field [in TA] is geared toward prevention rather than cure . . . fairytales provide children with different relationship models, some positive and some negative'. She maintains that through these stories, children learn about personal qualities which are important to social functioning such as empathy, determination and robustness. Children observe how people interact with each other in fairytale society and learn the importance of being able to seek and accept help from others when vulnerable, as well as being able to offer assistance to others when this is called for.

To the practitioner working with young people, all of these interpretations offer valuable insights into the child's world view and their understanding of how relationships operate at both social and psychological levels.

The concept of script

With reference to one of the central philosophical assumptions of TA i.e. that people decide their own destiny, and that these decisions can be changed, Lapworth, Sills and Fish (1993) comment that, in TA, emphasis is placed upon the individual's personal responsibility for their experience. From an early age, and with capacities which from a developmental perspective are naturally limited, the young child responds to the environment around them by making decisions, based upon their specific experience, which they then generalises out onto the wider world. They state:

> If we are personally responsible for our own experience, we must be responsible for the choices and decisions that we make about how we behave, how we feel, how we think and what we believe, even though many of these decisions may not be made in awareness. Even as children we made such decisions in response to the environments of home, school and society. Clearly, some of these decisions were misinformed, misperceived, skewed by immaturity, but nonetheless, the best we could manage in those early circumstances. Hope lies in the fact that new and reparative decisions can be made in the present to replace the now dysfunctional and maladaptive decisions of the past.
> (Lapworth, Sills and Fish, 1993: 4)

Those 'dysfunctional and maladaptive decisions' form part of the body of beliefs which, from a TA perspective, contribute to the 'script' of an individual. Berne (1972: 445) defined script as: 'A life plan based on a decision made in childhood, reinforced by the parents, justified by subsequent events, and culminating in a chosen alternative'.

From this reference point, script is viewed as the unconscious means by which, at best, an individual limits their options in life, and, at worst, brings about their own destruction. In TA, the alternative to script is autonomy, which consists in an ability to live life with awareness, spontaneity and intimacy with others, and therefore free from the shackles of script and predetermined outcomes.

Given the earlier descriptions of the individual's natural process to create themself through stories, these references to script do not appear to take account of a functional application of narrative and the life-enhancing process of story construction. Cornell (1988) assesses the influence of contributors to TA script theory and concludes that the major focus on script in TA literature has been on its pathological aspects. He points out that, of the early theorists, only English (1977: 290) speaks of script in a positive light:

> We all need a script. The child's need for a script reflects an inborn human need for structuring the time, space and relationships that are ahead of him, so that he can conceptualize boundaries against which to test his ongoing experience of reality . . . By constructing the outline of a script, he can hold together his hopes, his fantasies, and his experiences. This becomes a basic structure out of which he can develop a perspective about his life.

Cornell (1988: 281) continues:

> Although life script is not inherently pathological, it may be hopelessly imbued with pathological meaning in TA theory and practice. Transactional analysts need to either significantly challenge and broaden the current conceptualization of script or to introduce a second, parallel term – such as psychological life plan – to describe healthy, functional aspects of 'meaning-making' in the ongoing psychological construction of reality. Perhaps it would be more inclusive to use a term such as 'psychological life plan' to describe the ongoing evolution of healthy psychological development, with 'life script' used to describe dysfunctional, pathological constructions.

Thus it is possible to view the concept of life script from two traditions: as either a poisonous legacy describing pathology in the form of a fixated life story or, following the distinction Cornell makes between 'script' and 'psychological life plan', as the natural inclination in the individual to make stories that lend structure to their life, fulfilling a separate function from those aspects which have damaging connotations. Gobes (in Novey, 1993) contributes to this latter tradition when he refers to script as: 'a co-created narrative story providing new options: a healthy version of an ever-changing original life story in which it's OK to make mistakes'.

The concept of a 'psychological life plan' opens up a world of opportunity for harnessing inventive energy, and working with the creative flow of the individual. This has powerful and exciting implications in work with young people because, at this stage of their lives, they are still in the process of making decisions which may have far-reaching positive or negative consequences. In the face of sometimes bleak circumstances, practitioners working with children and adolescents are well-placed to make powerful interventions that can facilitate their clients to make alternative interpretations of their experience and reality, thereby creating for themselves a more hopeful new story or 'psychological life plan'. It is already too late for many of our young clients to have happy childhoods but, developmentally, they are still at a stage where their scripts are not set, not yet solidly entrenched. Earlier setbacks in their lives may have already caused them to draw powerful, and often negative, conclusions about themselves, the world and other people, but despite this, we, as Twelfth Fairies, can play an active part in script prevention and also contribute to our clients' construction of positive psychological life plans. We can offer them the opportunity to review earlier conclusions and previously excluded experiences, and present different options and outcomes, thereby facilitating them to strengthen their Adult ego state and to develop a new awareness and robustness in the way they deal with their lives.

Script prevention

As we have already seen, the Twelfth Fairy comes into the Sleeping Beauty's life at a time of crisis and responds to the emergency by seeking to improve a dire and life-threatening situation. As a result of her action, the princess's death is averted and a happy ending facilitated. The Twelfth Fairy's intervention in the life drama of the adolescent princess parallels that of practitioners working therapeutically with young people and calls to mind a description of script processes by Stewart and Joines (1987: 99):

You have written your own life story. You began writing it at birth. By the time you were four years old, you had

decided on the essentials of the plot . . . At seven you had completed your story in all its main details. From then until you were about twelve years of age you polished it up and added a few extras here and there. In adolescence you revised your story, up-dating it with more real-life characters.

This passage indicates that by adolescence the script is still not finally determined. At this stage the young person gathers information from their life experiences which confirm the hypotheses they have made in earlier childhood, and generally disregards or minimises the information which contradicts these conclusions. Although they will expect new people they meet to confirm their preconceptions, there is still a willingness on their part to be surprised and to have their frame of reference challenged, and thus a window of opportunity exists for 'real-life characters' to present this challenge. Change, although possible at any stage of life, is therefore developmentally more likely at this point, rather than later, when adolescence is complete and the script is firmly in place.

The aspect of prevention is one factor which differentiates therapeutic work with young people from work with adults. On script prevention, Campos (1986) states that in redecision work with adults, childhood decisions made out of awareness in response to early parenting, are uncovered as part of the process of making new, age-appropriate decisions. It follows, therefore, that in work with children and young people, practitioners can intervene at those critical points when the decisions are still in the process of being made. Campos contends that in early childhood the following five developmental processes contribute significantly to fixing the script in the child's mind:

- *Powerlessness* – in relation to adult carers.
- *Attachment and bonding* – to their caretakers, and the fear of not being taken care of.
- *Identification* (both positive and negative) – with the personalities and behaviours of the significant people in their lives (as well as with characters from stories).
- *Immature thinking process* – children are suggestible to the ideas of their carers, whether these are true or false.
- *Inadequate coping process* – children employ immature strategies for dealing with real-life problems and need help as they grow up to develop these strategies.

What is your name and how do you feel about being called this?
Do you have a nickname – who calls you this and how do you feel about it?
What do you like most/least about your appearance?
What do you like most/least about your personality?
What do you want to do when you leave school?
What does your mum/dad want you to do?
Did you enjoy being a child? Why/not?
How do you feel about being a teenager?
Are you looking forward to being an adult? Why/not?
Would you rather be male or female? Why?
Would you rather go to school or stay at home? Why?
What's your most important memory from being little?
Is there a story in your family about your birth?
What's the best/worst thing that your dad says or has said to you?
What's the best/worst thing that your mum says or has said to you?
When mum/dad is angry with you, what does s/he say to you?
What are you usually doing when mum/dad is pleased with you?
What's your favourite story/fairytale/film/TV show? Why?
Who is your favourite character? Why?
What does your mum/dad say about boyfriends/girlfriends/relationships?
What are your ambitions?
What would stop you achieving these?
How long do you imagine you're going to live?
How would you tell the story of your life?
If you had magic wishes, what would you wish for?

Box 15.1 Teenager's life script questionnaire (adapted from Campos, 1986)

Campos observes that in very early developmental stages up to the age of three, the child's script decisions will be primarily associated with the basic need to survive. After three years old, decisions are concerned with learning and doing. From four to six years, decisions connect with pre-operational logic and magical thinking, and eight- to twelve-year-olds make decisions to do with developing thinking and coping with reality. These earlier decisions and developmental processes influence the adolescent who is starting to experiment with free choice and self definition. Practitioners working with adolescents encounter the age-appropriate decisions connected with these issues, superimposed upon, and often inhibited by, earlier experiences. Campos' (1986) children's life script questionnaire is a useful tool to facilitate the uncovering of early script decisions. This is based upon questionnaires often used by transactional analysts with adult clients (see Berne, 1972; and Stewart, 1996) and is modified for the younger age group. In the same spirit I have adapted Campos' questions to suit work with teenagers (Box 15.1).

The teenage questionnaire provides information about the ego state structure of the adolescent: the potential toxicity of Parental messages; the wounds and unmet needs of the Child; the robustness and processing power of the Adult; and the vigour of the individual's drive to grow and develop i.e. *physis*. At this crucial time in young people's lives, the earlier script decisions can be explored in therapy, challenged and potentially changed. I say 'potentially', because although the redecision may not take place during therapy in adolescence, the therapeutic work can provide the foundations for decisions to be made later, in adulthood, when the young person has greater freedom and control of their life choices.

The healing relationship

What she needs is a good listening to.
(Slogan from an NSPCC advertising campaign, October 1992)

So what is it about the therapist/client relationship that is so important in the adolescent phase? Some students who come to me for counselling have parents and carers who are willing to develop supportive relationships, but the young women are protective of their carers' feelings to the extent that they believe that simply to mention having problems will be too much for their carers to cope with. For these clients, the counselling process enables them to practise talking to an adult outside their social circle about the issues that concern them. They develop emotional literacy as they explore their belief systems around expressing feelings, being vulnerable and asking for help. Following counselling, they often have the confidence to start to build the type of relationships they have previously yearned for, with the significant adults in their lives.

Some of the young women in my practice come for counselling because they do not have any other adults in their lives to whom they feel they can talk. For many, this perception is, in fact, sadly a reality. For a variety of reasons, the grown-ups in their lives are not available to listen to them and to invest energy into helping them learn to process their experiences and find strategies for dealing with the problems in their lives. This absence of relationship compounds the initial trauma and sets up a new set of problems as the young person struggles with the issue on their own. Trauma combined with the absence of a relationship is described poignantly in the following passage:

Much has been written about trauma and how traumatic events can leave psychic scars that influence a person's ability to function throughout life. Usually, however, it is not the traumatic event itself that creates such scars: it is the event unmitigated by healing through relationship. A single abusive experience is just that – an experience. For a child who can work through that experience in relation-ship with a caring and sensitive adult, the experience will become just one memory among many others. What is truly damaging is the absence of a healthy relationship following such an experience. When we have been traumatized by the actions of others or by some circum-stance of life, we need a reliable other who will listen and respond to our pain. The overwhelming, helpless-making nature of a traumatic experience threatens our cognitive and emotional stability as well as our physical security: it is natural and instinctive to reach out for help when such experiences occur. Following an undeserved punishment, a beating, or any other abusive experience, there is an intense need for someone who will talk with us about what happened and how we reacted, offer a realistic way of understanding the situation, keep us safe while we recover, and protect us from future trauma.

(Erskine, Moursund and Trautmann, 1999: 6)

The process of having counselling can also provide adolescents with another resource to draw upon when they experience difficulties as an adult. Young women are frequently referred to me by teachers when they are 11 or 12 years old. They have a course of counselling and move on, only to refer themselves for counselling on other issues at a later point in their school careers. This suggests to me that they have integrated into their strategies for dealing with life, the experience of talking about themselves as a healthy option that has benefited them, and which they are likely to seek out as a solution for difficulties in the future. In this context, Berne's (1961) metaphor of the pile of pennies is particularly apt: by being present in a child's life at a point before the pile gets too high on top of the bent pennies, or those out of alignment, it is possible for practitioners working with children and adolescents to play a part in reducing the number of kinks that would otherwise develop, thereby making for a straighter or more stable pile in later life.

In all of these situations I believe that the counsellor's input has echoes of the potency, permission and protection of the Twelfth Fairy. By being available to support the adolescent as they process difficulties, the counsellor offers the young client an opportunity for different outcomes; traumatic experience can be worked through and transformed, and can take on an altered significance in the individual's personal narrative and consequently in their future approach to life. As counsellors of young people we are not fairy godmothers with wings and magic wands. Nevertheless, the Twelfth Fairy can serve to remind us about the transformative impact our presence can have in the life stories of our clients.

References

Allen, J.R. and Allen, B.A. (1991) Towards a Constructivist TA. In Loria, B. (Ed.) *The Stamford Papers: Selections From the 19th Annual ITAA Conference.* Madison WI: Omni Press.

Berne, E. (1961) *Transactional Analysis in Psychotherapy: A Systematic Individual and Social Psychiatry.* New York: Grove Press.

Berne, E. (1972) *What Do You Say After You Say Hello? The Psychology of Human Destiny.* New York: Grove Press.

Bettelheim, B. (1976) *The Uses of Enchantment. The Meaning and Importance of Fairytales.* London: Penguin.

Campos, L.P. (1986) Empowering Children: Primary Prevention of Script Formation. *Transactional Analysis Journal*, 16: 1, 18–23.

Carter, A. (Ed.) (1990) *The Virago Book of Fairytales*. London: Virago Press.

Cornell, W.F. (1988) Life Script Theory: A Critical Review From a Developmental Perspective. *Transactional Analysis Journal*, 18: 4, 270–82.

Devlin, A. (1995) *Criminal Classes: Offenders at School*. Winchester: Waterside Press.

Doward, J. (2004) All Children Need Counselling at School, Says Hodge. *The Observer*, 18 April, p. 9.

English, F. (1977) What Shall I do Tomorrow? In Barnes, G. (Ed.) *Transactional Analysis After Eric Berne*. New York: Harper's College Press.

Erskine, R.G., Moursund, J.P. and Trautmann, R.L. (1999) *Beyond Empathy: A Therapy of Contact-in-Relationship*. Philadelphia, PA: Brunner/Mazel.

Lapworth, P., Sills, C. and Fish, S. (1993) *Transactional Analysis Counselling*. Bicester: Winslow Press.

Le Guernic, A. (2004) Fairytales and 'Psychological Life Plans'. *Transactional Analysis Journal*, 34: 3, 216–23.

Novey, T.B., Porter-Steele, N., Gobes, N. and Massey, R.F. (1993) Ego States and The Self-Concept: A Panel Presentation and Discussion. *Transactional Analysis Journal*, 23: 3, 123–38.

Stead, J. (2004) Talk Time. *Young Minds*, 68, p. 15.

Stern, D.N. (1985) *The Interpersonal World of the Infant. A View from Psychoanalysis and Developmental Psychology*. New York: Basic Books.

Stewart, I. (1996) *Developing Transactional Analysis Counselling*. London: Sage.

Stewart, I. and Joines, V. (1987) *TA Today: A New Introduction to Transactional Analysis*. Nottingham: Lifespace Publishing.

CHAPTER 16

Permission, Protection and Mentorship: Their Roles in Psychological Resilience and Positive Emotions

James R. Allen

Resilience is the positive adaptation to adversity, whether loss, challenging life circumstances, or physical problems. It is the ability to bounce back, and to resist the pull of the worst effects of misfortune, abnormal environments, and such internal vulnerabilities as chronic illness. For children, it implies the successful negotiation of developmental tasks despite such problems. It is due neither to the absence of vulnerability nor to some inherent characteristic of a person; rather, it is the outcome of reciprocal interactions between the individual and environment (Bronfenbrenner, 1977).

In their retrospective examination of the lives of a number of eminent and creative people including several Nobel Prize winners, Goertzel and Goertzel (1962) found that many had had very difficult childhoods indeed. Prospective studies have since documented that, despite high risks, 30 to 40 per cent of even severely disadvantaged young people do make it (Rutter, 1979; Werner, 1994) and that some stressors under certain circumstances, if not excessive, may actually enhance competence and increase resilience.

Such adolescent risk behaviours as school failure, early sexual intercourse, and substance abuse cluster together because of shared causation (Jessor et al., 1993; Jessor, 1995). Policies and programs for youth, however, have tended to focus on single problems and have been unable to document long-term effects (Scales and Leffert, 1999). Meta-analysis of Project Dare, which was directed against drug abuse and once was the most prevalent program in USA schools, for example, revealed that it did not significantly reduce that behavior (Ennett et al., 1994). On the other hand, the prevention programs which have been found to work best typically involve many aspects of young people's lives: peers, parents, teachers, school institutions, and community (Schorr and Schorr, 1988; Scales et al., 2000).

Over the years, certain factors have consistently been identified as important for the optimal development of the young and for the prevention of high-risk behaviors. These include:

- Relationships and connections with caring others.
- Development of a variety of competencies and skills.
- Development of positive self-perceptions, including a sense that one can impact one's environment and get one's needs met.
- Psychological mindedness.
- Effective and pro-social use of time.
- Positive connections to social institutions.

Grounded in the voluminous data on prevention, adolescent development and resilience, since 1989 the staff of the Search Institute of Minneapolis has conducted studies of some 600 communities in the USA (Scales, 1990; Benson et al., 1998; Scales, Leffert and Blyth, 1998; Scales and Leffert, 1999). From this, they have culled 40 building blocks that young people need to be healthy, caring, and productive, and grouped them into eight categories: external assets such as boundaries, expectations, empowerment, and the constructive use of time; and internal ones such as commitment to learning, social competencies, positive values, and positive identity.

Analysis of 99,462 young people in the sixth to twelfth grades in 213 different USA communities during the 1996–97 school year showed that the greater the number of these assets that young people had, the less likely they were to engage in risky behaviours such as alcohol and drug use or early unprotected sex and the more likely they were to engage in positive behaviours such as succeeding in school. This relationship was fairly consistent across age, sex, gender, race, ethnic, and socioeconomic backgrounds as well as across communities and regions of the country (Leffert, Benson, and Roehlkepartain, 1997).

Unfortunately, out of the 40 assets, the average USA adolescent had less than 20! On the basis of this work, Search Institute workers have now successfully helped a number of communities intervene at several levels: peers, parents, schools, and community institutions.

The positive psychology movement

Probably because it remained a largely therapeutic enterprise outside academic circles and because its proponents actively eschewed conventional empirical science, the humanistic psychology movement of the 1960s never really penetrated mainstream psychology. Recent research, however; has revived interest in the field, shifting our focus from pathology and victimhood to consideration of positive emotions such as hope and optimism, positive traits such as interpersonal skills, problem-solving, and future-mindedness, and positive institutions which encourage and amplify strengths. Such emotions, traits, relationships, and institutions are important both in their own right and because they actually serve us best in times of trouble (Isen, 2000; Danner, Snowdon, and Friesen, 2001; Fredrickson, 2001). Important examples of this research are provided in the latest work of Seligman and Csikszentmihalyi. Seligman (2002) a recent president of the American Psychological Association, designates the strengths which are most characteristic of a person as that person's 'signature strengths'. The highest success in living and the deepest emotional satisfactions, he finds, come from their use. This is a well-being grounded in authenticity. Csikszentmihalyi, for his part (Csikszentmihalyi and Rathunde, 1993), has been exploring states characterised by intense concentration and curiosity, loss of self-awareness, openness, and high levels of achievement and endurance. Such states he terms 'flow'. In Chapter 2 of this book, Trudi Newton picks up on the use of transactional analysis in transforming pathogenic interactions and feelings into positive ones. This paper looks more at the role of institutions and community organization, especially as exemplified in one group of adolescents.

Protection and permission

Much work on resilience and positive emotions can be conceptualized in terms of two basic principles: permission and protection. These strongly influence our personality development, the development of our ego states, our typical transactions, and the scripts which consolidate and modify our memories, and our sense of identity and direction.

Research over many years has delineated the effects of both accumulated risk and accumulated protective factors (Allen, 1998). Both occur in clusters, but, interestingly, protective factors seem proportionately more powerful than risk factors in terms of their later effects on young people in high-risk situations (Jessor, 1995). However, their effectiveness may differ according to the child's developmental level and sex.

Protection is directed against dangers and stressors of various types and at reducing their impact. Permissions, on the other hand, are aimed at the promotion of the social and problem-solving competencies that lead to an efficient use of whatever abilities a person has, as well as the promotion of self-esteem, self-efficacy, psychological-mindedness, and sense of responsibility.

Protection and permission frequently occur together. In direct therapeutic work with children and adolescents, we have found the concepts invaluable (Allen and Allen, 1997) whether we were dealing with environmental interferences such as inappropriate environmental demands or deficits; those developmental conflicts children traverse as a result of normal growth changes or changing external demands; interstructural conflicts (e.g. between different ego-state neural networks such as between Parent and Child), intrastructural conflicts (e.g. within different aspects of a single ego-state neural network such as between Free Child and Adapted Child), the externalisation of one of these conflicts onto the environment; deficits in the development of particular ego-state networks (e.g. in Child bonding); or with pathogenic script decisions. However, these concepts can also be applied in and extended for use in education (Pierre, 2002; Newton, 2003) and organizational and community development. As long ago as 1979, for example, Rutter was reporting substantial variations in children's outcomes depending on the specific schools they attended, even after he had controlled for differences at the time of admission.

Protection

Protection is one of the hallmarks of transactional analysis interventions. Children (and adults) need protection from life's dangers, as well as from both realistic and imaginary fears if they are to risk doing something new or risk refusing to listen to pathogenic messages, whether these come from within or from without. By the early 1960s, Caplan had pointed out that people in crisis were in a period of disequilibrium and could emerge better or worse. The major difference, he found, was the help they received. In keeping with this conclusion, he then elaborated a series of techniques for crisis intervention and decision counselling (Caplan, 1974). Those in the process of making changes also need to make sure that they will obtain positive strokes during and after so doing. People also need protection from making negative evaluations of themselves or drawing unwarranted or unfortunate conclusions (see the following section on permission to make/find meaning). Supportive individuals and groups are helpful for they imply, if not actually say, "We back you".

Normal young children need protection from such things as their fantasies of power and destructiveness, and normal adolescents need knowledge about real life as they begin to set career and relational priorities. For example, the author has found that artistically-gifted adolescents who are planning to make a career of their art form need to know such basic facts as that even in the best of economic times, 80 per cent of Equity (union) actors in the USA are unemployed, that art galleries routinely double the price of artists' work and take half, and that symphony orchestra members are at increased risk of burn out if they do not find venues such as chamber music or jazz improvisation to express their own creativity, but such knowledge should not and need not demoralise or paralyse them. If we wish to help vulnerable children, however, we need especially to focus on those protective processes that bring changes from risk to adaptation in their life trajectories. Rutter (1979) suggested four such categories:

1. Those that reduce risk impact.
2. Those that reduce the likelihood of negative chain reactions.
3. Those that promote self-esteem and self-efficacy.
4. Those that open up opportunities.

Expanding on this, we might subdivide protection into at least six categories:

1. Protection from real and potential dangers.
2. Protection from internal pathogenic messages.
3. Protection from external pathogenic messages.
4. Protection from finding oneself without support and positive strokes.
5. Protection from drawing pathogenic conclusions.
6. Accurate knowledge of the world so that evaluations and plans can be realistic and likely to succeed.

Permission

Children (and adults) need several different permissions if they are to function well. Like protection, permissions also have been one of the hallmarks of transactional analysis. While important at all ages, the need for each becomes more important during certain periods, then recedes, to arise again later in life. In addition, the same permission may need to take different forms at different ages. For example, a young child needs to feel close in the sense of feeling comfortable and secure with parenting figures. This involves frequent periods of alignment and resonance between the child's and the parents' behavioural and emotional states, a phenomenon associated with the development of important internal models of self with others. These early organising principles begin to form even before the use of words, perhaps by the seventh month, and exert major influences on our later relationships and expectations (Allen, 1998; Allen, 2003). The school-age child, on the other hand, needs permission and opportunities to feel close to peers, while adolescents need to feel comfortable with peers in a way that has growing intimate and sexual overtones.

Ultimately, each person needs to give themselves the permissions they need. However, therapists, counsellors, and educators as well as parents can directly foster an atmosphere which will facilitate this. Organisational and community development professionals and volunteers are in important positions to do so in the larger environment. However, it should be noted that what a person presents to the world influences the reactions of others, thereby shaping future experiences to which that person must then react.

In parent coaching in discipline and in child-rearing (Allen and Allen, 1983) as well as in direct therapeutic work (Allen and Allen, 1997) the author has found the following list of permissions especially useful. However, it needs to be adapted to one's particular clients and context (Allen et al., 1996; Allen and Allen, 2002; Allen and Hammond, 2003). One warning: as explicated later, an atmosphere rich in permissions is not an atmosphere of permissiveness or overindulgence.

- To belong.
- To exist.
- To exist with zest.
- To feel secure.
- To be close yet separate.
- To be aware of one's sensations, needs, and feelings.
- To express needs and have them met appropriately.
- To be oneself (i.e. one's appropriate age, colour, and ethnicity, including to be a child, and later, to be a grown-up).
- To trust appropriately.
- To be mutually responsive to and with others.
- To have an impact.
- To be OK, while letting others be OK.
- To receive accurate feedback and to interpret it accurately.
- To think clearly and solve problems effectively.
- To understand what is going on psychologically (mentalisation).
- To experiment and change and to use any failure productively.
- To be and to feel successful in love and work, however that be defined (including to be able to validate both one's own sexuality, work, hobbies, and career choices as well as those of others).
- To grow up and to leave home.
- To make/find meaning (in one's own life and in existence in general).
- To find cultural nurturance.

A fundamental sense that one is basically OK and that so are others, a fundamental sense of hope, and a basic belief that people can change for the better and that problems can be surmounted – these are all important for a healthful and productive life. The position that oneself, others, and the context all count is crystallised in the transactional analysis concept of basic existential positions. A sense that the odds can be surmounted was found to be the central component in the lives of the resilient individuals in Werner's 32 year prospective studies of a 11,698 babies born during a single year on the Hawaiian island of Kauai (Werner, 1994). In

addition, however, the opening up of opportunities as they entered their 20s led them to make major changes for the better.

The first and last permissions listed here need special comment. Every child needs to be wanted and accepted for themselves even before birth; even then, the permissions to be, to belong, and to be oneself are fused and intermixed. The last permission, permission to find cultural nurturance becomes more important as we grow older, for our cultural milieu, our beliefs, symbols, institutions, and artifacts become as important to our psychological well-being as oxygen is for our physiological existence. There are also two permissions whose importance I believe we will increasingly recognise in the next few years. The first is the permission to make/find meaning. This underpins much of parents', therapists', and even political spin propagandists' interactions as they highlight or downplay certain aspects of experience. At the social-political level, for example, Feitlowitz (1998) reported that during and after the Dirty Wars in Argentina, people in many communities could no longer freely say *capucha* (hood) or *parrilla* (barbeque). More recently, Susan Sontag (2004) has called our attention to US Secretary of Defense Donald Rumsfeld's refusal to use the word 'torture' after photos of torture at Abu Ghraib in Iraq were widely circulated. Indeed, during his trip there, a new complex was christened 'Camp Redemption'! The second permission we will likely appreciate better in the near future involves psychological mindedness, the understanding we have of our mental states and the mental states of others (Allen, Bennett and Kearns, 2004). Children's sense of their inner worlds forms from how they experience others experiencing and responding to them. Research suggests this is a necessary foundation for a healthy life and that it is central to resilience; it allows a person to observe dynamics and patterns in behaviour and to compare present situations with past experience, and so to be able better to predict what is likely to happen in the future. Recently, an international consortium including the Anna Freud Centre of University College, London, the Yale Child Study Center, and the Menninger-Baylor Human Neuroimaging Laboratory in Houston has been formed to study functional brain changes during this process of reflecting upon and making sense of experience.

Mentorship: A human relationship and practical advice

The concept of mentorship is now popular in business and educational fields. For older children, adolescents, and adults, it can involve a variety of things: helping them give themselves the permissions they need; helping them learn new skills; connecting them to needed networks; resources, and knowledge; and supporting them in analysing and solving problems effectively. Of great importance are the mentor's power to emphasise their strengths, to define or redefine reality, and to offer protection during times of re-decision and change. Experience from intergenerational mentoring programs suggests that a close one-to-one relationship with an unrelated elder can foster self-esteem and improved behaviour in troubled youth or children (Freedman, 1993). Among the most potent factors which were found to provide a second chance for the older high-risk youth in the Kauai study were: adult education programs in community colleges, voluntary national service, and confidence in some centre of value. For younger children, mentorship may include bonding, the development of insight into the basic components of human behaviour (psychological mindedness or the development of a theory of mind), and the application of this knowledge to the domain of emotions, and their regulation. For new mothers, mentoring involves help in all the areas necessary to facilitate good prenatal and postnatal care and appropriate bonding with their children. Lyons-Ruth, for example, has presented considerable evidence that the effects of later trauma are determined, at least in part, by a person's early security of attachment (Lyons-Ruth, et al., 1999).

Whatever the target group, however, mentoring includes two major aspects of social support: a human relationship and cognitive information, including practical advice (Caplan, 1974). Relationship experiences have a major influence on the brain because the circuits responsible for social perception are closely linked to or the same as those involved in the creation of meaning, the modulation of emotion, the regulation of body states, and the capacity for interpersonal communication (Allen, 2003). One of the important lessons from Werner's follow-up of high-risk babies in Kauai, for example, was that the resilient boys and girls found emotional support outside their families. Many had a favourite teacher who became a role model, friend, and confidant.

Lambert and Barley's (2001) meta-analysis of factors influencing the outcome of psychotherapy showed that only 15 per cent of positive therapeutic outcomes could be attributed to the specific therapeutic approach. Expectations were responsible for 15 per cent, external factors for 40 per cent, and general factors – including the patient-therapist relationship – for 30 per cent. This should not really come as a surprise, for it is a common observation that many people change in the context of a good interpersonal relationship, whether this be with a therapist, counsellor, teacher, confidante, or spouse. The resilient youngsters in Werner's Kauai study had had at least one person in their lives who accepted them unconditionally, and follow-up studies by Main's group in Berkeley have found a sub-group of young children characterized by insecure attachment who, as adults, could be classified as having an 'earned' secure attachment as the result of some good relationship later in life (Pearson et al., 1994). In summary, it seems that our underlying assumptions about self with others, the early internal working models in implicit memory that shape our perceptions and expectations of the world, self, and others (our basic existential positions in the terminology of transactional analysis) can be altered by later experiences (Allen, 1998).

When the mid-life outcomes of men in the Core City sample in the Harvard Study of Adult Development were evaluated when these men were 47 years of age, an almost complete differentiation was found between the top and bottom quartiles in terms of happy marriages, social competence, and regularity of employment. Most strikingly, the Boyhood Competence Scale, a scale based on the tasks of Erickson's stage of industry versus inferiority completed when they were boys; correlated most strongly with all facets of their adult development (Vaillant and Vaillant, 1981). The successful achievement of these tasks could be facilitated even in high-risk children by appropriate permissions, protection, opportunities, and mentoring in social, academic, and physical competencies.

Although mentoring is generally considered a powerful alternative education strategy for dropout prevention among students at risk (Reglin, 1998) or an effective addition to young people's education (Westhues et al., 2001;

Rhodes, 2002) research on mentoring in children and young people is unfortunately often rather difficult to evaluate because of significant differences in target groups, goals, objectives, and contexts, including the quality and quantity of protégé-mentor relationships, assessment criteria and length of follow-up, as well as because of problems in separating factors which are truly causative from those that are just correlated. In addition, there may also be significant differences between the effects on academic achievement, self-perceptions, efficacy, and self-esteem. The following are typical examples of this research: Linnehan (2003) found that at the end of a year, high-school students in a work-based program were more likely to report that school was relevant to their work if they had had a mentor than if they had not, and that those students who were highly satisfied with their mentor had higher levels of self-esteem. Karcher et al. (2002) found that after one year, elementary school children mentored by high-school students were better connected to their parents, school, and the future, but that the program's effects on spelling achievement were mediated by parental connectedness into middle school. Westhues et al. (2001) reported significant positive changes in self-esteem in third grade girls following a 6–8 week program designed to build positive relationships between little sisters and big sisters. In the Kauai study of high-risk children, scholastic competence at age 10 was positively linked with support from teachers and peers, and a sense of self-efficacy (self-esteem and internal locus of control) at age 18.

A greater sense of self-efficacy at age 18 was, in turn, linked to less distress and emotionality for the men at age 21 and to a greater number of sources of emotional support for the women in early adulthood.

Environmental disharmonies: too little, too much, or wrong time and a major locus for educational interventions

Children evolve in and through interaction with their environment and especially with their interpersonal environment. This interaction forges their abilities to organise their minds and to relate, and thereby is key in the development of cognition, language, and morality.

A poor fit between a specific child's needs and the environment can be termed an environmental disharmony (Allen and Allen, 1997). It is caused by one of two major phenomena: too little of something that particular child needs or too much. Sometimes, what might be appropriate at some point in a child's life comes at the wrong time and so is too much or too little.

Environmental disharmonies can lead to abnormalities in the development or functioning of the more frequently energized neural networks transactional analysts call ego states. This, in turn, may lead to an imbalance or conflict between ego states (an interstructural conflict as between Parent and Child ego states) or between different neural components of a single ego state (as between Adapted Child and Natural Child). Such disharmonies can also result in the child's drawing pathogenic conclusions and making unfortunate decisions about self and others, and about what to expect in this world, that is, their narrative identity or what transactional analysts call script. In reality, even small changes in the parenting or educational environment at the stage of environmental disharmonies can result in major changes in a child's life trajectory. This is an area where the efforts of educators and organizational development personnel are especially important, and potent.

Traditionally, mental health professionals have concentrated on the problems arising from too little. However, as Clarke et al. (2004) have described, too much can also have devastating consequences. Overindulgence by well-meaning but unskilled adults can lead to a cornucopia of pathologies: inflated Child demands and sense of entitlement, poor Adult competencies and coping skills, and a Parent driver to 'Get mine now!' These overindulged children have not been given appropriate permission and protection. In contrast, Rachman (1979) found that even such required helpfulness as community service was correlated with improved self-esteem, self-efficacy, and competence.

A culture of protection and permission

The term 'culture', it has been said, is one of the most complicated in the English language. It encompasses both civilisation's high achievements and its more prosaic ideas, attitudes, practices, and products. At times, the term has taken on quite negative connotations as in 'culture of poverty' or 'culture of violence', but we can also have cultures of health and richness. The author is currently engaged in a study examining resilience, positive emotions, developmental assets, and the underlying roles of permission and protection, including supportive but demanding mentors and institutions.

A group of severely artistically-talented youth

On the basis of competitive auditions, the Oklahoma Arts Institute, Quartz Mountain, accepts high-school students (modal age 17) for intensive summer programs in a variety of art forms: ballet, modern dance, poetry, film, orchestra, painting, sculpture, acting, and choral music. Students come from communities of all sizes throughout the state. All the students receive scholarships, which are funded in part by the state and in part by private philanthropy.

Eight hundred sixty-nine students were evaluated from 1998 to 2001 using a variety of paper and pencil tests addressing demographics and subjective experience as well as anxiety, depression, and other symptoms as measured by standardised tests. In addition, in 2000 and 2001, 471 students were also given the BarOn Emotional Quotient (BarOn EQ-i) (Bar-On, 1997) a test of 15 intrapsychic, interpersonal, adaptive, stress-management, and general mood indicators. Further details of this group and the study's findings will be presented elsewhere. However, as part of the study, five questions germane to this chapter were addressed:

- Are these artistically-accomplished adolescents characterised by factors which have been found significant for psychological resilience and optimal development in other populations of young people?
- If so, do they show evidence of specific differences from their high-school peers in terms *of* psychological distress, clinical symptoms, or behaviour problems?
- Are there significant intrapsychic or interpersonal differences between students involved in different art forms?
- If so, is there a significant correlation between art form and behavioural problems or experienced psychological distress?
- If so, can these differences be understood in terms of permission and protection?

Findings

1. Factors previously found important for psychological resilience:

1.1. Relationships and connections with caring others.

One third of the Search Institute's sample of almost 100,000 teenagers in the USA reported they had no family support. About three out of four reported a lack of positive family communication or a caring school or parental involvement in their education. Only 40 per cent reported a caring neighbourhood. In contrast, as a group the Quartz Mountain students described their families as supportive (mean of 4.3 on a 5 point scale). 74 per cent had a parent who participated in some art form, and 47 per cent of the parents still did. Of those students reporting two people especially supportive of their art form, it was their mother and father 45 per cent of the time and their mother and a teacher 20 per cent of the time. The odds of receiving emotional support from their families was 2.19 times higher for those students who received support for their artistic pursuits than for those who did not (95 per cent C.I, 1.67–2.89).

1.2. Consistent norms and expectations. Baumrind (1989) has found that a parental combination of demandingness and responsiveness (termed authoritative parenting) is associated with optimal competence in adolescence. In general, these characteristics seem typical of the families of the Quartz students, with the exception of the sculptors, whose parents were perceived as supportive but not challenging. Indeed, art forms in themselves offer a 'context of effort and demand' (Larson and Richards, 1994). These expectations were internalised by the Quartz students, as evidenced in their self-descriptions.

There is a considerable literature on the decisions of gifted children to become very serious about their art form during adolescence. This coincides, at least for some, with a switch from understanding their art from a more intuitive to a more cognitive point of view, a transition which causes some child prodigies great distress.

Among the Quartz students, the ballet, modern dancers, and choristers had decided to become among the top in their field, a major script decision, when they were 12 years of age (modal age) but photographers and painters did so at 16 years (F(8,211)=3.31, p<0.0014) with no gender differences. Actors, however, reported a commitment to be in the top group significantly more often than the average (p=.004) and poets significantly less (p=.007).

1.3. Effective use of time.
A 1992 Carnegie Institute study found that one-third of eighth graders in the USA spent five hours at home each day without anything useful to do. Similarly, the Search Institute's study of almost 100,000 adolescents showed that only slightly more than half participated in any youth program whatsoever and that only one in five spent any time in creative activities – and that even this constructive use of time declined between the sixth and twelfth grade. Yet, it is just such activities that provide opportunities to practice new skills, to develop a sense of competence, and to establish pro-social peer and mentor relationships.

As might be expected, the Quartz students spent little time just 'hanging out'. To begin with, they reported an average (mean) of 8.3 hours a week involved in their particular art form, although the range was from 11.1 hours (mean) for ballet dancers, 10.7 for modern dancers, and 10.2 for sculptors, to 5.6 for poets and 4.9 for film students.

A 1991 government report noted that the average teenager in the USA worked 20 hours a week outside the home (US General Accounting Office, 1992). Unfortunately, young people typically fail to take pleasure in this activity (Schmidt and Rich, 2000), and generally the jobs they find have little relevance to their later lives. Again, this contrasts markedly with the experience of the Quartz students, 70 per cent of whom expect to make a career of their art form and a full 96 per cent of whom (except poets and orchestra members) reported 'flow' while engaged in their art form. Even of the poets and choristers, however, 83 per cent and 82 per cent respectively had the experience (Chi-square(2)=9.26, p=0.01).

1.4. Connections to social institutions.
By participating in the Institute's programs as well as local school and youth orchestras, art shows, and the like, the Quartz students are actively involved in the social institutions of their communities – and doing something valued by the larger community. These are important experiences denied many adolescents in a country in which teenagers are commonly

regarded primarily either as a cause for social concern or as consumers to be courted because of their expendable incomes.

1.5. Development of positive self-perceptions.
Positive self-perception, in part, reflects awareness of real achievement. By admission itself into the program, each of the Quartz students has demonstrated significant achievement in his or her particular art form. In addition, each art form provides an opportunity to develop real-life skills. Indeed, 70 per cent intended to make a career in it. Some art forms, orchestra for example, give students an opportunity to learn to cooperate, to support one another, to trust, and to be trusted and the orchestra, ballet, and choral music students are very aware of this. Interestingly, management textbooks frequently use the metaphor of an orchestra for a well-functioning business enterprise.

The Bar-On Eq-i intrapersonal subscales address a number of areas of self-assessment: perceived self-awareness, assertiveness, self-regard, self-actualisation, and independence. The following graph depicts these for each of the art forms.

Self-regard is defined in the Bar-On *Technical Manual* (Bar-On, 1997: 16) as 'the ability to respect and accept oneself as basically good'. It is described as associated with general feelings of self-confidence and self-adequacy based on a fairly well developed sense of identity. On this scale, the actors, and especially the male actors (mean score 89) scored significantly lower than students in the other groups. Yet, this particular art form allows them to experiment with taking on new behaviours and new roles, a false identity, something presumably of protective value when they audition or perform.

The modem dancers scored the highest on the subtest for self-actualisation which is defined in the *Technical Manual* as 'the ability to realise one's potential abilities' (ibid.: 16). It is described as involving the development of enjoyable and meaningful activities, and of persistence in trying to do one's best and to accept oneself.

In summary, the Quartz adolescents have many characteristics that have been associated with psychological resilience: emotional support and direction by adults who care about them; clear boundaries and expectations; skill-training; solvable challenges; positive connections with social institutions; and reason to perceive

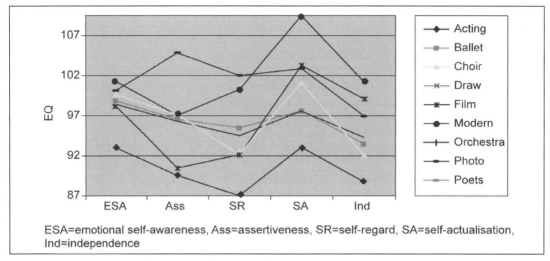

Figure 16.1   Intrapersonal EQ-i subscales (males and females)

themselves positively in terms of real achievements. Consequently, it might be expected that they would have fewer psychological symptoms and fewer behaviour problems than their peers.

2. Positive well-being and behaviour: differences from peers.

2.1. A. Academics.
81 per cent of the Quartz students are in the upper third of their class: only 3 per cent are in the lower third. Their mean ACT score, a nationally used academic achievement test in the USA, was 26.05 out of a possible 36. By way of comparison, the mean score for students in the Oklahoma City schools in 2001 was 18.08. For the state as a whole, it was 20.6. There were differences in art forms, however, with orchestra members and poets scoring highest, having a mean of 27, the score required by most competitive colleges. Sculptors had the lowest score: 22.

2.2 Alcohol and drug use.
Although the questions were not exactly identical, one year's self-reported use of alcohol and tobacco by the Quartz students was about equivalent to one month's use by their Oklahoma high-school peers (Oklahoma State Department of Mental Health and Substance Abuse, 2001).

2.3. Delinquency.
Self-reported delinquent acts were almost non-existent among the Quartz students. The one exception was school truancy, in which almost all

had participated. Only 4 of 283 Quartz respondents reported ever using a weapon in a fight. In contrast, the 2003 Oklahoma Behaviour Risk Study of high-school students found that 2.5 per cent of girls and 13.5 per cent of boys had actually carried a weapon on school property on one or more days during the previous 30 days (Oklahoma State Department of Health, 2004). This may be part of our legacy from the old 'Wild West'. It was only in 1907 that the Twin Territories of Indian and Oklahoma Territory (also known as Outlaw Territory) evolved into the State of Oklahoma.

Antisocial or pro-social behaviours are frequently conceptualised as outcomes, but they also have dynamic influences on their putative causes. However, 50 per cent of the Quartz students believed their art form responsible for keeping them 'on the straight and narrow'.

2.4. Psychological distress.
69 per cent of the female and 66 per cent of the male Quartz students reported what they considered significant psychological discomfort. Yet, they generally scored in the normal range on formal standardized tests such as The Spielberger Trait and State Anxiety Scales (Spielberger, 1984), and the Symptom Check List-90 (Derogatis and Lazarus, 1994). On the Beck Depression Inventory (Beck, Steer, and Garbin, 1988) only about 10 per cent had a score greater than 15 which is usually taken as a clinically significant cut-off point, although actors (mean score 9.7) and poets (mean

score 9.5) had significant higher scores than modern dancers (mean 5.19) choristers (mean 6.55), and orchestra members (mean 6.6). These low scores are significant in view of the fact that in 1999, the Oklahoma Department of Mental Health and Substance Abuse's survey of 5,003 Oklahoma teenagers found that 34.7 per cent reported feeling so sad or helpless almost every day for two weeks in a row that they stopped doing some of their usual activities (compared with 28 per cent of peers nationwide) and 29.4 per cent of these Oklahoma students had seriously considered suicide during the previous 12 months (compared with 18.1 per cent nationally) (Oklahoma Department of Mental Health and Substance Abuse, 2001).

Although there were significant difference between students in the different art forms, 92 per cent of the Quartz students reported that they have been able to use their art form to deal with psychological distress: 45 per cent 'very much', 47 per cent 'somewhat' – and had decided to do so consciously. Most strikingly, as the students' reported experience of distress increased, those in all art forms reported that their art form helped in dealing with it (MH(12) = 30.7, p = 0.0022).

In terms of the cultivation of positive emotions, it should be recalled that use of one's signature strengths in terms of some larger good, a decision, can be expected to lead to a sense of well-being and 'OK-ness' (Seligman, 2002). Concentration and absorption in an activity which fits their long-term goals, here a career, has been found to predispose to states of 'flow', a specific type of 'OK-ness' (Csikszmentmihalyi and Rathunde, 1993).

In summary, this group of accomplished young people show fewer emotional and behavioural problems than their state and national peers. It may be argued that they have had few trauma in their lives and so may not be good examples of resilience. For example, 72 per cent of their parents had remained married. Yet, these students are rich in terms of the developmental assets delineated by the Search Institute. Fifty-nine per cent believed that their experiences of psychological distress had helped them be a better artist but, as reported earlier, the greater their experienced distress, the greater they report the value of their art form in dealing with it.

3. Differences between groups.
Space does not permit a detailed description of differences between students in the different art

forms, and correlations between various art forms and reported psychological experience. Nevertheless, there were significant differences.

Total emotional quotients on the Bar On EQ-i were, in ascending order: acting, poetry, art, choir, orchestra, film, ballet, modern dancing, and photography. These differences were statistically significant (F(8,408) = 3.2, p = .0016).

Within art forms, however, there were significant differences, as depicted in the graph of their EQ-i Intrapersonal subscales reproduced earlier. Actors scored lowest on self-regard; poets, lowest on reality testing; photographers, highest in stress tolerance; and modern dancers, highest on sense of self-realisation.

Each of these findings needs special consideration. For example, the poets' low scores in terms of reality-testing would be a disturbing finding in a clinical sample of patients and had it not been accompanied by other characteristics such as higher scores in problem-solving and an average ACT score of 27. It is therefore probably best regarded as evidence of ability to be in touch with unconscious processes which they can then harness, 'regression in the service of the ego' or, put otherwise, of the importance of this art form in transforming unconscious processes into social communication. The modern dancers' very high sense of self-actualisation, especially when compared even with students in ballet, a discipline in which they all had previously trained, probably reflects the more democratic and less-hierarchical structure and tradition of modern dance and modern dance companies. Modern dancers put emphasis on self-expression as opposed to conformity, and in their world there is less need to live up to some one else's concept of the 'perfect' ballerina.

Interestingly, displacement is the one defence mechanism that allows a person to work on a problem without claiming it as their own, as any preschool teacher who reads stories to children has discovered. Indeed, young children can usually tolerate the idea of the mind as representing ideas and feelings so long as it is 'just pretend'. If such internal states are conceptualised as real and theirs however, they may be experienced as dangerous. Hence, the importance of working with children's displacements in play, stories, and activities (Allen and Hammond, 2003). This defence mechanism continues to play a significant role as we grow older, however, and remains evident along with symbolization in most of the art forms. In their less regulated forms, such activities can be seen as a form of active imagination, a way of giving the unconscious an outlet.

Although correlation is not causation, it seems that, quite apart from its role of providing a level of training not generally available in the state, the Oklahoma Arts Institute is a key link in a network of protective and permission-giving activities, relationships, and institutions for artistically-gifted adolescents. As such, it can be regarded as playing a significant public health role in fostering emotional well-being and pro-social behaviours and in the prevention of a variety of risky adolescent behaviours.

Summary: and a look to the future

First conceptualised as important in the therapy room, the roles of permission and protection have long been emphasized in the transactional analysis literature on treatment. Later, they were conceptualised in terms of the prevention of psychological dysfunction (Allen and Allen, 1983). Now, it is time to look at them in terms of the promotion of resilience and positive emotions. Together, they also form important aspects of mentorship.

When mental health practitioners speak of culture, we tend to emphasize the negative. However, we need also to look at how culture as well as treatment and education can support, facilitate, and enhance growth, resilience, and well-being (Tudor, 1991; Pierre, 2002; Allen, 2003; Newton, 2003); and how we,can provide appropriate permissions, protection, and role-models as well as expectations and demands within a broad socio-ecological matrix. This perspective highlights the importance of educators and organisational and community development personnel. It also fits with a multilevel, multi-factorial conceptualisation of human development, for risk and protective factors as well as risky or healthy behaviours occur in clusters, extend across multiple contexts (family, peers, schools, and communities) and influence each other reciprocally and synergistically over time.

Frameworks developed in the consulting room have understandably emphasised psychopathology and have tended to imply that well-being is just its absence. From early on, however, transactional analysts have emphasized 'OKness', albeit that the term was often misunderstood as a feeling rather than as a psychological stance towards oneself, others, and the contexts in which one lives, and out of which interactions and then feelings develop (Allen, 2003). At present, however, there is an explosion of interest in what has been called 'positive psychology'. This has resulted in a number of ongoing well-planned prospective research studies. Consequently, this aspect of transactional analysis can be expected to assume greater prominence in the near future and to become an area from which we will find increasing support for and applications of permission, protection, and mentorship.

References

Allen, J.R. (1998) Of Resilience, Vulnerability, and a Woman Who Never Lived. *Child and Adolescent Psychiatric Clinics of North America*, 7: 1, 63–71.

Allen, J.R. (2003) Concepts, Competencies and Interpretive Communities. *Transactional Analysis Journal*, 33: 2, 126–47.

Allen, J.R. and Allen, B.A. (1997) A Typology of Psychopathology and Treatment in Children and Adolescents. *Transactional Analysis Journal*, 27: 4, 256–64.

Allen, J.R. and Allen, B.A. (1983) Discipline: A Transactional-Analytic View. In Dorr, D., Zax, M. and Bonner, J.W. (Eds.) *The Psychology of Discipline*. New York: International Universities Press.

Allen, J.R. and Allen, B.A. (2002) Redecision Therapy as Brief Therapy. In Tudor, K. (Ed.) *Transactional Analysis Approaches to Brief Therapy or What Do You Say Between Saying Hello and Goodbye?* London: Sage.

Allen, J.R., Bennett, S. and Kearns, L. (2004) Psychological Mindedness: A Neglected Developmental Line in Permissions to Think. *Transactional Analysis Journal*, 34: 1, 3–9.

Allen, J.R. and Hammond, D. (2003) Groups Within Groups: Fractals and The Successes and Failure of a Child Inpatient Psychiatric Unit. *Transactional Analysis Journal*, 33: 4, 302–14.

Allen, J.R. et al. (1996) The Role of Permission: Two Decades Later. *Transactional Analysis Journal*, 26: 3, 196–205.

Bar-On, R. (1997) *Baron Emotional Quotient-Inventory: A Measure of Emotional Intelligence (Ba-ron Eq-I 7). Technical Manual.* North Tonawanda, NY: Multi-Health Systems.

Baumrind, D. (1989) Rearing Competent Children. In Damon, W. (Ed.) *Child Development Today and Tomorrow*. San Francisco, CA: Jossey-Bass.

Beck, A.T., Steer, R.A. and Garbin, M.G. (1988) Psychometric Properties of The Beck Depression Inventory: Twenty-Five Years of Evaluation. *Clinical Psychology Review*, 8: 1, 77–100.

Benson, P.L. et al. (1998) Beyond The 'Village' Rhetoric: Creating Healthy Communities for Children and Adolescents. *Applied Developmental Science*, 2: 3, 138–59.

Bronfenbrenner, U. (1977) Toward an Experimental Ecology of Human Development. *American Psychologist*, 32: 7, 513–31.

Caplan, G. (1974) *Support Systems and Community Mental Health: Lectures on Concept Development*. New York: Behavioral Publications.

Clarke, J.L, Dawson, C. and Bredehoft, D.J. (2004) *How Much is Enough? Everything You Need to Know to Steer Clear of Overindulgence and Raise Likeable, Responsible, and Respectful Children*. New York: Marlowe.

Csikszentmihalyi, M. and Rathunde, K. (1993) The Measurement of Flow in Everyday Life: Toward A Theory of Emergent Motivation. In Jacobs, J.E. (Ed.) *Nebraska Symposium on Motivation, 1992: Developmental Perspectives on Motivation. Current Theory and Research in Motivation*. Lincoln, NE: University of Nebraska Press.

Danner, D.D., Snowdon, D.A. and Friesen, W.V. (2001) Positive Emotions in Early Life and Longevity: Findings From The Nun Study. *Journal of Personality and Social Psychology*, 80: 5, 804–13.

Derogatis, L.R. and Lazarus, L. (1994) SCL-90–R, Brief Symptom Inventory and Matching Clinical Rating Scales. In Maruish, M.E. (Ed.) *The Use of Psychological Testing for Treatment Planning and Outcome Assessment*. Hillsdale, NJ: Lawrence Erlbaum Associates.

Ennett, S.T. et al. (1994) How Effective is Drug Abuse Resistance Education? A Meta-Analysis of Project DARE Outcome Evaluations. *American Journal of Public Health*, 84: 9, 1394–401.

Feitlowitz, M. (1998) *Lexicon of Terror: Argentina and The Legacies of Torture*. New York: Oxford University Press.

Freedman, M. (1993) *The Kindness of Strangers: Adult Mentors, Urban Youth, and The New Voluntarism*. San Francisco: Jossey-Bass.

Fredrickson, B.L. (2001) The Role of Positive Emotions in Positive Psychology: The Broaden-and-Build Theory of Positive Emotions. *American Psychologist*, 56: 3, 218–26.

Goertzel, V. and Goertzel, M.G. (1962) *Cradles of Eminence*. Boston, MA: Little, Brown.

Isen, A.M. (2000) Some Perspectives on Positive Affect and Self-Regulation. *Psychological Inquiry*, 11: 3, 184–7.

Jessor, R. (1995) Protective Factors in Adolescent Problem Behavior: Moderator Effects and Developmental Change. *Developmental Psychology*, 31: 6, 923–33.

Jessor, R. et al. (1993) Successful Adolescent Development Among Youth in High-Risk Settings. *American Psychologist*, 48: 2, 117–26.

Karcher, M.J., Davis, C. III and Powell, B. (2002) The Effects of Developmental Mentoring On Connectedness and Academic Achievement. *School Community Journal*, 12: 2, 35–50.

Lambert, M.J. and Barley, D.E. (2001) Research Summary on The Therapeutic Relationship and Psychotherapy Outcome. *Psychotherapy: Theory, Research, Practice, Training*, 38: 4, 357–61.

Larson, R. and Richards, M.H. (1994) *Divergent Realities: The Emotional Lives of Mothers, Fathers, and Adolescents*. New York: Basic Books.

Leffert, N., Benson, P.L. and Roehlkepartain, J.L. (1997) *Starting Out Right: Developmental Assets for Children*. Minneapolis, MN: The Search Institute.

Linnehan, F. (2003) A Longitudinal Study of Work-Based, Adult-Youth Mentoring. *Journal of Vocational Behavior*, 63: 1, 40–54.

Lyons-Ruth, K., Bronfman, E. and Parsons, E. (1999) Maternal Frightened, Frightening, or Atypical Behavior and Disorganized Infant Attachment Patterns. In Vondia, J. and Barnett, D. (Eds.) *Atypical Attachment in Infancyand Early Childhood among Children at Developmental Risk*. London: Blackwell.

Newton, T. (2003) Identifying Educational Philosophy and Practice Through Images in Transactional Analysis Training Groups. *Transactional Analysis Journal*, 33: 4, 321–31.

Oklahoma State Department of Health (2003) *Oklahoma Youth Risk Behavior Survey*. Oklahoma City, OK: Oklahoma State DoH.

Oklahoma State Department of Mental Health and Substance Abuse Services (2001) *Prevention Works: Examining High-Risk Behavior Among Oklahoma Youth*. Oklahoma City, OK: Oklahoma State DMHSAS.

Pearson, J.L. et al. (1994) Earned-and Continuous-Security in Adult Attachment: Relation to Depressive Symptomatology and Parenting Style. *Development and Psychopathology*, 6: 2, 359–73.

Pierre, N. (2002) *Pratique de l'Analyse Transactionnelle Dans la Classe avec des Jeunes et dans les Groupes* [Using transactional analysis in class with young people and groups]. Issy les Moulineaux ED ESF.

Rachman, S. (1979) The Concept of Required Helpfulness. *Behavior Research, and Therapy*, 17, 1–16.

Reglin, G. (1998) *Mentoring Students at Risk: an Underutilized Alternative Education Strategy for K-12 Teachers*. Springfield, IL: Charles C. Thomas.

Rhodes, J.E. (2002) A Critical View of Youth Mentoring. In Rhodes, J.E. (Ed.) *New Directions for Youth Development: Theory, Practice, Research*. San Francisco: Jossey-Bass.

Rutter, M. (1979) Protective Factors in Children's Responses to Stress and Children's Disadvantage. In Kent, M.W. and Rolf, J.E. (Eds.) *Social Competence in Children*. Hanover, NH: University Press of New England.

Scales, P.C. (1990) Developing Capable Young People: an Alternative Strategy for Prevention Programs. *Journal of Early Adolescence*, 10: 4, 420–38.

Scales, P.C. et al. (2000) Contribution of Developmental Assets to The Prediction of Thriving Among Adolescents. *Applied Developmental Science*, 4: 1, 27–46.

Scales, P.C. and Leffert, N. (1999) *Developmental Assets: A Synthesis of The Scientific Research on Adolescent Development*. Minneapolis, MN: The Search Institute.

Scales, P.C., Leffert, N. and Blyth, D.A. (1998) *The Strength of Developmental Assets: A Prediction of Positive Youth Outcome*. New York: The Free Press.

Schmidt, J. and Rich, G. (2000) Images of Work and Play. In Csikszentmihalyi, M. and Schneider, B.L. (Eds.) *Becoming Adult: How Teenagers Prepare for The World of Work*. New York: Basic Books.

Schorr, L.B. and Schorr, D. (1988) *Within Our Reach: Breaking The Cycle of Disadvantage*. Garden City, NY: Anchor Press/Doubleday.

Seligman, M.E.P. (2002) *Authentic Happiness: Using The New Positive Psychology to Realize Your Potential for Lasting Fulfillment*. New York: Free Press.

Sontag, S. (2004) Regarding The Torture of Others: Notes on What Has Been Done – and Why – to Prisoners by Americans. *New York Times Magazine*, 23 May, 42, 24–9.

Spielberger, C.D. (1984) *State-Trait Anxiety Inventory: A Comprehensive Bibliography*. Palo Alto, CA: Consulting Psychologists Press.

Tudor, K. (1991) Children's Groups: Integrating TA and Gestalt Perspectives. *Transactional Analysis Journal*, 21: 1, 12–20.

United States General Accounting Office (1991) *Child Labour: Characteristics of Working Children*. GAO/HRD91-83BR. Washington, DC: US Government Printing Office.

Vaillant, G.E. and Vaillant, C.O. (1981) Natural History of Male Psychological Health: Work as a Predictor of Positive Mental Health. *American Journal of Psychiatry*, 138: 11, 1433–40.

Werner, E.E. (1994) Overcoming The Odds. *Journal of Developmental and Behavioral Pediatrics*, 15: 2, 131–6.

Westhues, A. et al. (2001) Building Positive Relationships: An Evaluation of Process and Outcomes in a Big Sister Program. *Journal of Primary Prevention*, 21: 4, 477–93.

CHAPTER 17

Bringing up the Child: The Importance of Functionally Fluent Parents, Carers and Educators

Susannah Temple

This chapter looks at child rearing and growing up from a particular TA perspective. The 'functional fluency' model of human social functioning (Temple, 1999, 2004) is used to illuminate issues of human psychological development and to highlight the benefits of positive and enabling child rearing relationships. Upbringing is a relational process unique for each individual, in which what we do and how we do it can either support a positive growthful dynamic or hinder it. The question is, as Chess and Thomas (1999) put it, 'How good is the fit between the child's capacity and dynamic of growth and development and the carer's provision of challenge, stimulation and support?' Maintaining a good fit requires on-the-ball sensitivity and know-how along with empathic acceptance, firm guidance and creative ways to enjoy and share in the process alongside the child. In TA language, this means parenting from Integrating Adult, as the title of this book implies. Functional fluency is a term for the 'Integrating Adult in action' (Temple, 1999). The functional fluency model was developed as both a behavioural diagnosis of ego states and a practical framework for learning how to build positive relationships. It is a tool for enhancing emotional literacy (Steiner, 1999; Antidote, 2003). In education, this model helps people make sense of both intrapsychic and interpersonal dynamics so that they can maintain objectivity more easily and jump to conclusions less. This means that they are more likely to stay in charge of their responses, even when there is aggravation or anxiety, which in turn promotes positive communication. The model is presented here as a way to understand the effects of parenting behaviours and how to make them as helpful as possible.

The maturation process into adulthood takes many years, and in some cultures, such as our own, is prolonged past the stage of physical maturity and ability to survive, pair up and reproduce. As complex social animals, we have much to learn about how to relate to others and function as a productive member of the social group, whatever form that may take. We also need to learn much knowledge and many skills in order to fend for ourselves and provide for our own well-being and eventually for that of our children. Upbringing should provide that learning. The knowledge, skills and understandings needed vary immensely from culture to culture. Some of these variations are obvious and are linked to factors such as geography and climate. For example, consider the different learning necessary for the peoples of the Arctic circle and those of the Congo basin. Some of the variations are subtle and are more to do with tribal history and the psychology of the group concerned. However, the fundamental learnings necessary for all human beings are similar in essence – how to make or acquire shelter, find and produce food, protect water supplies and maintain the environment (Brody, 2001). Above all, as we are social animals and almost always live in groups, we have to learn how to co-operate and collaborate. As Hogan, Hogan and Trickey (1999) note, what human beings need to know is how to get along and get ahead. Succeeding in this is often termed being psychologically well adjusted. Upbringing, therefore, includes not only the passing on of knowledge down the generations, but also provides the relationships within which the children and young people develop their respective identities and abilities to relate to others in the social group.

What do we mean 'upbringing'?

As human beings are born entirely helpless, we need prolonged care and protection to survive.

Cultural and historical variation

Variation of cultural styles is immense. Different groups emphasise different priorities and follow different belief systems for making sense of their motivations and experiences. They care for their infants and prepare their young people for adulthood in different ways according to those belief systems and the various pressures for survival. For most of our evolutionary history, it has been the norm that infants are in physical contact with a member of their family day and night. Closeness has been a given. Human beings have grown up in small groups rarely coming across anyone whom they do not already know (Rowe, 1999). The norms of the group and the skills to be learned have been passed on by example and experience through the activities of the family and the group. In some cultures children are still cared for from a young age by barely older siblings. In industrialised countries with massed populations children are grouped according to age and are cared for during the day by specially designated carers, usually women. In many cultures going to school has become a 'normal' part of being educated and teachers do much upbringing. Children's total education, however, has always been, and always will be, the life they lead; and they learn, as ever, by example and experience from those who take responsibility for them. The times and ways in which children are expected finally to take responsibility for themselves vary hugely according to custom and necessity.

From the point of view of survival, human social behaviour is concerned with both the physical realities of life and the psychological dynamics of relationship. Mature social functioning includes the assessment of current reality for practical and relational problem solving, personally motivated energy output and energy output on behalf of others. Upbringing itself, therefore, has the same three-fold focus. There are many questions to be answered. The main one is: "Does the child benefit from the upbringing they receive?"

There are others: "Will the child survive – even thrive?", "Is the child cherished and supported, encouraged and inspired in ways that enhance a positive unfolding of identity?", "Does the child steadily achieve the competencies necessary and develop the confidence and motivation to launch out into adulthood, to be able to cope, earn a living and build positive relationships?", "Will the child be able 'to get along and get ahead?", "What are the key features of an upbringing that would make all this more likely?"

The functional fluency model is a tool for consideration of these issues.

The functional fluency model

A model for illustrating these matters and addressing these questions needs to apply to humanity in general and to work across cultural differences. It must be rooted in issues to do with survival of the species. No matter the geographical location and physical conditions for living; no matter what cultural differences there may be, human beings use their energy socially to grow up, survive and raise their young. These most basic matters are more fundamental than personality factors or traits, and intrinsic to the human condition (Gopnik, Meltzoff and Kuhl, 1999). The functional fluency model is a coherent framework for making sense of what we observe and experience in terms of growing up, surviving and upbringing.

It is these three categories of functioning that form the basis of the functional fluency model at a 'comprehensive construct' level. Kelly (1963) explained that complex concepts are layered, each level in turn becoming more precise and specific. The following three diagrams (Boxes 17.1, 17.2 and 17.3) show the three levels of construction of the functional fluency model. Each level is important in its own right as well as being a crucial part of the make-up of the final model of behavioural modes. Level one has three categories. Level two has five elements and level three has nine modes.

Level one

Level one comprises: social responsibility, reality assessment and self-actualisation. These three generalised categories are fundamental to our humanity and form the most basic level of the model (Box 17.1).

This first diagram shows the overarching generalised first level of constructs. In these three broad areas of social functioning we can say that we use energy on our own behalf, on others' behalf and for staying in contact with current reality. In considering our use of these three categories, we can estimate and compare our balance of energy between them. Is it even, or is there an imbalance? Do any imbalances reflect the demands of the current life situation?

Social responsibility

An important factor about this category is that it incorporates learned social roles that vary from culture to culture, for instance the roles of

Social responsibility	This is about *upbringing* and the role of *being in charge* carrying *authority*	This is how we use our energy on behalf of others in terms of: • grown-up self responsibility • parental responsibility • professional responsibility for others, maybe temporarily.
Reality assessment	This is about *survival* and being '*with-it*'	This is the basis for how we respond to life, here-and-now, moment by moment.
Self-actualisation	This is about *growing up* and *becoming myself*	This is how we use our energy on our own behalf. It is to do with identity and self-expression throughout life.

Box 17.1   Functional fluency model Level 1: Three categories of functioning

mother, father, teacher, guru, captain, leader, manager, etc. Many cultures systematically provide for their young people opportunities to try out and practise roles of being in charge, so that they are ready to take on the social responsibilities of adulthood when the time comes. Another factor is that we use energy in this category of functioning in three ways:

- Directly and actively on behalf of others so that they experience being guided and looked after.
- In modelling how to fulfil the roles, so that others learn about them by example.
- As an internal process of self-control and self-care, which is how in adulthood people take on the responsibility for guiding and looking after themselves.

Reality assessment

The central category of reality assessment, is directly about survival. It refers to a person's reality-testing facility for monitoring inner and outer current events, gathering and using data from internal processes including accumulated knowledge and experience, and externally both via the senses and by actively seeking information.

Self-actualisation

The category of functioning called self-actualisation relates to child and human development. It is to do with identity formation and expression of self.

Level two

At this second level of the model, the categories of social responsibility and self-actualisation are divided into two elements. The category of reality assessment stays as a single element and is given the name 'accounting'.

This second diagram, with the next level of subordination of constructs, reveals how this model echoes certain traditional transactional analysis ego state diagrams. It is vital both to understand the conceptual link with ego state theory and to realise that the functional fluency model is not another model of ego states! It is a model of *human social functioning* that provides a behavioural diagnosis of ego states. The key aspects of this second level are that all the five elements belong to the same level of abstraction and are value free. This important five-construct model is therefore conceptually consistent and logically derived, without qualitative bias. It is

	Social responsibility		
Guidance of others (and self)	*Control* element	*Care* element	Looking after others (and self)
	Reality assessment *Accounting* element		
	Self-actualisation		
Relating to and getting along with others	*Socialised self* element	**Natural self** element	Doing my own thing in my own unique way

Box 17.2   Functional fluency model Level 2: Five elements of functioning

important to note that no worthwhile measurement can be made using this level of abstraction because of the multidimensional nature of the constructs (Neuman, 1994).

Control and care elements

The two elements of social responsibility, control and care, delineate the two main areas of responsibility we take on when we are in charge of other people, whatever the context. The control element is about the responsibility we have for guiding, directing or steering those in our charge, also for providing appropriate expectations and boundaries for them. This requires decision-making on their behalf. The care element is about the responsibility for providing for their needs appropriately, for being available and responsive or 'there for them' in order to offer unconditional strokes and recognition for being.

Socialised and natural self elements

The division of the self-actualisation category into two elements highlights the issue of nature versus nurture. The natural self element is about the use of energy in expressing individual uniqueness by 'doing my own thing in my own way'. It is an individualistic and uncensored use of energy. The socialised self element is about the use of energy for relating to and getting along with others. The combination of elements in this category is about personal potency.

Accounting element

At this second conceptual level, the term for the use of energy in reality assessment is

'accounting'. As a term this is a double metaphor and key to how the model works. Firstly there is the mathematical connotation concerned with the organisation of data. Secondly there is the connotation of 'story-making': the fact that we are continuously construing and re-construing our own inner meanings, our own personal 'accounts'. This double metaphor relates strongly to Piaget's (1954) terms, translated from the French as 'assimilation' and 'accommodation', that he used in explaining aspects of children's learning. Accounting is an internal process giving a means of staying grounded in the here-and-now through awareness. Higher order thinking skills are needed to process the data available in order to assess significances, potential consequences and to compute resulting options. Accounting is learned and develops according to capacity of age and stage of cognitive functioning.

Level three

At the third level, the elements are divided once again, so that control and care, socialised self and natural self, all have both a positive and a negative mode. Accounting element, however, being an internal, value-free function, is different. It remains undivided and is called a mode at this third level, making nine behavioural modes in all (Box 17.3).

These nine modes of the functional fluency model are the unidimensional constructs that are suitable for measurement (Neuman, 1994), and that are used in the psychometric tool The Temple Index of Functional Fluency (TIFF) (Temple, 2002). The nine behavioural modes are

Negative control **Dominating mode**	Negative care **Marshmallowing mode**
Positive control **Structuring mode**	Positive care **Nurturing mode**
Accounting element **Accounting mode**	
Positive socialised self **Cooperative mode**	Positive natural self **Spontaneous mode**
Negative socialised self **Compliant/resistant mode**	Negative natural self **Immature mode**

Box 17.3 Functional fluency model Level 3: The nine behavioural modes

arrived at by asking certain questions with respect to the five elements (Box 17.2).

The question to ask with respect to care and control is "Do people benefit from the care and control used, or do they suffer from it?" In order to explore answers to this, it is necessary to divide both elements into a positive and a negative behavioural mode and to name and define each carefully. Thus there are four social responsibility modes: nurturing, structuring, dominating and marshmallowing.

The question for the socialised and natural elements of self is: "How effective are these two ways of functioning?" or, to be more precise, "What sort of satisfaction and recognition do I achieve by doing my own thing in my own way?" and "What are the outcomes of my efforts to relate to other people?" Again, for further exploration, it is necessary to make a positive and a negative mode for each element, so that there are four self modes: spontaneous, cooperative, compliant/resistant and immature.

In this model the term accounting is used at both element Level 2 (see Box 17.2) and mode Level 3 (see Box 17.3) as reality assessment is not divided. The issue with accounting is different from the other elements. It is primarily a quantitative matter. The question is: "Is there enough accounting going on in order to be effective, whether on my own behalf or on behalf of others?" An excess or a deficit of accounting is counterproductive. An excess of energy used up in internal processing makes it harder to get on and take action, while a lack of taking relevant factors into account may mean that action is unrealistic. An important point to note is that accounting is a value-free internal mechanism. Evidence for this emerged from the range of factor analyses of the research data from the pilot studies of TIFF (Temple 2002). Whatever the nature of the activity undertaken, whether it is for good or ill, an effective outcome requires sufficient accounting. In order to reinforce the use of accounting for achieving positive outcomes, it is presented and taught as one of the positive modes that will be of benefit to people and cause no harm. There are, therefore, five positive modes in the functional fluency model. In practice, these modes are now sometimes referred to as the 'Fabulous Five'!

The two pairs of negative modes can be thought of as sourced from the contaminated areas of Integrating Adult (Temple, 2004). There, the functional fluency model is shown superimposed on the structural ego state model.

The negative mode boxes then fall neatly over the Parent and Child contaminations. This suggests that dominating and marshmallowing modes are sourced from Parent contaminations and compliant/resistant and immature modes from Child contaminations. This, however, is somewhat simplistic, though likely, and useful as a basic idea. The reality is that any of the four negative mode behaviours could be derived originally from either Parent or Child contaminations. In-depth second order structural analysis of the respective Parent and or Child ego states within a therapeutic contract would reveal the details for a particular client. A diagram unique to that client could then be drawn up. For people learning about how to use the functional fluency model in educational and organisational contexts, it is useful simply to know that the negative modes derive from 'old teachings and old learnings' that we may still be using, even though they are out of date and possibly counterproductive. The process of learning how to transform energy used in those modes into use of positive modes involves the behavioural changes necessary for the relevant decontamination of Adult.

The social responsibility modes and parenting

The ideas for the four social responsibility modes were derived originally from 'four ways of parenting' (Illsley Clarke, 1978). To begin with the names were exactly the same, but the research showed that the name of the mode called 'criticising' needed to be more generalised, and that 'dominating' was considered to be a more useful and appropriate term. So now the name for negative control in the functional fluency model is the 'dominating mode'.

These four modes form neat pairs. They can be considered from the point of view of the two positives and the two negatives, or from the point of view of the two control modes and the two care modes (see Boxes 17.4 and 17.5). It depends on the purpose: whether one is considering the effectiveness of ways of being in charge, or two differing aspects of being in charge. It is important to realise that everyone uses all four modes at some time: we all have good and bad days! We may not realise which modes we are using, however, and one of the purposes of the model is to promote self-awareness.

Structuring mode	Nurturing mode
This is the term for **constructive control**, which empowers through inspiration and by enabling success. Guidance and help are given so that people feel safe to explore, learn and gain self-confidence.	This is the familiar term for **positive care** in action, which is responsive to need and offers the empathy and understanding that enables recovery and healthy growth of a positive sense of self.
The hidden message is: 'You can do it and succeed'.	**The hidden message is:** 'You are loveable and valuable'.

Boxes 17.4 & 17.5   The two positive social responsibility modes

It is important to understand the nature of all the modes and the fact that important 'messages' are conveyed at the psychological, or ulterior, level of communication: "It ain't what you say, it's the way that you say it"! The positive message of structuring is a permission, and that of nurturing an affirmation or attribution. Structuring and nurturing need to be thought of together. For positive parenting both are essential and need to be combined. This combination is extremely close to the style of parenting identified in the longditudinal studies by Baumrind (1991) as most closely associated with effective outcomes for the children. Baumrind's term for this combination was 'authoritative parenting' (Box 17.6).

It is important to note that Baumrind found that this most effective parenting style was warm and affectionate as well as having firm, clear expectations and boundaries. Similarly, the kindness and gentleness of the nurturing mode, along with the support and inspiration of structuring, have healthy and enabling effects on the recipients, who tend to thrive on the effects. There is an interesting phenomenon that Illsley Clarke has frequently pointed out in workshop settings: that, if nurturing is offered without some structuring to go with it, then the effect is the same as being marshmallowed: sweet but not

substantial and ultimately harmful. Similarly, if only structuring is offered with little nurturing, the effect is one of feeling dominated. Positive upbringing, parenting or internal support consists of a balanced combination of these two modes, with the combined hidden message 'You are lovable and capable'.

Boxes 17.7 and 17.8 illustrate the negative modes of social responsibility.

These negative modes are often used with the best will in the world and good intentions. Sometimes this is simply because of a lack of understanding about what sort of parenting behaviour works best in a given situation and sometimes it is because the parents are simply following a recipe from the past, recapitulating behaviour 'taught' by example from their own past parent figures. These 'old teachings' can be ingrained and seem right and inevitable until they are considered objectively and consciously transformed through a process of decontamination of the Adult ego state. A new and different sense of control can be gained by using the empowering characteristics of structuring instead of the coercion of dominating. The inconsistency and overindulgence of marshmallowing can likewise be transformed into the compassion and kindness of nurturing.

Authoritative parenting	With this parenting children tend to be
Exercises firm control. Communicates standards of conduct in a clear manner. Does not hem in the child with excessive restrictions. Uses reason and explanation in achieving their objectives. Demands relatively high level of achievement. Encourages verbal give-and-take. Respects the child's own wishes. Involves high levels of warmth and frequent expressions of affection.	More self reliant. Keen to achieve. Socially responsible. Content. Self-controlled. Co-operative with both adults and peers.

Box 17.6   Authoritative parenting style and resultant tendencies in children (after Baumrind, 1991)

Dominating mode	Marshmallowing mode
This is the term for **destructive control**, which disempowers through coercion and by focusing on the negative. It undermines self-esteem with criticism or put-downs, and may punish mistakes. **The hidden message is:** **'You are not good enough'.**	This is a new term designed to express the soft and hidden harmfulness of **negative care**, which gives too much attention, or the wrong sort, and which does too much for people while lacking clear boundaries or expectations. **The hidden message is:** **'You are inadequate'.**

Boxes 17.7 & 17.8   The two negative social responsibility modes

Most important are the hidden messages. When parents realise the covert, psychological messages of dominating and marshmallowing they find it easier to understand why the outcomes of these modes are so damaging, and why it is so important to structure and nurture instead.

The four self-actualising modes

These are known as the 'self modes'. They are concerned with identity and self-expression, and are about how we use energy on our own behalf, both for doing our own thing in our own way and for getting along with others. Both natural self modes have free-flowing, uncensored behaviours, while the socialised self modes have been learned in response to environmental, especially social demands. Both elements have positive and negative modes.

The four self modes do not relate in neat pairs. These modes are not the result of learned roles.

They are the manifestation behaviourally of an individual's personal development. They can be considered as an illustration of a dynamic developmental spiral. The root of the spiral, naturally, is in the immature mode: we all start here. The natural behaviours of young children reflect their age and stage. They still see things only from their own point of view and find it hard to appreciate the future social joys of 'sharing' and 'taking turns'. Their rudimentary sense of time-keeping and consequence make it hard for them to delay gratification or understand how long a wait for something might be. Hence the familiar cry of "Are we nearly there now?" and "Is it my birthday today?" It would be accurate (but maybe unfair) to call the resulting behaviours 'egocentric', 'selfish' ,'inconsiderate', 'unorganised' and 'reckless', as they are to be expected at a very young age and we know that it is likely that the child will grow out of them. We do *not* label the young child 'immature'; they

	Socialised element Cooperative mode	Natural element Spontaneous mode
Positive	This mode is the result of useful social learning that supports a person's ability to relate appropriately to others from an I'm OK – You're OK position, with mutual benefit. It enhances the person's enjoyment of working and playing with others.	This mode is the unrestrained, yet age- and context-appropriate, expression of a person's own unique liveliness and creativity. It enables playfulness at any age.
	Compliant/resistant mode	**Immature mode**
Negative	This mode includes the wide range of currently counter-productive social behaviours that are the result of previously learned ways to survive and get enough attention. They are the result of out-dated beliefs about self and need to be relearned.	This mode (in grown-up people) shows unrestrained self-expression inappropriate to age and context. The behaviours, natural to early childhood, have not yet been grown out of and interfere with adult social effectiveness. New learning is needed.

Boxes 17.9, 17.10, 17.11 & 17.12   The four self modes

simply *are* immature. However, supposing the child does not grow out of these behaviours, for lack of social opportunity, requirement, guidance or help, then the young person or adult still exhibiting them would rightly be said to be behaving immaturely. Such a conclusion would, of course, vary in the detail according to the cultural and social assumptions of what is expected and acceptable.

Upbringing and growing up combine in the continuation of the 'developmental spiral' because the nature of this spiral depends on the interactions and relationships the child has with their 'upbringers'. It is at this point that ideas of growing up and upbringing need to come together. The child needs to learn how to express their uniqueness and creativity from spontaneous mode, reflecting appropriately their maturity, so upbringing processes need to foster this individuality and help it to blossom and bear fruit. The child also needs to learn the pleasures and satisfactions of skillful social intercourse using cooperative mode, so that they can build positive relationships of mutual benefit. Upbringing, therefore, also needs to support, model and assist this social learning. Upbringers who structure and nurture appropriately offer the affirmations and permissions that the child needs to build healthy self-esteem and develop increasing competence. Empathic acceptance and understanding are mixed with the inspiration of high expectations and reliable help and support. For instance, children are shown how to take turns and share as soon as they are ready; they are helped to perceive others' points of view and to enjoy being considerate and collaborative; their creativity is appreciated and encouraged and they are cherished for their uniqueness. The foundations of the 'I'm OK – You're OK' life position are lived in the relationship through the respect and congruence of the adults and are 'caught' rather than 'taught'. In short, the child needs to move from immature mode to a combination and balance of Spontaneous and Cooperative modes, avoiding Compliant/ Resistant mode along the way (see Figure 17.1).

Habits of compliance and resistance are learned as self protection when the environmental and social demands are too great or too harsh for the child to cope with at that time. For instance, control may be more dominating than structuring. The habits so formed may need to be unlearned or relearned at a later date if the person doesn't transform them

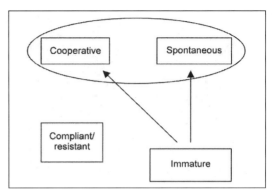

Figure 17.1   The journey from immature to spontaneous and cooperative modes

naturally as part of continuing growing up. On the other hand, the growing out of immature childishness may be hindered when care is of the marshmallowing variety and the child is stroked for, as Levin (1988: 18) puts it, 'staying little'.

The upbringing behaviours for fostering and assisting children's use of spontaneous and cooperative behaviours come from structuring and nurturing modes, well informed by accounting mode, and supported by the personal relationship building attributes of cooperative and spontaneous modes.

In addition to encouraging cooperative and spontaneous modes, upbringers need to stimulate and stroke effective accounting stage by stage so that gradually the child develops appropriate higher order thinking skills that promote the cognitive development necessary for moving out of immature mode behaviour. The provision of appropriate experiences for building up knowledge and skill is also important for fostering the accounting mode of functioning. Meanwhile, the modelling of structuring and nurturing provides a continuous example (for good or ill) of how to manifest these two modes. Later in life these absorbed examples will form the basis for how the person undertakes the social roles of 'being in charge of others'.

Temperament as an important factor in growing up and upbringing

The journey from immature mode to spontaneous and cooperative modes and the development of accounting, structuring and nurturing mode skills will need different learning experiences according to differing temperamental dispositions (Thomas, Chess and Birch, 1968). From within the overall modes of structuring and nurturing will need to come a variety of permissions, requirements, encouragements, boundaries and limits. It is unrealistic to think that it is 'fair' to treat all children the same way.

Chess and Thomas (1999) emphasise the fact that the newborn baby already has a well developed temperamental disposition. Also, as Bower (1977: 35) writes: 'The newborn begins life as an extremely competent learning organism, an extremely competent perceiving organism'. What is needed is a 'good fit' between the child's unique developmental needs, stage by stage, and what the upbringers provide so that the two way dance of upbringing and growing up supplies the right balance of demand and support for the child:

> With goodness of fit of infant and carer interaction, the child, with increasing biological and psychological maturity, faces correspondingly complex expectations and demands of the environment. As these interlocking events mount, the child with successive goodness of fit experiences, develops self-awareness, self-esteem begins to emerge, motivations and cognition become clarified and competencies begin to declare themselves.
>
> (Chess and Thomas, 1999: 46)

Thomas, Chess and Birch (1968) write about the term 'goodness of fit' as a principle for promoting change and expanding competence. They say that for optimal development in a progressive manner, the child's own capacities, characteristics and behavioural style need to be in accord with the environmental properties, opportunities and demands. To start with, this is in the context of feeding, bathing, dressing and the playful exchanges and routines that are the stuff of infant-carer interaction, and later of relationship-building and the progressive mastery of the environment by the infant. Sensitivity, knowledge, understanding, intuition and knowing the child well all contribute to appropriately helpful upbringing responses. Accounting moment by moment helps upbringers to monitor, reason and decide how to use structuring and nurturing for a particular child in order to create and maintain the 'goodness of fit' as outlined by Chess and Thomas. Appreciation of the child's temperamental characteristics, and sensitivity to the natural differences between children are vitally important in the process.

Thomas, Chess and Birch (1968) refer to temperament as behavioural style, that is, the child's way of being in the world and of doing things. They delineated nine temperamental characteristics: activity tempo; rythmicity; intensity of response; threshold of response; mood inclination; adaptability; response to novelty; persistence; and distractability. They pointed out that the initially identified pattern of these characteristics may be relatively unchanged, reinforced, heightened, diminished or otherwise modified by environmental influences during the developmental course. In other words they are not fixed. It is natural for a child to adapt to environmental demands; this is part of human survival. What is important is that the adaptation, or socialising process is in the child's best interests and proceeds along with the development of their individuality. In functional fluency terms, as described above, it is important that both cooperative and spontaneous modes are fostered.

Difficulties arise when the environment is stressful to the child. Stress comes in two main forms: frustration arising from the child's natural pace being held back, and anxiety when the child is not ready to cope with particular demands. These are similar to the 'Stay little' and 'Grow up' messages, identified by Levin (1988), that interfere with children's naturally unfolding developmental progress. Understanding the functional fluency model can help all those who take responsibility for children's upbringing, and those in therapeutic roles helping people to recover from their respective upbringings, to avoid these stresses. Learning how the model works helps to raise awareness of the possible effects of the four 'being in charge' modes, and also supports appropriate choice of strategy for responding to children and young people in ways that help them to develop positively.

Key aspects of the functional fluency model

The functional fluency model provides a framework for understanding the dynamic relationships involved in good upbringing. Everyone uses all the nine modes at some time or other, because we all use care and control, socialised and natural elements and we all do some accounting. What we need to be aware of is the nature of our use of these elements, so that we can learn to use our energy for greater benefit and reduce the stress of wasted and inappropriate energy use. This is true whether we are using the being in charge modes interpersonally on behalf of others, or intrapsychically on our own behalf. It is worth remembering that the ways we structure and nurture ourselves will impact on how we manage to structure and nurture others.

Some of the differences between the modes are subtle and it is these subtle differences that are of most importance in helping us shift from negative to positive behaviour. For instance, in terms of positive and negative caring, it is important to understand the difference between acceptance of the person (in nurturing) and over-tolerance of undesirable behaviour (in marshmallowing). Likewise, it is important to be clear that the authoritarian bossiness found in dominating mode is about exerting power *over* people, whereas the authoritative guidance from structuring mode is about using power *for* people.

With respect to the socialised and natural elements, firstly it is vital to grasp that cooperation is an 'I'm OK – You're OK' activity to be stroked and expanded, whereas compliance is an 'I'm not OK – You're OK' activity and needs transformation into assertiveness. Secondly, natural spontaneity is different from impulsiveness. Spontaneity includes the maturity of awareness and choice, whereas impulsivity is more simply an instant response to a stimulus, which, in adults, is a sign of immature behaviour patterns.

Another important difference is between certain aspects of the two negative self modes. On the one hand is the learned rebelliousness from compliant/resistant mode, and on the other hand is the oppositionality natural to the toddler stage of development. Oppositionality, when considered with respect to adult functioning, belongs in immature mode. The model thus helps us to understand that rebellious behaviour needs to be dealt with in a different way from oppositional behaviour. The former needs to be unlearned and transformed into assertiveness and personal potency and the latter needs to be grown out of. Age, stage, context and relationship will all have important bearings on the strategies to be used.

With regards to accounting, doing more of it than is necessary for a situation can be a sign of defensive cognitive patterns such as obsessing. Doing too little accounting may be a clue to discounting mechanisms or simply a lack of knowledge or of skill in how to think

productively. Increasing the relevant knowledge and skill necessary for a person who is struggling to problem solve can enrich the accounting process and make it easier and more effective. This in itself can reduce discounting so that whatever problem is being addressed is solvable, and the whole strategy helps to avoid pathologising. Accounting is the key mode for masterminding choices between the other eight modes. This requires some understanding of the nature of all the modes, both positive and negative manifestations.

The five positive functional fluency modes can be thought of as the ingredients of integrated and effective social behaviour which is also psychologically well-adjusted. Theoretically we can separate out the modes in order to explore meanings and improve our understanding of different aspects of behaviour. In practice, however, these ingredients are blended and balanced in varying proportions in order to respond appropriately to the situation. Learning about the model in detail can help us to enrich and expand our use of the positive modes and also to learn how to transform our use of the negative modes.

Functional fluency is especially important for parents, educators and all those of us who take responsibility for upbringing in one way or another. Children and young people are learning all the time, whatever we do or don't do, from both our example and the experiences we offer them. Increased self-awareness and understanding supports our sensitivity and perception of their needs so that we can develop our 'response-ability' and enhance the 'fit' we offer between upbringing and growing up.

References

Antidote (2003) *The Emotional Literacy Handbook.* London: David Fulton Publishers.

Baumrind, D. (1991) Parenting Styles and Related Child Behaviour. *Journal of Early Adolescence,* 11: 1, 56–95.

Bower, T. (1977) *A Primer of Human Development.* San Francisco, CA: W.H. Freeman.

Brody, H. (2001) *The Other Side of Eden: Hunter-Gatherers, Farmers and the Shaping of the World.* London: Faber and Faber.

Chess, S. and Thomas, A.C. (1999) *Goodness of Fit: Clinical Applications from Infancy Through Adult Life.* New York: Brunner/Mazel.

Gopnik, A., Meltzoff, A.N. and Kuhl, P.K. (1999) *The Scientist in the Crib*. New York: William Morrow.

Hogan, R., Hogan, J. and Trickey, G. (1999) Goodbye Mumbo-Jumbo: The Transcendental Beauty of a Validity Coefficient. *Selection and Development Review*, 15: 4, 3–8.

Illsley Clarke, J. (1978) *Self Esteem: A Family Affair*. Minnesota: Hazelden.

Kelly, G. (1963) *A Theory of Personality*. New York: W.W. Norton.

Levin, P. (1988) *Cycles of Power*. Deerfield Beach, FL: Health Communications.

Neuman, W.L. (1994) *Social Research Methods*. 2nd edn. Boston, MA: Allyn and Bacon.

Piaget, J. (1954) *The Child's Construction of Reality*. London: Routledge and Kegan Paul.

Rowe, D. (2000) *Friends and Enemies*. London: Harper and Row.

Steiner, C. (1999) *Achieving Emotional Literacy*. London: Bloomsbury Publishing.

Temple, S. (1999) Functional Fluency For Educational Transactional Analysts. *Transactional Analysis Journal*, 29: 3, 164–74.

Temple, S. (2002) *The Development of a Transactional Analysis Tool for Enhancing Functional Fluency*. Unpublished PhD thesis, University of Plymouth.

Temple, S. (2004) Update on the Functional Fluency Model in Education. *Transactional Analysis Journal*, 34: 3, 197–204.

Thomas, A.C. and Birch, H.G. (1968) *Temperament and Behaviour Disorders in Children*. New York: New York University Press.

Thomas, A.C., Chess, S. and Birch, H.G. (1968) *Temperament and Behaviour Disorders in Children*. New York: New York University Press.

CHAPTER 18

Transactional Analysis and Child Psychotherapy: A New Methodology

Maria Assunta Giusti

The early theories about childhood were developed from studies of clinical experience based on the observation of children with disorders rather than healthy children. In some instances they were based on retroactive data i.e. on what could be inferred from adult clients. Now, with the benefit of ultrasound imaging and neonatology, we can observe the foetus and the newborn child. In doing so, we have learned many new things which have challenged the view that the foetus in the mother's womb and the neonate do not have abilities and skills. Drawing on such observations, as well as ideas from attachment theory and self psychology, this chapter examines these findings and proposes a new methodology for TA child psychotherapy by means of four new assumptions:

- Going beyond Mahler's theory
- The responsibility of the therapist
- Trans-form-action
- From transference to transformation

What emerges from research

We now know that the infant has skills we never would have believed possible and that the mother-child relationship is not one that is based on the model of a mother who is the sole shaper of a passive child who is simply moulded. Together, mother and child form a system in which each influences the other and which becomes stronger as it develops. Thus, mother and child are both active in mutually shaping each other. The system is even more meaningful if the father is included as he is an integral part of the system and not at all the minor or background figure that he is often portrayed as.

The new picture that emerges consists of individuals who experience an inner and an outer world, in a dynamic relational contact. The internal worlds of the mother and of the child are made up of emotions, sensations, ideas, fantasies, wishes and needs. They mutually influence and mould each other, assisted by the presence, usually, of the father. Contact with oneself, and the development of a concept of self is the result of contact with the other. These interactions give rise to patterns of mutual influence and are regulated by the dimensions of space-time, emotion and self-regulation (Stern, 1998). Through these patterns the child creates familiar, recurring, and reassuring paths, so that they can learn to recognise, predict and remember. The outcome of the scientific observation of the child, of attachment theories and of studies on emotional intelligence, reminds us of what Berne (1961) talks about as 'the hunger for recognition and the hunger for structure'.

Drawing on attachment theory and self psychology, we can see and conceptualise a child who is biologically capable of forming a relationship. They attach to the mother through self-regulation, and at the same time are capable of psychologically and affectively recording the mental images relating to their experiences, thus creating an emotional world which resonates with the interactive regulations. The result of this process is the image of self and of the other.

The information that is issued simultaneously by the two parties constitutes a motivational model. There is a biological ability to receive and give information, and an inherent motivation to process and orde the information. O'Reilly-Knapp and Erskine (2003) suggest that we can speak of a motivational theory. Erskine develops Berne's writings through the concept of hunger for stimuli or sensations and hunger for recognition and structure:

- **Hunger for stimuli** – Stimuli operate simultaneously both internally and externally, and provide input for the feedback system that leads to the satisfaction of basic needs.
- **Hunger for structure** – An inherent drive towards wanting to organise experience and develop perception patterns that create meaning and prediction, and organise the continuity of experiences in time.

- **Hunger for relationship** – Satisfying this hunger depends on the awareness of relational needs, on what the individual believes about themselves and about others, and on the behaviour of the other in the relationship.

If the internalisation process is parallel to the organisation of mental representations, we can consider a person's psychic organs, which, according to Berne, were the mental organisers of the ego states, and the therapeutic setting as the scenario of a treatment. This jointly-built interactive process (defined by the contract) is in line with what Sandler, Tyson and Kennedy (1982) refer to when they speak about reciprocity, bi-directionality and co-construction – which are typical of the mother-child relationship and of any other relationship that involves the same degree of intensity.

Relationship and contact become at one and the same time contact with Self (perception of one's inner world), contact with the Other (external world), and the concept of Self-Other. This desire that the child has to achieve contact in the relationship is a two-way street: the infant responds to appropriate contact by initiating behaviours that indicate pleasure and comfort, and the adult taking care of them is rewarded by the response of the child (as are also those who do not have direct responsibility for the child). The satisfaction of feeling a tiny hand enveloping your finger and seeing a face that brightens up with a smile, is virtually universal. Even though the infant is incapable of expressing their satisfaction in words, we can certainly understand how relaxed they are from their outward and searching behaviour and from their affectionate smiles. This satisfaction is for the Other, contact with others, a primary experience of human behaviour. As human beings we fight for this from birth and, when we achieve it appropriately, we are universally rewarded (Erskine, Moursund and Trautmann, 1999).

Each individual is influenced and exercises influence, that is, they build a sense of self through what they do. The intrapsychic and the interpersonal levels thus interact, and so the need for self-protection deriving from self-regulation adds to the hunger for stimuli, structure and recognition (Berne, 1961; O'Reilly-Knapp and Erskine, 2003).

In the rest of this chapter I discuss four 'new assumptions' as the foundation for a new methodology of TA child psychotherapy.

First new assumption: going beyond Mahler's theory

The first new assumption arises from the observation of attachment towards self, where separation is necessary in order to reach individuation. Attachment is a biological (competence) and psychological (mutual satisfaction) process. Separation, as a natural consequence of attachment, expresses itself physiologically (e.g. birth) emotionally (sadness when separation occurs) and cognitively (awareness of the Ego-Other separation) (see Figure 18.1).

The introject leads to 'psychological individuation' – in that it is not possible to incorporate something from someone else without an internal place and the capacity to recognise it as being other from oneself – and to the ensuing formation of the self-other relationship. So the new process, instead of being 'individuation-separation', as Mahler claims (Mahler, Pine and Bergman, 1975) could instead be 'attachment-separation' with a mental process that facilitates the representation of self as the cause and effect of individuation. At this point the self-other becomes self with the other in a dynamic process of complementarity, sharing and transformation. Mahler stresses separation (at the age of three) rather than attachment. Attachment is seen as beginning with life itself. In my opinion separation is a natural consequence of attachment and not the beginning of the process as understood by Mahler. From separation-individuation we thus reach attachment-individuation.

Attunement between mother and child creates the possibility of a satisfying relationship that gives rise to a well-grounded attachment. Attunement is also an instrument used in psycotherapy to create a deep relationship and to allow individuals the possibility of reaching a state of intimacy.

In the psychotherapeutic setting, by encouraging the patient-therapist relationship, the individual is offered a sound and well-grounded attachment, a repertory of the patient's script experience. With adults, the therapist may encourage the transference in order to reactivate the attachment by processing the past in order to change the here-and-now. Working with children, this attachment function happens in the now (Figure 18.2).

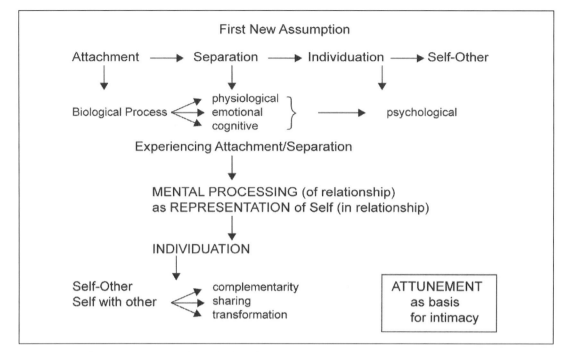

Figure 18.1   First new assumption: Beyond Mahler's theory

All this emphasises the importance of responsibility in therapy. Figure 18.3 offers a concise description of the relationship that the therapist has with the parent and with the child.

The internal dialogue is transformed because the child takes in new material from their parents and from the therapist in their Parent ego state. As a result of this introjection, the child has a new internal dialogue with a modified self-perception which becomes a stimulus for the parent and thus creates a new relationship.

At this point there is a further representation for the parent-therapist-child system, in which, by internalising the Parent model of the therapist (a new object of love) the child positions themselves differently vis-à-vis their natural parents. If the parents are helped to respond in a new way, they will, in turn, re-encode the external relationship with their child and the internal relationship with their self or their internal P-C dialogue.

It is as if there were a reverie that decontaminates the idea of the parent, that is, the Parent contamination of Adult. This can be introjected in a correct manner as it evolves or is re-encoded through a new experience with a parent that receives and assimilates this in a new

way. In this way the therapist enters into the system as an influential, influenced and influencing object (Figures 18.3 and 18.4).

Second new assumption: the responsibility of the therapist

What we have said previously brings us to Figure 18.4 which outlines the position of the therapist in the complex setting with the child. While the first assumption applies to Mahler's individuation-separation, the second assumption applies to the responsibility of the therapist and so rather than being the same, it is in fact a consequence of the first assumption.

The therapist must be aware of their responsibility on more than one level. For this specific reason the therapist is influential, influenced and influencing:

- **Influential** because their role is influential in the true sense of the word, both in the way it is experienced by the parent who gives them professional power, and for how it is experienced by the child who, at times, sees them as a parent.

Psychotherapy with adults

Reported Reality ⎰ family origin / actual relationships / colleagues...

↓

Not contacted by the therapist

Work on introjection, on 'here and then'

Elaboration of the past towards 'here and now' and vice versa

Attunement to Child ego state and Parent ego state

Attachment as a function to be reactived or to be corrected

↓

New conceptions of Script

Psychotherapy with children

family / school / operators... ⎱ Sharing Reality

↓

Contacted by therapist and active part of the setting

Work on parent's introject
Work with the real parent

Elaboration of 'here and now'

Attunement to real child and real Parent

Attachment as a current and natural function

↓

Process of the Script formation

Figure 18.2   Psychotherapy with adults and with children

- **Influenced** because, since we are talking about a system, the therapist changes during and after their experience with the patient. They are therefore, in turn, influenced by the relationship and the situation in which they take part, and through which they perceive themselves and their way of being with others. In other words, the image and concept of self are constantly evolving.
- **Influencing** because, by providing a therapeutic relationship, they operate as part of

the system, and as such they are necessarily introjected both in the Parent of the child and of the parents.

Awareness of all this goes beyond countertransference and attributes new strength to the Adult of the therapist. It adds to their ability to offer protection, permission and potency and thus increases the efficiency of the therapy. In fact the therapist's actions are attuned to those of the parents who develop new patterns

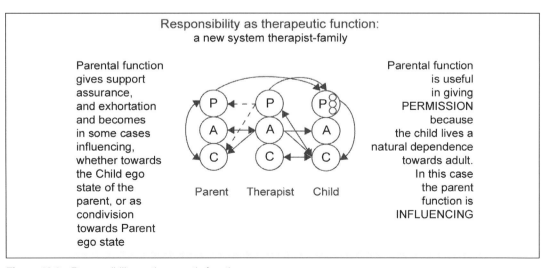

Responsibility as therapeutic function: a new system therapist-family

Parental function gives support assurance, and exhortation and becomes in some cases influencing, whether towards the Child ego state of the parent, or as condivision towards Parent ego state

Parent   Therapist   Child

Parental function is useful in giving PERMISSION because the child lives a natural dependence towards adult. In this case the parent function is INFLUENCING

Figure 18.3   Responsibility as therapeutic function

Second New Assumption

Child interiorises parent's model of the therapist (new object of love) and
behaves differently with his natural parent, who also responds in a new way.
It's like a reverie, that decontaminates the parent's idea before being
introjected or corrected in its becoming.
Therapist gets into the system as an influential, influencing and influenced
subject.

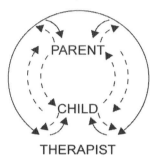

Figure 18.4   Second new assumption: the responsibility of the therapist

of behaviour towards their child. This therapeutic
and ethical responsibility towards the patient and
the setting is more complex but also more
complete if the therapist is aware of the
influential, influenced and influencing.

The work on the parent-child system, or
directly on the child who is inside the system,
enables change in the individual and hence in the
system and, in turn, in the therapist who, to some
extent, is part of the system.

All this is equally applicable to the therapeutic
relationship with the adult patient. Even though
we do not work directly with the parts of the
system we do enter into the mental fantasy world
of the patient and they enter ours. Taking care of
the patient also implies taking care of ourselves,
and their evolution is also ours. We may think
about this in terms of the transferential and
countertransferential relationship (see Figure
18.5).

To this figure, which is usually used to
represent transference, I have added a line that
represents the internal dialogue of the therapist,
who promotes within themselves the analysis of
the countertransference in the classical sense, and
the internal dialogue that exists independently of
the patient, or as a strict consequence of what the
patient has enabled emotionally. This is the

'reverie action' or processing of what the patient
has not yet the ability to feel emotionally. The
material which is processed during therapy,
especially with patients with regressive
disorders, both in adults and in children, triggers
new dimensions within the therapist and hence
promotes the analysis which enriches the
therapist.

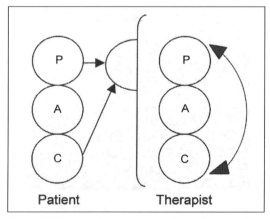

Figure 18.5   Transference transactions (developed
from Moiso, 1985)

Third new assumption: trans-form-action

Let us move on to the third assumption, pointing out that we should not speak only of transference but also of transformaction i.e. trans-form-action where trans = shift, form = model and action = evolution (see Figure 18.6). In Figure 18.6 we see the therapist in relation to their patient. If the patient were an adult we would have a transferential relationship. As, for our present interest, they are children, we have a request to the parents in the here-and-now.

The adult projects onto the therapist their Parent ego, while the child makes a request to the therapist stimulating the Parent ego state or a parenting function in the therapist. The patient (at any age) introjects the therapist and, as we have said, the therapist is influenced by the relationship. Together with the parents, the child builds a new map or system of reference possibly with a new life plan as the therapist has worked with both the parents and the child.

The healthy relationship and request enable the introjection of open routes and hence the possibility of reading different realities that lead the child to decisions and script beliefs different from those of the family system. Here the child is making a decision, not a *re*decision. If we think in terms of long-term psychotherapy that lasts many years, we can realise that some developmental steps are experienced and dealt with directly during therapy. Thus the therapist has the possibility in the here-and-now of intervening with the child, the parents and the relationship between the two. To echo what has been said before, the therapist is right in the script scene and not in the transferential re-edition of the script (as occurs when doing therapy with adults). In the adult setting we must enable the transference in order to reactivate an attachment function, whereas in the setting with a child this natural function is already there.

Even if the child's need has not been met, there is still the likelihood and time for it to happen once they start therapy. So the acting of the child is not only transferential but in most cases it is a possibility that the child gives themselves time to reach a positive conclusion to an open gestalt, and hence they review and correct the script decision which is still in the embryonic form (palimpsest).

This figure portrays the complexity of the relationship with the child and with the parent in the child therapy setting; we can see that the position of the therapist includes an action both with the child and on the Child. The therapist supports and reassures the parent, encourages them and, at times, exercises influence on the Child and Parent ego states of the parent. The natural parent then exercises their new Parent ego state on the child, and also acts from a new Child ego state, thus influencing the child on this level too.

The therapist also exercises a parent action on the young patient by giving permission to the child, who is living a natural and real dependency on the adult therapist. In this case the function is a true influencing function because the PAC system of the therapist is incorporated inside the P_2 of the child and, through the internalisation processes, it is introjected according to the experience of the child (P_1). By interacting in a different way with the adult and with the parent figure, the child will offer their natural parent different mechanisms and relationships which, in turn, will influence the parent-child and child-parent system.

Is there real transference in therapy with children? The answer, as shown in the diagram, (Figure 18.6) suggests a position which is more complex, a situation that produces a trans-form-action, in that the therapeutic response and proposal occurs during growth. Moreover, the diagram shows that there are two fields of therapeutic action i.e. that of the child and that of the parent. These reflect each other because they are systemic. The target of therapy is to reach a healthy decision, as an outcome of the therapeutic work done directly with the child, and indirectly with the parent who will influence their child by remodelling their Child ego state.

If we accept that the script evolves with the individual and with their life experiences, then we must take into account the fact that the therapist enters into the script of the patient both in reality and through transference, and that the patient also enters into our lives or scripts directly and through countertransference (Figure 18.7).

Kohut (1971) states that the child is physiologically predisposed to a given physical environment (food, oxygen and so on) and a psychic environment (the presence of self-objects that respond empathically). In the process in which the psychic structure is formed, it is possible to have a transmuting internalisation of the self-object that crystallises in the nuclear self of the child. We can then state that the autonomous self is not simply a repetition of the

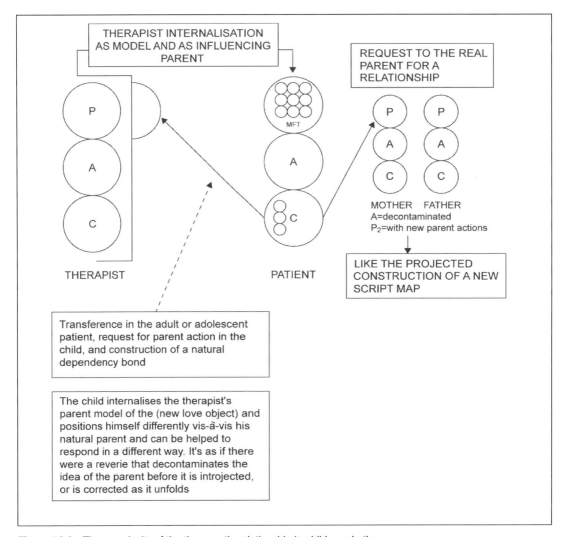

THERAPIST INTERNALISATION AS MODEL AND AS INFLUENCING PARENT

REQUEST TO THE REAL PARENT FOR A RELATIONSHIP

MFT

P   A   C

THERAPIST

PATIENT

MOTHER   FATHER
A=decontaminated
P$_2$=with new parent actions

LIKE THE PROJECTED CONSTRUCTION OF A NEW SCRIPT MAP

Transference in the adult or adolescent patient, request for parent action in the child, and construction of a natural dependency bond

The child internalises the therapist's parent model of the (new love object) and positions himself differently vis-à-vis his natural parent and can be helped to respond in a different way. It's as if there were a reverie that decontaminates the idea of the parent before it is introjected, or is corrected as it unfolds

Figure 18.6   The complexity of the therapeutic relationship in child psychotherapy

self-object, because it implies the subjectivity of the individual who can read reality according to their experience, even though the latter is configured as a stimulus. The therapeutic relationship hence influences the identity of the patient (Self) because it enables the patient to have a transferential relationship (repetitive relationship) and a transmutant relationship (necessary relationship) – which implies that the therapist is internalised as therapist-patient system in the here-and-now of the ongoing shaping of the script. This is possible both in the therapy with the child and with the adult, that is to say, in any setting in which we establish a

relationship. The system as such is mutually transmutant and may be represented thus.

If we accept the foregoing, we must admit that there is a here-and-now in the therapy, which, regardless of the age of the patient, provides the actualisation of a relationship involving all parties in the system.

Fourth new assumption: from transference to transmutation

At this point we have a broader view that leads us to the fourth assumption. Here we are moving

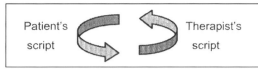

Figure 18.7　The mutual influence of the patient's and therapist's scripts

away from transference to transmutation, thereby suggesting a transmutation or transformation. If we speak about transference we must consider the subject along with their past. When we talk about transmutation, we must consider the actual material present in the here-and-now. The consequent change does not only include the patient (the therapist is behind the transference) but the patient and the therapist – as the transformation takes place in both. So the field of responsibility and of treatment is broadened.

All this leads us to a wider human and social dimension which goes beyond therapy itself. It leads to therapists being in a constant state of evolution together with the patient. The non-negotiated change (psychological contract) with the patient is the price and the consequence of a constantly evolving way of being for which we must be responsible and thankful to those who entrust their lives to us. The internalising process is not just simple absorption but an autonomous transmutation of the self-subjective perception of reality.

In the therapeutic relationship the fabric is created for a new identity or for a true identity (real self). Alongside the possible transferential relationship there is also the transmutant and necessary relationship which is based on the principle of attachment to the system and to the need of the individual for that system. The therapist enters into the script of the other with their life plan and offers themselves as a new scene which achieves a bi-directional dimension in the here and now. In order to verify what has been described so far, besides TA, I have used a fairly recent method called video micro-analysis.

Video micro-analysis came into being as a research instrument and it later took the form of a clinical tool. It was developed from infant research and its main representatives are: Stern (1985, 1995, 1998); Tronick (1989); Downing (1995); Beebe, Lachmann and Jaffe (1997); Beebe and Lachmann (1998, 2003). This methodology studies the child's interactions with the caregiver. The theme of the mother-child dyad becomes a system, and the relationship is significant,

differentiated and triangular. Given the importance of the research, the authors, who were using video micro-analysis, wondered whether it could be turned into a method for clinical intervention, and researchers such as Tronick, Beebe and Lachmann set to work to allow this methodology to take shape. They thus became the promoters of the video micro-analysis method which has contributed to observation and therapy with children as well as with adults. The therapist-patient dyad could be viewed as a mutually influencing system and the adult patient as an individual who is re-proposing circuits of request and attachment similar to those at work in the child.

This method is thus used both for preventive (and observational) purposes and also for treatment and supervision. (It is offered to parents in the setting with children, teenagers and with adults where the work focuses on the patient). The video facilitates insight, beginning with what happens in the here and now, with specific emphasis on the parent-child system. By working on experience we capture the intra-psychic dialogue and the various contaminations, using TA language. As Berne pointed out, we retrieve the internal dialogue in order to facilitate the understanding and possible variations of the intra-psychic so as to enable interpersonal opening.

If we promote a different internal dialogue in the parent, then a different relationship is also possible with the child. This relationship consists of a new interpersonal dialogue that in turn favours a more adequate and correct introjection. The work done with the parent becomes therapeutic in that it creates a new relationship with the child that is curative for the child itself: relational change as curative function (Figure 18.8).

I now borrow Stern's concept of relationship and the development of the individual which is summarised in the concept of internalised representation. Stern speaks of:

- The subjective experience of interaction, which creates a lived experience and thus an **internal representation** both in the child and in the mother (this can be compared to Berne's phenomenological diagnosis).
- **Observable and objectifiable interactive behaviour**, once again both in the child and mother (this can be compared to behavioural and social diagnosis).

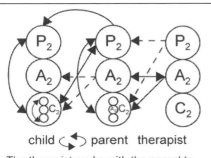

child ⟳ parent therapist

The therapist works with the parent to influence the relationship and hence the child-parent system.

The operators and the therapist work with the child to reinforce the relationship and verify the influence of the child on the parent-child system.

Figure 18.8 Working on the child–parent system

I use these elements and superimpose them onto a diagram of ego states to create the following parallel (see Figure 18.9):

As we can see the transactions can be represented by Cb and Mb and the internal dialogue by Cr and Mr. If we consider the script to be in a state of continuous evolution, new life experiences lead to the formation of a new life plan. The new relational situations give rise to new decisions and so to new pathways or

'positive scripts'. At this point we can make the assumption that the script evolves with the individual. It re-proposes primary scenes as Berne tells us, but it is also shaped by the changing of events. If mental representations and behaviour are related to each other, adjustment and assimilation constitute the constant and continuous work of life decisions and re-decisions. Perhaps we can speak of life decisions rather than script, especially when the individual works on themselves or goes into therapy.

Transactional analysis and video microanalysis

Let us now try and put together what we have said so far about the experience we have had with children and their families through TA and video micro-analysis. The therapist works on the mother's behaviour (or the parent couple) and on the child's, through the use of a video. This type of work, carried out using TA methodology and observation, set within the context of video micro-analysis, favours the insight in A_1 of the parent, because it is performed in a therapeutic setting. This understanding helps decode the internal dialogue and hence produces awareness of the phenomenological representation of the relationship (Mr). The diagram (Figure 18.10) shows how the therapist works with A_2 while watching the video.

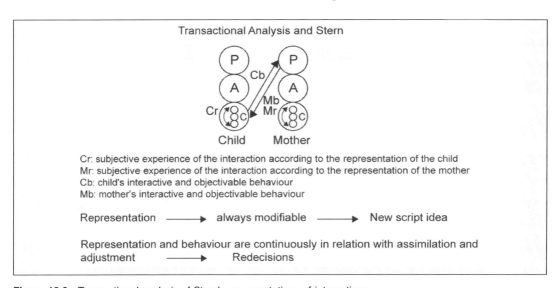

Figure 18.9 Transactional analysis of Stern's representations of interactions

The image (Mb-Cb) and the dialogue stimulate C_2 hence promoting insight (A_1) and awareness. The Adult elaborates the content of the material that emerges together with A_1 and builds up awareness about Rm. The parent can now discover a new internal experience that favours a different form of behaviour. The material enters into the parent-child system and has an impact on the experience of the child (Rb) who can change their behaviour (Cb). The same work is done by the other operators that the child works with (speech therapist, music therapist, movement therapist and so on). The therapist systematises and organises the child's experience, working in therapy individually with the child. As we can see, there are several interlocutors in the setting. When processing the video the interlocutors are the parents and the operator. When individual or group therapy is carried out the interlocutor is the child.

Change is systemic

Stern (1998) states that when parents have a different view of the child, the child begins to be transformed by their new gaze. This kind of work completes the therapeutic intervention as it takes care of all of its 'actors': the child, the parents, the operators (or the people around them) and the therapist, leading to a change in each one of them.

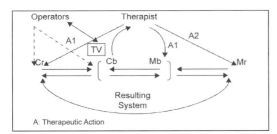

Figure 18.10 Transactional analysis and Stern

References

Beebe, B. and Lachmann, F.M. (1998) Co-constructing Inner and Relational Processes: Self And Mutual Regulation in Infant Research and Adult Treatment. *Psychoanalytic Psychology*, 15: 3, 1–37.

Beebe, B. and Lachmann, F.M. (2002) *Infant Research and Adult Treatment: Co-constructing Interractions*. New York: The Analytic Press.

Beebe, B., Lachmann, F.M. and Jaffe, J. (1997) Mother-infant Interaction Structures and Presymbolic Self and Object Representations. *Psychoanalytic Dialogues*, 7: 2, 133–82.

Berne, E. (1961) *Transactional Analysis in Psychotherapy: A Systematic Individual and Social Psychiatry*. New York: Grove Press.

Downing, G. (1993) *The Body and the Word*. New York: Routledge.

Erskine, R.G., Moursund, J.P. and Trautmann, R.L. (1999) *Beyond Empathy: A Theory of Contact-in-Relationship*. Philadelphia, PA: Brunner/Mazel.

Kohut H. (1971) *The Analysis of the Self*. New York: International Universities Press.

Mahler, M., Pine, F. and Bergman, A. (1975) *The Psychological Birth of the Human Infant: Symbiosis and Individuation*. New York: Basic Books.

Moiso, C. (1985) Ego States and Transference. *Transactional Analysis Journal*, 15: 3, 194–201.

O'Reilly-Knapp, M. and Erskine, R. (2003) Concepts at the Heart of Integrative TA. *Transactional Analysis Journal*, 33: 2, 168–77.

Sandler, J., Tyson, R.L. and Kennedy H. (1982) *The Technique of Child Psychoanalysis: Seminars with A. Freud*. Cambridge, MA: Harvard University Press.

Stern, D. (1985) *The Interpersonal World of the Infant: A View from Psychoanalysis and Developmental Psychology*. New York: Basic Books.

Stern D.N. (1995) *The Motherhood Constellation. A Unified View of Parent-Infant Psychotherapy*. New York: Basic Books.

Stern, D.N. (1998) *Le Interazioni Madre-Bambino nello Sviluppo e nella Clinica* [Mother-Child Interactions in Development and in the Clinic]. Milano: Raffaello Cortina.

Tronick, E. (1989) Emotions and Affective Communication in the Child. *American Psychologist*, 44, 112–9.

CHAPTER 19

Playing with Theory: A Relational Search for Self

Paul Kellett

Most of us feel that there must be something, some 'thing', within us which functions as the causal centre of all our activities, the 'I' that wills our actions. But must there be?
(Shotter, 1993: 133)

Jay arrives a little over ten minutes late for his 31st session, muttering to the secretary who lets him in, and makes a dash for the waiting room. He has spoken of how he doesn't like to wait in case there are other people around, and we have discussed my theory that his coming late in order to avoid his anxiety keeps him isolated and from getting the support he needs. Now I feel at once a pull between immediately dropping the work I started while waiting for Jay, or taking a minute to finish it off. Such impasses are familiar to Jay and to me in our work together, as well as in our own lives. I wonder briefly at my motivation in starting something while waiting for Jay, finish off the task at hand, and go to greet him.

Jay reluctantly follows me to our room, then takes an unusually long time to sit, circling the space between our chairs. I am reminded of a cat that circles before getting comfortable – yet Jay seems far more restless than this image suggests. I smile at him as he sits, thinking, as usual, to resist a version of the banal question "What do you want from today?" knowing what his familiar answer would be. Instead I say that he seems restless today, and he grudgingly agrees. I ask him "What's up?" and he replies with the familiar refrain I had intended to bypass: he doesn't know, he doesn't know, he just doesn't know.

Again, we meet at our impasse, bringing into play a core dynamic of Jay's being and our developing relationship. I begin to feel impotent and angry with myself for somehow slipping again into this repeated enactment. A 'mistake' that compounds that of my starting a task while waiting for Jay to arrive. I remind myself (defensively) that the many professionals involved in Jay's ongoing care view him as a very disturbed young man. They have many labels and theories for his way of being. During our year together I too have played with many such concepts. Playful resistor? Somehow Jay's intransigent despair is more existential than merely manipulative. Creative daydreamer? His withdrawal into a place of hopeless emptiness is more primitively schizoid than this catchy phrase evokes. For in this place, Jay cuts himself both as a rageful attack on a self that he hates, and as a reminder that he physically exists. Schizotypal? As a transactional analyst I have, as yet, no translation of this label – Fantastic Alien, perhaps?

I realise that, in musing on possible diagnoses, I have withdrawn momentarily from Jay. I look at him playing with his baseball cap and see that he too has withdrawn. We have lost each other and ourselves and, fleetingly, I remember my own adolescent experience of feeling lost. I ask him what it feels like for him not to know, "What's up?" – to feel stuck again with me here in this silence. He shrugs. I wonder aloud if, perhaps, we might discover something about what it's like if we stay together with this stuckness; if we see what comes up for us. He nods in a way that further empties me of hope and potency and, in this way we enter a non-linguistic realm that cannot be structured in language.

It is customary for authors to offer historical summaries of clients in order to contextualise their work. In so painting a portrait of their client, the author offers the reader, *a priori*, a framework with which to make meaning of the dynamics of the client and their relationship with the therapist, as well as an angle on the therapist's intentions and identity – a hook, as it were, on which to hang our frames of reference, our theories. In beginning as I do here I wish to avoid this kind of theoretical speculation, grounded in historical diagnosis, that can too often foreclose upon a rich, yet unnerving space, where exploration and play with meaning may flourish (Winnicott, 1971). Without such grounding, we are invited to let go of certainty (Cornell and Hargaden, 2005b) as well as the often defensive and somewhat narcissistic urge to impose our theories upon a world of possibilities, or rather, worlds of possibility. For while Jay, like all of us, can be partially shoe-horned into a familiar frame of reference, his all-consuming desire for a meaningful sense of self escapes theorisation, spilling over and outstripping any meaning I, or indeed he himself, may wish to assign.

So, before reading any further, take a moment to reflect upon the above account of my encounter with Jay. Imagine yourself as his therapist. Sit in silence with him and reflect, without rushing to make meaning, upon what images, recollections, feelings, and bodily sensations emerge. As you come out of this, note how old you imagine Jay to be. And now sit in Jay's chair and, as Jay, see what arises.

Developing theory: relational transactional analysis

Cornell and Hargaden (2005a) trace the emergence of a turn to relationality within transactional analysis in *From Transactions to Relations: the Emergence of a Relational Tradition in Transactional Analysis* (Cornell and Hargaden, 2005b). Relational transactional analysis, then, is a relatively 'young' theory or, rather, a young meta-theoretical perspective on therapeutic work, offering both an ontological and an epistemological framework within which theory can be played with and developed. It is ontological because relational philosophy addresses the nature of being, the always-already relational construction of selfhood. It is epistemological because it frames our construction of meaning, of interpreting our experiences as similarly forged in and through the processes of relating. One of the most significant practical consequences of this is that relational transactional analysis is concerned with interactions in which the whole person of the therapist – their intersubjectivity – is fundamentally implicated in the therapeutic encounter and the process of change. From this perspective the therapeutic relationship represents a mutual meeting of asymmetrical selves (Aron, 1996) leading to an ethic of *interactional* analysis.

The forging of a meaningful sense of self represents a lifelong process of coming-into-being (Stern, 1985, 2000) and is one of the most evocative and provocative challenges facing young people. From a relational perspective this process is socially mediated; our sense of self emerges in and through our relationships. In an attempt to capture what this sense of self may represent, Harré (1985: 262) states that 'to be a self is not to be a certain kind of being, but to be in possession of a certain kind of theory.' Thus, my project of developing theory within a relational ethic finds a parallel in Jay's quest for a good-enough theory of self. And so we meet in the consulting room, at the interface of this play with theory, in the search for meaningful senses of selfhood. For young clients, more fervently in the grip of the urgent desire that burns in this quest, this meeting is fraught with almost

unbearable tensions. For the therapist, as I illustrate, this encounter re-ignites their experiences of adolescent loss and desire. It is the therapist's willingness and ability to engage reflexively with these re-activated experiences that is crucial to effective relational practice, and is the focus of this chapter.

A repertoire of selves . . .

Summers and Tudor (2000) have eloquently described a sense of selfhood, comprising a fluid repertoire of socially situated relationships, roles and identities. In this view, the seemingly essential property, 'the self', is a *process*, a being-in-the-world (Heidegger, 1962) that comes into play in and through our relationships. Since ego state models may be seen as the transactional analytic conceptualisation of self (Novey et al., 1993), these models offer a metaphor for domains of being-in-relation, modes of interactivity, of dynamic processes. Building on Erskine's (1988) development of Berne's (1961) functional descriptions of the Parent, Adult and Child, the archaic ego states (Parent and Child) represent categories of fixated, or frozen ways-of-being; patterns of interactions or templates of past relationships that are reproduced with others in the present. In contrast, the Adult ego state represents an integrated and integrating way-of-being that is present-centred and reflexive (Tudor, 2003). Adult processes are spontaneous, relationally autonomous, and potentially fully contactful (Erskine, Moursund and Trautmann, 1999), where archaic ego state processes are never fully any of these (see Figure 19.1).

An important assumption of a relational approach is that all interaction between people, including client and therapist, includes both present-centred and past-centred ways of relating, in a constantly shifting balance. Thus, the integrated/integrating Adult function represents a meta-function, inclusive of archaic functions that have been, and continue to be integrated to a good-enough extent. How good-enough an extent will always be a contextual and relational judgement, situationally defined by our perception of the states of self and other. From this perspective, then, the model shown in Figure 19.2 represents a depiction of the ideally healthy self. All archaic senses of self are fully integrated within an integrated/integrating Adult that comprises both conscious and

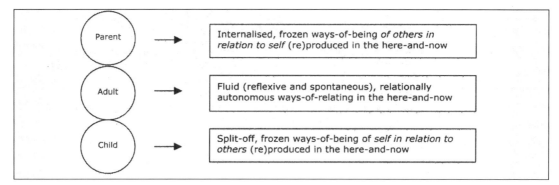

Figure 19.1   Ego states (based on Berne, 1961)

unconscious functions (Tudor, 2003). Though less neat, Figure 19.3 represents more fairly the personality of the therapist and, ultimately, the client, both striving towards a good-enough integration of self.

Ways of being incorporate thinking, feeling, action and sensation that coalesce to function as interpretive frameworks (Allen, 2003) offering particular kinds of narratives or stories with which we attempt to make meaning of diverse experiences. Such interpretation represents a process of *symbolising* experience that has been viewed in transactional analysis traditionally as both developmentally grounded and functional: that is, *ego states represent a metaphor for the development of function*. In this view, the newborn infant begins to symbolise repeated experiences of being with others through such interactive acts as turn-taking gestures and proto-conversations (Trevarthen, 1979, 1988) and, later, using symbols such as transitional objects (Winnicott, 1953). Learning and interaction become mediated by the use of cultural tools such as toys and eating utensils and, eventually, psychological signs, the meanings and values attached to such tools and symbols (Wertsch and Tulviste, 1998). Ultimately, in restructuring this diverse realm of signs and symbols, it is the acquisition of language that

asserts dominance over our ways of making meaning. With words, the child is ushered into the social order and provided with the once-in-a-lifetime membership of wider social and cultural domains of values and meanings. These values and meanings are thus part and parcel of our senses of self and ways of making meaning.

. . . in postmodernist societies

Contemporary Western culture, fuelled by capitalist principles and the values of hierarchical autonomy, power and wealth, has generated societies that have commercialised identity as a commodity. Hypnotised by a multiplicity of life-narratives, images and products that offer seemingly desirable identities, young people are seduced into investing in senses of selves that promise fulfilment and security. One need only reflect on the advertisements that crowd the public and private domains, tempting onlookers with a dazzling array of products linked to

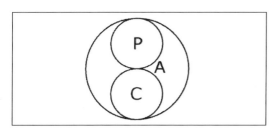

Figure 19.2   The ideal self

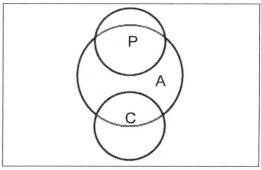

Figure 19.3   The good-enough self

images of idealised and demonised others. As such, it is the acquisition of a pre-fabricated image that determines identity; 'Ipod therefore I am' (Jones, 2005).

A number of authors have evaluated the impact of such dynamics upon the construction of selfhood. Of particular importance here are the ideas of Christopher Lasch (1984) and Kenneth Gergen (1992). Briefly, Lasch's (1984) vision of a 'minimal self' offers an image of a highly unstable sense of self in which the hungry individual is narcissistically dependent on others for self-definition and gratification. Attempting to squeeze themself into an array of partial identities, the young person's self-image is the product of a hall of mirrors, an endless regression of surface images that leads to emptiness and despair. In contrast, as a metaphor for a sense of self borne of the relentless acquisition of desirable images, Gergen (1992) describes a 'saturated self'. Bombarded by multimedia images, located in multiple social domains, and with endless possibilities for authoring various personal myths, the young person's sense of self can fracture and fragment in the pull between these diverse demands and desires, so that 'the narrative of self-identity is inherently fragile' (1992: 185). Together, both self portraits paint a picture of the individual as fragmented and transitory, oscillating between over-full and empty senses of self, motivated by the hallucinatory images of desired others. It is upon this tightrope that young people must forge their sense of selfhood.

A discourse without words
(Rabaté, 2003)

I mentioned above that, upon acquiring or adopting language, the child finds a new way to make meaning; a way that ushers in the values of the wider worlds of adults. One consequence of this re-writing is that experience is re-framed in such a way that there is no going back to a pre-linguistic realm; what cannot be signified in words is lost to conscious representation (Lacan, 1989). For example, upon adopting the position of 'me' or 'I', the child not only demonstrates an adult understanding, and thus acceptance of differentiation between self and other, but also takes on a symbolisation that pre-dates them; their sense of self, on a basic linguistic level, is

predetermined. In identifying with such a predetermined linguistic symbol, however, there is always something missing from, or in excess of, the identity into which the child inserts themself. Thus, this symbolic self-representation fails; there is no such thing as a perfect match between self and symbol, identification can never be complete. Lacan goes on to suggest that the sense of self that is left out of the child's insertion into the symbolic becomes repressed and, thus, represents the unconscious. As Redman (2000: 24) puts it: 'the unconscious does not pre-exist the symbolic but is brought into being through the child's insertion into it'. This view of the unconscious is fundamentally relational, 'an intersubjective space between people' (Elliott, 1994: 96).

Cornell and Hargaden (2005c) argue that an engagement with and reflection upon non-linguistic communication is *the* route to an engagement with such unconscious relational dynamics. Only by working with and within this domain can we hope to give voice to the dimensions of selfhood that become lost with the acquisition of language and projected into the relationships between people: 'the inarticulate speech of the heart' as Van Morrison puts it (cited by Hargaden and Sills, 2002: 45). But how might it be possible to connect with the relational unconscious, that which cannot be signified? For me, a crucial aspect of relational practice is the therapist's use of their own *fantasy* to connect with the client's unspoken yearnings. So let us return now to my encounter with Jay and see what fantasies emerged in my imagination as we sat in silence:

Jay turned away after a few minutes to look out of the window. Eventually, I followed his gaze. While the sky was an inviting pale blue, much of it was obscured by an ugly corrugated iron roof. I felt echoes of a childhood urge to fly out of the window and zoom around in that sky – but was brought quickly back down to earth by the worry that I might catch myself on the roof's jagged edge.

As I looked back at Jay I saw that he too was lost outside somewhere and felt both jealous that he might be able to enjoy his fantasy and annoyed that he wasn't engaging and allowing me to **be** *an effective therapist. At this point, a musical refrain began in my mind's ear. Round and round this tedious phrase ran. I tried to focus on it to see if it developed into anything else, but it stayed stuck, like a broken record. I sighed inwardly and asked Jay, almost for a distraction, what was going on for him. And I was actually surprised when he said that* **it** *never changes.*

Fantasies and reflections

What meaning might I make out of these fantasies and how might I use this insight to inform my work with Jay? While this extract is rich in evocative material, I briefly expand on my associations connected with just three images: Jay's circling, mentioned in the opening extract, the flying fantasy, and the elusive, monotonous musical theme.

Neither Jay nor myself were any more comfortable in the room after his circling. Upon reflection, this action felt both defensive and predatory. Defensive, since I was reminded of the wary, territorial checking out that fearful creatures engage in out in the open. Predatory since I imagined a hungry creature circling its prey before pouncing to devour. In what ways might we be circling each other, at once defensively and predatorily? Who feared being devoured, internalised by the other; or wanted to devour, to take in or to introject? What ambiguous desires might linger behind the dynamics within which Jay and I were enmeshed?

My associations with my flying fantasy appeared to develop further my sense of these desires, evoking a yearning for a lost sense of freedom, an emergence in a libidinal union of self and Mother Nature. This desire seemed cut-off by the jagged barrier of the metal edge barring this flight and I was here reminded of the serrated knives that play a prohibitive, self-regulating role in Jay's world. How envious and frustrated we may feel when contemplating the possibility of escaping such a barrier and flying free! Might a more intimate meeting of Jay and myself seem terrifying in its primary intensity? How might we wield the knife in our relationship as a defensive process? How might the pain that cuts us to the quick at one and the same time offer a way to remain connected to terra firma?

The musical tune stayed with me for some time as I could not identify it. Only upon waking the next morning did I recognise it as the theme tune of the film *Men In Black* (Sonnenfeld, 1999). The film stars the young, desirable media icon Will Smith and one of the focal themes is his character's transformation from cop to 'J'. As a cop, he lives in a mundane world on which he has a good angle, and in which he knows who he is. His identity of 'cop' is unproblematic and he identifies with this sense of self, without any reflection, though it appears at times to be unfulfilling. Through his job as a cop, through his performance of this role, he is suddenly plunged into a world in which he must search for an angle and a new sense of self, a world suddenly populated with aliens in which he feels alien. At a critical moment in his insertion into this new world, his colleague and mentor, K (played by Tommy Lee Jones) says to him, "Searching for a handle on the moment? I can't help you." J is on the threshold of taking on another sense of self: that of a man with radically different roles, functions and relationships. Confronted with an experience that he cannot yet integrate, cannot yet make sense of, J is without a handle, without an identity, without a theory.

Jay, like J, feels alien in an alien world and both struggle to find a place for himself, a sense of self that will be recognised, be accepted by others and from which he can act purposefully and intentionally. J looks to his mentor for guidance and K tells him explicitly that he cannot help, just as I, as Jay's therapist, tell him implicitly that I cannot do it for him and, indeed, at times, feel impotent to help. Like J the cop, Jay has not yet integrated into a more fulfilling, exciting, colourfully inclusive world, finding that the monotony of his familiar role and the rituals that comprise its performance 'never change'. An important aspect of this colourful quality, J's blackness, his difference in relation to the white-dominated world of *Men In Black* is only implicit in the film. Like Will Smith's otherness as a black man, is there, too, an invisible otherness between Jay and myself that we collude to dismiss as unproblematic? Furthermore, Will Smith's sexily desirable iconic status represents an invisible field of yearning that forms a central aspect of the film's popular status, particularly amongst younger people. What of the unspoken field of desire that generates the attraction for Jay and I to return week after week to our relationship in spite of our intermittent sense of hopelessness?

Framing meaning

The associations I have made from the above fantasies are in no way exhaustive, authoritative or definitive. Such associations are made within a realm of infinite possibilities, and are structured not only by our sense of our clients, but by our own frames of reference, which, centrally, coalesce around our theories: the sense we make of our relational being in the world. As I have

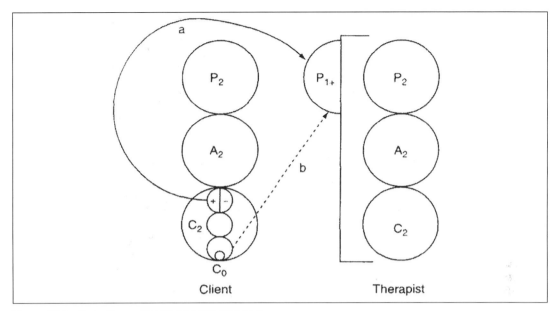

Figure 19.4   Projective and introjective transferences

argued, a relational perspective offers a promisingly broad enough framework by which such sense-making can be creatively and usefully explored.

The primary model for symbolising unconscious communication within relational transactional analysis is Hargaden and Sills' (2002) development of Moiso's (1985) structural representation of differing types of transference. This model operationalises the processes of projection, identification and introjection that transferential dynamics enact. In Figure 19.4 the client projects primitive self-regulatory ways of being (a), as well as split-off longings (b) onto their image of the therapist as lost and idealised self-(m)other. These represent categories of projective transferences (a) and of introjective transferences (b) respectively. In Figure 19.5, the client's split-off longings are communicated directly *into* the therapist. This radical shift in the unconscious intention of the client to contact the therapist's archaic sense of self is regarded as offering the opportunity for a transformation of the client's lost yearnings. The therapist who is open to receiving such communications is invited to detoxify and integrate these yearnings and find a way of feeding back the now digestible aspects of self for the client's integration.

It is through such transferential dynamics, then, that the client *recruits* the therapist as an essential other with whom and in whom the client's archaic, conflicting fixations can potentially be resolved. The client (and therapist) implicitly hope that the therapist can decode the client's unconscious communications; accurately empathise with the client's being in the world; detoxify what has been indigestible; and, in modelling a self-reflexive process that offers the key to re-integration, invite the client to unlock their own unspoken yearnings, and

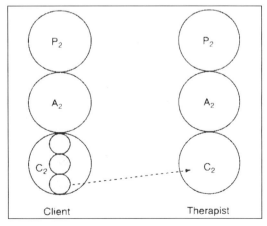

Figure 19.5   Projective identification (Hargaden and Sills, 2002: 60)

integrate these within a more inclusive sense of selfhood.

Since, as we have seen, the unconscious domain is a thoroughly relational one, representing a motivating field that emerges from the dynamics of relating, the therapist is implicated *a priori* in a co-transferential dynamic (Summers and Tudor, 2000). As a result, it is more useful to conceive of the client in their recruitment of the therapist as activating or re-igniting aspects of the therapist's whole self, particularly those aspects of being that are not yet fully integrated. That is, the client, and particularly the young client, by virtue of their developmental dynamic, inevitably touches upon the therapist's early narcissistic wounds. In this light, Moiso's, and thus Hargaden and Sill's model tends to portray the therapist as a passive recipient of the client's unconscious communications, rather than an active participant in the construction of unconscious relating. What Figures 19.4 and 19.5 omit, then, is the therapist's *reciprocal* transactions, their mutual participation in the relational unconscious field.

Sequentially then (and assuming a picture of a therapist who is integrated enough and a young client whose sense of selves represents a lesser degree of such integration) the client, unable to reflect adequately upon and integrate their own hidden yearnings comes to therapy, seeking solace, in part, in the fantasy of the therapist as an idealised self-(m)other. Through the transferential processes of unconscious, non-linguistic relating with the therapist (Figure 19.6) the client recruits the therapist in reflecting upon and making sense of the client's unspoken yearnings. Crucially, this is not a one-way communication, but an interaction, one in which the whole self of the therapist plays a reciprocal

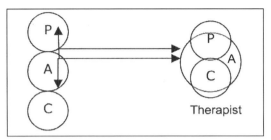

Figure 19.7   The therapist's interpretation

role. Indicated by double-headed arrowed interactions, these are shown as emanating from and impacting on the therapist at the vague boundary between their integrated and as yet unintegrated archaic selves, in order to allow for an uncertainty in the potency and ability of the therapist.

If the therapist is able to reflect upon and integrate these interactions to a good-enough extent, decoding and detoxifying the client's split-off senses of self, then they may be able to share this process of digestion with the client (Figure 19.7). In doing so, the therapist offers a model of integration that the client is invited to make their own, leading to a richer relational engagement (Figure 19.8).

Where the client's unspoken yearnings contact

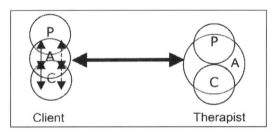

Figure 19.8   The client's integration

the therapist's as yet unintegrated archaic senses of selves, the therapist will need to resolve and integrate these if they are to provide a therapeutic frame in which the client feels safe and contained enough to change. The proper place for such integration is the therapist's own personal therapy and this integration is essential if the client is to be able to contact the therapist at this level. As Jung (1946, 1983: 35) argues:

A genuine participation, going right beyond professional routine, is absolutely imperative, unless of course the doctor prefers to jeopardize the whole proceeding by

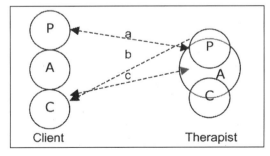

Figure 19.6   Unconscious communication: Projective transferences (a), introjective transferences (b), and projective identification (c)

evading his own problems, which are becoming more and more insistent. The doctor must go to the limits of his subjective possibilities, otherwise the patient will be unable to follow suit.' Indeed, it is often the client who invites the therapist to follow suit; the client invites the therapist to find them within a cocreated intersubjectivity.

Therapeutic impasses, as relationally co-constructed dynamics, are often propped up by such unresolved issues in the therapist. And while the therapist too will inevitably be transformed through their meeting with the client, the relational principle of mutuality within the therapeutic dyad does not imply equality (see Aron, 1996), it is the client's search for a meaningful self that must be held clearly in the foreground. The therapist's task of containing their own narcissistic wounds, while remaining available to reflect upon these in the service of the client, represents one of the biggest challenges of a therapeutic relationship, and one that a relational model and method makes explicit.

Finding Jay

How might I use the insights gained from my emergent fantasies and the consequent meaning I made of these within my therapeutic relationship with Jay? Cornell and Hargaden (2005a) explicitly warn of the danger of young theories becoming dogmatised. Such a process occurs through the rigid application of theories that are more usefully employed as frameworks for a play with meaning-making: they are not the meaning in and of themselves. Dogmatisation is motivated, in part, by anxious quests for certainty and unassailability, symptoms of unresolved and unintegrated issues within the therapist. Consequently, I find myself at another impasse. I have taken pains to avoid the style of 'case study' reporting using transcripts or direct quotations that often misrepresent the richly ambivalent process of therapeutic dialogue, and fixes in the minds of readers a seductive ring of truth. Like the imaginary mirror-image, such accounts offer misleading and fictitious ideals. Thus, I do not now wish to offer an account of my work with Jay that invites a dogmatic or authoritative fixing of theory and practice. Yet, at the same time, the 'how' of therapeutic practice is a crucial aspect in the development of theory, and omitting this aspect of my work with Jay also risks stifling this development.

As with the impasse I experienced with Jay outlined at the start of this chapter, this dilemma

finds a parallel in the therapeutic relationship: how to find a delicate and ever-shifting balance in the dialectic between offering insights with which to scaffold the client's growth (Bruner, 1986), while still providing a creative space in which the client can safely play with theory in order to make their own meanings. With this caveat, I offer the following account of our next session. This session proved the first of a number of significant turning points for Jay; sessions that, above all else, began to nurture his sense of hope in his ability to develop a meaningful theory of self. As this fledgling sense of a wider and more inclusive repertoire of selves developed, Jay began to imagine a future that was less fixed and more creatively uncertain:

Jay cancels his next session, telling the receptionist he doesn't feel well. She looks at me like I could do with the break, and I realise that, though I have no doubt Jay will come next week, I am disappointed not to see him this week. I miss him.

The following week he is early, for perhaps the first time, and sits in the waiting room rather than standing impatiently. Yet he bounds up the stairs ahead of me and, as soon as the door of our consulting room is closed, asks if I got his message last week. He really wants an answer. I say that I did, and thank him for letting me know. He smiles shyly and says it wasn't anything to do with the previous session, the one in which we didn't say much. I ask him what he has made of that session and, rather than his familiar refrain, he appears to struggle to put something into words. He wants to ask me something but says he doesn't know how – that it's embarrassing. He looks at me directly and I have a powerful sense of his struggle. I say that it can be hard for us to put some things into words here. He becomes animated, points at me and says "That's it. That's right!" He seems to have found something of himself in what I have said. Yeah, it's hard for both of us. I say that perhaps we are both wary of each other at times, when what we're trying to say feels risky, shameful . . . that at times like that we can feel alone, out of place . . . alien, perhaps.

He sits back and looks out of the window. I wait, oscillating between the hope that what I have offered might eventually flower, and the resignation that I've missed Jay and that we'll stay stuck a while longer. He looks at me out of the corner of his eye and says "Yeah" in such a world-weary way that I am genuinely surprised. He looks back down at his battered cap, then up at me directly and says that no one knows what it is to feel as alone as he does, that I am the only person he speaks to all week. The silence that follows is different in tone to that of the last session. I tell him that perhaps the other week he invited me to feel something of what it's like for him to feel so alone and his nodding response seems a far cry from his dismissive shrugs or despairing 'don't knows'.

Towards the end of the session he shares a particularly painful 'don't know': his uncertainty about his sexuality. Crucially, he tells me that the reason he felt ashamed to tell me was because he has been so certain that I know about myself, that I am sure, secure in my sense of who I am. He has no idea how anyone could know that about himself and, he adds very quietly, he has felt like an alien; alienated from his body and from others.

Summary

Our sense of self comprises a repertoire of relational selves borne of and through our relationships, forged from the interpretive meanings we invest in our relational experiences and constituting our being-with-others-in-the-world. This sense of selfhood is socially situated and mediated by language. If our sense of selfhood is to be rich, integrated and coherent we must acknowledge and hold what cannot be symbolised: the lost yearnings of unconscious desire that always outstrip symbolisation. One way to connect to this unknowable realm is through fantasy. It is through fantasy that we can commune with the unknowable. Through his free associations, the therapist can connect with his own integrated unconscious dynamics, accurately empathising with the client, and inviting the client similarly to reflect upon his subjectivity. Thus the therapist reflectively models the process of good-enough integration needed to hold the unknowable.

Work with young people re-ignites the loss and desire that burns in adolescence within the whole person therapists of all ages. The therapist must have integrated these lost senses of self to a good-enough degree if they are to be able to digest the client's unspoken yearnings, and to offer their insight in such as a way as to facilitate the client's own self-discovery. Young clients need to fashion their own meanings within the world of others, to make their own theories. Where the therapist is willing to play with meaning and theory both within and outside the therapeutic encounter, there will be opportunities for change and transformation. The relational project within transactional analysis, with its focus on non-linguistic communication in the forging of a good-enough sense of relational selfhood offers the opportunity for such creative, shared change. As Barnes (2005:6) puts it: 'If you want people to change, you have to change, I have to change, we have to change, our theories have to change.'

References

Allen, J. (2003) Concepts, Competencies and Interpretative Communities. *Transactional Analysis Journal*, 33: 2, 126–47.

Aron, L. (1996) *A Meeting of Minds: Mutuality in Psychoanalysis*. Hillsdale, NJ: The Analytic Press.

Barnes, G. (2005) The Political is Personal and the Personal is Political. *The Script*, 35: 3, 1–6.

Berne, E. (1961) *Transactional Analysis in Psychotherapy*. New York: Castle Books.

Berne, E. (1972) *What Do You Say After You Say Hello?* New York: Grove Press.

Bruner, J. (1986) *Actual Minds, Possible Worlds*. Boston, MA: Harvard University Press.

Burr, V. (1995) *An Introduction to Social Constructionism*. London: Routledge.

Cornell, W. and Hargaden, H. (2005a) Introduction. In Cornell, W. and Hargaden, H. (Eds.) *From Transactions to Relations: the Emergence of a Relational Tradition in Transactional Analysis*. Chadlington: Haddon Press.

Cornell, W. and Hargaden, H. (Eds.) (2005b) *From Transactions to Relations: the Emergence of a Relational Tradition in Transactional Analysis*. Chadlington: Haddon Press.

Cornell, W. and Hargaden, H. (2005c) Reflections. In Cornell, W. and Hargaden, H. (Eds.) *From Transactions to Relations: the Emergence of a Relational Tradition in Transactional Analysis*. Chadlington: Haddon Press.

Elliott, A. (1994) *Psychoanalytic Theory: An Introduction*. Oxford, Malden MA: Blackwell Publications.

Erskine, R. (1988) Ego Structure, Intrapsychic Function, and Defence Mechanisms: A Commentary on Eric Berne's Original Theoretical Concepts. *Transactional Analysis Journal*, 18: 1, 15–9.

Erskine, R., Moursund, J. and Trautmann, R. (1999) *Beyond Empathy; a Therapy of Contact-in-Relationship*. New York: Brunner-Routledge.

Gergen, K. (1992) *The Saturated Self*. New York: Basic Books.

Hargaden, H. and Sills, C. (2002) *Transactional Analysis: A Relational Perspective*. London: Brunner-Routledge.

Harré, R. (1985) *The Philosophies of Science*. Oxford: Open University Press.

Heidegger, M. (1962) *Being and Time*. New York: Harper and Row.

Jones, D. (2005) *Ipod Therefore I Am*, London: Weidenfeld and Nicolson.

Jung, C. (1983) *The Psychology of the Transference*. Hull, R. Trans. London: Routledge and Kegan Paul. (Original work published 1946).

Lacan, J. (1989) *Ecrits: A Selection*. Sheridan, A. Trans. London and New York: Routledge. (Original work published 1966)

Lasch, C. (1984) *The Minimal Self: Psychic Survival in Troubled Times*. New York: Norton.

Moiso, C. (1985) Ego States and Transference. *Transactional Analysis Journal*, 15: 3, 194–201.

Novey, T, Porter-Steele, N. Gobes, L and Massey, R. (1993) Ego Sates and the Self-Concept: a Panel Presentation and Discussion. *Transactional Analysis Journal*, 23: 3, 123–38.

Redman, P. (2000) *The Subject of Language: The Theorisation of Identity in Cultural Studies*. Buckingham: Open University.

Rabaté, J-M. (2003) *Lacan's Turn to Freud*. In Rabaté, J-M. (Ed.) *The Cambridge Companion to Lacan*. Cambridge: Cambridge University Press.

Shotter, J. (1993) *Conversational Realities: Constructing Life through Language*. London: Sage.

Sonnenfeld, B. (Director) (1999) *Men in Black* [Film]. New York: Columbia Pictures.

Stern, D. (1985) *The Interpersonal World of the Infant*. London: Karnac Books.

Stern, D. (2000) *The Interpersonal World of the Infant* 2nd edn. London: Karnac Books.

Summers, G. and Tudor, K. (2000) Cocreative Transactional Analysis. *Transactional Analysis Journal*, 30: 1, 23–40.

Trevarthen, C. (1979) *Communication and Co-operation in Early Infancy: A Description of Primary Intersubjectivity*. In Bullowa, M. (Ed.) *Before Speech*. Cambridge: Cambridge University Press.

Trevarthen, C. (1988) Universal Co-Operative Motives: How Infants Begin to Know The Language and Skills of the Language of their Parents. In Jahoda, G. and Lewis, I. (Eds.) *Acquiring Culture*. Beckenham: Croom Helm.

Tudor, K. (2003) The Neopsyche: The Integrating Adult Ego State. In Sills, C. and Hargaden, H. (Eds.) *Ego States*. London: Worth Reading.

Wertsch, J. and Tulviste, P. (1998) *L.S. Vygotsky and Contemporary Developmental Psychology*. In Faulkner, D., Littleton, K. and Woodhead, M. (Eds.) *Learning Relationships in the Classroom*. London and New York: Routledge, Open University.

Winnicott, D. (1953) Transitional Objects and Transitional Phenomena. *International Journal of Psychoanalysis*, 34: 89–97.

Winnicott, D. (1971) *Playing and Reality*. London: Tavistock Publications.

Appendices

An Annotated Bibliography of TA Books on Working with Children and Young People*

Keith Tudor

The Happy Valley by Eric Berne (1968) New York: Grove Press.

The first TA book for children which Berne himself described as his first 'unpsychiatric' book, illustrated by Sylvie Selig. The characters include a mixed-up python, an obedient rabbit, a wide little man, a friendly sheep, a dutiful princess, an explorer, a billy goat, a kind prince and three robbers. The happy valley, called Lamador, describes a place where everyone is polite and happy and does what they like best, whilst still managing to satisfy their conscience – things which, in a comment on the flyleaf of the book, Berne acknowledges he would like to do himself.

TA for Kids (and Grown Ups Too) by Alvyn M. Freed (1971) Rolling Hills Estates, CA: Jalmar Press.

The first of three books in a series 'Transactional Analysis for Everybody'. Written for children aged 9 to 13, this book outlines concepts such as ego states, life positions ('I'm OK, You're OK'), trading stamps, transactions, games and rackets, scripts, and contracts for change. The book is pleasantly illustrated and reasonably easy to understand, but, in places lacks clear theoretical grounding.

TA for Tots (and Other Prinzes) by Alvyn M. Freed (1973) Rolling Hills Estates, CA: Jalmar Press.

The second of three books written by Freed and, as its title suggests, written for a younger age group, most likely for grown ups to read to children. It portrays a traditional, very basic and inaccurate view of ego states e.g. that we have three people inside of us: 'Bossy me', 'Thinking me' and 'Feeling me'. It introduces the concepts of strokes by means of 'warm fuzzies' (good strokes) and 'cold pricklies' (bad strokes), and life script by means of prinzes (winners) and frogs (losers). Freed also published a 24 page companion volume, the *TA for Tots Colouring Book*.

---

*Books published in English.

TA for Teens by Alvyn M. Freed (1976) Rolling Hills Estates, CA: Jalmar Press.

The third book in the series, this one aimed at young people in the transition to adulthood. Whilst the book again takes a simplistic approach to the theory of ego states, it is generally more thorough in its language and presentation of TA. It introduces more complex concepts such as ego state pathology (contaminations); process scripts; time structuring; life positions; discounting and passive behaviour; games; decisions; strokes; and permissions. There is an emphasis on values and what Freed describes as the goals of TA: autonomy, spontaneity, integrity and authenticity. There are good chapters on school and home; drugs; relationships and sex; and divorce and death, which, despite their slightly dated language, still read well and are relevant today.

A Warm Fuzzy Tale by Claude Steiner (1977) Rolling Hills Estates, CA: Jalmar Press.

This beautifully illustrated book for children introduces the terms 'warm fuzzies' and 'cold pricklies' to describe positive and negative strokes, respectively, in the context of a fairy story. The book is a classic and, as such, worth reading, but is very wordy to use with children and very dated. The 'Hip Woman' comes and gives strokes to children 'even when not asked', which is both dated and dubious, especially in the light of Steiner's own ideas about the stroke economy, in response to the regulations and injunctions of which he encourages people to reject the stroke they don't want.

Circle-Face Symbols by Elisabeth Kleinewiese (first English edition 1988) Berlin: Institut für Kommunikationstherapie

This book provides a visual representational model of ego states through circles with different faces drawn to represent various ego states. It is both simple and sophisticated in moving beyond the functional model of ego states to encompass and represent the structural model (first and second order), and applications to the egogram, drama triangle, miniscript, and for use in multiple chair therapy.

Lumps and Bumps by Denton Roberts (1992) Privately circulated publication, available from Denton Roberts, 5840 Richmond Avenue, Dallas, Texas 75206, USA.

Described as a children's book for parents and a parents' book for children, this is a short story, illustrated by Ayako Grace Kim, which uses the metaphor of lumps and bumps to describe what happens when we feel stuck or bad. It introduces the figure of a 'bump shrinker' who knows how to help people with their lumps and bumps.

Improving Behaviour and Raising Self Esteem in the Classroom – A Practical Guide to Using Transactional Analysis by Giles Barrow, Emma Bradshaw and Trudi Newton (2001) London: David Fulton Publishers.

This book is designed to address the needs of teachers working with children who face challenging behaviour in their classrooms. It provides a methodology for developing a positive school culture, facilitating learning and development and reducing conflict, using TA models including functional fluency, three-cornered contracts, drama an winner's triangles, life positions and cycles of development. It is well-structured and user friendly, offering strategies, notes and resources for improving interpersonal relationships and communication with both children and colleagues.

Walking the Talk edited by Giles Barrow and Trudi Newton (2004) London: David Fulton Publishers.

This book follows on from *Improving Behaviour and Raising Self-Esteem in the Classroom* and is made up of a series of case studies describing the implementation of TA concepts in a range of practical contexts. The contributors are all practitioners who work directly with children or who offer support and advice to schools, and the book offers ideas, resources and evidence of the effectiveness of TA methods for working with children and young people.

An Annotated Bibliography of TA Articles on Working with Children and Young People*

Roger Day and Keith Tudor

The *Transactional Analysis Journal* is available through the International Transactional Analysis Association at www.itaa-net.org.

Articles published in the *Transactional Analysis Journal* (2005–1973)

A Transactional Analysis Model for Psychological Work with Pediatric Patients with Hearing and/or Speech Problems. Anna Rita, Carone Craig and Francesco Craig (July, 2005)

A description of a multisystem method approach for working with children with hearing and/or speech problems and their families. The method is a form of group therapy involving a number of families with similar problems. Research into this method is described, including observations of the therapy and progress of two groups. The efficacy of this approach is demonstrated, even when intervention is possible only with parents.

Fairy Tales and Psychological Life Plans. Agnès Le Guernic (July, 2004)

(This and the following two articles appeared in a special themed issue of the *TAJ* on 'TA and Education', edited by Newton (2005) see Introduction).

A description of how fairy tales provide children with different relationship models, the article proposes a positive triangle of social roles: the guide, the helper and the beneficiary. It is based on the premise that the field of education in general and educational TA in particular are preventive rather than curative endeavours.

Script Interventions in the School Setting. Ferdinando Montuschi (July, 2004)

A brief discussion of the practice and ethics of interventions in the educational setting at the

level of script, and of the teacher's boundaries in this. The article introduces the concept of expanding script.

Dealing with Fear of Failure: Working with Script Concepts in the Classroom. Miriam Toth (July, 2004)

A second article (in the same issue) on script in education discusses how script theories can help teachers to understand why children act as they do, and offer options for responding specifically to support children to change their self-limiting behaviour.

Every Child is a Group: The Girl of the Snakes. Dolores Munari Poda (January, 2004)

The presentation of a case study of therapeutic work with a girl which focuses on the parental figures present in the attributions, drivers and injunctions and, thus, the internalised family group.

A Letter to Parents about Child Therapy. Dolores Munari Poda (January, 2003)

A description, in the form of a letter to parents, of the meaning and value of child therapy for both the child and their parents.

A Chance to Thrive: Enabling Change in a Nursery School. Trudi Newton and Gill Wong (January, 2003)

The presentation of a case study of a 3 year old boy with severe behaviour difficulties. The authors describe a multicornered contract for change involving the child, his father, the school and staff.

Little Pipa and Other Ghosts: Short-term Psychotherapy with a Child. Dolores Munari Poda (October, 2002)

The therapeutic journey of a seven year old girl over eight months, shown through the evolution of a story about a gentle giant, created and illustrated by the patient herself. Emphasises the importance of a strong therapeutic alliance and the development of new, vital permissions.

---

*Published in the *Transactional Analysis Journal* (*TAJ*) and the *Transactional Analysis Bulliten*. The *TAJ* is available on disk from www.tajdisk.co.uk.

The Girl of the Wind: The Story of Miriam. Dolores Munari Poda (October, 2001)

The therapeutic journey of a 12-year-old girl who initially sees herself pushed by the wind but who eventually finds direction. The therapy makes important use of her drawings, which are reproduced.

The Fern Monster: A One-session Cure with Dreamwork. Margaret Bowater (October, 2001)

The outline of work with a 13-year-old boy who presented for therapy having had a one-off scary dream about a fern monster. An excellent explanation of one approach to dream work, with parallels with Jung's concept of the 'Shadow self'.

Violence: Early Childhood, Family and Context. James R. Allen and Barbara Ann Allen (April, 2000)

A look at the onset of violence in children, the development of aggressive and violent behaviours and issues around attachment and projection. Violence is explored as a contribution to family dynamics.

Integration of Play Therapy and Transactional Analysis. Edward Conning (April, 1999)

A consideration of ways of using Axline's play therapy in a TA way with clients, both children and adults. It covers awareness of how rackets and authentic behaviour manifest themselves, and the therapist's ability to feedback the analysis of the dynamics of play.

Child Play Therapy from a Transactional Analysis Perspective. Edward Conning (October, 1998)

A reflection on play therapy and the way it parallels TA theory. The author also examines aspects of script based on Steiner's joyless, mindless, and loveless script types. He proposes areas for research on boundaries and injunctions, the playroom, toys, boundaries, attention span and contracts.

A Typology of Psychopathology and Treatment of Children and Adolescents. James R. Allen and Barbara Ann Allen (October, 1997)

The identification of six basic categories of child and adolescent psychopathology, and the development of a useful seven-stage redecision work model specifically for work with child and adolescent clients.

Is a Happy Teenager a Healthy Teenager? Four Levels of Adolescent Anger. Tony White (July, 1997)

The report on an approach based on the assumption that expression of anger by teenagers is healthy as part of breaking the bonds with parents. Such anger can be shown in an antisocial way, a passive way, a healthy way, or not at all.

Redecision Therapy with Incarcerated Disturbed Youth. Leonard P Campos (October, 1995)

A write up of the author's experiences in applying redecision therapy in the group treatment of incarcerated youth in California. He describes three levels or stages of treatment work and some problems associated with it. He concludes that redecision therapy is effective for the majority of this population.

Self-Reparenting with Female Delinquents in Jail. Gloria Noriega Gayol (July, 1995)

A research project using Muriel James's self-reparenting techniques with female delinquents in a prison in Mexico. The results show a significant improvement in the teenagers' behaviour. The programme has become a part of the ongoing treatment at the juvenile jail in Mexico City.

Which Child – Which Family? Heather M. Millard Veevers (October, 1991)

The outline of a simplified form of TA theory in social work situations, specifically using injunctions and permissions to make an appropriate choice of parents for a child needing permanent placement in a new family.

Children's Groups: Integrating TA and Gestalt Perspectives. Keith Tudor (January, 1991)

Integration of TA concepts with the gestalt contact cycle to facilitate educational and therapeutic work with children in groups as a way of promoting positive mental health.

Systemic Contexts for Therapy with Children. Sharon D. Massey and Robert F Massey (October, 1989)

A case study illustrates how scripting occurs in multigenerational contexts and how to use an understanding of systemic processes in the effective treatment of children.

Systemic Contexts for Children's Scripting. Robert F. Massey (October, 1989)

Integration of experiential and social-psychological contexts provides a comprehensive understanding of scripting and a multidimensional framework for selecting appropriate therapeutic interventions with children.

A Treatment Program for the Child Referred by Parents. A. J. Elliott (April, 1988)

(This and the following seven articles formed the special themed issue of the *TAJ* on 'TA and Children', edited by Bonds-White (1988) (see Introduction)).

Description of a treatment process involving the parent-referred child and the parents, including techniques to enable the child to talk about feelings, with examples and case histories, and showing ways to help the child alter negative scripting or self-destructive patterns of thinking.

Empowering Children II: Integrating Protection into Script Prevention Work. Leonard P. Campos (April, 1988)

Discussion of the role of protection in empowering children, integrated into the permission structure of play therapy. Examples are given of how children try to empower themselves in their play and how the therapist can integrate protection with permission to change any unhealthy script formation.

An Application of the Drama Triangle to Family Therapy. Marjory Zerin (April, 1988)

A description of the use of Karpman's drama triangle to promote rapid structural change in a multi-problem blended family. This removes focus from the identified patient, generates awareness of each other's perceptions, stimulates openness, and facilitates separation and individuation through contracting for change.

Systemic Assessment and Treatment Considerations in TA Child Psychotherapy. Petruska Clarkson and Sue Fish (April, 1988)

The categorisation of difficulties exhibited by children needing psychotherapy into six major types of problems. Three sub-systems are identified, and the pros and cons of different therapeutic formats are discussed.

Systemic Integrative Psychotherapy with a Young Bereaved Girl. Charlotte Sills, Petruska Clarkson and Roland Evans (April, 1988)

A report on combining individual work with family therapy to provide brief focused therapy for a traumatised 12-year-old girl whose response to her mother's suicide stabilised and fixated the bereaved family so that the mother's loss could be avoided and denied.

Ego State Dilemma of Abused Children. Petruska Clarkson (April, 1988)

Discussion of the intrapsychic dynamics of the abused child as well as the perpetuation of Parent ego state and Child ego state responses to abuse. The psychotherapist may on occasions assume the role of the abusing parent, supported by anti-child assumptions embedded in some psychological theories, and a colluding socio-culturual environment.

The Developmental Function of Play and Its Relevance for Transactional Analysis. Diana Shmukler and Marle Friedman (April, 1988)

The experience of enough Free Child activity lays the foundation for the development of a healthy Adult. Examination of the conditions that facilitate development and expression of play in children and the importance of Winnicott's 'holding environment', relating these conditions to Berne's description of the therapy process.

A Systemic Approach to Treating Children with their Families. Robert F. Massey and Sharon Davis Massey (April, 1988)

When children are treated with their families, valuable information and additional resources for change are available. Discussion of the advantages and procedures of family therapy, and the elaboration of TA and family systems techniques for use with children.

'Mama Stop Doing MMMMM': TA in the Treatment of Autistic Children. Julia Bala (October, 1986)

The description of a general treatment plan for autistic children in a day-school setting, with phases of therapy where TA is used as an explanatory framework. A segment of therapy with an autistic child is offered to demonstrate the possibilities of applying TA with this specific population.

An Evaluation of Self-Esteem: A Family Affair. David J. Bredehoft (July, 1986)

The evaluation of the effectiveness of Illsley Clarke's eight-week programme on self-esteem with families that have adolescent children aged 11 to 19. Families were randomly assigned to the treatment or control group, and were measured for self-esteem, family adaptability, family cohesion and family conflict. The programme is presented with implications for TA research and practice.

Empowering Children: Primary Prevention of Script Formation. Leonard P. Campos (January, 1986)

The application of redecision therapy to the treatment of childhood disorders with the goal of preventing later, unhealthy script behaviour in adulthood. The author gives general intervention principles and family and child interventions designed to interrupt the unhealthy script in formation, and develops a children's life script questionnaire.

Legal Issues Surrounding Psychotherapy with Minor Clients. John E. B. Myers (July, 1983)

Discussion of several legal issues of concern to psychotherapists working with minor clients, such as informed consent to treatment, confidentiality and the minor's legal capacity to enter the therapeutic relationship. Suggestions are offered to help the clinician deal with these legal issues.

A Model of Family Development and Functioning in a TA Framework. Merle Friedman and Diana Shmukler (April, 1983)

A model derived from a systems conceptualisation. This superimposes a TA concept on a systems approach to families, describes a developmental process within functional families, and offers implications for both the understanding and treatment of problems in families.

Self-Esteem: A Family Affair. Jean Illsley Clarke (October, 1982)

An outline of an eight meeting workshop that teaches TA concepts such as stroke theory, levels of discounting and parenting skills to groups of parents and others involved in childcare.

The Feeling Wheel: A Tool for Expanding Awareness of Emotions and Increasing Spontaneity and Intimacy. Gloria Willcox (October,1982)

Based on the artistic work of the Gestalt therapist, Joseph Zinker, the author develops a feeling wheel and various games to play in order to highlight feelings. Half the sectors on the wheel are to do with the feeling of joy.

A Family Systems Context for Life-Script Analysis. James J. Magee (October, 1980)

The elaboration of four principles developed by family systems models of psychotherapy: cataloguing folklore of the extended family; recording the influence of gender and ordinal positions of siblings; recognition of any family member's tendency to assume a consistent position on the drama triangle; and identification of intergenerational and inter-individual boundaries.

TA with Children: Visual Representation Model of the Ego States. Elisabeth Kleinewiese (July, 1980)

A look at a way of using a system of visual representations with preschool and school age children. The author outlines her experiment in using a visual ego state model with forty children in a home for children from problem families in Berlin, Germany. Practical applications of the circle faces in diagnostic and therapeutic work are discussed. (Later developed into a book – see Appendix 1.)

Changing Your Own Children's Script. Patricia Emerson (April, 1979)

As TA emphasises the creation of new scripts, suggestions and examples are given for parents to assist their children in this process.

Introducing TA in the Public School System. Christine Garrison and Ronald Fischer (July, 1978)

A report of how TA concepts are successfully introduced into classrooms with children aged between 8 and 11 to improve communication between students. New ways to handle conflicts with self, others and the situation can contribute to a preventative approach to community mental health.

Developmental Principles with TA and Children. Norman E. Amundson (April, 1978)

Effective use of TA with children requires considering the principles of Erikson and Piaget. Such a perspective may lead to new developments in both theory and practice. A description of a new ego state vocabulary.

Dealing with the Rebellious Teenager. Marian Hansen (July, 1978)

The rebel is a potent, exciting person who often lacks thinking skills with which to develop a plan or direction. An outline of how, using TA approaches, including the Palmer currency wheel, these energetic youth can acquire thinking skills. The potential for changing our world and some of its antiquated systems can then be positively realised.

'Stroking up' Our Children. Mavis Klein (October, 1977)

Healthy child development can be described in terms of different kinds or amounts of parental stroking. An outline, with diagrams, of the stroking needs at each stage in the child's development.

A TA Approach to Children's Feelings. Boyd Bloomfield and Gay Goodman (July, 1976)

The report of a course to identify and describe anger, sadness, happiness and embarrassment which was taught to pre-adolescent, emotionally disturbed children in a day programme at an institute of psychiatry. The course combined TA vocabulary with a behavioural curriculum and was designed to improve communication. Maladapted behaviours decreased; the improvement is positively related to abstract reasoning ability.

A Summative Evaluation of the 'Transactional Analysis with Children' Educational Program. Norman E. Amundson and D. Donald Sawatzky (July, 1976)

A summative evaluation of a study reported in the *TAJ* is made (see below). Through teaching of the 'Transactional Analysis with Children' programme to primary school children, significant increases in self-esteem and peer acceptance were noted.

TA with Elementary School Children: A Pilot Study. Norman E. Edmundson (July, 1975)

An outline of the author's own TA programme for work with children aged 8 to 11, which he developed and piloted with nine year olds. The article also outlines his criterion for research.

The Effects of a TA Group on Emotionally Disturbed School-Age Boys. Tim J. Arnold and Richard L. Simpson (July, 1975)

An investigation of the influence of TA on boys aged 10 to 16 who were described as behaviourally disordered or socially maladjusted. Numerous positive results are reported but the

authors suggest that more research of this sort is needed to justify the use of TA to educational professionals.

TA Work with Child Abuse. Rita Justice and Blair Justice (January, 1975)

A report on pioneering group work using TA with couples where one or both parents had been legally charged with child abuse. The results show high levels of success in preventing further abuse and improving relational satisfaction. In most cases children who had been removed from the home were returned on the recommendation of the authors.

Children's TA Glossary. Kathryn J. Hallett (October, 1973)

Amusing and revealing anecdotes of what children from TA families come out with in conversation.

Articles published in the *Transactional Analysis Bulletin* (1970–1962)

(The *Transactional Analysis Bulletin* was the predecessor of the *TAJ*; its issues are unavailable except through second-hand bookshops and internet booksellers. A volume of selected articles, which contains only one of the articles noted here – Steiner's fairy tale – was published by the TA Press in 1976 and is now also out of print.)

A Fairy Tale. Claude Steiner (1970)

An original draft of what became the *A Warm Fuzzy Tale* (see Appendix 1).

Don't be Close: A Note on the Replacement of a 'Witch-Mother' Message in Psychotic Five-year-olds. James R. Allen (1970)

The write up of research involving four boys in which experimental use of sensory and perceptual isolation had different effects. The author puts a TA perspective on the research and draws some important conclusions about P_1 messages.

TA and Family Counselling. John Cooper, John Dusay, Gordon Haiberg and Dorothy Jongeward (1969)

An interesting report on verbal discussions about different perspectives regarding family therapy from various practitioners.

Transactional Analysis with Children: The Initial Session. Muriel James (1969)

A detailed description of how the author structures the first session, including layout of the room, questions to ask, contracts to make and homework to do between sessions.

TA with Children and Adolescents. Sydney B. Mannel, William Piehl and Mary Edwards (1968)

Discussion of various approaches to therapeutic work with children and adolescents, with practical ideas and results.

Children's Groups. Jacqui Schiff (1966)

A brief description of groupwork with children aged from infancy to adolescence, separating groups into behaviour disorders and psychiatric disorders. The author includes her views on how small children perceive strokes and the Parent, Adult, Child ego state model.

Children Raised with Structural Analysis. David Kupfer (1962)

After 18 months in a TA group, a 30 year old single woman decides to acquaint her three small daughters with the structural analysis of ego states. Various anecdotes of the results are included in this fascinating article, showing children's insights into TA principles.

Signs and Symptoms of Abuse

Mica Douglas

Abuse encompasses physical abuse, emotional abuse, sexual abuse and neglect. Each form of abuse has both physical and behavioural indicators.

Physical abuse

Physical indicators

Unexplained bruises, welts, lacerations, abrasions:

- On face, lips, mouth, ears
- On torso, back, buttocks, thighs
- In various stages of healing
- Clustering, forming regular patterns
- In the reflected shape of an article such as a belt, or buckle
- On several different surface areas
- In the form of bite or fingernail marks.

Unexplained burns, e.g.

- Cigarette or cigar burns, especially on soles, buttocks, palms or back
- 'Immersion' burns where hands, feet, buttocks or body have been forcibly immersed in very hot water
- Rope burns on arms, legs, neck or torso
- May be patterned – from an electrical burner, an iron, etc.

Unexplained (multiple or spiral) fractures

- To skull, nose, facial structure
- In various stages of healing

Behavioural indicators

- Flinching when approached or touched
- Reluctance to change clothes for physical education lessons or swimming
- Wariness of adult contacts
- Being difficult to comfort
- Crying or irritability

- Apprehension when other children cry
- Being frightened of parents or carers
- Being afraid to go home
- Rebelliousness in adolescence
- Apathy
- Depression
- Poor peer relationships
- Panic in response to pain
- Includes behavioural extremes: aggressiveness, impulsiveness, withdrawal, compliance.

Emotional abuse

Physical indicators

- Failure to thrive
- Delays in physical development or progress

Behavioural indicators

- Sucking, biting, rocking
- Anti-social, destructive
- Sleep disorders
- Inhibition in play
- Compliant, passive, aggressive, demanding
- Inappropriately adult or regressed
- Impairment of intellectual, emotional, social or behavioural development
- Rapid swings of behaviour

Sexual abuse

Physical indicators

- Difficulty in walking, sitting down
- Stained or bloody underclothing
- Pain or itching in genital area
- Bruising, bleeding, injury to external genitalia, vagina and/or anal areas
- Vaginal discharge
- Wetting and soiling
- Excessive crying
- Sickness
- Pregnancy
- Sexually transmitted diseases.

Behavioural indicators

- Bizarre, sophisticated or age-inappropriate sexual behaviour or knowledge
- Promiscuity
- Sudden changes in behaviour
- Running away from home
- Wariness of adults
- Feeling different from other children
- Unusual avoidance of touch
- Reporting of assault
- Substance abuse e.g. glue sniffing or misuse of drugs
- Emotional withdrawal through lack of trust in adults
- Over-compliance with requests of others
- Frequent complaints of unexplained abdominal pains
- Eating problems
- Sleep disturbances
- Poor peer relationships.

Neglect

Physical Indicators

- Constant hunger
- Poor hygiene
- Inappropriate dress
- Consistent lack of supervision for long periods, especially in dangerous activities
- Unattended physical problems or medical needs
- Abandonment.

Behavioural indicators

- Begging
- Stealing
- Not being collected on time from playgroup or school on a regular basis
- Constant fatigue, listlessness.

TA Assessment Sheets

Anita Mountain

Intake Sheet

Name

Male/Female   **DoB**

Ethnic origin   **Religion**

Legal status

Reason for intake:

Key worker's understanding of reason for intake:

Young person's understanding of reason for intake:

Observations

This part of the form is completed by the key worker after they have had time to interact with the young person. Please complete this within the first week of admission.

Primary ego state functioning of the young person (structural model):
(Please tick or draw ego state portrait)

Parent ego state

Adult ego state

Child ego state

Evidence for this: including differences, if any, when with peers or adults

Egogram: (complete in red and green pen where possible)

−NP	−CP	+NP	+CP	AA	+FC	+AC	−FC	−AC

Karpman drama triangle:

This young person seems to be mainly in: (please tick)

Persecutor   Rescuer   Victim

Basic life position on the OK Corral: (please circle)

I am Not OK	I am OK
You Are OK	**You Are OK**
(one down position)	*(healthy position)*
I am Not OK	**I am OK**
You Are Not OK	**You Are Not OK**
(hopeless position)	*(one up position)*

Evidence for this:

Family constellation: (parents, siblings, significant others)

Fostering history: e.g. number of placements, reason for breakdown, etc.

Special relationships: any relationships which the young person wishes to maintain whilst at [the home] e.g. with relatives, friends, significant others

General comments: e.g. suicide attempts – including how attempts were made; substance abuse – including the types of drugs if known (including alcohol); other at-risk behaviour

Positive Parenting Strategy Guidance Notes

Diane Hoyer

These guidance notes for the therapist are designed to encourage creative and reflective thinking on the issues. Record the responses of all parties, note relationship dynamics, and differing perspectives.

List the top 5 'day to day' parenting issues

Encourage parties to be specific about the issues, rather than stating 'tea-time', or 'rainy days'. For example, what precedes the behaviour, whom they deem to be 'responsible', etc.

Focus on the Child

What understanding parents or carers have of developmental milestones and needs, etc. Have good literature to hand (e.g. Levin, 1974; Illsley-Clarke, 1978/1998). Encourage parents and carers to actively seek out information to inform their judgements.

Do parents and carers understand the principle of 'delay'? Discuss attitudes and values relating to competition, failure, labelling, etc.

Discuss trauma as a concept, including vulnerability, resilience, and temperament. Emphasise the dynamic nature of trauma responses i.e. "We can move on from this". Explore attitudes to scapegoating, blaming, etc., and whether there is any investment in perpetuating the trauma.

Introduce the concept of development being a collection of information and experiences for 'filing'. Are the 'papers' in good order, can the knowledge or skill be found when it is needed.

Do parents and carers value the communications of the child? Is behaviour seen as a form of communication? NB: As we grow we learn lots of ways of getting needs met, some more healthy than others; at times of stress we may revert to previous methods.

Can parents and carers accurately anticipate, or identify the needs of the child? Ask about indicators of tiredness, anger, anxiety, fear, and ill-health.

Do parents and carers have 'usual' sayings or phrases that they use to reassure, discipline, encourage, or gain the child's attention? Are these appropriate to the child's current needs?

Can parents and carers see the impact of a life-time of positive or negative responses to the child, and the effect this has on aspects of development? Discuss examples such as not being encouraged to think for yourself, or being teased for getting things wrong.

Focus on the Adult

Recognise the ego state of parents and carers as they respond to the task or question. Do they engage with the process, discount, avoid, or sabotage it? Continually reflect your observations during sessions to the parents. It is more important and potent to work with the presenting process than to complete the questions.

Make regular 'checks' on whether the task is being understood.

Reflect tensions between the observable needs of the parents and carers, and those of the child, e.g. "It seems hard for you to accept that those actions don't help your child, as if the 'little you' inside feels hurt, rejected, or scared". Give affirmations and encouragement bearing in mind permission, protection and potency.

Utilise adult awareness as often as possible to anchor the work in the most resourceful part of the parents' or carers' own filing system.

Give specific examples of useful phrases, gestures, postures, and voice tones for positive parenting, and set tasks that involve practising them.

Where possible make the work fun and stimulating, 'Catch the kid' in them.

References

Illsley-Clarke, J. (1998) *Self-esteem: A Family Affair*. Center City, MN: Winston Press/Hazelden. (Original work published 1978)

Levin, P. (1974) *Becoming the Way We Are*. Menlo Park, CA: Trans Pubs.

Psychotherapy with Children: Principles, Aims and Guidelines for Training

Psychotherapy with Children

Principles, Aims and Guidelines for Training

UK COUNCIL FOR PSYCHOTHERAPY

PART I: Principles

A training in psychotherapy with children should be such that any accredited practitioner, in any modality, should be able to justify a decision to undertake psychotherapy with a child and be able to show how using the approach of their particular modality would competently address the needs of that child at that time. All trainings should be consistent with 'UKCP Psychotherapy Training Standards: Policy and Principles' and 'Psychotherapy with Children: UKCP Guidelines for Training', incorporating the specific Generic Learning Outcomes for Psychotherapy with Children as outlined within this document.

2. OVERALL AIMS:

2.1 These guidelines are informed by the recognition that psychotherapy with children differs from that with adults, and that training organisations must have a separate set of guidelines and a specific curriculum that meets the different needs of these client groups, which must be subjected to separate assessment by the Section or accrediting organisation. These guidelines are based on the Generic Training Outcomes for UKCP Psychotherapy Training Standards for work with adults, but additionally incorporate particular and specific training outcomes relating to psychotherapy with children. All such courses should be subject to the normal course accreditation and approval process of the Sections and to regular monitoring and review processes. Sections may also wish to develop additional Section-specific Training Outcomes for Psychotherapy with Children, reflecting the values and principles, and the methods of working, of the modalities represented within that Section.

2.2 The intention is to create a framework for trainings that is flexible and can encompass the different modalities within the UKCP whilst providing a sound basis for good practice for psychotherapy with children. In all cases, the student/trainee will be expected to demonstrate a depth understanding of child development and of the nature of psychotherapy with children within the modality which they are practising, to be able to locate this within the wider context of understanding of other psychotherapeutic approaches to work with children within different sectors and disciplines; and to practice skills of psychotherapy with children in a range of settings and contexts appropriate to their modality. They should acquire a depth appreciation of the particular dynamics and practical issues involved in psychotherapeutic work with children in different settings, and the ethical and legal issues concerned.

2.3 The onus is upon the Training Organisation to demonstrate the means by which the curriculum and assessment of trainees will achieve these learning outcomes, and upon the Section or Accrediting Organisations to provide the framework for supporting the unique characteristics of particular modalities. These guidelines are intended to apply to full trainings in psychotherapy with children, but also have application to shorter courses intended to build on prior trainings eg in working with adults or in other professional arenas.

2.4 Training Organisations, Accrediting Organisations and Sections should also have specific Ethical Guidelines and Codes of Practice relating to psychotherapy with children to which all those accredited on the basis of these trainings will be expected to adhere.

3. Guiding Principles for Trainings in Psychotherapy with Children:

The guidelines for trainings in psychotherapy with children additionally are informed by overriding principles which give recognition to:

3.1 The child's individual human rights, including the right to self-determination, within the reasonable constraints of their needs for safety, protection and care in keeping with the law relating to Child Protection and rights of parents and carers.

3.2 Given the right support and conditions, the capacity for the child to access impeded developmental impulses and re-establish the potential for psychological well-being.

3.3 The importance of considering the experience of children and young people in the context of the overall matrix of their lives. The child's experience cannot be considered in isolation from their relationship with significant others who may continue to play a part in determining their future

3.4 The need to recognise the value and validity of the child's experience and to recognise the creativity and resilience of infants and children in responding to the circumstances of their lives as best they can, within their developmental capabilities and emotional resources, even where this manifests in ways that present challenge and difficulty in the adult world; to recognise that the child alone is not 'the problem'.

3.5 The particular dependency and vulnerability of the infant, child and young person, emotionally, physically, psychologically and spiritually. The particular nature of the child's experience that characterises the several developmental stages and tasks involved in growing up into mature relationship in the world

3.6 The multiple implications of the child's position in relation to the world, and the centrality of family, social, cultural, religious/spiritual and political systems which frame the reality of their lives.

3.7 The need to support children in developing the skills and resources they need to deal realistically with the circumstances of their lives, as well as to emerge more fully with their own potentialities and to build trust.

3.8 The importance of interdisciplinary dialogue and exploration.

PART II: Generic Learning out comes for Trainings in Psychotherapy with Children

Knowledge Base

4. KNOWLEDGE AND UNDERSTANDING

The trainee will be expected to be able to:

4.1 formulate a model of childhood development and psychotherapeutic change within their chosen modality, with reference to other major modalities

4.2 demonstrate a sound knowledge of the developmental stages of infancy, childhood and adolescence with particular reference to the psychological, existential, cognitive, developmental and relational tasks, and the different needs and experiences of children and young people at particular stages in their development. This will be underpinned by appropriate levels of experiential knowledge and the development of observational skills.

4.3 demonstrate an advanced and detailed level of understanding of the theoretical and clinical principles of psychotherapy with children within the modality they are studying, against an overall historical and critical perspective on the development of psychotherapy and psychotherapeutic work with children. Trainees should additionally have an understanding of the principles of adult psychotherapy and be able to articulate this understanding insofar as it impinges on work with the adults who form part of the child's world including the therapist themselves.

4.4 formulate concepts of serious mental illness - not only in infants, children and young people, but also in adults as this impinges on children's lives; formulate an understanding of assessment, diagnosis, management and therapeutic intervention as it relates to the modality within which the student is training and with reference to other major frameworks for assessment.

4.5 develop and awareness of and alertness to recognise the range and continuum of special educational needs, of physical and learning disabilities which together affect a significant number of children and how these needs and disabilities may present specific challenges to the therapist in establishing an effective therapeutic relationship; be able to identify and consult with appropriate professionals who can assist in the assessment of suitability of certain therapeutic practices for children with specific needs or disabilities and who can advise on necessary modifications where appropriate; be aware of the potential limitations of one's own modality in relation to psychotherapeutic work with children manifesting specific disabilities or special educational needs.

4.6 demonstrate a general level of understanding of other major models and approaches to psychotherapeutic work with children.

4.7 demonstrate an understanding of the effects of psychological trauma, neglect, sexual and physical and emotional abuse and how these manifest; formulate a theoretical framework for understanding and evaluating memory in relation to traumatic events, and the impact of such events on the psychological development and behaviour of the child.

4.8 show an ability to understand and evaluate research methods

relevant to all models of psychotherapy with children, and critiques of evidence-based research within models. Be aware of the importance of keeping up to date with innovations in psychotherapy with children, parents and families, and the evaluation of these.

4.9 demonstrate a knowledge of family and cultural dynamics including the roles which may be attributed to children in general as well as the roles which may be constructed with this child in particular and how within these contexts of family and culture there will be resources as well as restraints which may contribute significantly towards the child's past, present and future development

4.10 demonstrate an understanding of the role and involvement of education, social services, health services and other public service sectors, and the implications of these for the dynamics of the psychotherapeutic work in different settings.

4.11 demonstrate an understanding about other work done with children and families within other sectors and disciplines, and the role of inter-disciplinary working in different contexts.

4.12 demonstrate a sound knowledge of Child Protection procedures and guidance, the legislative framework relating to children, and the ethical issues involved relating to safety and well-being of the child or young person, and to boundary issues and confidentiality. To show a practical knowledge of special procedures in the settings within which the work is undertaken (eg statementing for special needs).

4.13 demonstrate a sound understanding of the issues relating to the use of medicines in the mental health treatment of children (eg where there is a diagnosis of ADHD), and an ability to engage in multi-disciplinary reflection on the validity or otherwise of such treatments and the ethical considerations involved

5. ANALYSIS AND APPLICATION

The trainee will be expected to be able to:

5.1 formulate an understanding of how children function in the various contexts of their lives, including an understanding of individual child development and psychotherapeutic change, using the theoretical approach of their chosen modality or approach to psychotherapy with children.

5.2 also formulate an understanding of adult functioning within this framework, especially as it relates to family dynamics and other interactions which impinge upon the child.

5.3 use the above model to analyse complex situations and conceptualise a range of psychotherapeutic interventions, acknowledging areas of incomplete knowledge, inconsistency or uncertainty in order to retain flexibility of clinical intervention.

5.4 demonstrate a knowledge of specific skills and approaches related to working with children of particular age-groups or special characteristics which will form the core of the psychotherapist's practice.

5.5 be able to work with parents, carers and other relevant adults in ways which make use of their psychotherapeutic understanding and which recognises the significance of the psychotherapeutic relationship whether or not this is considered a central vehicle for change.

5.6 demonstrate a depth understanding of the particular power dynamics and depth relational issues involved in working with children and young people, including an appreciation of issues relating to transference and counter-transference (or alternative formulations corresponding to different modalities), even where the relationship is not seen as the primary vehicle for the work.

5.7 this will include a particular understanding of the dynamics or interactive realities relating to the place of the child or the young person in the family and in the other contexts of their lives.

5.8 demonstrate a capacity to analyse the impact of the role and involvement of other agencies or individuals, and the implications of this in particular settings.

5.9 demonstrate an awareness of and sensitivity to prejudice; show an ability to respond openly and appropriately to issues of race, gender, age, sexual preference, class, disability, and ethnic, spiritual/religious and cultural difference.

6. SYNTHESIS AND CREATIVITY

The trainee will be expected to be able to

6.1 use a high level of theoretical knowledge to develop hypotheses and generate psychotherapeutic responses to clinical problems relating to psychotherapy with children

6.2 show a willingness to acknowledge the limitations of this and to retain appropriate flexibility and creativity in psychotherapeutic intervention

7. EVALUATION

The trainee will be expected to be able to:

7.1 use critical reflection and undertake ongoing supervision with an experienced supervisor with extensive relevant experience to assess and report on their own and others' work with clients/patients. (see para. 10.3 below)

7.2 critique the chosen model of psychotherapy, assess its limitations and compare it with alternative approaches, drawing on evaluative and evidence-based research and clinical experience.

7.3 critically evaluate the implications of issues of culture, religion, race, gender, sexual orientation and disability in psychotherapy.

Person Skills

8. PSYCHOTHERAPEUTIC AND PERSONAL SKILLS

The trainee will be expected to be able to:

8.1 assess clients/patients for suitability for their chosen psychotherapeutic modality/approach, and justify the decision to offer to undertake psychotherapy with a child or young person in the context of the child's total situation and the needs of that child.

8.2 pick up and differentiate indications of deeper disturbance or areas of specialist need that cannot be addressed within the modality being practised or in the setting in which the work is being offered.

8.3 negotiate appropriate contracts and boundaries with all parties concerned.

8.4 establish and work with a psychotherapeutic relationship congruent with the chosen modality of approach and the level of intensity of the work being offered. Specific skills should be offered which relate to working with the children of particular age-groups or special characteristics, needs or disabilities which will form the core of the psychotherapist's practice.

8.5 this will include skills in communicating and establishing relationships with children at a range of age-levels, working with parents and children, with families, or with other parties involved, as appropriate within the modality offered and the settings for the work. Irrespective of modality, some skills in working with parents and families, and with other significant parties should be developed.

8.6 understand the child's need to be able to express feelings, thoughts and beliefs in the context of a safe and secure environment which includes the therapist being able to accept their expression in a non-judgemental and non-prejudicial way.

8.6 formulate and apply appropriate psychotherapeutic processes, make appropriate psychotherapeutic interventions and manage appropriate endings.

8.7 demonstrate a capacity for appropriate participation in inter-disciplinary working, and managing the relationships involved in working with children in different settings.

8.9 use an advanced level of theoretical knowledge to develop hypotheses and generate psychotherapeutic responses to clinical situations.

8.10 synthesise their own personal integration of theory and clinical practice.

8.11 develop a capacity for reflecting on one's own process in relation to working with children, through an appropriate combination of personal enquiry, experiential work and supervision.

9. SELF-APPRAISAL, REFLECTION ON PRACTICE

The trainee will be expected to be able to:

9.1 critically and consistently reflect on psychotherapeutic process and on their own functioning in order to improve practice.

9.2 engage with their own psychotherapeutic process and self-development at a depth congruent with the work being undertaken, and to a level that enables the practitioner to develop a high level of insight into their own issues as they arise in the work.

9.3 demonstrate a method of understanding, recognising and responding to transferential and counter-transferential issues (or alternative formulations corresponding to other modalities) in a manner congruent with the approach practised and with the context in which the work is being done.

9.4 have a realistic appreciation of the value and limits of the chosen psychotherapeutic approach and of the psychotherapist's own capabilities; and to be able to refer to other resources as required.

9.5 demonstrate that regular on-going supervision and continuing professional development (CPD) are part of being a psychotherapist, and to appreciate the particular CPD and supervisory requirements for psychotherapeutic work with children, which should be appropriate to the context, specialisation offered, and level of intensity of the work being undertaken including an understanding of why on-going supervision is necessary in working with children..

10. PLANNING AND MANAGEMENT OF LEARNING/PRACTICE

The trainee will be able to

10 1 demonstrate the ability to autonomously use resources for learning

10.2 engage in appropriate placements and observational work required within the specific training curriculum in order to develop observational skills and awareness.

10.3 prepare for and make effective use of supervision appropriate to the context, specialisation offered and level of intensity of the work being undertaken, with a supervisor who has extensive experience of psychotherapeutic work with children or extensive relevant skills and a background of relevant experience with children. This should include the supervisor's understanding of the effects on the child of any adult psychopathology which may be present in the child's family or social environment and which may be directly impacting on them

10.4 identify, clarify, assess and manage resolution of most clinical problems.

11. COMMUNICATION AND PRESENTATION

The trainee will be expected to be able to:

11.1 engage confidently and respectfully in appropriately professional communication with others involved in the life of the child

11.2 present their clinical work for discussion and mutual learning in the context of others who are also undertaking psychotherapeutic work with children

12. INTERACTIVE PROFESSIONAL AND GROUP SKILLS

The trainee will be expected to be able to:

12.1 negotiate and handle conflict confidently and respectfully. This will include ability to relate not only to children and young people, but also to parents, teachers and other professionals, or others with whom they are required to have dealings who may be dismissive, seek to break boundaries or otherwise challenge the psychotherapeutic space

12.2 work co-operatively with others within the reasonable boundaries of the agreed psychotherapeutic contract.

12.3 where this is part of the approach, work effectively with psychotherapy groups and/or with co-therapists or other professionals; and handling consultations with family members or other interested parties.

12.4 have a clear appreciation of the place of the psychotherapeutic work in the context of the overall well-being and care of the child. To have a realistic appreciation of the value and limits of the chosen psychotherapeutic approach, and of appropriate indicators for referral.

Context of Practice

13. CHARACTERISTICS OF PROFESSIONAL SETTING AND PRACTICAL MANAGEMENT SKILLS

The trainee will be expected to be able to demonstrate:

13.1 awareness of the setting in which psychotherapeutic work with children takes place, and awareness of the need to hold boundaries against challenge (e.g. confidentiality, privacy, non-disruption, dedicated space and time-tabling). Given the crucial significance of the school setting for children, it is particularly important for those trainees who are likely to be working within or closely with the education system to develop an understanding of the specific social contexts of the primary, secondary and special schools; and of the challenges that teachers and support workers face and the importance of the therapist establishing good liaison and working relationships in the interest of appropriate referral, attendance at sessions and confidentiality.

13.2 ability to adapt the approach or take innovative action if deemed necessary in particular circumstances where not to do so would result in the psychotherapy being curtailed or undermined to the disadvantage or damage to the child. In such cases, steps taken to preserve the value of the psychotherapeutic work should not undermine the integrity of the psychotherapeutic approach (this relates in particular to the circumstances which might prevail when for example undertaking work in a school or another non-psychotherapeutic setting)

13.3 awareness at the outset of the need to assess what might not be possible in a particular professional setting

13.4 awareness of boundary issues, including confidentiality, in specific settings and in relation to the particular obligations relating to psychotherapy with children.

13.5 a capacity to handle complex, unpredictable and specialised situations.

13.6 an ability to understand and handle contracts between child/school/parents and other professionals; manage the dynamics and role relationships within different organisational settings, and professional relationships within and between professional teams and in multi-disciplinary settings where this applies.

13.7 demonstrate an understanding of systems of referral (policies, criteria and processes, and motivation for referral) in different settings and a readiness to take responsibility within this area.

14. RESPONSIBILITY

The trainee is expected to demonstrate

14.1 autonomy in professional practice

14.2 responsibility for self-monitoring including the appropriate use of supervision (see 9.5, 7.1 and10.3 above)

14.3 awareness of particular issues and procedures relevant to the professional practice of psychotherapy with children

15. ETHICAL UNDERSTANDING

The trainees should be able to formulate the general ethical principles and value base for working with children within their chosen modality, and to show how this relates to the overall principles formulated within the UKCP Guiding Principles for psychotherapy with children outlined above and the UKCP Ethical Guidelines. They should be able to demonstrate the practical application of these principles through their adherence to the specific ethical guidelines and codes of practice of their particular training organisation, modality or Section relating to psychotherapeutic work with children.

The trainee will be expected to be able to demonstrate:

15.1 awareness of the ethical and professional practice responsibilities of being a psychotherapist working with children.

15.2 awareness of and ability to manage the implications of the particular ethical issues and dilemmas relating to work with children and young people in the particular contexts within which the work is being undertaken, including a recognition of the child or young person's right to confidentiality and self-determination in the context of the complementary right of care and protection and the parental right in relation to decisions about their chilights.d. This would reflect the legal framework of parental

15.3 an awareness of the ethical issues and multi-disciplinary implications of the use of medicines in relation to the mental health treatment of children

15.4 a sound knowledge of legal issues relating to psychotherapy with children, and of other issues relating to the safety, wellbeing and protection of the child.

15.5 ability to work proactively with others to formulate potential solutions.

15.6 ability to predict and manage consequences of applied solutions.

Submitted by Laura Donington and Anne Murray
To the Training Standards Committee
December 2003

Throughout the document the term "child" and "children" will be used and should be taken to encompass all ages from birth to age of 18.

About the Editor and Contributors

Keith Tudor is a qualified social worker, a qualified and registered psychotherapist, group psychotherapist and facilitator. He has worked for 30 years in the helping professions in a number of settings, for 20 of which he has been involved in transactional analysis, and is now a Teaching and Supervising Transactional Analyst. He has an independent, private practice in Sheffield offering therapy to children and young people as well as adults, supervision, training and consultancy. He is a Director of Temenos, also based in Sheffield where he is Director of Education and Training and of its MSc in Person-Centred Psychotherapy and Counselling. He runs a specialist supervision group, comprising TA practitioners working with children and young people. He is a widely published author in the field of social policy, mental health and psychotherapy including over twenty chapters and articles on TA; and seven books, including *Group Counselling* (Sage, 1999), and (editor) *Transactional Approaches to Brief Therapy* (Sage, 2002). He is the series editor of *Advancing Theory in Therapy* (published by Routledge), and an Honorary Fellow in the School of Health, Liverpool John Moores University. His website is: www.keithtudor.com

James R. Allen, MD, FRCP(C), MPH is Professor of Psychiatry and Behavioural Sciences and Rainbolt Family Chair in Child Psychiatry at the University of Oklahoma Health Sciences Center, Oklahoma City, Oklahoma. He is the current President of the International Transactional Analysis Association.

Chris Davidson has been involved with groups of varying kinds for over 20 years and with the former Group Relations Training Association. He is a Provisional Teaching and Supervising Transactional Analyst (Organisational). He works in a variety of organisations and has a range of training expertise, including group work, team development, and communication skills. For the past six years he has worked full-time for Mountain Associates.

Roger Day is a Provisional Teaching and Supervising Transactional Analyst, a Certified Transactional Analyst and a UKCP registered psychotherapist, experienced in working with children and families. He is also a Certified Play Therapist, and a registered counsellor (UKRC Healthcare Faculty). He lives and works in Romania, where he provides consultancy, training and supervision in working therapeutically with children. He has edited various books and magazines, including the Institute of Transactional Analysis's magazine *TA UK*. He is the author of many articles and eleven books, including four children's novels in the Pressure Points series and, with his wife Christine, *Help! I'm Growing Up: A Child/Parent Guide to Sex and Puberty*. His latest book for children, *Being Mad, Being Glad* (Raintree, 2004) is an illustrated book on emotions for children aged 5 to 8. His website is: www.therapyinromania.org.uk and his email address is: romaniaretreat@hotmail.com

Kath Dentith MSc (TA Psychotherapy), DIPSW, Certified Transactional Analyst and UKCP Registered Psychotherapist. Kath operates a private practice in South Manchester and offers therapy to individuals, couples, families and adolescents. She is a registered Social Worker and has worked across statutory and voluntary social work services. Kath is currently in the employment of a voluntary childcare agency. Her role involves therapeutic work with families, parents and children experiencing complex difficulties. She provides counselling to young people in a number of inner city comprehensive schools. Kath continues to develop a multi-faceted approach in order to offer therapeutic services in a wide range of settings.

Mica Douglas CQSW, CTA(P), PTSTA(P), MA in Social Work, MSc TA Psychotherapy, provides therapy for children and adults and supervises therapists, social workers and foster parents. Mica is Director of Fostering at By the Bridge, Independent Fostering Organisation, from where she runs the first TA-based, university-accredited Certificate in Therapeutic Fostering for social workers, foster parents and managers. Mica is currently writing a book on understanding difficult behaviour displayed by children with complex or abusive backgrounds. She has worked with people since 1989 as a social worker, therapist and manager of therapeutic services to children and foster parents.

Maria Assunta Giusti has a degree in philosophy from Perugia University and a degree in psychology from Rome University. She trained in TA at the Istituto di Analisi Transazionale in Rome and became a Certified Transactional Analyst in 1990 and a Provisional Teaching and Supervising Transactional Analyst in 1997. For the last twenty years she has worked as a psychotherapist in a rehabilitation institute with patients with psychotic, autistic and borderline disorders. She has used TA in individual and group settings with both children and adults. She is the author of three books on working with children: *La Trans-formazione Possibile* (The Possible Trans-Formation; Del Cerro, 1996), *Analisi Transazionale e Psicoterapia* (Transactional Analysis and Child Psychotherapy; Istituto Torinese di Analisi Transazionale, 2005), and *La Piccola Principessa* (The Little Princess; Istituto di Analisi Transazionale/Associazione Italiana di Analisi Transazionale, 2006), and of various articles published in the international *Transactional Analysis Journal*, and in *Neopsiche*, and *Psicologia e Salute*. She teaches and supervises at the Specialist Psychotherapy School in Turin and Naples, and for Integrative TA Counseling courses in Rome and Arezzo.

Diane Hoyer has been employed by the National Society for the Prevention of Cruelty to Children (NSPCC) since 1989, working with children who have experienced abuse, and their families. This has included undertaking assessments of need and risk; therapeutic work with parents and key adults; development of therapeutic work packages; counselling adult and child survivors of sexual abuse; play therapy with children who have experienced abuse; assessment and treatment of children with harmful sexual behaviours; and training and development work with other professionals. Alongside this she has worked within a Social Services Access Team, in a specialist unit for adult survivors of sexual abuse, and, independently, as a trainer and consultant. She is qualified, having a NNEB, Diploma in Transactional Analysis (Counselling), PGDip/MA in Non-Directive Play Therapy (York), DipSW (Open University) and AASW (York).

Laura Hyatt is a qualified and registered social worker. She has worked with children, young people and families for over 15 years in statutory and voluntary agencies undertaking child protection, children in need, permanence, and therapeutic work. She has trained in transactional analysis psychotherapy and runs her own counselling, psychotherapy, training, life coaching, and supervision business. Laura also works as a training and development officer for a local authority fostering service, and assesses social work degree students on placement. She holds a BSc Honours degree in applied social sciences, and a Diploma in Psychology (both from the Open University), a Diploma in Social Work, a Diploma in Life Coaching, and is a graduate member of the British Psychological Society. Laura can be contacted by email on l.hyatt@btinternet.com

Paul Kellett MSc Psychotherapy (Middlesex), MSc Psychology (Open University), Clin.Dip. Transactional Analysis Psychotherapy (Metanoia), CTA(P), is a MBACP accredited counsellor and UKCP registered psychotherapist. He spent two years as the Counselling Service Coordinator for *Off The Record*, a young person's counselling service in Croydon and currently runs a private practice in South London. He is an associate therapist with the Project for Advice, Counselling and Education, which provides support services to sexual minority groups, an affiliate with Ceridian, an EAP, and a member of the Directory of The Pink Therapists. He has published articles, reviews and letters in *Transactions*, the *EATA Newsletter*, *The Script*, and the *Transactional Analysis Journal* of which he is currently on the editorial board. He can be contacted through www.paulkellett.net

Jean Lancashire is a MSc in Transactional Analysis Psychotherapy, PTSTA(P), CTA(P), Dip.SW and a UKCP registered psychotherapist. Her main employment is with Foster Care Associates (FCA), a national foster care agency working with foster families, adults and children, in which she provides training and consultation for the staff and foster carers. In this role she specialises in working with children and young people who have complex emotional needs relating to attachment, separation, loss and behavioural difficulties, and who are 'looked after' by the Local Authority. She also has a private practice and offers supervision to people working with adults, children and young people.

Anita Mountain MSc, Certified Transactional Analyst and Teaching and Supervising Transactional Analyst (both in both Organisational and Psychotherapy specialities) has a background in youth and community work. For over ten years Anita was the consultant to a Social Services children and young people's home. During that time she trained all the staff in transactional analysis and offered consultation and support to staff regarding their work with young people. She has written a number of articles for the *Transactional Analysis Journal* and had two publications produced by the National Youth Bureau, now the National Youth Agency. Her most recent publication is *The Space Between: Bridging the Gap Between Workers and Young People* (Russell House Publishing, 2004). Currently she works nationally and internationally in large and small organisations, undertaking a range of organisational developmental processes. Anita is the founding partner of Mountain Associates, which she runs with her partner Chris Davidson. Together they also facilitate open Developmental TA training programmes. Contact: www.mountain-associates.co.uk or email: ta@mountain-associates.co.uk

Dolores Munari Poda is a Teaching and Supervising Transactional Analyst in private practice in Turin and Milan, Italy. She works with children and parents and also teaches Transactional Analysis child therapy in Milan (at the Scuola di Specializzazione in Psicoterapia), Turin (at the Istituto Torinese di TA), and Padua (at the Scuola di Specializzazione in Psicologia Clinica dell'Università di Padova). She is the author of five books on working with children: *La Storia Centrale* (The Central Story); *L'Adolescenza Accade* (Adolescence Happens), *Piccole Persone, Piccoli Copioni* (Little People, Little Scripts); and *La Stanza dei Bambini* (The Children's Room), all published by La Vita Felice, 2003, and *Il Bambino Curzio* (A Child named Curzio, Treni in Transito, 2003). She has also had articles published in *Rivista Italiana di Analisi Transazionale, Quaderni di Psicologia, Analisi Transazionale e Scienze Umane* and the international *Transactional Analysis Journal*.

Marie Naughton is a UKCP registered psychotherapist working in private practice in Manchester. For the past seven years she has run a counselling service in an inner-city girls' high school. In her former life as an educator she worked for over twenty years as a teacher in schools and university and she now works as a freelance trainer and supervisor, contributing to training programmes in the UK and abroad. She is currently studying for a Masters degree in Ethnicity and Racism. She likes to spend time gardening and walking the dog with her family in the beautiful countryside of the north of England.

Trudi Newton is a Teaching and Supervising Transactional Analyst in the Educational field of application. She has over 40 years experience of working with young people and adults as a social worker, youth leader, counsellor, educator, trainer and consultant. She now specialises in supervision and training consultancy for educational behaviour support services, adult learning programmes and coaching development. She has a number of publications in print, including, with **Rosemary Napper** *TACTICS* (TA Resources, 2000), which looks in detail at the process of learning and teaching. She is a co-director of the Cambridge Institute for Transactional Analysis, and works locally, nationally and internationally. She has recently directed a four-year training programme for educators and school psychologists in St Petersburg, Russia, and is currently collaborating with a TA psychotherapist in undertaking research for the European Association for Transactional Analysis into relational aspects of adult learning.

Pete Shotton is a certified transactional analyst and Provisional Teaching and Supervising Transactional Analyst in both the education and psychotherapy fields. He has worked in education settings since 1978, as a subject teacher, a special needs co-ordinator, a head of year, and a local authority advisory and support teacher. From 1999 to the summer of 2007 he established and led a pastoral mentoring support team in an inner-city boys' high school in Manchester. He provides training on inclusion in education to PGCE teacher training students, and has recently taken up a part-time role providing education support to a foster-care agency. He is also a partner in a psychotherapy, supervision and training practice.

Graeme Summers has over 20 years experience of coaching and training people working in a diverse range of contexts including corporate, statutory and voluntary organisations. He has an honours degree in psychology and is a UKCP registered TA psychotherapist. He worked for ten years with children and young people in social services, education and the voluntary sector, during which time he ran a number of children's workshops with Keith Tudor. He provides TA training to foster carers and social work professionals at Foster Care Associates. He is a former Director of Training for the Counselling and Psychotherapy Training Institute in Edinburgh and a former coaching trainer for the Scottish Network of Business Psychologists. He is now an associate tutor for the London Business School and provides executive coaching and coaching training through his own consultancy: Co-creativity.com

Susannah Temple PhD, PTTA, is an Educational Transactional Analyst. She has experience in many educational settings including being a schools counsellor for seven years. Susannah is the author of both the Functional Fluency model of human social functioning and the Temple Index of Functional Fluency (TIFFÕ), a TA psychometric tool for behavioural diagnosis, personal development and research. In July 2003 she was awarded a Silver Medal by the European Association for Transactional Analysis for this doctoral work. Susannah works in Bristol as a researcher, consultant and trainer and is continuing to develop TIFFÕ academically and also commercially through licensing TIFF Providers. Email: sftemple@care4free.net; website: www.functionalfluency.com

Mark Widdowson is MSc (TA Psychotherapy), Grad. Dip. Couns, ECP, TSTA. Mark lives in Glasgow, where he has a private practice offering psychotherapy for individuals and couples, with both adults and adolescent clients, and supervision for both individuals and groups working in private practice and voluntary sector agencies. He is Director of Training for the Counselling and Psychotherapy Training Institute in Edinburgh where he is also tutor for the foundation and fourth years. Mark is also an Academic Tutor and Supervisor at The Berne Institute in Kegworth, and a Lecturer in TA and Integrative Psychotherapy at Therapia, The Laboratory of Liberal Studies, in Athens. Mark is registered as a psychotherapist with both the United Kingdom Council for Psychotherapy and the European Association for Psychotherapy.

Author Index

Subject Index

Russell House Publishing Ltd

We publish a wide range of professional, reference and educational books in these areas:

Families, children and young people – parenting, support, safeguarding and caring

Child abuse and neglect – working with victims, carers and perpetrators

Looked after children and young people – caring, adoption, wellbeing

Young people in need, young people in trouble – health and wellbeing, caring and safeguarding, drugs and alcohol, anti-social and offending behaviour

Working with young people – learning and skills, policy, service delivery, management

Communities – neighbourliness, participation, safety

Adults in need, adults in trouble – mental health, homelessness, drugs, alcohol, offending

Social work – learning and skills, policy, service delivery, managment

Care of older people – learning and skills development, policy, management

Care and health – learning and skills development, policy, management

For more details on specific books, please visit our website:

www.russellhouse.co.uk

Or we can send you our catalogue if you contact us at:

Russell House Publishing Ltd, 4 St George's House,
Uplyme Road Business Park, Lyme Regis DT7 3LS, England.
Tel: 01297 443948. Fax: 01297 442722. Email: help@russellhouse.co.uk

The space between

Bridging the gap between workers and young people
By Anita Mountain

Offers groupwork approaches to work with young people who are at risk – for any reason – of being in contact with the juvenile justice system, coming before the courts, or being received into care.

It introduces **transactional analysis** "in a way that is intended to be of use to those working with young people in the field . . . Part One explains the theory . . . It may well cause the worker to consider themselves and their own practice, but from this I expect they will develop a better knowledge of the emotionally driven traps we are all at risk of falling into with young people . . . and how our resultant responses can inhibit our work and the development of those we are seeking to help. Part Two takes the form more of a workbook. It contains a range of straightforward group-work exercises aimed at addressing the most common difficulties facing young people, such as anger management, accommodation and racism, but with transactional analysis in the background as an aid to good practice . . . any practitioner worth their salt should be able to adapt the tasks as the need arises." *Young People Now.*

978-1-903855-37-9   2004

Adolescence   SECOND EDITION

Positive approaches for working with young people
By Ann Wheal

This new edition has been praised: "We need more books like this one . . . packed with helpful, practical advice for those working directly with adolescents." *Young Minds.* "Toolbox of ideas, strategies and research evidence to support working with adolescents in meaningful ways . . ." *Community Practitioner.* "Comprehensive, accessible . . ." *Care & Health.*

Each chapter is divided into numerous, clearly identified sections, making it possible to use the book like an encyclopaedia, without disrupting what is a good read. "**Frank and clear . . .** The chapters are threaded with real examples of the issue in hand and bring life to the text . . . full of information and advice on how to work effectively with young people . . . it provides an adolescent's perspective on situations where all too often only a 'professional' view is given." *Young People Now.*

Ann Wheel advocates the use of TA in this book: "**Anyone who is serious about improving their communication skills will benefit from studying transactional analysis.** TA simplifies and explains the psychology of the communication process."

978-1-903855-42-3   2004

Tips: Tried and tested ideas for parent education and support

By Ginnie Herbert and Rosemary Napper

"Practical help for facilitators in running and setting up parenting groups . . . not prescriptive about the debates that surround parent education . . . particularly useful . . . a valuable reference guide for people with a variety of experiences." *Community Care*. "Very accessible." *Adult Learning*.

Photocopiable, it is built on the belief that the best resource people can use is other people and that equality of opportunity is fundamental to parents and children. It stands apart from other parent education resources by stressing the crucial importance of negotiating with parents what they want to include in the time spent learning with you. It gives you guidance on: what leading a parenting group involves

- how learning takes place

- getting started and putting the word out

- the first, all-important session

- negotiating a programme

- awareness raising

- skills development

- dealing with tricky situations

- checking the effectiveness

- resources.

All the ideas are based on actual experiences of parents and parent educators. **Rosemary Napper is a writer, qualified trainer, counsellor and Transactional Analyst**. She teaches tutor training programmes and Masters in psychodynamic counselling and psychotherapy.

978-1-898924-81-4   2000

The child and family in context

Developing ecological practice in disadvantaged communities

By Owen Gill and Gordan Jack

Child welfare research increasingly focuses on the 'ecology' of childhood. The child is at the centre of interdependent systems including the household, the wider family, the local community and formal institutions such as schools. This approach to children's lives and seeing the 'whole child' has also underpinned key initiatives such as the Assessment Framework for Children in Need, and service developments such as Sure Start, the Children's Fund, extended schools and children's centres. However, the authors of this book argue that, in spite of these developments, much mainstream child welfare practice fails to adequately make the connections between the child and family, and the local communities of which they are a part.

The book reviews research on the impact of living in disadvantaged communities and develops the concept of 'ecological practice', which links community and family elements of children's well-being, and tries to work creatively with the connections between different parts of the child's life.

Practice examples from different communities including large peripheral estates, inner city refugee communities, and rural market towns are used throughout the book. The implications of linking community and family approaches are drawn out for safeguarding and promoting the well-being of children and young people, developing support for parents, involving children and parents in regeneration and tackling crime, and working to support disabled children and young people and their parents. The challenges of the approach are also explored – particularly those faced by agencies, practitioners and evaluators.

The practice approach that the authors advocate for working with individual children in their family and community contexts will be important and highly topical for practitioners, service managers and those involved in organisational and policy aspects of delivering children's services, as well as researchers, lecturers and students.

978-1-905541-15-7   2007